Dickens The Novelist

Also by F. R. Leavis

∗

FOR CONTINUITY
NEW BEARINGS IN ENGLISH POETRY
REVALUATION
EDUCATION AND THE UNIVERSITY
THE GREAT TRADITION
THE COMMON PURSUIT
D. H. LAWRENCE: NOVELIST
'ANNA KARENINA' AND OTHER ESSAYS
ENGLISH LITERATURE IN OUR TIME
AND THE UNIVERSITY

with Q. D. Leavis
LECTURES IN AMERICA

with Michael Yudkin
TWO CULTURES?

with Denys Thompson
CULTURE AND ENVIRONMENT

Edited by F. R. Leavis
DETERMINATIONS
MILL ON BENTHAM AND COLERIDGE

∗

also by Q. D. Leavis
FICTION AND THE READING PUBLIC

DICKENS

THE NOVELIST

By

F. R. Leavis
and Q. D. Leavis

PANTHEON BOOKS

A DIVISION OF RANDOM HOUSE

NEW YORK

Library of Congress Catalog Card Number: 77-135367

ISBN: 0-394-46860-0

Printed in Great Britain
First American Edition

Contents

*

We dedicate this book to each other as proof, along with *Scrutiny* (of which for twenty-one years we sustained the main burden and the responsibility), of forty years and more of daily collaboration in living, university teaching, discussion of literature and the social and cultural context from which literature is born, and above all, devotion to the fostering of that true respect for creative writing, creative minds and, English literature being in question, the English tradition, without which literary criticism can have no validity and no life.

'I suppose so remarkable an author as Dickens hardly ever lived who carried so little of authorship into ordinary social intercourse. . . . Though Dickens bore outwardly so little of the impress of his writings, they formed the whole of that inner life which essentially constituted the man.'

FORSTER, Life of Dickens

' "It always struck me they missed my little point with a perfection exactly as admirable when they patted me on the back as when they kicked me in the shins. By my little point I mean – what shall I call it? – the particular thing I've written my books *most* for. Isn't there for every writer a particular thing of that sort, the thing that most makes him apply himself, the thing without the effort to achieve which he wouldn't write at all, the very passion of his passion, the part of the business in which, for him, the flame of art burns most intensely? . . . The order, the form, the texture of my books will perhaps some day constitute for the initiated a complete representation of it. So it's naturally the thing for the critic to look for." '

HENRY JAMES, The Figure in the Carpet

'I have said that Dickens felt criticism, of whatever kind, with too sharp a relish for the indifference he assumed to it; but the secret was that he believed himself to be entitled to a higher tribute than he was always in the habit of receiving.'

FORSTER, Life of Dickens

PREFACE

IT seems well to state clearly and briefly in front of this book what we offer to do in it. We have not undertaken a general survey of Dickens, believing that all such enterprises are merely academic, and unprofitable critically. Our purpose is to enforce as unanswerably as possible the conviction that Dickens was one of the greatest of creative writers; that with the intelligence inherent in creative genius, he developed a fully conscious devotion to his art, becoming as a popular and fecund, but yet profound, serious and wonderfully resourceful practising novelist, a master of it; and that, as such, he demands a critical attention he has not had. We should like to make it impossible for any academic authority to feel that, in 'doing' assorted 'Dickens characters' with histrionic gusto he pays the recognized appropriate tribute to the creative gift, or for any intellectual–academic, journalist or both–to tell us with the familar easy assurance that Dickens of course was a genius, but that his line was entertainment, so that an account of his art that implies marked intellectual powers–a capacity, for example, to read and understand Bentham–is obviously absurd. We wish to make it impossible for such critics to assert, or assume, that any character from the novels of Dickens's maturity might have equally appeared in any other of the novels than the one in which it in fact functions as an inseparable part of the whole. And we have thought it essential to register specific protests against the trend of American criticism of Dickens, from Edmund Wilson onwards, as being in general wrong-headed, ill-informed in ways we have demonstrated, and essentially ignorant and misdirecting.

In this connection we should perhaps explain our preference for Forster's Life of Dickens as a source, over modern, more 'correct' biographies, whether British or, still less acceptable, American. The fact is that Forster, whatever his sins of omission, suppression, or alteration of some letters or documents to give himself greater importance in relation to Dickens in the eyes of his world, does give the only convincing representation of Dickens as the creator of the novels for those capable of reading them with critical perception and disinterestedness–witness the quotations from Forster's Life in our Epigraphs. And Forster, with his intimate personal knowledge of his friend (a friendship which survived storms), gives us the sense, as no other biographer does or now can, of being in the same room as Dickens, and even, more important, of being really inward with Dickens's personality and character, and without being concerned to make out a case by 'interpreting' his subject. The ineptness of scholars as literary critics is a notorious fact. Essential ignorance can consort with a great deal of scholarly industry in assembling irrelevant data, and misrepresentation with interpreting that so-called 'factual matter', owing to a more or less unconscious bias, and with insinuating, through critical stupidity, false assumptions about the subject's art, character, personality and history: the subject often becoming a victim. In these respects the older biographers are much the safest, and even, surprisingly, the most useful still, for they shared and understood the age of which they wrote. They are also less pretentious as critics, have no modern psychological jargon, and were more really knowledgeable in presenting their subjects, as well as more truly respectful and essentially more inward with them. George Eliot's widower thus contrives to provide an intimate, indispensable and unsurpassed portrait of, and understanding of the inner life of, Miss Evans and G. H. Lewes's consort, without Mary Anne- or Marian-ing her in an ineffectual attempt to achieve familiarity, such as we have met in recent biographies from which after all no such appreciation or clear portrait is obtainable. Thus for instance Professor Edgar Johnson's biography of Dickens cannot claim to have superseded or even to rival Forster's, or Professor Gordon Haight's to be as illuminating a guide to George Eliot the novelist as John Cross's, while the biographical notices and memoirs of anyone who knew D. H. Lawrence and wrote of him without malice are undoubtedly to be preferred to Professor Harry T. Moore's. The untenable position of those academics and journalists who are determined to explain away Dickens's creative *œuvre* as the uncontrolled product of childhood obsessions or experiences, or of a psychological abnormality, or of a consistent lifelong exhibition of manias, is examined in a Note below.

The method we decided on was to take the six great novels as lending themselves peculiarly to the purpose when considered in relation to the development of Dickens's powers, and to discuss them each in terms of intrinsic interest but in chronological order and in reference to each other. The book was conceived as a book: the fact that a chapter is devoted to each of these novels doesn't reduce it to a collection of essays. The purpose is everywhere there as the informing spirit, determining approach and presentation, and the chronological order belongs to the sustained argument.

The fourth chapter, that on *Hard Times*, originally appeared in *Scrutiny* as inaugurating this approach to Dickens, and more generally to the Novel, as early as Spring 1947, being the initial essay in a series the title of which, 'The Novel as Dramatic Poem', conveyed the idea of the enterprise. Received at the time with ridicule, this title and this essay have since been accepted as marking a new approach both to Dickens (and effecting a revolution in Dickens criticism) and to the art of the novel generally. It was reprinted as something in the nature of an appendix to *The Great Tradition*, where its inclusion testified to the convinced and emphatic recognition of Dickens's status. The inclusion was strongly urged by the other of the collaborating pair; both in fact realized that the complete omission of Dickens from the book would be ridiculous, and if its inclusion looked odd, it was meant as an avowal at any rate of default in respect of Dickens and of a deferred commitment to making the default good. The critical significance of the slowness to recognize Dickens's pre-eminence among English novelists—he may be seen surely as the Shakespeare of the novel—is touched on explicitly in the beginning of the first chapter (on *Dombey and Son*), and is implicitly developed in the book as a whole.

The critique of *Dombey and Son*, originally written as introducing the book for its inclusion (which was cancelled later by the publishers on financial grounds) in a series of English classics, was published only in an American quarterly (*The Sewanee Review*, 1962)—still with the limitations entailed by the original conditions of writing. In Chapter I there is the completer treatment of *Dombey* conceived in relation to the stated plan and purpose of our book. Some changes of the same kind will be found in Chapter IV.

No notes of the kinds exemplified above are called for by the four chapters initialled 'Q.D.L.'. These were all written *ad hoc* as constituent parts of the book when it had been conceived as something to be undertaken forthwith, and worked at in an intensive and sustained way until completed. The last of the four—it concludes the book—is a study of Dickens's use of illustrations as accessaries of his art in conveying his meaning to his readers; it has an immediate relevance to the central critical themes of this book. And since it was in the earlier part of his creative career that Dickens first habitually asserted a positive and authoritative interest in the illustrating of his text, the chapter, it seems to us, adds to the direct discussion of the major work an appropriate recall of the earlier work out of which the great novelist emerged. It stresses moreover the importance for Dickens of having such a live tradition of illustration and a public which understood it—of being able to assume this and develop it for the purposes of his art; while showing that the death of the tradition, owing to the characteristic and fundamental change in the later Victorian ethos, meant a serious narrowing of taste which pointed to a corresponding impoverishment of art, poetry and literature generally, so that Dickens's death marked the end of his era.

As for the mode of collaboration, the collaborators have in their respective chapters—as will no doubt be noted—been guided by the spontaneities of the personal judgment and the personal habit of approach, and also by the experience they both have of the most profitable method of criticizing Dickens derived from many years' individual teaching of university students. The authors here started by knowing that they were in essential agreement about Dickens and about the kind of book needed. The differences of idiosyncrasy, it seemed to them, could only be an advantage in the execution of the collaboratively conceived project, and the upshot, they judge, answers reasonably to their idea of what was required and what they are prepared to stand by. To repeat the insistence, it asks to be read as a book, and not as a collection of essays.

There is a note to be added under the head of 'acknowledgments'. As Chichele Lecturer at Oxford in 1964, the writer of Chapter V discussed *Little Dorrit* together with – in a minor way – *Hard Times* – under the title: 'Dickens, Art and Social Criticism'. The different emphasis entailed by the present undertaking necessitated for Chapter V, not only an extended, but a re-thought treatment of *Little Dorrit*. Nevertheless, the given collaborator is very conscious that the attention he devoted to that great novel in preparing the Chichele Lectures has told decisively in the critical discussion offered here, and he would like to express the gratitude he feels to All Souls' College for the opportunity and intellectual stimulus the appointment as Chichele Lecturer gave him. Parts of Chapter II, on the relation between Dickens and Tolstoy, and with regard to the two levels at which Dickens may be read, were delivered as lectures by the other collaborator at the universities of Bristol and Aberdeen.

F.R.L.
Q.D.L.

NOTE

The Marxizing and other ideologically-slanted interpretations of Dickens's achievement were comparatively harmless and are now a dead letter, but the echoes and elaborations of Edmund Wilson's theory of Dickens's art—as being the volcanic explosions of a manic-depressive—are still with us on the air, in print and in lectures being given in this centenary year to academic audiences and learned societies. Alternative accounts are that Dickens's art is evidently the product of 'an anal dandy', that it is based on and conditioned by childhood terrors and fantasies from nurse's story-telling, or by the brief spell the boy Dickens endured in the blacking-factory. The favourite method is to amalgamate these and others with the assumption that the art can be explained away in the light of such miscellaneous and quite unconnected data (or alleged data) as: the uninhibited capers of Dickens's youth; the outbreaks common to men of letters against exploitation by their publishers and the touchiness and irritability almost inevitable in literary genius; the trials of an unsatisfactory marriage and the wholly conjectural torments of a possibly unsatisfactory *liaison*; the physical exhaustion of an overworked, much-tried and over-convivial editor and journalist who, in the manner of his day and profession, kept himself going ultimately with stimulants, undermining his health; the nervous shock and physical damage due to a railway accident late in life, while writing *Our Mutual Friend* (during which accident, however, he behaved with admirable self-control); and finally the greatly exaggerated accounts and implausible explanations of his dramatic readings from his novels at the end of his life. No discouraging scepticism has, as far as one knows, been incurred by these amateur psychologists of our academic scene; but no trained psychologist seems to have condoned, much less supported, any of these assumptions and theories. Besides the evident fact that such self-indulgent vapourings give no satisfaction to anyone but their perpetrators (for they shepherd us away from the texts and can only misdirect for the approach to Dickens's creative achievement), they reveal in their authors a refusal, or an inability, to read the novels as literature: for the complex sensibility, in general so marvellously controlled and directed objectively into a unique form in each of the novels of Dickens's maturity, gives the lie to such crude and cheap attempts to dispose of the created entities.

The theories are also a travesty of the facts that we know of Dickens's personality and behaviour. What a weight of academic capital has been made of that innocent hornpipe danced by the young man outside that window! – Quilp-like comparisons have even been made on the strength of that and similar lively capers and pranks in the young manhood of poor Charles – bearing witness only to the innocence of these academic minds as to normal youth and also as to the manners, running naturally to high jinks, of that phase of English social life Dickens was reared in, of the tone and habits of which he inevitably partook. Dickens's was a pre-Victorian England of course, with the uninhibited licences of the Regency lower-middle-class, plus a temporary plunge by him into the raffish underworld (as Mr Micawber's son) which extended into the society of the debtor's prison, and the streets in which old Mr Weller boasted that he had provided his son with an essential education when (like Dickens) Sam was 'wery young'. If Dickens was in these respects abnormal, so was practically everyone else in his youth. Cruikshank, a much older man than Dickens and a favourite companion, was a great deal more 'eccentric', wildly unconventional (that is, by later Victorian standards, which were prim) and more startling in his antics than Dickens was ever known to be, while a gentleman like Thackeray could waggle his legs out of his carriage window in triumph as he drove past without arousing adverse comment. The habitual buffoonery, amounting to licence, of another gentleman who was also a cleric and nearly a bishop, Sydney Smith, was welcomed in the highest society as well as the most intellectual of the day. Practical jokes of the most unrefined kind and even savagery, histrionics and travesty for fun, hoaxes or 'flams', uninhibited punning and broad jests, excessive tippling, as well as a now unknown degree of sentimental susceptibility, were characteristic of the age Dickens was formed in. But what was characteristic of *him* is surely that he grew or raised himself out of its influences instead of being their victim – the change from the author of *Pickwick* to the author of *Dombey* is as decisive as impressive.

Social historians and literary-critical historians once knew such facts of life. G. M. Young in his *Victorian England: Portrait of an Age* rightly stresses the characteristic 'exuberance' of the earlier Victorians, as when audiences even at Bowood sobbed at Tom Moore's songs, 'when Ministers sometimes wept at the Table; when the sight of an infant school could reduce a civil servant to a passion of tears . . . an age of flashing eyes and curling lips', and concludes that 'out of the horse-play of sentimental Cockneys [came] Dickens'. Dickens moreover had worked in a law-office, and the society of Dick Swivellers (are Dick's capers to be taken as pathological?) can only have encouraged the normal adolescent histrionic tendencies which Dickens exploited for humorous purposes – a conditioning to which purposes was inevitable at first. Such deliberate playfulness and exaggerated whimsicality has been solemnly taken for morbidity, as in the case of his prolonged drama of frustrated passion for the young Queen and jealousy of Prince Albert, though well understood for what it was by Forster who mentions that it was a joint jape with two friends of Dickens's. Professor Oliver Elton in his *Survey of English Literature* (1830–80) had made similar points to G. M. Young's in citing the (inevitable) literary influences of this period on Dickens as a young novelist and a man of his time. He mentions as typical Theodore Hook, 'farce-maker, journalist, essayist, novelist, punster, practical jester, impromptu rhymester, and Bohemian' whose characters were a source of early characterization for Dickens, and that Hook actually relates in his novels some of his own outrageous 'flams', adding that while Hook and Surtees and others of that kind were 'not exactly literature', they were 'the cause of literature in others', for instance, Dickens. Yes, indeed, and deductions therefore from the contents and tone of the early batch of Dickens's novels must be checked by such considerations (a precaution ignored by Edmund Wilson) – for how, as a hard-driven young aspiring writer could Dickens fail to be of his ambience, draw on his predecessors, and satisfy such a public's tastes? 'Even allowing for the change of taste, there is a vulgar callousness about most of them that is not amusing. The cheaper jokes of Sydney Smith, the sarcasms of Macaulay, the horse-play in Marryat's novels, the manners of old Lady Holland, the illustrations of Cruikshank and Douglas Jerrold's merry and vulgar work – all belong, if we will, to a more robust age (pre-Victorian at first)' says Elton, writing in 1920 as a later Victorian gentleman. Such data show us the matrix in which Dickens was originally shaped as a writer and a person, and no suppositious tracing to childhood impressions is needed to find the source for Dickens's use at first of grotesque, savage and violent activities and personalities in his fictions, for they were the commonplaces of Grub Street and High Society alike. [One might as well allege a death-wish in the writer for the frequent deaths of children, babies and wives, but of course these were factual in the first half of the 19th century.] What distinguishes Dickens is that he could make of a Quilp a study in sadistic malice, showing his critical detachment from the inheritance of his literary and social environment, and his own better informed insights, the insights of a genius and one fortunately informed also, through his literary tastes, with better influences from a finer past of English literature–his two greatest assets. We should not however under-rate the range of possible or permitted feeling in this uninhibited society, for along with the ribald jests, the noisy waggishness and the appearance even of Mr Punch, in Sydney Smith there was, as in others of his world, not only brilliant wit but the unexpected capacity for a sensibility of another order: Fanny Price in *Persuasion* was 'one of his [Smith's] prime favourites'.

As to the recent fashion for attributing as characteristic of Dickens's art deforming terrors and fixations set up by nursery tales of horror, folk-tales and fairy-tales imparted in his childhood, it is surely decisive that he never, in any novel, to my knowledge, shows a child suffering from such an heritage but, on the contrary, stresses that children essentially need the old folk-lore and fairy-tales and the magic cycle of the Arabian Nights, as part of their full imaginative development. That he should write up for purposes of journalism, with obvious playfulness and pleasure in blood-curdling reminiscence, tales of horror and popular nursery bogies of the time (such as Susan Nipper harmlessly uses to chasten little Miss Floy) is quite beside the point. Dickens the journalist was a lightly assumed personality very often, and we can surely gather from his style and tone how seriously to take him on such occasions. What his letters show, besides the same histrionic attitudes and high spirits, is the confident and devoted writer for whom his profession was the main consideration in his life. Dickens's consistent courtesy, generosity and unstinted helpfulness to his contributors as an editor, and his high standard of conscientious professionalism throughout his writing life and in spite of his later physical and other handicaps, suggest that he had exceptional self-control and was as far as possible from being dependent on moods or uncontrollable drives in any direction, and this is borne out by the experience of many who knew him in his maturity. It is also borne out, as we argue in discussing the later fiction, by the evidence from the creative work itself, that he was not a psychically sick man or anything like a 'case'. This is the only deduction possible to the literary critic.

The arguments drawn from Dickens's passion at the end of his life for giving dramatic readings from his novels is a more interesting and not so simple a question as is implied in the claim that Dickens thus killed himself and that his satisfaction in the readings was the morbid one of sending his audience into fainting fits. In common with other literary artists, such as Henry James and T. S. Eliot for example, who launched deliberately into play-writing for the purpose, Dickens obviously, as his hold on life began to fail, felt the need, overpoweringly in his case as in theirs, for a visible instead of an invisible audience, to prove that the public were still responsive to his powers as an artist: the only difference in Dickens's case was that, with his early and never-satisfied impulse to become a professional actor, he made himself his own vehicle for the purpose, taxing his exhausted physical strength and giving at times (the accounts vary widely) performances in poor taste with over-acting, and subsequently expressing excitement at the audiences' violently responsive reactions. We should however remember such reports of an opposite kind as Annie Thackeray's (Lady Ritchie) of 'the last London reading from *David Copperfield*' to which she was taken by her friend Kate Dickens:

> It was for all the rest of my life that I heard his voice. . . . The slight figure stood alone quietly facing the long rows of people. He seemed to be holding the great audience in some mysterious way from the empty stage. Quite immediately the story began; Copperfield and Steerforth, Yarmouth and the fishermen, and then the rising storm, all were there before us. It was not acting, it was not music, nor harmony of sound and colour, and yet I still have an impression of all these things as I think of that occasion.

Intimate with the Dickens household from childhood, her testimony to Dickens's personality is valuable since she knew everyone in art and literature in her time, and she writes of Dickens as always impressing her by 'that curious life-giving power of his' which he exercised on others 'quietly', adding: 'I know not what to call that power by which he inspired everyone with spirit and interest'. Dickens is not a case for the simple-minded or the amateur psychologist to exercise himself upon; what a crazy structure even academic 'Dickens specialists' have reared on selected, confidently interpreted, miscellaneous or incompatible, so-called facts! One notes that a distinguished specialist like Russell Brain, in the book cited in Chapter 6 below, *Some Reflections on Genius*, though he recognizes in Swift a well-known and unfortunate type of case, whose disabilities in life and consequent constricted and damaged creativeness he understands and can account for, he has no such impression of Dickens but only, in the essay devoted to him, admiration for his exceptional range of intuitive powers and his objective interest in life. It would be wiser to bear in mind Jung's caution:

> The creative aspect of life which finds its clearest expression in art baffles all attempts at rational formulation. Any reaction to stimulus may be causally explained; but the creative act, which is the absolute antithesis of mere reaction, will for ever elude the human understanding. It can only be described in its manifestations; it can be obscurely sensed but never wholly grasped.

Q.D.L.

CHAPTER ONE

THE FIRST MAJOR NOVEL: 'DOMBEY AND SON'

I REMEMBER to have somewhere heard in childhood, feelingly rendered, the Victorian song that was inspired by *Dombey and Son*:

What are the wild waves saying
Sister the whole day long?

I cannot pretend that it struck me as anything but an eminently fit tribute to the book. The book was vividly in my mind; I had heard it read out, and read admirably, by my father, for family reading was still an institution in those days, and Dickens of course was before all others the classic for such use. He suffered, I think, a consequent disadvantage in one's later experience–a disadvantage not shared, for instance, by Shakespeare, with whom also one had a vivid early acquaintance through much family reading of him. Shakespeare, once one could read him at all, one inevitably went on reading, and he could never be thought of as a writer qualified for fullest appreciation in one's less mature and sophisticated days.

But that is just how, looking back, one naturally thought of Dickens. With so much else before one that *had* to be read–so much that there was the need and the urgent impulsion to read, one remembered Dickens as the classic it was perhaps on the whole best to leave, piously and affectionately, to the memory and associations of the early acquaintance. When one dipped one found very readily the kind of thing one had recalled, though divested now, where some of the most cherished manifestations of the Dickensian genius were concerned, of some of the magic. And one could too easily light on places where the wonderful vitality clearly ran too much to repetitiveness or to the cheapnesses and banalities of Victorian popular art.

Resistances and reluctances, then, in the way of the serious re-reading of many, at any rate, of Dickens's novels (that an exceptional kind of strength, challenging a mature appreciation, is to be found in certain of them is generally recognized) have been, I think, a common experience.

I

I myself confess to a very long abstention from *Dombey and Son*, which I remembered vividly and thought I remembered fully enough.

Dombey and Son marks a decisive moment in Dickens's career; he offered it as a providently conceived whole, presenting a major theme, and it was his first essay in the elaborately plotted Victorian novel. There can be no denying that the theme in actuality serves as licence for end-less overworked pathos, for lush unrealities of high moral insistence, for childish elaborations of sensational plot, and for all the disqualifying characteristics (a serious theme being proposed) of melodrama – Victorian melodrama. On the other hand, of course, the genial force of Dickens's inexhaustible creativity is also strongly present, in the vigour of the per-ception and rendering of life, the varied comedy, the vitality of expres-sion as manifested even in the melodramatic high moments and *tours de force* and in the flights of rhetorical and sentimental art to which we don't respond, at any rate in the massive way proposed to us. But there is, to make *Dombey and Son* remarkable, something more than this account suggests. There is a kind of strength that, while it is profoundly Dickens-ian, cannot be thought of as characterizing Dickens's work in general. No one is likely to have carried a full and fair memory of it from a child-hood acquaintance with *Dombey and Son*; it is too closely associated in that elaborately planned novel with the copious other – the varied and quite different, yet certainly not less Dickensian – qualities, and in any case it demands some maturity of experience in the reader for a full recognition.

Yet, for anyone starting to re-read, it is a strength that makes its im-pact immediately; it is there, and very impressively, in the first chapter, which must be as good an opening chapter as Dickens ever wrote. The scene of the death, with its economy, its precision, and its delicate sure-ness of tone and touch, is something that only Dickens could have done; yet, as the description I have given must suggest, it is not ordinarily Dickensian: the genius functions with an unusual intensity and there is a control from an unusual depth. It is a bold, rapid and highly simplifying art that evokes and establishes Dombey – his brand of pride and self-importance, and the cold inhumanity of his egotism – in so brief a space. Yet, close as it might again and again seem to caricature, it has none of the limitations that that description would suggest.

'The house will once again, Mrs. Dombey,' said Mr. Dombey, 'be not only in name but in fact Dombey and Son; Dom-bey and Son!'

The words had such a softening influence, that he appended a term of endearment to Mrs. Dombey's name (though not without some hesitation, as being a man but little used to that form of address): and said, 'Mrs. Dombey, my–my dear.'

A transient flush of faint surprise overspread the sick lady's face as she raised her eyes toward him.

'He will be christened Paul, my–Mrs. Dombey–of course.'

She feebly echoed, 'Of course,' or rather expressed it by the motion of her lips, and closed her eyes again.

'His father's name, Mrs. Dombey, and his grandfather's! I wish his grandfather were alive this day!' And again he said 'Dom-bey and Son,' in exactly the same tone as before.

We respond as to the fulness of immediately felt life: this is poignantly –the more poignantly because of the pathos of Mrs. Dombey's past life –a death-chamber. What I have called the boldness of the art is something that we feel to be one with the intensity of the realization, sensuous and imaginative:

'Well, Sir,' said Doctor Parker Peps, in a round deep, sonorous voice, muffled for the occasion, like the knocker; 'do you find that your lady is at all roused by your visit?'

'Stimulated as it were?' said the family practitioner faintly: bowing at the same time to the Doctor, as much as to say,

'Excuse my putting in a word, but this is a valuable connexion.'

Mr. Dombey was quite discomfited by the question. He had thought so little of the patient, that he was not in a condition to answer it. He said it would be a satisfaction to him if Doctor Parker Peps would walk upstairs again.

Mr. Dombey's sister does think of her sister-in-law:

'Well!' said Mrs. Chick with a sweet smile, 'after this I can forgive Fanny everything!'

It was a declaration in a Christian spirit, and Mrs. Chick felt that it did her good.

This element of robust ironic comedy, which figures so much in the scene, plays its essential part in effects of the greatest delicacy and actually ministers to the total solemn pathos. Dombey's inhumanness of personified Pride tells so strongly because of the way in which, by Dickens's astonishing art, human life is evoked in its fulness. The self-important professionality of the two doctors is beautifully got, but we feel no

3

surprise when (unlike Mr. Dombey) they turn out to be capable of compassion:

> There was such a solemn stillness round the bed; and the two medical attendants seemed to look on the impassive form with so much compassion and so little hope, that Mrs. Chick was for the moment diverted from her purpose. But presently summoning courage, and what she called presence of mind, she sat down by the bedside, and said in the low precise tone of one who endeavours to weaken a sleeper:
> 'Fanny! Fanny!'
> There was no sound in answer but the loud ticking of Mr. Dombey's watch and Doctor Parker Peps's watch, which seemed in the silence to be running a race.

The close of that illustrates in the most obvious of ways what I meant above by 'intensity of sensuous and imaginative realization'. The two watches 'running a race' – with what a sharp precision that peculiarly and impertinently insistent noise is evoked, giving us in immediacy the stillness of the death-chamber, and giving it as the fact and presence of death. The close of the chapter might seem to be utterly remote from any conceivable note of ironic comedy, but it comes in perfect consonance:

> The race in the ensuing pause was fierce and furious. The watches seemed to jostle, and to trip each other up.
> 'Fanny!' said Louisa, glancing round, with a gathering alarm. 'Only look at me. Only open your eyes to show me that you hear and understand me; will you? Good Heaven, gentlemen, what is to be done?'
> The two medical attendants exchanged a look across the bed; and the physician, stooping down, whispered in the child's ear. Not having understood the purport of his whisper, the little creature turned her perfectly colourless face, and deep dark eyes towards him; but without loosening her hold in the least.
> The whisper was repeated.
> 'Mamma!' said the child.
> The little voice, familiar and dearly loved, awakened some show of consciousness, even at that ebb. For a moment, the closed eye-lids trembled, and the nostrils quivered, and the faintest shadow of a smile was seen.
> 'Mamma!' the child cried, sobbing aloud. 'Oh dear Mamma! oh dear Mamma!'
> The Doctor gently brushed the scattered ringlets of the child aside

from the face and mouth of the mother. Alas how calm they lay there: how little breath there was to stir them!

Thus, clinging fast to that slight spar within her arms, the mother drifted out upon the dark and unknown sea that rolls round all the world.

What Dickens does later in the book with the potentialities of pathos in his theme we know, and it is impossible to say that there is not the clearest continuity of relation between the effect struck in this close to the opening scene and the later insistent lushness that plays so large a part in *Dombey and Son*. Yet what we have here in the treatment of Mrs. Dombey's death is all the same an essentially different kind of effect. The theme as Dickens is possessed by it here is a very different thing from what it becomes. For he *is* possessed by it: he is possessed by an intense and penetrating perception of the real–his theme here *is* that. The art that serves it does not run to the luxuries of pathos and sensation or to redundancies. And it is astonishingly sensitive and flexible.

It is in the second chapter that the theme represented by Mr. Dombey gets its most pregnant poetic and dramatic definition. There is the problem of keeping the baby alive. 'Couldn't something temporary be done with a tea-pot?' asks Mr. Chick. The question, put as it is to Mrs. Chick, has the air of being just a random (if apt) snubbability of the snub-attracting Mr. Chick, Dickensian figure of comedy; but it illustrates fairly the peculiar strength of the humour in the supreme ranges of Dickens's art. If a solution of the tea-pot kind could have been found, Mr. Dombey would have been spared his painful and characteristic inner conflict. Actually, of course, the cruel irony of the situation for Mr. Dombey is that, to save the baby's life, what is needed is a living agent, a woman and a mother, and that, if she can be found, she will inevitably, in the nature of the case, be of the lower orders. The need of a wet-nurse is desperately urgent, yet Mr. Dombey viewed, we are told, 'with so much bitterness the thought of being dependent for the very first step towards the accomplishment of his soul's desire, on a hired serving-woman who would be to the child, for a time, all that even *his* alliance could have made his own wife, that in every new rejection of a candidate he felt a secret pleasure'.

We see his pride as in essence a stultifying self-contradiction; his egotism, in its inhumanity, as inimical to life and inevitably self-defeating. The profundity of the effect of Dickens's treatment of the theme depends upon the force and adequacy with which he makes present to us the opposite of the pride and the egotism–that which they outrage and frustrate and blight. The focus of the presentation of 'life' as the positive invoked in the irony is of course Polly Toodle the wet-nurse. The scene in which Polly is engaged gives us the truly great Dickens, the clairvoyant artist wholly commanded by a profound theme–a Dickens profoundly serious, that is, as well as genially creative: indeed, all that has to do with Polly or what is associated with her is strong.

> 'Still,' resumed Miss Tox, 'she naturally must be interested in her young charge, and must consider it a privilege to see a little cherub so closely connected with the superior classes gradually unfolding itself from day to day at one common fountain. Is it not so, Louisa?'

The irony is that Mr. Dombey's inner being, his egotism, vehemently repudiates the community, though his child's survival, which this egotism demands with the same passionate will, depends on it. *He* doesn't see why Polly must be interested in her young charge; he desires her to be no more interested than a tea-pot would be. Strong in his wealth, he is confident that this *desideratum* can be virtually achieved; money will do it. Money will induce her to forgo, for as long as the son and heir of wealth may need her, any 'interest' she may have in her own children, and money will ensure that when no longer needed, she will not, yielding to the 'natural' temptation (the nature of the lower orders being that in question), use as an exploitable advantage the having inevitably been something other than a tea-pot.

> 'Oh, of course,' said Mr. Dombey. 'I desire to make it a question of wages altogether. Now, Richards, if you nurse my bereaved child, I wish you to remember this always. You will receive a liberal stipend in return for the discharge of certain duties, in the performance of which I desire you to see as little of your family as possible. When these duties cease to be required and rendered, and the stipend ceases to be paid, there is an end of all relations between us. Do you understand me?'
> Mrs. Toodle seemed doubtful about it; and as to Toodle himself, *he* had evidently no doubt whatever, that he was all abroad.
> 'You have children of your own,' said Mr. Dombey. 'It is not at all in this bargain that you need become attached to my child, or that my child need become attached to you. I don't expect or desire anything of the kind. Quite the reverse. When you go away from here, you will have concluded what is a mere matter of bargain and sale, hiring and letting; and you will stay away. The child will cease to remember

you; and you will cease, if you please, to remember the child.'

Mrs. Toodle, with a little more colour in her cheeks than she had had before, said, 'she hoped she knew her place.'

'I hope you do, Richards,' said Mr. Dombey.

This, with a change of proper names, might have come from *Hard Times*, a book eight years or so in the future when (1846–7) Dickens was writing *Dombey and Son*. As yet, however, Coketown and the industrial world had not made their impact on him; it was under the aspect that would strike an observer for whom the centre was London–Thackeray's London–that he knew the hard and hateful ethos with which both books deal. The stress falls on the reinforced spirit of class, with its cold, brutal and extreme repudiation of what Lawrence calls 'blood-together-ness'. 'Oh! Exclusion itself!' says Miss Tox, recommending Mrs. Pipchin's establishment to Mr. Dombey. His second marriage allies him with the aristocracy. But the particular spirit of class he represents depends without disguise on the new money-power, and openly identifies its power with that. His is not industrial England, but it is an England whose prevailing ethos is that of *Hard Times*. Dickens, indeed, explicitly associates Dombey with the utilitarian orthodoxy and its formulations. 'Some philosophers', he remarks, discussing the nature of Dombey's devotion to his son, and intimating plainly enough that we are to see this representative of the City (' "A pecuniary Duke of York, my love, and nothing short of it!" said Miss Tox') as representative of the spiritual world expressing itself in the 'hard' philosophy, 'tell us that selfishness is at the root of our best loves and affections.'[1] And Dombey himself, reproving the act of generosity that entangled Solomon Gills, does so with the distinctive orthodox sanctimony.

Money-pride and money-faith, egotism, the closed heart, class as 'exclusion'–these in *Dombey and Son* are aspects of the same theme. It is presented with subtlety as well as force. To the life the Dombey 'pride'

[1]Regarding the egotism of Dombey's devotion to his son Dickens has already recorded this observation:

'For all his starched, impenetrable dignity and composure, he wiped blinding tears from his eyes as he did so; and often said, with an emotion for which he would not, for the world, have had a witness, "Poor little fellow!"

'It may have been characteristic of Mr. Dombey's pride, that he pitied himself through the child. Not poor me. Not poor widower, confiding by constraint in the wife of an ignorant hind who has been working "mostly underground" all his life, and yet at whose door Death never knocked, and at whose table four sons daily sit–but poor little fellow!'

repels, represses, insults and sacrifices – the generous life that, acting as foil
to it, shows up its mean and lethal inhumanity for what it is – Dickens
has given a figuring presence that is more inevitable in its representative
authority than the Horse-riding of *Hard Times*. As the natural motherly
woman, Polly Toodle is perfectly done. But she does not stand alone;
she has her special context in the Toodle family and the Toodle milieu.
Mr. Toodle is in his way as remarkable a triumph as Polly. Brought by
Miss Tox and Mrs. Chick with the family on the exhibitionary visit that
is to reassure Mr. Dombey, he plays his characteristic and significant part
in the interrogatory:

> 'You have a son, I believe?' said Mr. Dombey.
> 'Four on 'em, Sir. Four hims and a her. All alive!'
> 'Why, it's as much as you can afford to keep them!' said Mr.
> Dombey.
> 'I couldn't hardly afford but one thing in the world less, Sir.'
> 'What is that?'
> 'To lose 'em, Sir.'

The irony of that repeated 'afford', the repetition bringing to one
sharp focus the opposed habits of valuation, the opposed kinds of 'success'
in life, is pregnant. In the context Toodle's reply carries no suggestion of
pertness. He is naïve, mannerless and unaggressively direct – simple
humanity (in a double sense of the noun). That, after the ironically fore-
shadowed death of Paul, is his rôle in the scene (chapter XX) at the railway terminus where, standing by his engine, he accosts Mr. Dombey:

> During the bustle of preparation at the railway Mr. Dombey and
> the Major walked up and down the platform side by side. . . . Neither
> of the two observed that in the course of these walks, they attracted
> the attention of a working man who was standing near the engine,
> and who touched his hat every time they passed; for Mr. Dombey
> habitually looked over the vulgar herd, not at them; and the Major was
> looking, at the time, into the core of one of his stories. At length,
> however, this man stepped before them as they turned round, and
> pulling his hat off, and keeping it off, ducked his head to Mr. Dombey.
> 'Beg your pardon, Sir,' said the man, 'but I hope you're a doin'
> pretty well, Sir.'
> He was dressed in a canvas suit abundantly besmeared with coal-
> dust and oil, and had cinders in his whiskers, and a smell of half-slaked
> ashes all over him. He was not a bad-looking fellow, nor even what
> could be fairly called a dirty-looking fellow, in spite of this; and, in
> short, he was Mr. Toodle, professionally clothed.

'I shall have the honour of stokin' of you down, Sir,' said Mr. Toodle. 'Beg your pardon, Sir. I hope you find yourself a coming round?'

Mr. Dombey looked at him, in return for this tone of interest, as if a man like that would make his very eyesight dirty.

' 'Scuse the liberty, Sir,' said Toodle, seeing he was not clearly remembered, 'but my wife Polly, as was called Richards in your family–'

A change in Mr. Dombey's face, which seemed to express recollection of him, and so it did, but it expressed in a much stronger degree an angry sense of humiliation, stopped Mr. Toodle short.

'Your wife wants money, I suppose,' said Mr. Dombey, putting his hand in his pocket, and speaking (but that he always did) haughtily.

'No thank'ee, Sir,' returned Toodle, 'I can't say she does. *I* don't.'

Mr. Dombey was stopped short now in his turn: and awkwardly: with his hand in his pocket.

'No, Sir,' said Toodle, turning his oilskin cap round and round; 'we're a doin' pretty well, Sir; we haven't no cause to complain in the worldly way, Sir. We've had four more since then, Sir, but we rubs on.'

The whole passage is consummate in its ironic trenchancy and its natural truth. Dombey's imputation of the money-motive recoils on himself. The stoker, in the simple decency of his human feeling, registers nothing to resent–sees no insult; it hasn't occurred to him that, in such a situation, there *could* be any intention to snub. His mention of 'my wife Polly as was called Richards in your family' reminds us of the will expressed in that substitution: the will to preclude as far as possible any but the barest functional relation between the stoker's wife and the infant of class ('Exclusion'). While 'Richards' is functioning as she is paid to do, her human ties shall (for the due monetary consideration) have ceased to exist; when, once more Polly Toodle, she goes back to her children, 'Richards' the nurse will have ceased to exist, and with her any possibility of human relations there may have been a danger of her establishing. The name reminds Dombey too, reminding him at the same time of the humiliating way in which, when little Paul was dying, that will had had to confess its defeat. But the truly horrifying aspect of the concentrated irony is that this humiliation of outraged pride should so predominate in Dombey's present pang of bereavement. To be reminded that the stoker 'foster-father' has a redundancy of children who live–that is bitter enough; but the climax of bitterness is when Dombey espies the crape on the stoker's cap, and realizes that it is worn for the dead Dombey heir. How dare *he*, the stoker, presume to flaunt *his* sympathy; how dare he make this implicit and insufferable claim to a common humanity?

The painful imaginative impact, which is shockingly real, brings to a new sharp focus our recognition of the truth that this pride is of its very nature an enemy to life. We renew our sense of the central irony that it should have been this confident spirit that killed Paul Dombey himself. For essentially it did, having with righteous deliberateness taken the risk. Polly's crime was unforgivable; she had yielded to her human feelings and gone to see her children. Therefore, although the proven perfect nurse for the motherless Paul, she must go:

> 'Ah, Richards!' said Mrs. Chick, with a sigh. 'It would have been more satisfactory to those who wish to think well of their fellow-creatures, and much more becoming in you, if you had shown some proper feeling, in time, for the little child that is now going to be prematurely deprived of its natural nourishment.'

The pride represented by the child and the child's vital interests being weighed against each other, there could be no question which was to be sacrificed. So Paul lost 'his second mother–his first, so far as he knew –by a stroke as sudden as that natural affliction which had darkened the beginning of his life' (and that the 'natural affliction' was the work of the same ethos is a reflection we make without further prompting).

The criminal expedition to Staggs's Gardens (chapter VI) that led to Polly's dismissal is a good instance of what occurs a great deal in *Dombey and Son*: the characteristically Dickensian (as it must strike the reader) that has a strength *not* characteristically Dickensian till *Dombey and Son* makes it so. Polly and Susan Nipper, with Florence and Paul, visiting the humble, populous and happy home of the Toodle family–it is a highly Dickensian occasion, and it is done with all the vivacity, force and humour of Dickens's genius. But the force goes with economy; there is no overdoing. The Toodle family and milieu, as we have noted, stand for that which is repressed and denied by the Dombey code: human kindness, natural human feeling, thriving human life. But there is nothing that seems to us sentimental or as the least inclined to be soft or too facile: it all affects us as real.

Dickens for his positives and foil has not, as in *Hard Times*, gone outside the common actualities of every day. The Toodles are, we don't question, just a working-class family belonging to the workaday Victorian world. The conditions that enabled Dickens to use them with a convinced sense of realism in the way he does are given, in very large part at any rate, in his account of the 'great earthquake' that has rent the Camden Town through which the little party finds its way to Staggs's Gardens. The description of the driving-through of the railway that was to have Euston for its terminus is in its vigour, vividness and clear authenticity a magnificent document of the early Victorian age. It reminds us of those drawings, paintings and engravings in which the artists of that time record their sense of the Titanism and romantic sublimity of the works of man. In a like spirit Dickens is profoundly impressed by the energy and the promise:

> In short, the yet unfinished and unopened Railroad was in progress, and, from the very core of all this dire disorder trailed smoothly away, upon its mighty course of civilization and improvement.

With much to justify him in the actualities he contemplates, he sees the railway as the triumphant manifestation of beneficent energy. And, characteristically, the beneficence that he acclaims manifests itself in terms of immediate human betterment. It is figured directly and representatively in Toodle himself – Toodle and his family. 'Where have you worked all your life?' Mr. Dombey asks him at that first intreview.

> – 'Mostly underground, Sir, till I got married. I come to the level then. I'm a going on one of these here railroads when they comes into full play.'

The prosperity and happiness of the Toodle family are associated with the 'coming into full play' of the railways – and seen as a representative accompaniment. When Dickens comes to write *Hard Times*, which is to register a disturbing contact with industrial England, he will not be able to use the working-classes in that way as a foil to Gradgrind, or to associate the Titanism of contemporary civilization with any beneficent action on humble life.

As I have noted, the 'hard' ethos celebrated in *Hard Times* figures explicitly enough in *Dombey and Son*. Where Education is in question we have it in the episode of the Charitable Grinders and Mr. Dombey's act of charitable generosity.

> 'The number of her son, I believe,' said Mr. Dombey, turning to his sister, and speaking of the child as if he were a family coach, 'is one hundred and forty-seven.'

II

It is remarkable that an art so strong, a moral insight and a grasp of realities so sure, should be associated as they are in *Dombey and Son* with things so different. The association is in many ways close and embarrassing, though the essential distinctions are easy to make–they make themselves. The impressive, the truly great, art I have been considering forms part of an elaborately plotted novel written–and written with conviction–for the Victorian market. With conviction: Dickens, it is plain, would have told us that the book had a long-pondered unifying theme and was conceived as a whole. He would have told us this in good faith: there is evidence enough of that. If, however, we are to do justice to what impresses us most in *Dombey and Son* we have to judge that the book is not a whole conceived in any unified or unifying imagination– and that it is certainly not, in its specious totality, the work of that genius which compels our homage in the strong parts. The creative afflatus goes in other, characteristic and large parts of the book with a moral *élan* that favours neither moral perception nor a grasp of the real.

I speak of 'creative afflatus' advisedly. We pass our adverse judgment, but we can't help perceiving–for all the evidence we have of the anxious calculating eye he kept upon the public and the sales-returns–that here too Dickens writes with the conviction, the triumphant conscious power, of the inspired artist. In fact, to arrive at a full recognition of the nature of his greatness, it is necessary to recognize how far, as a creative force, he was from being either a Romantic genius or a Flaubert. If we look through the chapters of Forster's *Life* covering the period during which (to take the instance under consideration) *Dombey* was written, that truth comes home to us. As, in the summer and autumn of 1846, he wrote the first two numbers, he felt that he was doing something superlatively good. Yet, after agonies of worry and hesitation, he laid the new and prospering work aside in order not to miss producing the annual Christmas tale this year, *The Battle of Life*.

It was not a rival creative compulsion, though it was a characteristic scruple of the actual great creative force Dickens was, that took him from *Dombey*. Simply, the Christmas tale had become an institution, and to defeat the expectation of the public, he felt, would be to damage his status. But the 'simply' must not be taken to suggest that this last clause portends an altogether simple state of mind (as we read Forster it is easy enough to understand, but less easy to analyse). There was certainly profit-and-loss calculation–Dickens was never a less than eager money-maker–but equally what we must call a sense of duty entered in. Was it not his status–his genius–to be *the* public entertainer? The public entertainer had as such his obligations to the public. Of closely related significance (records of such exchanges forming a constantly recurring element in the *Life*) are the anxious discussions with Forster as to whether the public will stand *this* contemplated development of the now-appearing story, or whether it wouldn't respond more favourably to *this*, which could very well be contrived.

To this kind of calculation Dickens commits himself without uneasiness or any sense of offending against the artist in him. That artist, in fact, needs, feels he ought to need and to have, and actually has, a sense of solidarity with the nation-wide public for which he writes–we have here a condition or essential aspect of his peculiar creative greatness. To observe which truth, of course, is not to abstain from noting the attendant disadvantages. We see the disadvantages in *Dombey* in Dickens's failure to maintain, and in his offences against–his worst departures and inconsistencies amount to that, the strength of the opening. The spectacle of the great writer at his greatest disturbing, and then deserting, the creative drive for the sake of an uninspired and unnecessary Christmas production may well strike us as ominous. And, actually, when he does, having incurred fatigue to the point of illness, take up *Dombey* again, calculations and inspirations that do not belong with the opening strength turn out to have established their claim to a major part in the development.

We may recall some admonitory modulations into an art that is disconcertingly Victorian in the pathos of the dying Paul and of the neglected Florence's goodness and beauty. But Dickens's rendering of Paul's fate and the cruel irony of the father's pride mustn't be dismissed with such a reference: nowhere is the poet-novelist's genius more apparent than there. The irony of the child's immolation is the irony of the father's pride, a pride that, of its nature, destroys life in painfully thwarting itself. And that pride (money-pride) is the theme so potently realized by Dickens in the strong half of the book, Dombey himself being the victim of the society that formed him and of which he is the honoured representative.

Life, of course, in the pages dealing with Paul's education, is above all –is focally and insistently–the child, the emergent sentience and awareness, and these pages give us childhood with the unique Dickensian vividness, delicacy and truth. And we are made to recognize that this power of recall is not something apart in Dickens; that it is beneath, or implicit in, the penetration and strength of his response in general to human life–the immediacy and insight with which he renders it. He has not forgotten; in achieving the rare maturity his genius represents he has lost nothing. The genius is an intense concern for the real, and Dickens, when under its command, isn't tempted to sentimentalize. The acuteness with which we are made to feel Paul's ache of deprivation, his hunger for love, depends on that and our utter conviction of it.

'little people should be tired at night, for then they sleep well.'

'Oh, it's not at night, papa,' returned the child, 'it's in the day; and I lie down in Florence's lap, and she sings to me. At night I dream about such cu-ri-ous things!'

And he went on warming his hands again, and thinking about them, like an old man or a young goblin. Mr. Dombey was so astonished, and so uncomfortable, and so perfectly at a loss how to pursue the conversation, that he could only sit looking at his son by the light of the fire, with his hand resting on his back, as if he were detained there by some magnetic attraction. Once he advanced his other hand, and turned the contemplative face towards his own for a moment. But it sought the fire again as soon as he released it; and remained, addressed towards the flickering blaze, until the nurse appeared, to summon him to bed.

'I want Florence to come for me,' said Paul.

'Won't you come with your poor nurse, Wickam, Master Paul?' inquired the attendant, with great pathos.

'No, I won't,' replied Payl, composing himself in his armcha again, like the master of the house.

Invoking a blessing upon his innocence, Mrs. Wickam withdrev and presently Florence appeared in her stead. The child immediatel started up with sudden readiness and animation, and raised toward his father in bidding him goodnight, a countenance so much brighter, so much younger, and so much more childlike altogether, that Mr. Dombey, while he felt greatly reassured by the change, was quite amazed at it.

After they had left the room altogether, he thought he heard a soft voice singing; and remembering that Paul had said his sister sung to him, he had the curiosity to open the door and listen, and look after them. She was toiling up the great, wide, vacant staircase, with him in her arms; she singing all the way, Paul sometimes crooning out a feeble accompaniment. Mr. Dombey looked after them until they reached the top of the staircase–not without halting to rest by the way–and passed out of his sight; and then he still stood gazing upwards, until the dull rays of the moon, glimmering in a melancholy manner through the skylight, sent him back to his own room.

The emotional situation presented here has a complexity that positively disclaims anything like a sentimental purpose. Paul himself isn't the ideally *sympathique* child-victim. He is a victim, right enough, but that doesn't make certain of the characterizing traits the less disconcerting. It isn't Wickam (not yet in the room) or Mrs. Pipchin and Mrs. Blimber who here see Paul as 'like an old man or a young goblin', but we ourselves and (for we take the suggestion) Dombey. Of course, those traits are very largely the products of the substitute for love that Dombey, with the devoted co-operation of his friends and allies, makes the formative spirit of the child's upbringing. But in this passage itself we have the intimation that the child is the son of his father:

'No, I won't,' replied Paul, composing himself in his armchair again, like the master of the house.

The irony for Dombey is that he has to see this admirably decisive firm-ness of the worthy successor, the born master, exerted in a characteristic demonstration of the love for Florence that he hates but daren't obstruct. That it belongs to a world wholly alien to him, from which he is ex-cluded, and in which the Dombey criteria of success have no meaning, is brought cruelly home to him when, opening the door, he looks and listens as Florence carries her brother up to bed. Something more than utterly disinterested love and absolute trust is involved in the evocative power (it suggests Lawrence) of that last paragraph of the passage I have quoted. As Florence toils (and toils happily) up the staircase, 'singing all he way', Paul croons an accompaniment, 'his head lying on her shoulder, one of his arms thrown negligently round her neck'. The 'old man', the goblin 'slyness', and the *enfant terrible* disconcertingness have disappeared, and been replaced by the relaxed and absorbed spontaneity of childhood.

The spontaneity is the flowing of life, emotional and imaginative. But Dombey's confident scheme has no place for spontaneity—for life that finds by living its own nature and need. 'There is nothing of chance or doubt before my son', he tells Mrs. Pipchin: 'His way in life was clear and prepared, and marked out before he existed.' She on her part re-assures him about the undesirable attachment to Florence: 'the studies he would have to master would very soon prove a sufficient alienation'. Mrs. Pipchin (the 'child-queller') in her self-enclosure is inertly malign, but it's not apprehension she awakens in Paul:

> He was not fond of her; he was not afraid of her; but in those old, old moods of his, she seemed to have a grotesque attraction for him. There he would sit, looking at her, and warming his hands, and looking at her, until he sometimes quite confounded Mrs. Pipchin, Ogress as she was. Once she asked him, when they were alone, what he was thinking about.
>
> 'You,' said Paul, without the least reserve.
>
> 'And what are you thinking about me?' asked Mrs. Pipchin.
>
> 'I'm thinking how old you must be,' said Paul.
>
> 'You mustn't say such things as that, young gentleman,' returned the other. 'That'll never do.'
>
> 'Why not?' asked Paul.
>
> 'Because it's not polite,' said Mrs. Pipchin snappishly.
>
> 'Not polite?' said Paul.
>
> 'No.'
>
> 'It's not polite,' said Paul innocently, 'to eat all the mutton-chops and toast, Wickam says.'

There is no suggestion of archness about the 'innocently' here; Paul, 'quaint' though he may be, *is* innocent; the *enfant terrible* element in him is the child's fresh, 'unsocial', directness of vision and judgment—frank because 'frank' is a word he hasn't learnt the use of.

> 'Berry's very fond of you, ain't she?' Paul once asked Mrs. Pipchin when they were sitting by the fire with the cat.
>
> 'Yes,' said Mrs. Pipchin.
>
> 'Why?' asked Paul.
>
> 'Why!' returned the disconcerted old lady. 'How can you ask such things, Sir! why are you fond of your sister Florence?'
>
> 'Because she's very good,' said Paul. 'There is nobody like Florence.'
>
> 'Well!' retorted Mrs. Pipchin shortly, 'and there's nobody like me, I suppose.'
>
> 'Ain't there really though?' asked Paul, leaning forward in his chair, and looking at her very hard.
>
> 'No,' said the old lady.
>
> 'I'm glad of that,' observed Paul, rubbing his hands thoughtfully. 'That's a very good thing.'
>
> Mrs. Pipchin didn't dare to ask him why, lest she should receive some perfectly annihilating answer.

The quality and nature of Mrs. Pipchin's apprehensiveness have been made manifest to us; it is the correlative of 'innocence'. For of Dickens's 'annihilating', too, we note that it isn't to be taken as cliché-colloquial. Paul, and not the less because he couldn't have expressed the judgments analytically, sees that, while she neither is loved nor wants to be (an oddity that makes her an object of fascinated contemplation to him), she relies with utter confidence on devoted services that imply love. The full conscious perception is not one she could have lived with (what she wants is unqualified selfish comfort), and when she is forced by Paul's unsocial innocence (which is 'not polite') to share it, she feels her own supreme reality (guaranteed as it is by an habitual sense of social corroboration) suddenly menaced with destruction.

The *enfant terrible* disconcertingness derives from Paul's own aching need – the deprivation that has conditioned his rapid 'quaint' development, and engendered the 'old man' or 'goblin' in him, his precocity. That comes out plainly in the scene (chapter VIII) which begins: 'Papa! what's money?'

The abrupt question had such immediate reference to the subject of Mr. Dombey's thoughts, that Mr. Dombey was quite disconcerted.

'What is money, Paul?' he answered. 'Money?'

'Yes,' said the child, laying his hands upon the elbows of his little chair, and turning the old face up towards Mr. Dombey's: 'what is money?'

Mr. Dombey was in a difficulty. He would have liked to give him some explanation involving the terms circulating medium, currency, depreciation of currency, paper, bullion, rates of exchange, value of precious metals in the market, and so forth: but looking down at the little chair, and seeing what a long way down it was, he answered: 'Gold, and silver, and copper. Guineas, shillings, half-pence. You know what they are?'

'Oh yes, I know what they are,' said Paul. 'I don't mean that, papa. I mean what's money after all?'

'What is money after all!' said Mr. Dombey, backing his chair a little, that he might the better gaze in sheer amazement at the presumptuous atom that propounded such an inquiry.

'I mean, papa, what can it do?' returned Paul, folding his arms (they were hardly long enough to fold), and looking at the fire, and up at him, and at the fire, and up at him again.

Mr. Dombey drew his chair back to its former place, and patted him on the head. 'You'll know better by and by, my man,' he said. 'Money, Paul, can do anything.' He took hold of the little hand, and beat it softly against one of his own, as he said so.

DICKENS

But Paul got his hand free as soon as he could; and rubbing it gently as if his wit were in the palm, and he were sharpening it–and looking at the fire again, as though the fire had been his adviser and prompter–repeated, after a short pause:

'Anything, papa?'

'Yes. Anything–almost,' said Mr. Dombey.

'Anything means everything, don't it, papa?' asked his son: not observing, or possibly not understanding, the qualification.

'It includes it: yes,' said Mr. Dombey.

'Why didn't money save my mama?' returned the child. 'It isn't cruel, is it?'

'Cruel!' said Mr. Dombey, settling his neckcloth, and seeming to resent the idea. 'No. A good thing can't be cruel.'

'If it's a good thing, and can do anything,' said the little fellow, thoughtfully, as he looked back at the fire, 'I wonder why it didn't save me my mama.'

He didn't ask the question of his father this time. Perhaps he had seen, with a child's quickness, that it had already made his father uncomfortable.

The child's directness, we see, has for Dombey the same effect as for Mrs. Pipchin; it makes him feel that the reality in which he has invested his life is threatened with annihilation. But Dombey has a resource that Mrs. Pipchin hasn't; he can propose to wean Paul from his childishly destructive irrationality by means that he is peculiarly in a position to exploit. Seizing on the opportunity offered by Solomon Gills's misfortune and Walter Gay's appeal, he tries to awaken and foster in Paul a pride that shall exploit his development into full Dombey adulthood.

'If you had money, now.' said Mr. Dombey; 'as much money as young Gay has talked about; what would you do?'

'Give it to his old uncle,' returned Paul.

'Lend it to his old uncle, eh?' retorted Mr. Dombey. 'Well! When you are old enough, you know, you will share my money, and we shall use it together.'

'Dombey an Son,' interrupted Paul, who had been tutored early in the phrase.

'Dombey and Son,!' repeated his father. 'Would you like to be Dombey and Son, now, and lend this money to young Gay's uncle?'

'Oh! if you please, papa!' said Paul: 'and so would Florence.'

'Girls,' said Mr. Dombey, 'have nothing to do with Dombey and Son. Would you like it?'

'Yes, papa, yes!'

'Then you shall do it,' returned his father. 'And you see, Paul,' he added, dropping his voice, 'how powerful money is, and how anxious people are to get it. Young Gay comes all this way to beg for money, and you, who are so grand and great, having got it, are going to let him have it, as a great favour and obligation.'

The potentiality is there in the child, as his immediate response shows:

Paul turned up the old face for a moment, in which there was a sharp understanding of the reference conveyed in these words: but it was a young and childish face immediately afterwards when he slipped down from his father's knee, and ran to tell Florence not to cry any more, for he was going to let young Gay have the money.

'Young Gay' is Florence's 'Walter', and Dombey, a little later, has the satisfaction, for all the 'uneasy glances' he bestows on the sister thus distinguished by the Son, of watching Paul 'walk about the room with the new-born dignity of letting young Gay have the money'.

Poignantly felt privation remains, of course, the determining condition in Paul. It is behind what I have been referring to as the *enfant terrible* in him. The phrase, in fact, is too glib, with a glibness that slights the delicacy and penetration of Dickens's insight. We can't help realizing that in the acutely affecting scene of Paul's introduction to the Blimber academy, when he makes his reply to the Doctor—the reply that is so heart-piercing in its brevity and finality. Blimber, unlike Mrs. Pipchin, isn't malign; he is merely stupid, with the confident collective stupidity of the world to which he belongs:

'Ha!' said the Doctor, leaning back in his chair with his hand in his breast. 'Now I see my little friend. [Paul has been lifted on to the table.] How do you do, my little friend?'
The clock in the hall wouldn't subscribe to this alteration in the form of words, but continued to repeat 'how,is, my,lit, tle,friend? how,is, my,lit, tle,friend?'
'Very well, I thank you, Sir,' returned Paul, answering the clock quite as much as the Docotr.
'Ha!' said Doctor Blimber. 'Shall we make a man of you?'
'Do you hear, Paul?' asked Mr. Dombey. Paul being silent.

Paul's intuitive recognition that this is a frighteningly inhuman world, one bent, in its blind mechanical cheerfulness[1], on annihilating *him*, is

[1]'As to Mr. Feeder B.A., Doctor Bimber's assistant, he was a kind of human barrel-organ . . . .'

conveyed in that 'answering the clock quite as much as the Doctor'. There is no sang-froid in the characteristic directness of his reply, when it comes:

'Shall we make a man of him?' repeated the Doctor.
'I had rather be a child,' replied Paul.

The poignancy of this has its dreadful piercingness because we know so well that Paul is doomed: no adult present will be pierced, and the righteous personnel of the academy, unlike Mrs. Pipchin, can't be disconcerted by the menace of being made to see itself.

'Indeed!' said the Doctor, 'Why?'
The child sat on the table looking at him, with a curious expression of suppressed emotion in his face, and beating one hand proudly on his knee as if he had the rising tears beneath it, and crushed them. But his other hand strayed a little way the while, a little farther–farther from his yet–until it lighted on the neck of Florence. 'This is why,' it seemed to say, and then the steady look was broken up and gone; the working lip was loosened, and the tears came streaming forth.
'Mrs. Pipchin,' said the father, in a querulous manner, 'I am really very sorry to see this.'
'Come away from him, do, Miss Dombey,' quoth the matron.[1]

The exploitation of childish tears plays no part in the heart-rending pathos of Paul's life and death as Dickens evokes it. The other occasion on which Paul expresses with as intense and overt a directness the extremity of his case–the starvation and the ache–is when he asks Florence, 'where's India, where that boy's friends live?'

'Oh, it's a long distance off,' said Florence, raising her eyes from her work.
'Weeks off?' asked Paul.
'Yes, dear. Many weeks' journey, night and day.'
'If you were in India, Floy,' said Paul, after being silent for a minute, 'I should–what is it that mama did? I forget.'
'Loved me,' answered Florence.
'No, no. Don't I love you now, Floy? What is it?–Died. If you were in India, I should die, Floy.'
She hurriedly put her work aside, and laid her head down on his

---

[1] " "Never mind", said the Doctor, blandly nodding his head, to keep Mrs. Pipchin back. "Ne-ver mind; we shall substitute new cares and new impressions, Mr. Dombey, very shortly. You would still wish my little friend to acquire —?" '

pillow, caressing him. And so would she, she said, if he were there. He would be better soon.

'Oh! I'm a great deal better now!' he answered. 'I don't mean that. I mean I should die of being so sorry and so lonely, Floy!'

Dickens doesn't simplify. And his concern, childhood being the theme, to present the essential varied and related expressions of the reality he perceives, and knows, so fully in imaginative possession, precludes, where his genius is engaged, all possibility of sentimentalizing. The privation that makes Paul so hungry for love and so devoted to Florence manifests itself also in his attachment to Old Glubb. Love frees and licenses his spontaneity–the spontaneity that is, of its nature, imaginative and creative. To repress the spontaneity in children as the Blimber academy does is to thwart and discourage life. Paul is still a living child, and he sees, among other things of importance to himself that he doesn't mention to the academic staff, 'lions and tigers climbing up his bedroom walls' and 'grim sly faces in the squares and diamonds of the floor'. The attraction of Old Glubb is that he represents, for the starved and thwarted child, the life-fostering indulgence in creative 'wonder' (the 'wonder' that Gradgrind is to deplore and ban[1]) for the lack of which, though knowing he will have the rationed company of Florence and love at intervals, he wilts:

'What a dreadful low name!' said Mrs. Blimber. 'Unclassical to a degree! Who is the monster, child?'

'What monster?' inquired Paul.

'Glubb,' said Mrs. Blimber, with a great disrelish.

'He's no more a monster than you are,' returned Paul.

'What!' cried the Doctor, in a terrible voice. 'Aye, aye, aye! What's that?'

Paul was dreadfully frightened, but still he made a stand for the absent Glubb, though he did it trembling.

'He's a very nice old man, ma'am,' he said. 'He used to draw my couch. He knows all about the deep sea, and the fish that are in it, and the great monsters that come and lie on rocks in the sun, and dive into the water again when they're startled, blowing and splashing so, that they can be heard for miles. There are some creatures,' said Paul, warming with his subject, 'I don't know how many yards long, and I forget their names, but Florence knows, that pretend to be in great distress; and when a man goes near them, out of compassion, they open their great jaws, and attack him. But all he has got to do,' said

[1]See page 191 below (the attitude summed up in: 'You are not to wonder').

Paul, boldly tendering this information to the very Doctor himself, 'is to keep on turning as he runs away, and then, as they turn slowly, because they are so long, and can't bend, he's sure to beat them. And though old Glubb don't know why the sea should make me think of my mama that's dead, or what it is that it's always saying–always saying! he knows a great deal about it. And I wish,[1] the child concluded with a sudden falling of his countenance, and failing in his animation, as he looked, like one forlorn, upon the three strange faces, 'that you'd let old Glubb come here to see me, for I know him very well, and he knows me.'

The significance of old Glubb comes out in the way in which, though the child starts tremulously, his spontaneity asserts itself and takes charge as he gets launched on the theme of his initiation. The legends he retails may be grotesque, but there is a terrible pathos in the naïve and eager good faith with which he commits himself to the flow of the recital–terrible, because of the 'three strange faces', and because the reception will demonstrate the extremity of his need and the hopelessness. Later he makes a desperate appeal to Cornelia, whom he strains himself to please:[1]

'Oh, Dombey, Dombey!' said Miss Blimber, 'this is very shocking.
'If you please,' said Paul. 'I think if I might sometimes talk a little to old Glubb, I should be able to do better.'
'Nonsense, Dombey,' said Miss Blimber. 'I couldn't hear of it. This is not the place for Glubbs of any kind.'

A few pages on we have this correlative observation:

Such spirits as he had in the outset, Paul soon lost of course. But he retained all that was strange, and old, and thoughtful in his character: and under circumstances so favourable to the development of those tendencies, became even more strange, and old, and thoughtful than before.
The only difference was that he kept his character to himself. He grew more thoughtful and reserved, every day; and had no such curiosity in any living member of the Doctor's household, as he had had in Mrs. Pipchin's. He loved to be alone. . . .

[1]'It was not that Miss Blimber meant to be too hard upon him, or that Doctor Blimber meant to bear too heavily on the young gentleman. Cornelia merely held the faith in which she had been bred; and the Doctor, in some partial confusion of his ideas, regarded the young gentlemen as if they were all Doctors, and were born grown up. Comforted by the the applause of the young gentlemen's nearest relations, and urged on by their blind vanity . . . .'

The profound, far-reaching and (disturbing to think!) representative irony of Paul's fate was conceived by the major Dickens who, as a conscious and supremely intelligent artist, was aware both of the advance represented by what he had done and of the difficulty of completing the book as a realized, total conception at the level of what he must have known to be the magnificent and marvellously original first part. He wrote to Forster on the 19th of September, 1847:

> Dombey takes so much time, and requires to be so carefully done, that I really have serious doubts whether it is wise to go on with the Christmas book.

He did go on with the Christmas book, and it was a tired Dickens, desperately needing to relax, who came back to the problem facing him; the problem of a writer who, committed to holding his immense addicted public in instalments written rapidly for the printer, was committed by his new sense of his genius to developing at the same time, if he could, an exactingly profound and pregnant conception and remaining creatively possessed by it. What we have to observe is the demonstration that he couldn't; the defeat, in the circumstances, striking as it is by reason of the paradoxical contrast it involved, can hardly be cause for wonder. The decisive turn comes with the development of the main theme that was proposed for *Dombey and Son*—a development in perfect keeping, it must have seemed to the rushed, but resourceful and confidently productive, Dickens. The theme, money-pride and money-dominance as enacted by the representative Mr. Dombey, now becomes that of the Bought Bride. This takes Dickens into a realm where he *knows* nothing. What he takes for knowledge is wholly external and conventional; determined, therefore, unresistingly by all the theatrical clichés and sentimental banalities of the high-life novelette and the equivalent drama. It lends itself congenially to the elaborations of the plot to which he is committed—villainies of the flashing-toothed villain, coincidences, sensations, reversals and melodramatic *dénouement*. We have the quality of his essential imaginative engagement in the pairing of Edith with a beauty in low life, a natural cousin who has a mercenary Mrs. Brown for a mother to match Mrs. Skewton, and who, for further link with Edith, has herself had a place in the life of the wicked Carker. Dickens means this ingeniously revealed pattern to have a serious moral significance in relation to his theme. It enables him, while observing all the Victorian proprieties, to throw the lurid light of the word 'prostitution', which he doesn't bring in explicitly, on Edith's marriage-contract with Mr. Dombey.

Alice, she also beautiful, belongs unequivocally to low life–she has just returned from some years of exile as a transported felon, but she not only maintains towards her mercenary mother the proud accusing attitude of Edith towards Mrs. Skewton; she holds forth on her own position and history with a finished rhetorical eloquence indistinguishable from Edith's. It is an eloquence that bears no relation to anything real, and that Alice, the returned convict, should speak it, and speak it (one gathers) with an educated accent, is no more absurd than that the well-born lady should. The whole business of Edith's 'proud' attitude to Dombey is unreal–as unreal as Dombey's use of Carker for intermediary in order to humiliate her. It is impossible to make moral sense of her attitude towards her marriage, and only in the world of melodramatic rhetoric could there be any illusion to the contrary. That Dickens, yielding in response to protests, should have changed his mind and saved her 'virtue' at the expense of the sensationally thwarted villain adds nothing essential–it couldn't–to the unreality. But we are to take it as a moment of high moral significance, the emotional poignancy depending on that, when, in the final meeting with Florence, Edith is able to declare herself 'innocent'.

That Dickens changed his mind about Walter Gay and, instead of letting him go to the bad, brought him back to marry Florence, also made no difference that mattered. The art of this Dickens runs no less, and more acceptably, to the unrealities of the happy ending (as of course to the frustration of the villain). Its spirit proclaims itself frankly here: 'A wandering princess and a good monster in a story-book might have sat by the fireside, and talked as Captain Cuttle and poor Florence talked– and not have looked very much unlike them.' This is only speciously an unequivocal placing note: Carker's villainy–though *he*, ostensibly, re-presents the real world of Dombey and Son's counting-house–belongs to the same ethos of unreality, along with the drama of his frustration. And so much of the play of Dickens's humorous and comic abundance, even when it issues in the sinister-grotesque, serves the ends of implicit reassurance: reassurance that works by implicitly discounting the serious-ness of the drama–by intimating that what we have to do with does not, at bottom, make any claim to be the world where the sanctions, con-ditions and inexorabilities of real life hold without remission. Personally, I find Captain Cuttle–and not only Captain Cuttle–boring. But there is an immense deal of Dickens's comic creation that, in its genial and self-justifying liveliness and force, gives us what we acclaim as the expression of his genius, and yet, in the respect referred to, belongs with Captain Cuttle – with Captain Cuttle rather than with the Toodles. The Toodles represent what we have in the strongest part of *Dombey and Son*, and it is this strength that I have been intent on distinguishing. The Toodles have their essential part – and it is performed with what might strike us as an un-Dickensian economy – in an art that offers an astringent and wholly serious 'criticism of life'.

But I must not appear to be suggesting that, on the side of humorous creation, what goes decidedly with the supreme strength of *Dombey and Son* rather than with Captain Cuttle is confined to the Toodle family. The case is of course far otherwise. The book contains Susan Nipper, Mr. Toots, Mrs. MacStinger, Cousin Feenix – a quartet whom, in their variety, I permit myself to specify as a reminder of the actual wealth. This Dickens, compelling observer and recorder of life, there is very obvious point in describing as Shakespearian (consider the vitality – the surprisingness combined with felicity, dramatic and poetic – of the speech in which he so largely renders these characters).

It is a commonplace that Captain Cuttle represents, in his Victorian way, the influence of Smollett, but some of Dickens's strongest art reveals an essential kind of indebtedness to his education in the eighteenth-century masters that is an utterly different thing. This is an episode from the visit to Warwick Castle (chapter XXVII):

'Ah, ma'am!' cried Carker, stopping short; 'but if you speak of pictures, there's a composition! What gallery in the world can produce the counterpart of that?'

As the smiling gentleman thus spake, he pointed through a doorway to where Mr. Dombey and Edith were standing alone in the centre of another room.

They were not interchanging a word or a look. Standing together, arm in arm, they had the appearance of being more divided than if seas had rolled between them. . . . So unmatched were they, and opposed, so forced and linked together by a chain which adverse hazard and mischance had forged: that fancy might have imagined the pictures on the walls around them, startled by the unnatural conjunction, and observant of it in their several expressions. Grim knights and warriors looked scowling on them. A churchman, with his hand upraised, denounced the mockery of such a couple coming to God's altar. Quiet waters in landscapes, with the sun reflected in their depths, asked, if better means of escape were not at hand, was there no drowning left? Ruins cried, 'Look here, and see what We are, wedded to uncongenial Time!' Animals, opposed by nature, worried one another, as a moral to them. Loves and Cupids took to flight afraid, and Martyrdom had no such torment in its painted history of suffering.

Again and again in *Dombey* we meet with this manner, a rhetoric where the moral and pictorial have been transmuted by a truly poetic imagination. While the passage quoted reminds us forcibly of the Virginia Woolf of *To the Lighthouse* (as do so many others of the same kind in this book), and though it consorts naturally with what is most impressive in *Dombey and Son*, and even, in its strong way, strikes us as characteristically Dickensian, yet the relation to Hogarth is plain. We are reminded how radically pre-Victorian Dickens was in his upbringing, education and temperament, in other matters besides his eighteenth-century tastes in art and literature. But here it is a crucial indebtedness to the eighteenth-century artist that we have to note: the indebtedness to Hogarth that is beyond question a major, if not generally recognized, fact of Dickens's development.

That Dickens had an intense admiration for, and real understanding of, Hogarth is on record: Forster quotes a tribute at some length in the *Life*. What still, oddly enough, has to be insisted on is the significance of the admiration. We hear a good deal of the influence on Dickens of Smollett, but that is a small affair, and the influence even of Fielding doesn't amount to much compared with that of Hogarth. We can see that Dickens's moral and creative imagination was deeply affected by Hogarth's work, and that, striving to achieve the expression of his own vision and sensibility in an art that should convey his profoundest sense of life, he drew habitually on Hogarth; he responded intensely to him and used him creatively. Only a great original writer, a great poet, could have done with Hogarth what Dickens did; but to say that he did it *with* Hogarth–that in such a passage as that quoted above we have a creative adaptation of Hogarth–is plainly justifiable. And there is more in the way of Hogarthian influence to be seen in *Dombey* than this pointing–a proper emphasis–to passages of magnificent Dickensian prose might convey: it is surely more than a guess that the idea of Dombey's second marriage came to him from *Marriage à la Mode*. In any case, Hogarth was one of the sources of life and shaping inspiration from the English past that gave Dickens, as a novelist in the English tradition, such immense advantage over any French contemporary.

But as *Dombey and Son* exemplifies very copiously, he *was*–inevitably–
Victorian. He was Victorian, pre-Victorian, and, at his greatest, a genius
of a kind one doesn't label with any adjective that–with limiting intention or not–emphasizes period characteristics. He was, in fact, in his
own way, very complex. What I have been insisting on is that his way
was that of a great genius, and that there is a much greater Dickens than
the traditional cult has tended to recognize. Can we imagine conditions
under which we might have had more of him, or had him in a 'purer'
form? The actual Dickens, it is true, was 'uneducated', in the sense that
he had had no such education as might have given him a maturity of
critical consciousness in respect of the new art his genius was developing.
But, after all, there is little point in such a speculation; for when one asks
oneself what such an education could have been there is no answer. His
distinctive genius *was* the ability to respond freely and expansively to the
inspirations of popular taste, popular tradition and the market, and, in
doing so, to evolve for himself (and for the world) a high intellectual art.
The evolving, in all conscience, was rapid–rapid and superlatively intelligent.

Contemplating the diverse and disparate elements brought together
into a specious unity in *Dombey and Son* (specious, because to be just to
Dickens one must insist that the strength represented by the early treatment of the theme of money-pride and the conventional nullity of the
treatment of pride and scruple in Edith remain at odds), one asks how
the confident show of unity is achieved, and is perhaps inclined to reply
that it is done through the dominant resonance on the moral side of the
sentimental and melodramatic–with which so much of the humour and
comedy consort quite happily. An answer fairer to Dickens's genius
would be to point to the poetic conception of his art that this first elaborate novel of his gives proof of, and to the inexhaustibly wonderful
poetic life of his prose. One may not feel the faintest velleity of serious
response to such effects as that in which the refrain 'Let him remember
it in this room in years to come!' figures; yet they have their place in
the wonderfully varied and flexible play of what, considering the use of
language, and the use of imagery and symbolism and dramatic enact-
ment, one has to call poetic means. For the characteristic higher use of
poetic means, consider this:

The passive desolation of disuse was everywhere silently manifest
about it. Within doors, curtains, drooping heavily, lost their old folds
and shapes, and hung like cumbrous palls. Hecatombs of furniture,

27

still piled and covered up, shrunk like imprisoned and forgotten men, and changed insensibly. Mirrors were dim as with the breath of years. Patterns of carpets faded and became perplexed and faint, like the memory of those years' trifling incidents. Boards, starting at unwonted footsteps, creaked and shook. Keys rusted in the locks of doors. Damp started on the walls, and as the stains came out, the pictures seemed to go in and secrete themselves. Mildew and mould began to lurk in closets. Fungus trees grew in corners of the cellars. Dust accumulated, nobody knew whence nor how; spiders, moths, and grubs were heard of every day. An exploratory black-beetle now and then was found immovable upon the stairs, or in an upper room, as wondering how he got there. Rats began to squeak and scuffle in the nighttime, through dark galleries they mined behind the panelling.

The dreary magnificence of the state rooms, seen imperfectly by the doubtful light admitted through closed shutters, would have answered well enough for an enchanted abode. Such as the tarnished paws of gilded lions, stealthily put out from beneath their wrappers; the marble lineaments of busts on pedestals, fearfully revealing themselves through veils; the clocks that never told the time, or, if wound up by any chance, told it wrong, and struck unearthly numbers, which are not upon the dial; the accidental tinklings among the pendant lustres, more startling than alarm-bells; the softened sounds and laggard air that made their way among these objects, and a phantom crowd of others, shrouded and hooded, and made spectral of shape. But, besides, there was the great staircase, where the lord of the place so rarely set his foot, and by which his little child had gone up to Heaven.

The evocations of the Dombey house–evocations of varied dramatic mood and tone–are very impressive in their characteristic Dickensian power: the Hogarthian passages sort well with other kinds that are also in their different ways strong. See, for instance, in chapter IX the account of the second-hand shop ending:

> Of motionless clocks that never stirred a finger, and seemed as incapable of being successfully wound up, as the pecuniary affairs of their former owners, there was always great choice in Mr. Brogley's shop; and various looking-glasses, accidentally placed at compound interest of reflection and refraction, presented to the eye an eternal perspective of bankruptcy and ruin.

> Mr. Brogley himself was a moist-eyed, pink-complexioned, crisp-haired man, of a bulky figure and an easy temper–for that class of

Caius Marius who sits upon the ruins of other people's Carthages, can keep up his spirits well enough.

Everywhere, in description and narrative and dramatic presentation and speech, we have exemplified that vitality of language which invites us to enforce from Dickens the truth of the proposition that in the Victorian age the poetic strength of the English language goes into the novel, and that the great novelists are the successors of Shakespeare. In fact, it is hard not to see a significance in the habitual way (the habit is very marked in *Dombey and Son*) in which Dickens quotes from Shakespeare and alludes to him–in the familiarity with Shakespeare he assumes in the reader and in the evidence he gives of the active presence of Shakespeare in his own creative mind. That he developed an art so different from anything he could have learnt from Smollett or Fielding–or Ben Jonson, in whom he was also interested, or the theatre of his own time–was of course a manifestation of his genius; but that his genius was fostered on the side of its characteristic strength by the potent fact of Shakespeare, not only in his own life, but in the life of the English people for whom he wrote (a fact making itself felt at the level of popular entertainment), is very much a point to be made. When it was that Shakespeare ceased to be a popular institution I do not know; he was certainly that in Dickens's formative period. Looking at the characteristics of form and method of the novel as Dickens was aspiring to create it in *Dombey and Son*, we can see that the influence of the sentimental and melodramatic theatre was not the only dramatic influence that counted, or the most profound.

One cannot, then, rest happily on the formula that Dickens's genius was that of a great popular entertainer: the account is not unequivocal enough. Exalting the 'great French novelists' in general, and Balzac in particular, over 'their fellows here,' a well-known Sunday-paper critic not very long ago wrote:

> George Eliot, deeply influenced by the French, was the first English writer, I belive, to think of fiction as a major art. . . . Thackeray, Dickens and Trollope, like their eighteenth-century predecessors, were satisfied to offer entertainment, often weighted with moralizing.

It is an ignorant and unintelligent *parti pris*, the Francophil convention of 'Bloomsbury', that comes out, amusingly, in that 'deeply influenced by the French'. But what immediately concerns us is the bracketing of Dickens with Thackeray and Trollope–an absurdity that *Dombey and Son* is enough to dispose of. Dickens was in the fullest sense a great national artist. His genius responded with inexhaustible vitality to the new, the unprecedented conditions of a rapidly developing civilization. In catering for the tastes and needs of a nation-wide public he found congenial employment for his powers—he found what his powers were and he found the inspiration he himself needed. His art was wonderfully original, and no great writer was ever more remote from being troubled or limited or guided by scruples that could in any sense be called academic. Yet, as we have seen, Dickens's uninhibited freedom of practice as a great popular artist did not prevent him from having his essential creative relations with the classical past of English literature and English art. And if we are to say that he saw himself as a popular entertainer, it must not be with any suggestion that he did not think of himself, and with justice, as having, *qua* artist, a penetrating insight into contemporary civilization, its ethos, its realities and its drives, that it concerned him to impart. And if we are to talk of fiction as a 'major art', then, faced with explaining what we mean and how the 'art' established its right to be considered in that way, we have to recognize that Dickens had a very important—a major—part in the history. He may, in the habit and conditions of his work, have been very unlike Flaubert, but he nevertheless thought of himself with the conscious pride of responsibility as an artist, and with a developing earnestness pondered the claims of his art. His *œuvre*, in fact, presents the critic of 'fiction as a major art' with a central, delicate and testing challenge.

APPENDIX

Dickens and Smollett

Dickens was an enthusiastic reader of Smollett in his boyhood[1] and paid tribute to him not only explicitly, as in making Roderick Random, Peregrine Pickle and Humphrey Clinker the imaginative sustenance of David Copperfield in his boyhood—along with such authentic immortals as Don Quixote, Tom Jones, the Vicar of Wakefield and Robinson

[1]'Supposing one wrote an essay on Fielding, for instance, and another on Smollett, and another on Sterne, recalling how one read them as a child (no one read them younger than I, I think) and how one gradually grew up into a different knowledge of them, and so forth—would it not be interesting to many people?'—Letter, quoted by Forster, Sept. 5 1847.

Crusoe–but, as has been frequently pointed out, by including, in his earlier novels at least, a line of cruder comic characters in the Smollett image of such, with their external humours and coarse knockabout. However, after *Pickwick Papers* such obtrusive borrowings can be seen to have been transmuted into the Dickensian art: they have an inherent psychological interest in themselves (like Dennis the hangman in *Barnaby Rudge*) and are absorbed into the totality of the novel in which they occur, and this seems not as yet recognized by literary criticism, though it should be part of the larger tribute paid to Dickens which he himself felt owing to him and deplored his never receiving. Even in an early novel like *The Old Curiosity Shop*, Dick Swiveller and Codlin and Short, for instance, are very different from similar types in Smollett and not merely in having been made acceptable to a more refined age. It is in the first great Dickens novel, *Dombey*, that what Dickens made of his Smollett originals may be most profitably studied. In Captain Cuttle, 'a very salt-looking man indeed', with 'a hook instead of a hand', a nose all over knobs like his stick, a farcical hard glazed hat and 'such a very large coarse shirt-collar, that it looked like a small sail', we have a character visibly close to Smollett's rough sea-dogs, a character who would not have been there at all but for the Smollett originals, who has the customary eccentricities of speech and manners of such Smollett types and who gets involved in the customary comic humours (with the vixen Mrs. MacStinger, the still more Smollettian Captain Bunsby, the artful Rob the Grinder, etc.). But Captain Cuttle is not sentimentalized in order to make such a type tolerable to a Victorian reading public which would not have borne Smollett's brutal humour, though the Captain's having been endowed with qualities of feeling such as chivalry and some delicacy, as well as with a vein of shrewdness that may seem incompatible with such worldly simplicity as he manifests habitually, may make him dubiously plausible. We are obliged by the quality of Dickens's art in *Dombey* (and there are three chapters before the Captain appears) to reflect that human nature is more complex even in the apparently simplest and least cultivated of us, than is recognized in Fielding's and Smollett's novels, and that Dickens is the superior of his predecessors if only in asserting this and consistently providing for it. Moreover, Captain Cuttle is not a mere grotesque who could be as well in one novel as another, a peripheral figure of fun or a cog in the plotting as in a picaresque novel, but falls within the stylization of the whole theme of the unique work of art in which he plays an essential part.

For example, he is the necessary complement to Sol Gills for the nurturing of Walter Gay, in contrast to Mr. Dombey's, Mrs. Pipchin's and the Blimbers' of little Paul: even more an orphan than Paul, and in addition poor, Walter is shown to receive from his foster-parents the love and imaginative food for lack of which the rich man's son pines and dies; and that Captain Cuttle is a sailor with, it is shown, the reverence for the mysteries of life ingrained in him by the experiences of seafaring, associates him with Old Glubb in the meaning of the book, as well as with the nautical instrument-maker Sol Gills, these standing in contrast to Dombey himself, Carker, Major Bagstock, the Blimbers and the other land-sharks preying on little Paul and Florence, who ignore the sea and its voices. Another aspect in which Captain Cuttle relates to the whole meaning of the book is in his faith in the amount of capital represented by his silver teaspoons, sugar-tongs and watch, not by any means merely the occasion for a trivial kind of humour. His belief in the value of these objects, his 'property', is either ridiculous or touching, as you care to take it, and Dickens allows for both reactions, making it plain that he sees Cuttle's belief is preposterous to Mr. Dombey and likely to be found absurd by the sophisticated reader; yet Dickens thus intimates to us that, to the hard-working pilot and skipper, such a pitiful accumulation, plus an annuity of a hundred pounds a year, is the reward for a life of honest service to the Dombey society (Dombey makes his money by trading overseas). It is also a proof that the Captain's life has been passed among those to whom his little heap of silver objects and the contents of his tin canister of savings represents wealth, so that his confidence in its impressiveness when he goes with Walter to negotiate a loan for Sol Gills in chapter X is natural. And we are perforce touched by the Captain's willingness to give his all, his annuity as well as his pathetic little heap of property laid out on the table before us, to save his friend from bankruptcy, when we are shown in contrast Mr. Dombey's mean prudence in correcting Paul's instinctive 'give it to his old uncle' to 'lend it to his old uncle'—mean, seeing that 'he' is Walter who has done the whole Dombey family a service in rescuing Florence and that the required sum is nothing to Mr. Dombey. As part of the theme of the novel Dickens is showing that the poor man can put forth such flowers of the spirit as generosity and a delicacy of feeling not known to the successful merchant, a delicacy which is not the product of education or contacts with social superiors. We meet this again in Hard Times in the contrast between the horse-riding people and the Gradgrind-Bounderby class in their attitudes to Sissy's loss of her father. Captain Cuttle is thus seen to be a necessary element in the novel, casting an ironic light on that Victorian idea of Property as a value and its acquisition an end in itself which is later to be satirized both by Dickens in Wemmick's assertion of everyone's obligation to acquire Portable Property and by Tennyson's insight into the effects of this assumption (that it superseded all real human values) in his brilliant poem 'The Northern Farmer, New Style'. Without going into the subject exhaustively, we can see in the case of Captain Cuttle that a Smollett type of character has been by Dickens's profounder genius turned to uses inconceivable to Smollett.

Q.D.L.

CHAPTER TWO

DICKENS AND TOLSTOY: THE CASE FOR A SERIOUS VIEW OF 'DAVID COPPERFIELD'

i

D AVID COPPERFIELD is a long novel, uneven in quality and more complicated than it may seem; snap judgments on it are certain to be not merely inadequate but falsifying. Therefore there seems to me an interesting point which must be raised before anyone can begin to discuss it at all: What novel is it? For evidently, for Tolstoy it was a very different novel from what it was for its English contemporaneous admirers or equally from what (quite other) it is for its latter-day denigrators – I note that in the opinion of the more recent trans-Atlantic thesis-writers (there is always a smart Dickens book in vogue with the academics and literary journalists, and those favoured at the moment seem to be Garis[1] and Dabney[2]) the valuation of *David Copperfield* should be low indeed. The view of it held from the moment of its publication in 1850 and till modern Dickens criticism ousted that, was shown in its being bracketed invariably in esteem with *Pickwick Papers*, the pair being accepted as the high-water mark of Dickens's achievement (with *The Christmas Carol* often thrown in) – *David Copperfield* was 'second only to *Pickwick* in immediate and lasting popularity', wrote Forster, Dickens's biographer and business confidant. This was the valuation not only of the average un-critical member of Dickens's reading-public but also of the most intellectual men of the age, who thus made it clear that they saw Dickens only as a writer to relax with. 'I was told by Lord Morley', wrote Harold Laski in his Introduction to Mill's *Autobiography*, 'that few people enjoyed more, or read more often, *Pickwick Papers* and *David Copperfield*' than – John Stuart Mill. Lord Acton, I note, wrote in 1880 in a letter: 'It is beginning at the wrong end to read *David Copperfield* first, but he

[1] R. Garis, *The Dickens Theatre: A Reassessment of the Novels* (Oxford, 1965).
[2] Ross H. Dabney, *Love and Property in the Novels of Dickens* (Chatto and Windus, 1967).

34

[Dickens] is worth anything to busy men, because his fun is so hearty and so easy, and he rouses the emotions by such direct and simple methods. I am ashamed to think how much more often I return to Dickens than to George Eliot'. Perhaps comment is unnecessary, but my deduction that he thought Dickens, at what Acton took to be his best, could serve only for the relaxation of serious citizens, and rather shamingly at that, is borne out by another statement in his letters: 'Dickens is far below Thackeray in his characters', and it appears that he didn't think much of Thackeray at that.[1]

Quite logically, from this reading of and valuation of *Copperfield*, Forster saw Dickens's subsequent novels as a steady falling-off, increasingly less amusing and more 'unpleasant' (for instance, he complains that Skimpole is a very disagreeable successor to Micawber), while the only drawback to *Copperfield's* perfection he finds is the insertion of the unnecessarily 'unpleasant' Rosa Dartle. An acceptance of this reading of *Copperfield* is implied in Henry James's low opinion of Dickens generally, as in this comment in his non-fictional book *English Hours*: 'You go on liking *David Copperfield*–I don't say you go on reading it, which is a very different matter–because it is Dickens'. Supporting this view of Dickens we have James's statement in his essay on Turgeniev in 1884 expressing surprise that 'Turgeniev should have rated Dickens so high' and explaining that it *must* have been 'merely that Dickens diverted him, as well he might'.

Tolstoy on the contrary *did* go on reading it, having singled out *David Copperfield* from his first encountering the Russian translation[2] and then grappling with it in English with the aid of a dictionary in order to do it justice.[3] We know from numerous independent sources of Tolstoy's

[1] I quote from letters printed in *Lord Acton and his Times* by David Mathew.

[2] When he was 24, not, as he alleged in 1896, before he was 20–though his putting the influence of *David Copperfield* back in memory to his adolescence, the most formative period, is significant.

[3] Dickens was highly esteemed by the Russian intelligentsia and early translated, *David Copperfield* appearing in Russian translation in both 'The Contemporary' and 'The Muscavite' in 1851. Tolstoy refers to it first in his diary for Sept. 2 1852, where he wrote: 'Read *David Copperfield*–a delight', and in Dec. 1853 wrote to his brother: 'Buy me Dickens's *David Copperfield* in English, and send me Sadler's English Dictionary, which is among my books'–I quote from an essay, 'Tolstoy and Dickens' in *Family Views of Tolstoy*, ed. Aylmer Maude, to which I was referred by Dr Theodore Redpath, on consulting him with respect to my interest in Dickens's influence on Tolstoy. There N. Apostolov says that Dickens's

conversation throughout his long life, as well as from his own written tributes, that *David Copperfield* was a serious and indeed fundamental influence on his work as a novelist. In 1905 he told Makovitsky: 'How good Dickens is! I should have liked to write about him'. Though he seems never to have done so directly, I think by examining his novels we can see what he would have written about Dickens if he had been able, from the use he makes of Dickens and the understanding of Dickens's themes and intentions that he shows in *War and Peace* and *Anna Karenina*. Recalling in conversation with friends in 1905 the influence Dickens had on him when he began writing he said that it was second only to Stendhal's; but in general he placed Dickens above all other novelists and *Copperfield* above all his other novels: his family quoted him as saying: 'If you sift the world's prose literature, Dickens will remain; sift Dickens, *David Copperfield* will remain'. He also said: 'Dickens was a genius such as is met with but once in a century' and 'on me he had a great influence'. Between this admiration for Dickens in his youth and his old age there are also similar references to his frequenting Dickens's novels–e.g. in 1886: 'Dickens interests me more and more', and he used to read Dickens to his visitors. While to us it may on reflection seem surprising that a young Russian aristocrat with a wild youth and an army officer's experiences, living as a privileged member of an archaic society which had an autocrat at one end of the social scale and serfs at the other, accustomed to only a monastic form of Christianity and generally being as remote as a European can be imagined from in-

translations in Russian magazines 'crowded out' all other English and French writers, Dickens's popularity in Russia being at its height in the 1840s and 1850s; Russian critics approved of Dostoevski's imitating Dickens, for example. While Apostolov stresses a general debt of Tolstoy to Dickens, he does not specify anything more than Tolstoy's finding congenial Dickens's 'humorous treatment of his themes' and 'the socio-ethical bearing of his novels' generally. Dickens himself was soon made acquainted with his success in Russia; a Russian man of letters sent him a translation of *Dombey* into Russian 'informing him that his works, which before had only been translated in the journals, and with certain omissions, had now been translated in their entire form by his correspondent', ending: 'For the last eleven years your name has enjoyed a wide celebrity in Russia .... Your *Dombey* continues to inspire with enthusiasm the whole of the literary Russia.' This seems to have been in 1849 (*v*. Forster, Book VI, § IV) but Dickens's work was widely known in Russia by 1844. It was as well that Tolstoy struggled with *David Copperfield* in English, for Russian translators made free with Dickens's text, and the translator of *David Copperfield* has been found guilty of many hundreds of ad libbings.

dustrialized Victorian England–that such a member of such a society should be so excited and stimulated by the wholly alien fictions of a self-made member of a Protestant English lower-middle-class–yet it is only because of an overall likeness to Dickens's of Tolstoy's two great novels that we do not register as improbable this surely remarkable state of affairs. Would Tolstoy's novels have been as they are and what they are but for their author's having encountered the translation of *David Copperfield* at the formative phase of his writing life? Even Tolstoy's autobiography *Childhood, Boyhood and Youth* has been found by Russian critics to contain 'evident traces of *David Copperfield*' in 'the characteristics of conduct and even the grouping of characters and the selection of facts'. It was in fact this novel that Tolstoy again and again specified as for him the most important work of the greatest of novelists. And not only as a novel: when in 1896 he drew up a list of the books which had made a strong impression on him in his youth, in the highest category he placed *Copperfield* (along with Rousseau and the Gospel of St. Matthew); at the age of 80 he told his doctor that the English *book* he thought the highest of was *David Copperfield*.

This surely gives us something to think about. It is not lessened but made clearer by the remark I notice Gorki recorded that Tolstoy made to him in his old age, that 'On the whole Dickens was a sentimental, loquacious and not very clever writer, but he knew how to construct a novel as no one else did' (*Reminiscences of Tolstoy* by Maxim Gorky). Tolstoy was evidently not a blind worshipper of Dickens, he saw his faults and weaknesses just as Henry James did, but to Tolstoy these seemed negligible (and 'clever' may well convey a contempt for novelistic arts as such)–negligible compared with what Dickens had to offer him as a great genius whose insights and preoccupations inspired his own and who was a master of the art of composition, for this is what he must have meant by *constructing* a novel. And as we now, unlike Henry James, see that Tolstoy himself was the creator of miracles of construction and meaningful complexity, a master of the art of the novel whose opinion of a novelist's achievement must be respected, we must take it that Tolstoy's consistently high valuation of *David Copperfield* must mean that Dickens's intentions and achievements there, in some fundamental way (below the superficial level of the social, linguistic, economic, religious and historical differences in the two novelists' habitats), were perceived by Tolstoy to have an immediate relevance to his own creative problems, in helping him to formulate what he, through Dickens's eyes, saw as the essential difficulties of living that pressed on him.[1] Now if Dickens in *Copperfield* were merely providing the kind of entertaining fiction his contemporaries, as we've seen, saw it as being, indeed, if Dickens were merely (or at all) the kind of novelist assumed by H. House[2] or were Garis's Dickens (the compulsively theatrical and factitious entertainer) or Dabney's victim of the Victorian relation between Love and Property, then he could not have been of use to Tolstoy at all, still less held by Tolstoy for over half a century in the highest esteem. Nor if Edmund Wilson's view of his novel was just: '*Copperfield* is not one of Dickens's deepest books; it is something in the nature of a holiday' [*The Wound and the Bow*].

Yet what a novelist thinks of another novelist is best deduced not from what he says critically but from what he says creatively, in the use he makes of the other's art, and it is in *War and Peace* and *Anna Karenina* that we must look for the proofs of what *David Copperfield* meant to Tolstoy.

Tolstoy, who, as we've seen, actually translated his pre-adult experiences into the forms of *David Copperfield*'s in writing his own autobiography, must have therefore felt the power and essential truth of its representative selection of experience as a child's, boy's and youth's in 19th-century society, or in the parts of that common to Dickens's England and Tolstoy's Russia. Forster, who was by no means so stupid as he often seems to be in his criticism of Dickens's novels, was shrewd enough to note that one of the reasons for the great popularity of *Copperfield* was that 'it can hardly have had a reader, man or lad, who did not discover that he was something of a Copperfield himself', thus bearing witness to its relevance for Englishmen of that age. The parts of Tolstoy's first major fiction, *War and Peace*, which he wrote nearly twenty years after first reading *Copperfield*, that struck me as so interestingly like parts of

[1]R. F. Christian, the Tolstoy scholar and critic, has two generalizations of interest in this connexion. He writes of Tolstoy: 'There is no doubt that he seized avidly at any confirmation of his ideas in other people's work and even borrowed their examples' and 'A study of the drafts of Tolstoy's novels confirms the suspicion that problems of structure and composition were often in the forefront of his thoughts' (*Tolstoy's 'War and Peace': A Study*, Oxford, 1962).

[2]H. House, *The Dickens World*, ignoring the surely essential and obvious fact that Dickens was a creative artist, treats his novels as accurate or inaccurate sources of facts, implying in Dickens ignorance or dishonesty in the latter case; in addition to this crass and dangerous approach to the works of Dickens he constantly insinuates misleading valuations or fatuous generalisations, e.g. that Pip's history is 'a snob's progress', that Dickens habitually and characteristically 'flattered the public's moral feelings', and so on.

Copperfield that I started looking for extra-fictional evidence of Tolstoy's interest in this novel, with what astonishing results and confirmation I have described–these parts, though not integrated into *War and Peace* nor really prepared and accounted for there, show that Tolstoy had grasped the importance of Dickens's theme in *Copperfield* and the nature of Dickens's use of symbolic action and dialogue in isolating for examination psychological truths of radical importance to the young man of his own time even, it appears, in Russia too. Before I give my account of what I take to be Dickens's theme and the nature and technical means of his presentation of it, I had better distinguish the parts of *War and Peace* I have in mind. To begin with, consider the married life of Prince Andrew which Tolstoy chose to open the novel with so abruptly, though we know he took immense trouble with this and that Prince Andrew went through numerous changes of character and appearance before becoming the protagonist he is. The stress this episode gets seems out of proportion to its relevance to the plot of the novel, though after studying its origin in *Copperfield* I think we can understand why for Tolstoy it had this importance.

Tolstoy's curtain rises on a drawing-room in the highest society where Lisa, beautiful, gay and childlike, but already married long enough to be visibly pregnant, is the centre of admiration, engaged on an empty-headed flirtatious conversation with the gentlemen. Her husband alone is unresponsive to her charm, treating her with a cold and insulting politeness that we soon see covers the exasperation of a clever and sensitive man who finds he has fallen in love with and married a silly trivial creature; she is however a loving child, who has enough feeling to sense that her relation with her husband has gone wrong and to complain that his present indifference (to her unaccountable) is cruel. He then tells his friend Pierre that he has nothing to accuse his wife of except that he is disappointed with marriage, even though he had chosen as wife a girl who is the type approved by his society. He has decided to solve his matrimonial difficulties by leaving his wife to bear their child at his father's country home and going off to the war, in the likelihood of being killed. He takes her there and his sister Mary, a tender-hearted and spiritually-minded girl, tries to make the best of what she sees as a wrong to poor little Lisa, by persuading her brother to look at his wife in a more compassionate light:

'She was so tired that she has fallen asleep on the sofa in my room. Oh, Andrew! What a treasure of a wife you have,' said she, seating herself of the sofa opposite her brother. 'She is quite a child: such a dear, merry child. I have grown so fond of her!'

Prince Andrew was silent, but the princess noticed the ironical and contemptuous look that showed itself on his face.

'One should be indulgent to little weaknesses; who is without them, Andrew? Don't forget that she was educated and brought up in society. Besides, her position now is not a rosy one. We should enter into every one's situation. *Tout comprendre, c'est tout pardonner.* Think what it means to her, poor thing, after what she has been used to, to be parted from her husband and to remain alone in the country, in her condition! It is very hard.'

Prince Andrew smiled as he looked at his sister, as we smile at those we think we thoroughly understand.

As his sister tells him, 'You are good in every way, Andrew, but there is a kind of intellectual pride in you, and that is a great sin'.

She tries again:

'As I was saying to you, Andrew, be kind and generous as you always were. Don't judge Lisa harshly,' she began. 'She is so sweet, so kind, and her position now is a very trying one.'

'I do not think I have blamed my wife to you, Masha, or complained of her. Why do you say all this to me?'

Red patches appeared on Princess Mary's face and she was silent, as if she felt guilty. . . .

'Know this, Masha: that there is nothing I can reproach *my wife* with; I have not reproached and never shall reproach her, and I cannot reproach myself with anything in regard to her. . . . But if you want to know the truth, if you want to know whether I am happy? No! Whether she is? No! But why this is so, I don't know.'

But his father, the eccentric Prince Nicholas, says to him, by way of showing his sympathy:

'It's a bad look-out, eh?'
'What is, father?'
'The wife!' said the old prince, shortly and significantly.
'I don't understand!' said Prince Andrew.
'Yes, it can't be helped, lad,' said the prince. 'They're all alike; one can't unmarry. Don't be afraid! I'll tell no one, but you know it yourself.'

The son sighed, thus admitting that his father had understood him.

Neither father nor son seems to see any other attitude to Lisa as possible, but the son is to learn more about himself when, seriously wounded on the battlefield, he has some kind of mystical experience that softens what his sister has called his 'intellectual pride'. He now realizes 'the unimportance of everything I understand and the greatness of something incomprehensible but most important', so that he returns able to feel sorry for his wife as well as himself, and contrite towards her. We return in advance of him to the household where false news of Andrew's death has been received just as Lisa is expecting the birth, but though when he comes home at last he is anxious to show her he has had a change of heart towards her (" "My darling! " he said–a word he had never used to her before. "God is merciful. . . ." ') she is too far gone in labour ever to recognize him before she dies.

> She lay dead in the same position he had seen her in five minutes before, and despite the fixity of the eyes and the pallor of the cheeks, the same expression was on her charming, childlike face. 'I love you all, and never did any one any harm; and what have you done to me?'–said her lovely pathetic dead face. . . . And there in the coffin was the same face, though with closed eyes. 'Ah, what have you done to me?' it still seemed to say, and Prince Andrew felt that something gave way in his soul; that he was guilty of a sin he could neither remedy nor forget. He could not weep.

Later he puts up a white marble statue of an angel over his wife's tomb and the angel's short upper lip seems raised in the childlike smile that characterized his wife; in consequence he feels the angel's expression is one of mild reproach like that he saw on her dying and then her dead face: 'Oh, why have you done this to me?' Of course this expresses his sense of guilt towards her, now inexpugnable.

Yet in spite of the brilliant and moving delineation of a typical situation, which is of course that of David and Dora in *Copperfield* translated into Russian terms, with Princess Mary as Agnes, it has no before or after in *War and Peace*; it merely fixes a subject that Tolstoy, it seems to me, had been struck with in making the acquaintance of a Dickens masterpiece. It has no apparent bearing on Andrew's subsequent second love for Natasha, though I suppose it may be seen as a trailer for the many-stranded subject of love and marriage and the achievement of happiness that determines the 'Peace' section of the novel and which is also the subject-matter and theme of *David Copperfield*. But it inevitably raises questions in the reader's mind that Tolstoy has not provided for, such as: How comes it that so intelligent and sophisticated a man as Andrew should accept a Lisa, who is merely the incarnation of a frivolous

society's ideal, as suitable to pass his life with, since *he* despises the drawing-room world that is her only existence? Neither his father nor his
sister, both of whom he loves and respects, has any difficulty in seeing
what Lisa is. We can't on Tolstoy's showing accept Andrew's marriage
as plausible,[1] though the detailing of his disenchantment and unhappiness
is; and the indications of Andrew's moral growth and the creation in
him of a sense of guilt, though minimal, are remarkable imaginative
feats, proofs of Tolstoy's genius for the novel. We can't but wonder
whether, in these circumstances if Lisa had survived, Andrew's remorse
would have withstood the trials of her social habits and her conversation
for long and whether his new-found spirituality would have been able
to survive prolonged contact with her triviality and egotism. While we
are bound to feel that Tolstoy's handling of Dickens's subject is wholly
serious and so really painful, we also perceive, I hope, that Tolstoy has
not such an unquestionable advantage over Dickens as critics generally
assume (e.g. 'Dickens was not a Tolstoy: it was quite beyond his range
to show in fiction a great man's struggles towards new moral forms'–
H. House, *The Dickens World*). There is something to be said, surely,
for Dickens's lighter hand which with humour relieving, and at the same
time heightening, the dilemma, allows shades of feeling and complexities
of meaning and subtleties of attitude that have no equivalent in the tragic
affair of Prince Andrew's marriage, where the situation is quite barely
stated instead of, as in *Copperfield*, comprehended in its whole social and
psychological context and implications. For Dickens does not leave us
rebellious because of unanswered or rather unanswerable questions, like
Tolstoy in his rendering of the same theme, questions which we can't
help positing. We don't need to know that Dickens wrote during the
composition of *Copperfield*: 'I feel the story to its minutest point'. This
is evident from the start, not only in the imaginative understanding of
how a child feels[2] and thinks and acquires ideas–for instance, in David's

[1]'Why did he marry Lisa?' asks R. F. Christian. 'We are not told.' Thus Mr.
Christian expresses a natural surprise at such an improbable marriage.

[2]Tolstoy has been greatly admired for his understanding of children and sympathetic insight in his novels into a child's and boy's modes of feeling, but has it
been noticed how much these insights owed to Dickens's in *David Copperfield*?
Not only is his rendering of children's feelings and behaviour Dickens's, but scenes
are of a similar kind. David's lessons with his step-father seem to have made such
an impression that they are reflected in both Tolstoy's great novels–in Princess
Mary's misery at her mathematics lessons from her bullying father, and Serezha's
lessons and unhappy relations with his father Karenin (who like Miss Trotwood has

confused feelings about his unknown father outside in his grave shown in his immediate fear, on being told he has a new father, that the dead man has come out of it, or his wondering whether the sundial misses the sun–and of the next stage when he has left behind the infant's egocentric universe and become self-conscious in his awareness of the community he is part of, so that he inevitably imagines how he appears to others in his (genuine) grief for his mother's death and how it affects his status.[1] No, it is most evident in the construction which *required* Dickens, as he had realized, to start before David's birth with establishing the nature of his parents' relation to each other in a typical Victorian marriage, and where the presence of Miss Trotwood is necessary not, as it is now fashionable to assert, as the bad fairy at the christening, but in order that she may provide the astringent comment of an unromantic adult wisdom on those aspects of the Copperfield parents' marriage which need such exposure, since they are to form the unborn child's attitudes in important matters.

ii

The masterly construction of *Copperfield* is the more surprising when one reflects that its only predecessor as an integrally conceived novel was *Dombey*, and that that broke down, changing direction and mode, with the death of little Paul, losing its previous steady focus on the theme. *Copperfield* is only a year later but what an advance it shows in planning, complexity of conception and consistency from the first chapter right through to the schematic ending! (leaving out the last chapter, which provides a pantomime transformation scene–a concession to the reading-public which Dickens never again makes. There are no happy endings after *Copperfield*).[2]

the peculiarity of being unable, though apparently a hard, cold, character, to bear the sight of tears). Serezha instinctively hates Vronsky for coming between him and his mother even while Vronsky is not openly Anna's lover, as David was hostile to Mr. Murdstone before he knew he was courting his mother, feeling a threat to himself from the man touching his mother's hand.

[1]Not, as Cockshut asserts (*The Imagination of Charles Dickens*, 1961) intending a sneer, that it shows he is an actor; but to make us aware that David's consciousness is now outward-directed. All parents and teachers will recognize this feature of the now self-conscious schoolboy David as normal and typical.

[2]Dickens was perfectly well aware of the advances he made both as an artist and in educating a reading-public, as these two excerpts from letters show: 'I hope David Copperfield will do for your correspondent. The world would not take

Unlike Tolstoy in *War and Peace* Dickens has pondered his theme so as to provide an answer for the question raised by the why of Prince Andrew's marriage, and which Tolstoy avoids by opening with it as a *fait accompli*. David is not a Prince Andrew who should have known better. He is an innocent, by the circumstances of his childhood and upbringing, simply passive in being imprinted with the age's 'best' ideals of love, marriage, conduct of life and what is desirable in a woman. He is deliberately chosen to be representative, in order to examine current ideas; we should note that he is otherwise colourless, and impossible to visualize physically in any respect—seeing how gifted Dickens is at communicating personal characteristics and how naturally this comes to him, only concentration on this conception of his protagonist could have stopped Dickens from providing David with a full, vivid individuality (the same is true of Pip in *Great Expectations*, for the same reason). It follows that David's relation to Dickens is nothing like what it has generally been alleged to be,[1] I have already quoted Forster's witness to the universality of Copperfield in his age, and the passage in his life of Dickens that ends thus should have been enough to warn critics off confusing a novel written in autobiographical form with an autobiography or, as Mr. Cockshut calls it, a fake autobiography. Forster wrote:

> 'Too much has been assumed, from those revelations [of facts of Dickens's experiences] of a full identity of Dickens with his hero, and of a supposed intention that his own character as well as parts of his career should be expressed in the narrative. It is right to warn the reader as to this . . . it would be the greatest mistake to imagine anything like a complete identity of the fictitious novelist with the real one, beyond the Hungerford scenes; or to suppose that the youth,

another Pickwick from me now, but we can be cheerful and merry, I hope, notwithstanding, and with a little more purpose in us' (to Costello, April 1849); 'I am glad to say that there seems to be a bright unanimity about Copperfield. I am very much interested in it and pleased with myself. I have carefully planned out the story, for some time past, to the end, and am making out my purposes with great care. I should like to know what you see from that tower of yours. I have little doubt you see the real objects in the prospect' (to the Rev. James White, July 1850).

[1] Too much has been made of the possible psychological implications of the fact that the novel's hero and the novelist have the same initials in reverse and of Dickens's being unaware of this or startled when Forster pointed it out to him. Dickens's first two choices of name for the hero had been 'David Mag' and 'Thomas Mag, and it was the novel *David Copperfield*, not its hero, that Dickens called his 'favourite child'.

who then received his first harsh schooling in life, came out of it as little harmed or hardened as David did. . . . The character of the hero of the novel finds indeed his right place in the story he is supposed to tell, rather by unlikeness than by likeness to Dickens, even where intentional resemblances might seem to be prominent.

Forster is correct, but the key to all this has escaped his notice, since he was deaf and blind to Dickens' art,[1] though invaluable in the insights he gives us into Dickens the man. We ought to reflect that D. C. could not possibly have written C. D.'s novels, even if some of Charles Dickens's experiences were made use of–in the usual manner of writers–in the history of his hero, though apart from the episode in boyhood in the wine-business and London low life, David Copperfield does not get mixed up in Dickens's own history. The other parts of Dickens's feelings and adventures drawn on are there, deliberately chosen, because they are typical, such as his adolescent love-affair with Maria Beadnell. Whoever David is, he isn't his author, and very obviously less so even than Levin

[1]The most striking instance is that of his well-intentioned but revealingly stupid objection to the masterly 'History of a Self-Tormentor' chapter in *Little Dorrit*, which he thought should have been part of the narrative. Dickens used his better judgement, but the letter Dickens wrote justifying himself and expressing despair at not being understood is important to an appreciation of the difficulties under which he worked: 'In Miss Wade I had an idea, which I thought a new one, of making the introduced story so fit into surroundings impossible of separation from the main story, as to make the blood of the book circulate through both. But I can only suppose, from what you say, that I have not exactly succeeded in this.' This did not prevent Forster's blandly confident assertion, in the *Life*, of the shortcomings, as he saw them, of *Little Dorrit*: 'the want of coherence among the figures of the story, and of a central interest in the plan of it . . . . some of the most deeply considered things that occur in it have really little to do with the tale itself. The surface-painting of both Miss Wade and Tattycoram, to take an instance, is anything but attractive, yet there is under it a rare force of likeness . . . and they must both have had, as well as Mr. Gowan himself, a striking effect in the novel, if they had been made to contribute in a more essential way to its interest or develop-ment.' He adds, with incredible fatuity: 'The failure nevertheless had not been for want of care or study, as well as of his own design as of models by masters in his art' [the classical and 18th century picaresque novelists, who all use the autobiography of a character inserted into the narrative for variety and other purposes, for instance; he thinks Dickens failed to emulate them in Miss Wade's history] and he goes on to cite the letter from Dickens I have quoted above. We may also observe there his criterion of 'attractive' in operation, that of his age. This Dickens was courageous enough to ignore, and to stand by his own lights, as he implies in another letter of self-defence when he wrote: 'Wrong or right, this was all design, and seemed to me to be in the fitness of things'.

is Tolstoy. David incarnates the kind of youth the age demanded–sensitive, modest, upright, affectionate, but also resourcefully industrious and successful in rising in the world. Now whatever Dickens was he was not a Daisy, and his habit of referring to himself as 'The Inimitable' does not sound at all like David either. While Dickens was a colourful personality David is colourless and intentionally uninteresting in himself–only a type. I doubt if Dickens admired David as unreservedly as his public did, or endorsed him fully as writers even now assume–David is necessarily sensitive and lacking in guile, the evidence for this exists in the text of the novel itself, but I will return to this later–just as Pip is later explicitly constructed to be 'morally timid and very sensitive', both being shown to be the product of childhood conditioning and therefore, for the purposes of each novel, typically significant. As also is *Little Dorrit's* Arthur Clennam, though a fully human and characterized exponent of a Victorian disease, however, being in a novel of a different kind from *Oliver Twist*, *David Copperfield* or *Great Expectations*. We can therefore dismiss the kind of charge of dishonesty now brought against Dickens, represented characteristically by Cockshut's assertion that Dickens wrote *David Copperfield* in order to present his past and himself in a favourable light–'the self-criticism has no sting'. Not only is David's life not Dickens's past, but even though, as Forster noted, the young male reader of his time naturally identified himself with David, there is no compulsion to identify with him uncritically as there is, for instance, for the reader of *Jane Eyre* to do so with the heroine. In fact, those critics who *do* identify C. D. with D. C. and complain that Dickens didn't realize that David was stupid not to see through Dora, or reprehensible not to blame himself, merely expose their inability to read what Dickens has offered them. Dickens had started to write his autobiography, it is true, and abandoned the project when he decided to write the novel instead; but this must have been because he *did* want to examine *impersonally* the experience of growing up in the first half of the 19th century, with the problems that a young man of that generation incurred, an examination needing the kind of objectivity that inheres in the novelist's art, but still one best exposed through the autobiographical form. [*David Copperfield* was his first novel in this form and it is interesting that in his next novel, *Bleak House*, he decided to combine the advantages of the fictional autobiography with the freer possibilities available to the writer of narrative, so that this novel is divided into halves technically, with alternations of each form sandwiched together. Whatever advantage he found in this, it was presumably not successful enough to be worth repeating, and when he needed a first-person narrative again, he re-read *David Copperfield*, as we know, before writing *Great Expectations* in the *Copperfield* form.] David's relation to Charles Dickens is even less close than Levin's to Tolstoy–who is Tolstoy not only without the genius but without being Vronsky either (as Tolstoy was or had been). What Tolstoy evidently saw in *David Copperfield* was that real issues were raised in it that were *not* personal to Dickens.

The questions Dickens was asking himself more or less consciously before writing *David Copperfield* must have been similar to and often identical with those we can see Tolstoy, alerted to them by Dickens, asking himself in the Peace sections of *War and Peace*; Tolstoy's fiction is formed to state and explore these questions by dramatizing them, and we may well ask whether Tolstoy's answers would have been worked out on Dickensian lines, or even if he would have been conscious of such questions, if he had not come on Dickens's novel in his wild youth. Yet Dickens's questions arise from a painful if not yet bitter feeling (as later in *Great Expectations*) that a young man is misled by taking the new Victorian pilgrim's path to the Promised Land. David's history is a model one in that buoyant era which believed or held that every man had the prospect of achieving comfort and respectability, even riches and distinction, at any rate happiness, if he would choose the path of thrift, austerity, perseverance in hard work, and self-improvement. This David does, and he accepts the reward that his society had given him to understand would then make him happy: domestic bliss which would be guaranteed by marriage with the incarnation of a feminine ideal he had been conditioned to accept as lovable. Dickens had done so too, and evidently had now reached the point of asking himself: Why then am I not contented? If society is right, what went wrong? Or was it the wrong prescription? What should it have been? These questions are explored through the history of David Copperfield, but there is no such uncontrollable passionate identification of the author with the protagonist as we resent at times in *Jane Eyre* or find embarrassing in *The Mill on the Floss*, for not being David, Dickens is not concerned to make a hero of him.

The theme is preluded before David's birth, in his mother's typical marriage. Clara Copperfield is the girl-wife whom her son registers as the ideal woman because, fatherless, and isolated with her in a male infant's paradise of having his mother entirely to himself, turned in on her, surrounded with love and tenderness till a suitor appears, he inevitably associates love of woman with her personally, with her curls, gaiety, vanity, her pettishness even, and extreme youthfulness. These were in fact generally considered winning feminine characteristics then, though David as an uncritical child sees them ideally without recognizing his mother's weaknesses, of course. Dickens's note for Clara in the original plan for the first number[1] was 'Young mother–tendency to weakness and vanity'; the phrase 'Brooks of Sheffield' also occurs there, showing that Dickens intended David's innocence to be exploited from the start, thus launching the two themes together[2]. This innocence is shown to be the result of David's sheltered life among women combined with his need for affection. The innocent trustfulness which makes him ridiculous so often as well as unhappy in the event is inherited, we must note. In the opening chapter, before David's birth, Miss Trotwood extracts from Mrs. Copperfield the admission that the house was called The Rookery by David's father (of the same name) under a mistake. ' "David Copperfield all over!" cried Miss Betsey. "David Copperfield from head to foot! Calls a house a rookery when there's not a rook near it, and takes the birds on trust, because he sees the nests!" ' This striking and suggestive generalization applies to both Davids and is to alert us to later events. Dickens wrote *Why Rookery* and underlined it in his plan for chapter I, showing the significance he attached to the point. We have this heritage revived for us when David's reception into Miss Betsey's home is marked by constant references to 'David's son' and 'David's son David'. The mistakes David makes, we are to understand then, are inherent in the upbringing and heredity of such a child; the cloistered infancy is virtually repeated in his second existence as the sheltered schoolboy fostered by Miss Trotwood and Agnes and the guileless Dr. Strong, though a different kind of idealism is provided by them. Miss Trotwood and Agnes are very different and–to us–superior to his mother, but how can they supplant her in his imagination since her early death in peculiarly

[1]The plans for *David Copperfield* are given in *Dickens at Work* by John Butt and K. Tillotson (1957).

[2]In looking at Dickens's 'Plans' I personally have been struck by the confirmation they give to my deduction–that Dickens was predominantly interested in thematic construction after the first batch of impromptu fiction-writing before *Dombey*– that I have made from studying the novels themselves. But Tillotson and Butt, ignoring this evidence of Dickens's concern for construction in the Tolstoyan sense, discuss the Plans simply as evidence for the handling of the plots only, whereas we can see that the themes determined the plotting.

painful circumstances has stamped her image on his memory as she was before a stepfather came between them? (Owing to whose advent, he remembers, he was turned out of his mother's room where he had slept in a closet–whether the stepfather was actually 'a Murderer' or not he would of course have seemed one to the child as murderer of his happiness, in coming between him and his mother.)

The woman who fulfils the maternal function in practice for David, his real mother, is also a Clara, and David tells us that he loved her (Clara Peggotty) equally but in a different way from his mother; he loved her because he recognized that she loved him truly (unselfishly) and was indispensable–he says he could never have borne to lose her (though he bore the loss of the other Clara). It is evident that for his purpose of examining the rôle of woman Dickens has split the dual nature of it into separate identities, the two Claras.

The Plan for chapter IX that Dickens made says: 'close with the idea of his mother as she was, with him as *he* was, in her arms'–surely the most striking proof of the seriousness of Dickens's commitment to this novel as an impersonal work of art. It is impossible to imagine this major theme–the relation of mother and son–handled with more delicacy, insight and firm control in its understanding of the dilemma involved. The idea is psychologically true in conception and richly and interestingly rendered. Underlying it is Dickens's strikingly intelligent apprehension of the need for both romantic tenderness and devoted services to sustain the male ego in its struggle with the conditions of living in such a world as the Dickens world, in a competitive society; and the impossibility of combining these qualities in a single personality. The emotional complexity of David's situation as the boy-child who, as a posthumous son, had been from birth in sole possession of his mother, until her remarriage banished him from her, is made tolerable for him when, returning from school, he finds his mother with a new baby boy at her breast and instead of feeling jealous identifies with him because of his overwhelming desire to be that babe again. David has first heard Clara's voice singing in the tone he remembered from his infancy before he saw the baby, and this predisposes him to the identification, of course, though we are left to deduce this[1] for ourselves. The accompanying illustration (and we know

[1]This is only one of the innumerable occasions in *David Copperfield* where we should take heed of the statement in a letter Dickens wrote to G. H. Lewes: 'The truth is, I am a very modest man, and if readers cannot detect the point of a passage without having their attention called to it by the writer, I would much rather they

Dickens kept a tight hand on his illustrators, often specifying the illustration or criticizing the drawing to get it right) shows a worn-looking Clara suckling the infant with David opening the parlour door; on his face is a curious mixture of surprise and perplexity, over the head of the nursing mother is a portrait of her as the girlish mother of his earliest memories, flanked by two Biblical pictures chosen in the Hogarth tradition for the symbolic nature of their content: they are the infant Moses being taken from the bulrushes, and the Prodigal Son being embraced by his father again. The lovely idyll of the evening David then spends, encircled in the love of the two Claras, is completed when he returns next time from school to his mother's funeral and hears Peggotty's account of her 'sweet girl's' pining and death-bed; it has the effect of wiping out the intervening period for David, and establishing forever their old relation of being all in all to each other and of Clara as eternally girlish, for Peggotty had mothered them both, and this I conclude is why Dickens forbore to have a direct death-bed scene, witnessed by David:

> From the moment of my knowledge of the death of my mother, the idea of her as she had been of late vanished from me. I remembered her, from that instant, only as the young mother of my earliest impressions, who had been used to wind her bright curls round and round her finger, and to dance with me at twilight in the parlour. What Peggotty had told me now, was so far from bringing me back to the later period, that it rooted the earlier image in my mind. It may be curious, but it is true. In her death she winged her way back to her calm untroubled youth, and cancelled all the rest.
> The mother who lay in her grave, was the mother of my infancy; the little creature in her arms was myself, as I had once been, hushed for ever on her bosom.

There is nothing finer in Tolstoy's novels, and it is 'Tolstoyan' before Tolstoy. The whole conception and treatment is perfectly free from sentimentality. It is a supreme example of Dickens's 'feeling the story in its minutest point', as he truly said, for it is an insight which can owe nothing to Dickens's personal experience. It is the understanding of the way we deal with the deepest human feelings which only a great genius

lost it and looked out for something else'. 'Readers have done just that. They have been so dazzled and so satisfied by the richness of the immediate effects that they have neglected the subtler shadings.'–thus Professor Harry Stone comments on this statement when reviewing the first volume of the new edition of Dickens's letters in the quarterly of the University of Illinois Press.

DAVID COPPERFIELD

could arrive at, and it is made the basis and starting-point of a typical
male history in that age. Dickens was as far as possible from having a
Freudian attachment to his mother. But–a proof of genius–he had observed that the other was the more usual condition of man, and had
pondered, and worked out, its implications. This passage presages David's
escape from a second phase of misery in order to find a substitute home
and mother, which he does at Dover with his great-aunt, where he is
reborn as Trotwood, goes to school all over again, is launched into the
world of London on his own a second time, where he–in a dreamlike
or Alice-in-Wonderland world–strays into the previous dimension inhabited by the figures of his previous state–Steerforth, Micawber, Traddles, the boat household at Yarmouth, and meets the double of his
mother, Dora. Dora is naturally to repeat his mother's history, in fading
away for the same reason. Dickens's original idea seems to have been to
keep Dora alive, but it was a sound instinct that made him, however
reluctantly, (and only deciding at the last possible instalment) kill off
Dora (as he put it)–not, as has been alleged by those who do not grasp
the theme and structure of the novel, because he wanted the spurious
pathos of a death-bed scene.

   That David's love of his mother is the love of Woman, and that he is
always looking for her image, a pettish, wilful, childish, loving playmate,
is shown as the pattern of his emotional life. He has first encountered in
childhood Little Em'ly, whom he was thrown with both at the time of
first being separated from his mother and again when he is desolate after
her funeral. These two episodes give prominence to this part of the theme
and indicate its nature very delicately. David is impressed by Emily's being loving, tender-hearted, spoiled, pretty and gay, she even has the
necessary curls (characterized as running over her uncle's hand like water)
so that David goes to sleep praying that he 'might grow up to marry
little Em'ly'. Emily also prefigures Dora (and echoes his mother whose
manner he had recognized–but only after her remarriage–as 'pettish and
wilful') in her response to David's juvenile courtship, calling him 'a silly
boy' as she 'laughed so charmingly', in fact she has all the marks by which
he recognizes the feminine character. He then thinks of their marriage as
one where they would 'never grow older, never grow wiser, [be] children
ever' etc. Growing older and wiser is associated with the Murdstones'
programme of educating Clara which was to denature her. When David
meets Agnes he notices at once that what characterizes *her* is that though
a child she is her father's housekeeper with the household keys at her side.

51

The charge of the housekeeping keys was an issue between David's mother and Miss Murdstone, marking the victory of the latter. This therefore becomes a symbol for David, and is picked up in Dora's case when her response to David's request to her to take charge of the household is to 'tie the key-basket to her slender waist' but use the keys only 'as a plaything for Jip. She was quite satisfied that a good deal was effected by this mode of make-belief of housekeeping'. David identifies Agnes with her dead mother's portrait, as Agnes's father does—she is to both of them not a child but a little *woman*. Agnes isn't gay and girlish but calm, staid and responsible, so David realizes that: 'I love little Em'ly, and I don't love Agnes—no, not at all in that way', so she can be only loved as a sister. Maturity in a woman is chilling to him.

Of course this was a typical Victorian dilemma, and at the centre of Dickens's theme as he understands it. Idealizing immaturity stabilized it and inhibited maturity in women, but this was not the product of a morbid or irrational desire in the man since the qualities that Dickens shows as being associated with feminine immaturity of the Clara-Em'ly-Dora kind represented a real emotional need for men living in the world that the 19th century became. [George Eliot's observation, that the serious, intellectual Dorothea Brooke was unattractive to the average man in her social sphere, who recognized the 'infantile fairness' of Rosamund Vincy as being the right idea in a woman, conveys the contempt of a superior woman for the weakness of the male of her time.] Of course the dilemma was that the qualities needed in a satisfactory wife (as efficient household manager and mother) were of a conflicting kind with the other need. Dickens made two attempts to resolve this dilemma, in his creative experiments. The first was with Mrs. Peerybingle in *The Cricket on the Hearth* (1845), the gay young wife of a much older and very staid man; her name is Mary but her husband calls her Dot, she has a baby and is represented as the goddess of the hearth, where the chirping cricket typifies the spirit of Home, but she combines the housewife's virtues with girlish disclaimers of efficiency, calling herself 'little woman' and 'your foolish little wife' like Dora, and ultimately explaining to her husband: 'And when I speak of people being middle-aged, and steady, John, and pretend that we are a humdrum couple, going on in a jog-trot sort of way, it's only because I'm such a silly little thing, John, that I like, sometimes, to act a kind of Play with Baby, and all that: and make believe'. In short, maturity is only tolerable if disguised as a children's game. The other attempt came at the end of Dickens's work, showing that he never got much beyond this point in his thinking. Bella Wilfer, the heroine of *Our Mutual Friend*, his last completed novel, is a resolute effort on the novelist's part to take a winning type of girl into womanhood by the disciplines of misfortune, good fortune, a sacrifice of her prospects by a marriage to a poor man, and motherhood. Bella, for all her curls, coquetry, follies and charms, has capabilities beyond those of a 'little woman', and indeed aspires to be something more. In her own words, 'I want to be something so much worthier than the doll in the doll's house'. This is promising, but once married she is described in exactly those terms, playing at housekeeping in a fascinating way and, when she has a baby, 'acting a kind of Play with Baby' just like Dot Peerybingle, having rehearsed for it with her father beforehand; afterwards, so that we shall be under no misconception, her father 'justly remarked to her husband that the baby seemed to make her younger than before, reminding him of the days when she had a pet doll and used to talk to it as she carried it about'. Bella (a name in the Clara-Dora tradition of course) is shown using the baby Bella as a toy and as an instrument for flirting with her husband in an embarrassing way. By this time Dickens had had ten children and must have known that a baby is no joke. The obstinate unreality of his image of a charming wife, from Dot and Dora to Bella, would of itself suggest that he would be unlikely to achieve marital happiness in the form of husband to the mother of many children

A historical example of how the dilemma could be made tolerable in practice is available in the case of Disraeli's marriage. He was remarkably intelligent in knowing that he (also a novelist) needed the same qualities as David Copperfield for his domestic happiness and in being prepared to put up with the concomitants. He wrote to his future wife that he needed to be surrounded with love; it was tenderness and sympathy at home that made his political life possible. Though much his senior in age and previously a widow, Mrs. Disraeli was juvenile in manner, gay, overflowing with affection, and adored her husband, so that she made him happy in spite of being generally considered by his society a silly woman, 'foolish and at times even ridiculous', noted Lady Battersea. Disraeli minded this not at all, and seems not to have repined at her accompanying childlessness either; he seems positively to have enjoyed her 'not knowing who came first, the Greeks or the Romans', and the similar examples of her Dora-like conversation. She was in fact widely loved, though Disraeli was commiserated for having a wife whose conversational follies made her a joke, and respected for his stoicism in ignoring this. He snubbed a friend who questioned his indifference to his wife's shortcomings by saying that unlike other men *he* could feel gratitude (he did not mean for his wife's very moderate private income). Mrs. Disraeli however was unlike Dora in being, or being able to afford, a good housekeeper, and also in being unselfishly devoted to her husband; she did not merely hold his pens but corrected his proofs (or thought she did). Dizzy's undoubtedly sincere love for his wife lasted into her old age and her death left him desolate.

It is inevitable, then, that at the next phase of a man's life, as adolescent, David meets his mother's image again, in Dora Spenlow, [Dickens himself had fallen seriously in love at 17 with Maria Beadnell who provided Jip as well as typical features of Dora and David's courtship, though Dora seems to have assimilated as well – very naturally since the point of Dora is her typicality – relevant qualities of Catherine Hogarth's, whom Dickens subsequently married since Maria was denied him.] Dickens is in firm control of his theme here as throughout the novel, beautifully indicating David's conditioned helplessness by his becoming 'a captive' at first sight of the curls etc. A less predictable factor is David's complete lack of surprise at finding Miss Murdstone in command of the household; as she was his mother's jailer it is natural she should be Dora's and he reveals his unconscious train of thought by regarding Miss Murdstone not as Dora's protector but more like a life-protector which is 'a weapon of assault'. Her presence, together with her subsequently forcing a breach between David and the object of his love, made the parallel between Clara Copperfield and Dora Spenlow inescapable for the original readers, who might well have forgotten the earliest instalments of the novel by now. 'Phiz' the illustrator helped bring out Dickens's idea (as so often) by showing Clara-like portraits of Dora over the mantelpiece in every interior Dora figures in. This girlish portrait of Dora appears finally in the central position of the sitting-room where David and Agnes sit surrounded by their children, pointing the contrast with the matronly Agnes.

As Dora on further acquaintance shows herself an exact replica of Clara, David's heart is satisfied in spite of the occasional misgivings of his intelligence, so that when Traddles tells him about his useful, Agnes-like fiancée Sophie, and David says, 'I compared her in my mind with Dora, with considerable inward satisfaction' – our irritation at his fatuity is tempered by our having been put in command of the reasons why he can't help it. A dazzling piece of supplementary insight into the situation is shown by providing Dora with Jip as a pet's pet and playmate, who is more important than David to her and whose death coincides with hers not merely on the plane of sentimental effectiveness, and about whom David can be more explicit–he has to tolerate Jip though Jip is an insufferable nuisance, irrational, and cannot be trained, like his mistress, and parodies Dora in using the cookery-book as a plaything; after their marriage he lives in a doll's-house in the form of a pagoda which is always in the way.[1] Dora is rightly felt to be pathetic–as a pet is, of its very nature–as well as exasperating, and Dickens has been so successful in showing that her charm for David is potent in spite of her folly and rejection of reality, that not only in the Victorian Age but even in our own sophisticated literary world Dora has found masculine defenders on both sides of the Atlantic, who see her through David's eyes instead of through Dickens's or an intelligent reader's. Alternatively, some ungallant (English) critics reproach David for his stupidity in not recognizing Dora for what she was, repeating Miss Trotwood's refrain of 'Blind, blind, blind!' as though Dickens himself had not taken so much trouble to provide for this by the earlier part of his history.

That Dickens put an immense amount of work and thought into the theme of this novel is seen in the numerous tendrils of associations between the Clara and Dora sections. Another line of association is that between David and his mother and father; he is shown to have inherited from the former 'her affectionate nature' and from his father the 'blind' trustfulness that gets him into so many disasters (both are of course characteristic Victorian features and values). That his case-history is a repetition of his father's is brought out for us by Miss Trotwood's description of David Copperfield senior as one 'who was always running after wax dolls from his cradle', a 'wax doll' being her contemptuous comment on the masculine weakness for a woman as a pet and plaything. She also says of the boy: ' "He's as like his father as it's possible to be if he wasn't so like his mother too" ', the likeness to his father being stressed by their having identical names[2] and by Mr. Dick's repeatedly calling him 'David's son David'. Behind this of course is the new scientific

[1]Life obligingly provided Dickens with a perfect piece of symbolism when, on taking his wife to call on his old flame, he was able to observe in the hall the original Jip, dead and stuffed.

[2]Dickens preserved this feature through all the changes his titles for this novel passed through–'Thomas Mag the Younger', 'David Mag the Younger', 'David Copperfield the Younger', 'David Copperfield, Junior' etc.

interest in heredity characteristic of Victorian literature and a corresponding new interest in what determines conduct, which superseded the previous such interest that was based on the teachings of theology.[1] Forster writes, very appositely: 'The question of hereditary transmission had a curious attraction for him, and considerations connected with it were frequently present to his mind. Of a youth who had fallen into a father's weaknesses without the possibility of having himself observed them for imitation, he thus wrote on one occasion; "It suggests the strangest consideration as to which of our failings we are really responsible, and as to which of them we cannot quite reasonably hold ourselves to be so. What A. evidently derives from his father cannot in his case be derived from association and observation, but must be in the very principles of his individuality as a living creature"' (*Life*, Bk. VIII, § II, footnote).

The problem represented by the marriages of the two David Copperfields is both more profound and more representative than seems commonly realized, and Dickens investigates it with concern since it was a problem that necessarily involved himself as an insoluble one. David the elder is reported by his widow as having tried to train her, but the demands the middle-aged man had made on his young wife are represented by her only as a pedantic insistence on accuracy, though he had eventually recognized that 'a loving heart was better and stronger than wisdom and that he was a happy man in hers'. We are told this by Clara when she is justifying herself on her death-bed against the killing demands to change her character that her second husband has made on her, and we are therefore to take it very seriously. David the second comes to the same conclusion in due course as his father had done, but David's demands on Dora were not pedantic or inhuman: he wanted to share his thoughts and interests with her and find support in his troubles, a natural claim. Her refusal to accept responsibility for managing the household is only a symptom of what he has to complain of, and not the main complaint he makes to himself, as Dabney and others allege.

Yet David repeats his father's experience in deciding that tenderness is, in the marital relation, better than a wife's being 'wise' or sensible even, though the terms in which David describes his decision are revealingly different from the confident expression of a truism that his mother had offered us. David explains: 'I could not endure my own solitary wisdom:

[1] *Wuthering Heights* is another example of this interest. *v.* my essay in *Lectures in America* (F. R. & Q. D. Leavis).

I could not reconcile it with her former appeal to me as my child-wife'. Yet we can't help questioning–are obliged to question, by the novelist's art–the quality of this freely available affectionateness in a wife which is seen not only as making up for the absence of almost everything else but also as justifying an obstinate selfishness. Both Clara and Dora justify themselves thus, Clara repeating:

> 'Whatever I am, I am affectionate. I know I am affectionate. I wouldn't say it, if I wasn't certain that I am. Ask Peggotty. I am sure she'll tell you I'm affectionate.'

–which Dickens has put in such a form that it sounds more like an ob-session than a testimonial. We therefore immediately reflect that it is 'affectionateness' without 'wisdom'–without enough affection for David to consider her child's welfare[1]–which had made her sacrifice him by a re-marriage that ignored Peggotty's warnings against Mr. Murdstone. David himself notices her 'wilful, pettish manner' after his disillusion-ment following the marriage. And Dora's 'loving' nature is repeatedly seen to be immune to David's appeals to her alleged affection. ' "I am sure I am very affectionate" ' Dora asserts in response to David's asking her to behave more considerately.[2] At an almost surface level therefore Dickens was making it evident to the reader that there are awkward questions involved in his age's easy assumptions as to the superiority and adequacy of 'a loving heart', suggesting that it may be a cloak for a selfish will, for Dora's callousness and Clara's cowardice (in leaving David to suffer for her mistake and not interfering to protect him against his stepfather). Miss Trotwood, whose insights are never deflected by sentimental con-siderations, significantly characterises Clara's 'affectionateness' as 'the best part of her weakness' when accusing Mr. Murdstone of having played on it.

Yet there is no doubt Dickens had arrived at a really important truth–important most of all to him–in spite of the perplexities it involved.

---

[1] That Dickens intended us to make this reflection is shown by Miss Trotwood's making this very point when she asks Mr. Murdstone if Clara had made no settlement upon her boy when she remarried, and it then appears that David's father was equally guilty in having left his young wife 'the what's-its-name Rookery without any rooks in it' unconditionally. To underline this point, there is a Biblical picture on Miss Trotwood's drawing-room wall in this scene, called 'Jacob's Garment'.

[2] Dickens's notes for the chapter 'Our Housekeeping' contain this one, underlined as important: *Carry through incapacity of Dora–but affectionate*.

David, who is a novelist, even if not a very impressive one, is shown to need, as Dickens himself supremely did–and recognized that it was a more than personal need–gaiety, and tenderness, and companionship in the fantasies of nonsense, that were the soil from which his creativeness sprang. [In life Dickens himself seems to have got them not from his wife (who was not, or soon ceased to be, a Dora) but from his children and circle of friends, and no doubt that is why he was such a splendid father to his children when they were small but lost interest in them when they were growing up.[1]] Dora the child-wife is these things and nothing else; to appeal to her reason is to alarm her and insult her–' "I didn't marry to be reasoned with" ' she sobs; she expects to be talked nonsense to and refuses to live by the rules of common sense, balancing the wholly rational Miss Trotwood in the scheme of things. David's recognition of the supreme value to him of such a personality made even more poignant the insoluble problem of how to reconcile this need with the other need of a housekeeping, child-bearing and burden-sharing wife, though all these functions except that of actual child-bearing could be delegated. And it seems that Dickens had intended to keep Dora alive, probably supplementing her by Agnes as the Peggotty of this next generation– Agnes having been described as 'the real heroine' in Dickens's notes for Number V. Forster quotes a letter as late as May 7 1850 (the novel having been first discussed early in 1849, and possibly conceived in the previous year) where Dickens, then writing Number XIV, says: 'Still undecided about Dora but MUST decide today'–and he decided only reluctantly to 'kill' her. But her premature death makes the parallel with Clara complete: the Little Blossom withers away in the unsuccessful attempt to become a mother–an excellent piece of symbolic thought. [The deep impression made on Dickens in July 1848 by the death-bed of his sister

---

[1]Forster's *Life* is a mine of interesting documentation here. The incredible number of letters dashed off to his friends with which Dickens, as it were compulsively, filled the chinks of his editorial duties and novel-writing and social activities, is explicable only as the result of this need–they overflow with high-spirited fun and nonsense that it seemed he must share with someone. He was a wonderful conjuror, a giver of outstanding children's parties, and brought all his children into his theatrical activities in the home, as part of this need. His insight into the necessity of play-activities and imaginative fostering for the child's psychic health is generally recognized, since it is explicit in most if not all of his novels; but this is part only of his general theory, as a creative artist, of the adult's need also for love and art, which is basic to *Hard Times*, and in *David Copperfield* produced this characteristic enquiry into the nature of happiness in marriage.

Fanny, resigned to her 'early decay', as he wrote, was heightened by the death soon after of her little child, whose pining away and other characteristics had been embodied in little Paul Dombey. Fanny had played an important part in Dickens's childhood (even as Florence did to little Paul) and her death contributed to the genuine feeling conveyed in the death of David's mother.] That Dora's death from pregnancy was felt to represent a psychological truth is implied by George Eliot's endorsement in using the same situation and image (even if an unconscious borrowing) in her tale 'Mr Gilfil's Love Story' (1856) where her childlike tiny heroine 'Tina' comes to a similar end: 'the prospect of her becoming a mother was a new ground for hoping the best. But the delicate plant had been too deeply bruised, and in the struggle to put forth a blossom it died.'

The detailing of David's difficulties with Dora after their marriage has been anticipated by his uneasiness during their engagement, when he had found his first attempts to enter on a more satisfactory relation with her invariably frustrated. He could not risk losing her, so postponed facing the problem until after the honeymoon, when it at once surfaces in his realization of what the irresponsibility of romantic courtship had landed him in: after 'the romance of our engagement' now, he finds, they have 'no one to please but one another—one another to please for life', where the possibility of happiness has evidently turned into the realization that it is in fact a sentence of imprisonment for life. Marriage after all was a most serious matter when divorce was impossible and separation not respectable; but neither of such alternatives would have touched the trouble here. David's problem is eternal. David is helpless in the face of Dora's refusal to listen to reason, and his patient efforts to make her meet him on other than playmate terms are really touching though seen with humour which precludes any sentimental stressing. He tries to share his thoughts and interests with her and 'to "form her mind" '; Miss Trotwood when appealed to makes him see that she cannot consent to take the part Miss Murdstone did in his mother's second marriage, and that he is in danger of repeating that situation. He then tries alternative tactics in the hope of getting Dora to grow up; these are in the line of those adopted by his father in his mother's first marriage. Eventually it dawns on him that Dora is immutable, and he must, as his aunt had pointed out, enjoy the qualities she has, for which he fell in love with her, and put up with their drawbacks. Realizing that he risks losing everything that made her precious to him by frightening her, he gives up, seeing that he would otherwise be in the position of 'always playing spider to Dora's fly'. 'I had been unhappy in trying it; I could not endure my own solitary wisdom; I could not reconcile it with her former appeal to me as my child-wife'. He has learned the folly of 'trying to be wise', for after all, like Disraeli, it was not 'wisdom' that he ultimately needed from a wife but the relief and the stimulus of relaxing from 'wisdom', and it is this instinctive wisdom that Dora has, always characterizing herself as 'stupid', 'foolish', 'silly', 'a poor little thing' and so on, and taking it as a compliment and a testimonial when her husband calls her a Mouse, which is a tiny, helpless, timid, scampering, amusing little creature [Dickens used this as a term of endearment in his own courtship of his wife. It was a traditional English term of endearment in love-play – cf. Hamlet's instructing his mother not to let his uncle call her his mouse – and still current in the early 19th century, but Dickens undoubtedly reactivated its implications that made Dora insist on identifying herself with it in her character of being a creature for love-play only. In a similar context it recurs in *Our Mutual Friend* when Bella's father says to her, in loving praise on her wedding-day, when she behaves 'as if she had never grown up': 'What a silly little Mouse it is'.] And Dora therefore feels that she must be a failure when he is 'cruel' enough to reason with her. David is then convincing when he says: 'I told her I feared . . . the fault was mine. Which I sincerely felt, and which indeed it was'. The whole detailed investigation of David's courtship and married life strikes me as a marvel of delicate insight and moreover as exhibiting the impersonality of true genius. The case is completed by David's attempt to imagine a self who had not known Dora and what she represents: 'Sometimes the speculation came into my thoughts, What might have happened, if Dora and I had never known each other? But she was so incorporated with my existence, that it was the idlest of all fancies, and would soon rise out of my reach and sight, like gossamer floating in the air'. We see that this is associated with the fact, of which he is vaguely aware, that Dora's identification with his mother is what makes her 'incorporated with his existence'. We remember that during David's ordeal in his journey, the flight from the warehouse-Micawber-Murdstone phase of his life to start afresh at Dover, he understood the source of his dogged persistence in trying to reach a home and happiness: 'I seemed to be sustained', he noted, 'and led on by my fanciful picture of my mother in her youth, before I came into the world. It always kept me company'. Surely this is a remarkable aspect of the theme so imaginatively created for us here.

It is in consonance with these perceptions that Miss Trotwood was created, to play the complex and inevitably ridiculous part of Reason or systematic rationality; but she is not left as a Blakean idea, Dickens worked very hard on her, one sees, and she does not eventually figure as a concept for ridicule but as a very human case-history who is sympathetic because she can admit she has been misguided. This is seen in her ultimate distress at her share in Clara's tragedy which makes her show her contrition by her very different attitude to Clara's successor Dora, whom she not only tolerates but humours, forcing herself to show her exactly the same forbearance as she does Jip. Her uncompromising rationality in the first chapter is *meant* to be felt as inhuman because it is unfeeling. This is embodied in the grimness of her aspect, her 'fell rigidity' and her 'stalking' movements, her gruff voice, and the unforgettable image of her peering in at the window (this was chosen very rightly for the frontispiece to the novel) which terrifies poor Clara into hiding in a corner, only to be driven out by the clockwork movement of the eyes following her round the room, a metaphor implying an automaton ('like the Saracen's Head in a Dutch clock', Dickens writes)–Reason, as the unnatural and life-threatening machine, horrible in its relentlessness. There is an essential humour in bringing her up at once against that basic mystery of Nature, childbirth, with its human sufferings (against which she stops her ears with cotton-wool in an attempt–unsuccessful–to protect herself from feeling in sympathy) and unpredictability (her assurance of getting the girl baby her egotism demands is thwarted, to her indignation, which she vents on the doctor as a failure at his job). We are here invited to enjoy the spectacle of the defeat of rationality by Nature–we note however that even she cannot completely subdue her own humanity, for she can't bear the sight of tears[1] in spite of their being an illogical weakness: she softens to Clara when she cries, and immediately takes in the vagabond David when he breaks down in tears though

[1] I have always thought that Tolstoy was struck with the psychological insight shown in this trait and that the result was his Karenin, who is afraid of feeling and can't bear the sight of tears, but once develops a fully human self owing to the appeal of the helpless neglected baby his wife has borne that is not his. His realization thereby that Anna's adultery is something he is involved in, and thence that if it were not for the moral conventions of his society they could find a *modus vivendi* which would not turn her out of her home with the loss to him of the baby is his first tentative effort towards a moral rebirth. It is thwarted, unlike Miss Trotwood's, and he dries up.

she has started, characteristically, by 'making a chop in the air with her knife'[1] at him and declaring '"No boys here!"' This is taken up to show, after her gradual humanizing, her complete yielding to natural sensibility when, on learning of David's engagement to Agnes that she had long desired, 'she immediately went into hysterics, for the first and only time'; she has previously been reconciled to Peggotty, her very opposite, and is last seen sharing with Peggotty the nurse's rôle for David's children and, having got the long-desired namesake, 'spoiling' her.

When David is introduced into the Dover household he finds there the deranged Mr. Dick, through whom Miss Betsey demonstrates her refusal to admit that final defeat of reason, madness: constantly 'triumphant' when she has elicited dubious proofs of his having sense (' "*That* man mad!"' etc.) Similarly she refuses to admit the fact of sexual attraction instead of accepting it as inevitable, employing maids 'expressly to educate [them] in a renouncement of mankind, and who generally completed their abjuration by marrying the baker', having herself consistently protested against the conditions of marriage by reverting to the status and mode of living of a spinster.[2] We are made to wince at her harshness in relegating people into categories–Clara is always and from the first sight a Baby to her, and the most she can do in sympathy for her after her death is to prefix it with 'poor' or 'poor dear'; Dora she classifies as something subhuman as 'Little Blossom'. Yet she had recognized that reason alone is inadequate to live by; as she later admits rather pathetically to David: ' "It was a gleam of light upon me, Trot, when I formed the resolution of being godmother to your sister Betsey Trotwood"', for her yearning for a human link was defeated: ' "Where was this child's

[1]Dickens cannot be said to have meant this as a symbolic threat of murder or castration at a conscious level, but it is undoubtedly the right gesture to express the attitude Miss Trotwood has taken up, just as the Doll's Dressmaker characteristically makes two pricks in the air with her needle when angered, symbolically blinding those she dislikes. To use–or invent–characteristic gestures for his personae is one of the means a novelist has to convince the reader of his insight, of course, and Dickens is peculiarly gifted in being able to uncover such authentic expressions of a unique inner life.

[2]Her humanization towards the end of the novel is shown by her acceptance of woman's fate–'aiding and abetting' her last maid's marrying a tavern-keeper and 'crowning the marriage-ceremony with her presence', as well as in spoiling her god-daughter when she gets one. The half-way stage is marked by her declaring to David her refusal to try to help him improve Dora's character: ' "I want our pet to like me, and be as gay as a butterfly"'. Dora is now 'our' pet, in effect an acceptance of the idea.

sister, Betsey Trotwood? Not forthcoming. Don't tell me!"' It was after this, we learn, that she took Mr. Dick into her care, as a substitute. The shortcomings of rationality in furnishing self-knowledge are beautifully implied in the dialogue with Mr. Dick (where, as so often in *David Copperfield*, humour not merely reinforces serious insights but is a mode of presenting them effectively):

> 'Ah! his sister, Betsey Trotwood, never would have run away.' My aunt shook her head firmly, confident in the character and behaviour of the girl who never was born.
> 'Oh! you think she wouldn't have run away?' said Mr. Dick.

His innocent question undermines for the reader in advance the assurance of her over-emphatic answer to the seeds of doubt thus sown in her own mind as well as ours.

Dickens also allows for the real usefulness of sharp unsentimental good sense, as in her enlightened treatment of Mr. Dick, her understanding of what the Murdstones are, her upbringing of David, her immediate 'placing' of the Old Soldier and Mrs. Crupp, – but undoubtedly another and important function is to show, in her devastating comments which do not allow for the feelings of others,[1] and the unanswerable conclusions she draws in opposition to the facts of experience, that there is something to be said for the illogical, irrational, tender-hearted female accepted then as the norm. As is the mode of *David Copperfield*, she is offered, it seems, playfully and apparently for our entertainment, but this should not disguise the serious uses Dickens makes of her, and the importance of her contribution to the meaning of the novel, as one of its conflicting possibilities. We must surely recognize the inventiveness and spontaneous ingenuity with which Dickens brings this about. I must say that I used personally to resent his apparently unworthy tactic of saddling Miss Betsey with what I took to be a gratuitous trait of aggressive mania – the donkeys whose intrusion on to the green which she claims to own, that she spends so much time in resenting, and her banging the donkey-boys' heads against the wall, as rather too suggestive of the vulgar Victorian

---

[1] A contrast in the same novel to Miss Trotwood's fallacious use of logic is provided by Miss Dartle's brilliantly witty use of logic to expose the fallacies of the Steerforth assumptions, based on class contempt for the lower orders, when in reply to James Steerforth's conventional dismissal of their right to consideration as not being sensitive like 'us', she retorts: 'Really! Well, I don't know, now, when I have been better pleased than to hear that. It's so consoling! It's such a delight to know that, when they suffer, they don't feel!'

idea of a strong-minded woman, as though Dickens felt obliged to make a concession to vulgar prejudice. But on second thoughts one sees it is psychologically right: the aggressiveness belongs to her condition and the touch of mania against the opposite sex sees the donkey-drivers as suitable objects for her animus against mankind, just as she saw in the helpless and victimized child-man, Mr. Dick, a suitable object for her protection and sympathy. Again we see Dickens combining the rôles of entertainer and serious novelist.

iii

At this point I will return to the comparison with Tolstoy. We have seen that Dickens has rooted the David-Dora marriage into the psychological as well as the sociological context of his age, as Tolstoy has not–what evidently struck Tolstoy in reading *David Copperfield* was mainly the fact of such a marriage and its bearings on a man's happiness. So Tolstoy, unlike Dickens, leaves us rebellious against his *fait accompli*. Did Prince Andrew's courtship give him no doubts about the wisdom of his choice of a wife, we ask, especially since he is not shown as having such need for childlike gaiety as David Copperfield had? And we note that nevertheless Dickens does show, with the greatest delicacy, that in David's prolonged courtship he has misgivings in the many causes for uneasiness which he registers more or less consciously, particularly in the way Dora takes the news of his loss of Miss Trotwood's fortune and her response to his consequent demands on her for support and co-operation. He does try to cope with her, but he is very young, and inexperienced, and as he cannot do without her his doubts have to be suppressed: we see that he can only allow himself to admit the truth about Dora in his dreams–Dickens's intelligent interest in the underlying factors of consciousness make dreams and delirious states an important means of exploring experience in his novels. For instance, David dreams he is at 'an imaginary party where the people were dancing the hours away, and I heard the music incessantly playing one tune, and saw Dora incessantly dancing one dance, without taking the least notice of me'. And again, his waking self had bravely seen his future in this sanctioned form: 'What I had to do, was, to take my woodman's axe in my hand, and clear my own way through the forest of difficulty, by cutting down the trees until I came to Dora' (the suggestion of a fairy-tale hero implies a consciousness of this activity's being unrealistic in his very different circumstances, also that he sees that his Dora belongs to a fairy-tale world.) Yet when dozing over the fire this recurs in a hopeless recognition of the actuality as 'thinking how I could best make my way with a guitar-case through the forest of difficulty, until I used to fancy my head was turning quite grey'.

Tolstoy's very rationality and his consistently logical use of language seem to put him at a disadvantage compared to Dickens in such a complex matter. Thus Andrew's guilt is for having deserted his wife and been dead to her appeals for affection, but that does not prevent his forming a satisfactory attachment later to Natasha, who though undisciplined, spoilt and girlish is shown to be capable of maturing through her love for him. Andrew's penitence after his experience of suffering (virtually death) on the battlefield, had no basis in genuine feeling for Lisa, it is only a new consciousness of the moral claims of others instead of the hard superiority, the egoism, of his father. Yet Tolstoy in giving his own version of Dickens's theme in *War and Peace* does take it to a more satisfactory issue. We all feel–though the Victorian public didn't for the most part– that the schematic marriage to Agnes, theoretically the right wife, is hollow and unconvincing, that all the reality is in David's feelings for Dora. Of course Dickens had no experience of a satisfactory marriage and his sister-in-law Georgina, who carried out so successfully the housekeeping and child-rearing functions in his home, did not arouse feelings of love or romantic tenderness in him: this kind of woman seems to have evoked in him only gratitude plus some irritation (he wished she would marry though he knew he could hardly spare her). Agnes is only a willed concession to the Victorian ideal–seen always as the angel on the hearth, in the light from a stained glass window, 'pointing upward', or with her 'patient smile'. Moreover, she has been established as in essence a sister-figure to David, and there is an unpleasant suggestion in the Sister-and-wife combination corresponding to the 'O my father and my husband' of the Strongs' marriage, neither of which Dickens at bottom found appealing, we can see, for he can't make them either attractive or plausible.

But what about Dickens's other models for a happy marriage–are they any more satisfactory? He has tried hard with the Traddleses, and with some success. Sophie, 'the dearest girl in the world', *is* a convincing presence; for one thing, she isn't envisaged as forever static with a holy smile on her face like Agnes, and she has the playfulness and vivacity that for Dickens was the essential feminine allure without having also Dora's or Clara's folly and selfishness. But she also is essentially schematic, and too much of her consists of turning Dora upside down without sacrificing Dora's desirable qualities. Sophie, says Traddles, 'is quite as much a mother *to* her mother, as she is to the other nine [sisters]'; she is older than Traddles and used to narrow means, so altogether she can take the burden of marriage to a struggling professional man and train herself to be a helpmeet. Dora can only hold the pens for her overworked husband in, as usual, a make-believe of wifely duty (actually this makes her a hindrance to David's writing but he acquiesces in the fiction, having enough imagination to realize, Dickens shows, that she needs to believe that the marriage is thus put on a more equal footing—David was *not* a Prince Andrew). But Sophie really uses the pens herself to serve Traddles as the necessary copying-clerk he can't afford, and disciplines herself to write a stiff masculine law-hand. Yet Sophie is also a source of unfailing gaiety and youthful feelings—to establish this we are shown her romping with 'the girls' in Traddles's legal chambers, singing innumerable children's songs from memory, and so forth; so she is satisfactory on every score. Yet is the Traddles marriage any more than a daydream? We can't help noting that their private life is that of grown-up children, and the novel ends with further illustrations of this fact though Traddles has somehow, very improbably, developed legal maturity to the degree required for becoming a Judge.[1] There is a similar absence of realism in the Micawber marriage, where, though the attachment of husband and wife to each other is in itself convincing enough, yet in Mrs. Micawber's theme-song, that she will never desert Mr. Micawber, and in his, about the comfort of mutual confidence, Dickens seems to be using the couple as a means of making fun of the *clichés* of the Victorian marriage theory, and almost to make it impossible to take seriously the mutual explanations of the Strongs in chapter XLV, which the Micawbers unconsciously burlesque subsequently in their comic scene in chapter LII.

For the other couple Dickens has worked hard to produce as a model is a very surprising one indeed, almost shockingly perverse, and calls for some investigation. Their symbolic name of Strong suggests that it has Dickens's full endorsement—but at what level? Annie, we learn, was only 17 when she was persuaded into marriage with the learned classical

---

[1]Scott, who like Dickens was greatly interested in the psychology of the legal profession besides being a lawyer himself, showed in *Guy Mannering* an eminent lawyer enjoying himself in an atmosphere of high jinks, but in the sanctioned smoking-room tradition of masculine relaxation, which is very different from Traddles's childlike diversions.

scholar and headmaster aged 60 who had been her father's old friend and her own teacher from childhood, and whom she has continued to think of as a father-figure. He provides all the wisdom while she contributes girlish gaiety, singing, and relaxation for him; she is always seen symbolically kneeling at his feet, first buttoning up his gaiters and later in reverence towards him, or else contentedly but uncomprehendingly listening to him reading from his projected dictionary. In spite of Dickens's efforts in making the Doctor chivalrous and kind-hearted, it has an inescapable grisly likeness to that later marriage of the kind, Dorothea Casaubon's, and Dickens throws in, perhaps involuntarily, some features that support this view (e.g. the marriage is childless, the Doctor's life's work is represented as rather ridiculous pedantry and unreal, not being even remotely possible of completion in his lifetime, and so on). Worse still, the marriage has to us inevitably a really unpleasant morbid aspect which Dickens seems to reveal in spite of his conscious intentions, as in Annie's 'O my father and my husband' speeches and attitudes–isn't there something very wrong in her contentedness with this situation? we ask. Dr. Strong, 'the old scholar', needs youth and gaiety and tenderness, too,–in Dickens's eyes they are, as we saw, indispensable to a man's happiness; but we can't be satisfied seeing the price Annie has to pay that he may enjoy them, and note with disapproval Dickens's determination to believe that Annie is really fulfilled in such a marriage.[1] Here I think we must not impute dishonesty to Dickens but recognize the Balaam prophetic vein at work that is a part of every true artist's endowment and that must surface at the right time. In fact, the Strongs are so presented that they posit these doubts inevitably. The technique here is that which characterizes *David Copperfield*–not ambiguity but a novel that can be read at two levels, a popular one (humorous, sentimental and moralistic) and that of art, complex, serious, poignant, subtly suggestive, though devious in presentation and its argument subterranean.

[1] A better treatment of the unequal marriage had already appeared in *The Cricket on the Heath* (1845) where the gay young wife is thought by her sober and older husband to have a lover; after some saddened self-reproach he decides to separate from his wife without allowing blame to attach to her since he ought not to have tied a young girl to middle age. He finds however, in the general *dé-nouement*, that his wife truly loves and honours him and enjoys the disparity as an excuse for a game of make-believe. Dickens can carry this off with a light hand in a Christmas fairy-story, and the couple's having a baby and a convincingly realistic working-man's home makes the marriage more acceptable.

As a pendant to Dickens's attempt to cover the matrimonial possibilities in his age, he gives us Miss Trotwood who, having made an unhappy choice and finding herself deceived in her husband's character,
follows the voice of Reason in separating herself from her husband and
quite logically reverting to spinster status. But a rational solution to the
problem of an unhappy marriage, a legal separation, can't make happiness. She is shown living a rigidly monotonous existence in which her
tending of Mr. Dick is (till David enters her life) her substitute for husband and child and the natural instincts for intimate human relations—
she has to vindicate her own judgment against society's. But by giving
her a thoroughly bad man for a husband Dickens has spoilt his argument,
for it was necessary to show that it was her inflexibility in the face of the
process of readjustment and mutual concession that marriage demands,
that caused the breakdown of her marriage. I imagine this was his original
intention, since it fits the part Miss Trotwood enacts in the schematic
novel, but that getting fond of Miss Trotwood as a person, as the novel
progressed, he could not bring himself to treat her afterwards with the
impartiality required. Otherwise we might have had a parallel to the
Murdstone marriage with the sexes reversed, which would have completed the schematic argument.

We must admit therefore that Dickens in *David Copperfield* is not able
to provide an adequate answer to the question of Victorian man's happiness that he set out to tackle. He has, however, shown us very fully,
delicately and seriously what is involved in that question, and has refused
to simplify the issues. We may recollect that Chekhov defended *Anna
Karenina* against critics by saying that we must not demand that a novelist
solves our problems for us; that all we are entitled to require of him is
that he should state the problems correctly. This Dickens has certainly
done, to the best of his ability, in *David Copperfield*, and we need not, I
suggest, think less of his novel if we compare it with the comparable art
of Tolstoy's work that he inspired. However we must note that Tolstoy
was in fact able to take further steps towards suggesting helpful answers
to the problems Dickens first raised and that Tolstoy in his turn undertook to dramatize in his first large-scale novel. Dickens makes David,
after the long enchanted courtship, during which, through no fault of his
own, he has failed to make of Dora anything but a pet, feel alarm once the
marriage has taken place and he must live with her in the everyday world.
Dickens shows him, in one masterly phrase, realizing that the courtship
has turned into a prison sentence: they have now, David reflects, 'no one

to please but one another–one another to please for life'. And their married life continues to the end unchanged, in the chapters called 'Our Housekeeping' and 'Domestic', which explore the marriage between the lines, as it were, as a hopeless dilemma, while maintaining a sufficient appearance, in its humorous tone, of being the stock joke about a young couple's housekeeping troubles and little quarrels, that Dickens's reading public would not find disturbing. Tolstoy was able to show through his Natasha the growth into maturity of the delightful girlish creature who has revived in the despondent Prince Andrew a desire for life and happiness. Unlike his dead child-wife Lisa, Natasha is potentially a woman. In the proposal scene we learn that both of the lovers realise that they are now responsible for each other:

> Prince Andrew held her hands, looked into her eyes, and did not find in his heart his former love for her. Something in him had suddenly changed; there was no longer the former poetic and mystic charm of longing, but there was pity for her womanly and childish weakness, fear in face of her devotion and trustfulness, and an oppressive yet joyful sense of the duty that now bound him to her for ever. The actual feeling, though it was not so bright and poetic as the former, was stronger and more serious.
>
> 'Is it possible that I–the chit of a girl, as everybody called me.' thought Natasha, 'is it possible that I am now to be the *wife*, the equal of this strange, dear clever man, whom even my father respects? Can it be true? Can it be true that I can no longer play with life, that now I am grown up, that on me now lies a responsibility for every word and deed of mine?'

And after this and its development we see Natasha pass through a succession of painful experiences (which include nursing Andrew to his death) and finding happiness in a marriage with Pierre, who has progressed to that marriage by his own self-discoveries which started with the disastrous mistake of letting himself be seduced into marrying a vicious society beauty. Pierre and Natasha's happiness is shown to be founded on domestic tastes and mutual respect, so that Natasha is able to discard her girlish personality altogether without risking losing her husband's love:

> Natasha did not follow that golden rule, advocated by clever folk, especially the French, which says that a girl ... must be more careful of her appearance, and must fascinate her husband as much as she did before he became her husband. Natasha, on the contrary, at once

abandoned all her witchery. . . . She gave it up just because it was so powerfully seductive. . . . She felt that the allurements instinct had taught her formerly to use would now be merely ridiculous in the eyes of her husband, to whom she had from the first given herself entirely–that is, with her whole soul, leaving no corner of it hidden from him. She felt that her unity with her husband was not maintained by the poetic feelings that had attracted him to her, but by something else–something indefinite, but as firm as the bond between her own body and soul. To fluff out her curls, put on fashionable dresses, and sing romantic songs, to fascinate her husband, would have seemed as strange to her as to adorn herself to attract herself.

Dickens does not write and could not write such things, but we cannot but recognize that they are implied in his analyses of what was wrong with the society that formed David's ideal for him and that formed Dora.

At the same time, while Tolstoy was able to formulate and dramatize convincing positives of Dickens's negatives, and successes to correct Dickens's failures, we note that he is in Dickens's debt for the idea of the good marriage. It may have struck some of Tolstoy's other readers, as it has always done me, that the Victorian bourgeois ideal of marriage is unexpected, almost disconcertingly so, in its context in *War and Peace* and from the pen of a Russian aristocrat. The marriage of Nicholas Rostov with Princess Mary, the alternative happy marriage to Pierre's and its complement, is a realistic version of David's second marriage, and Nicholas Rostov's feelings for his wife–also an angel-wife–are those of David for his Agnes.

This is what had attracted Nicholas Rostov to Princess Mary originally:

Nicholas was struck by the peculiar beauty he observed in her at this time. That pale, sad, refined face, that radiant look, those gentle graceful gestures, and especially that deep and tender sorrow expressed by all her features, agitated him and evoked his sympathy. In men Rostov hated to see an expression of lofty spirituality (that was why he did not like Prince Andrew) and he spoke of it contemptuously as philosophy and dreaminess, but in Princess Mary, just in that sorrow which revealed the depth of a whole spiritual world foreign to him, he felt an irresistible attraction. 'She must be a wonderful woman! A real angel!' he said to himself.

Tolstoy's society and Dickens's are evidently similar in a need to localize in woman-as-wife the spiritual values which the man cannot afford to accept in his own life of manly aggressiveness and struggle–even though Tolstoy's had a powerful aristocracy and court and only an insignificant bourgeoisie. Tolstoy as novelist incarnates the Victorian ideal of Woman, the Victorian ideal of marriage, and in his novels as in our own Victorian novels a culture based on the family, the countryside, the farm and the great house still counts for more than the city; there is no question as yet of the emancipation of woman either from domesticity or from male dominance. But Agnes is seen pictorially and her inside never examined, she has no life of her own like Princess Mary, in consequence Agnes's spiritual attributes are little more than uplift. But even though this is not so with his Mary, Tolstoy does not, like Dickens, accept the idealisation as sound. He makes the point quite clearly that an average man like Nicholas Rostov sequestrated spirituality, which he knew he lacked but needed, as a right and desirable quality in Woman, feeling that these same qualities were in practice a weakness in a man because incompatible with his own duties as provider for a family:

> . . . this untiring mental effort, of which the aim was the children's moral welfare, delighted him. If Nicholas could have analysed his feelings he would have discovered that his steady proud love for his wife was founded on wonder at her spirituality and at the lofty moral world almost beyond his reach–in which she had her being. . . . Countess Mary's soul always strove towards the infinite, the eternal, and the absolute, and therefore could never be at peace. A stern expression of secret lofty suffering, of a soul burdened by the body, appeared on her face. Nicholas glanced at her. 'Oh God! What will become of us if she dies, as I always fear when her face is like that?' he thought.

It is because Tolstoy rejected the position of the man's placing the responsibility for moral goodness on his wife that he ends his novel with the state of mind of 'little Nicholas', Prince Andrew's son and Nicholas Rostov's nephew. The boy turns away with dislike from his practically minded uncle and takes as his hero Pierre who was his dead father's friend and whom he identifies in his dreams with his father, the two together being the inspiration for the boy's idealism; he determines to do something glorious in life that *they* would approve of. For Pierre, we are shown, the source of values is not a Victorian idealization of Woman but for him it exists in the disinterested life of the spirit, shown in the artist's, scientist's and philosopher's spheres of mind and vocation. And it is for this, we are told, that Natasha respects as well as loves him. Here

Tolstoy has made it very clear that he sees a better alternative than Dickens's idea for David Copperfield of a satisfactory ideal of marriage, where Agnes is described by her husband as 'the source of every worthy aspiration I had ever had; the centre of myself, the circle of my life', though Tolstoy's ideal of married life is equally founded in the life of hearth and home. And yet we note also that Tolstoy in Natasha has provided a thoroughly Victorian conception of the right and proper relation of wife to husband, one that is neither aristocratic nor enlightened but decidedly bourgeois. Natasha cannot comprehend or share, is often irritated by and even jealous of, Pierre's preoccupation with what is outside the scope of her wholly domestic life, yet she knows he must have this life in the outside world of the mind and spirit to make him the man she can look up to. [Kitty, Levin's wife in *Anna Karenina*, is placed in exactly the same relation to her husband, showing that this was a part of Tolstoy's beliefs that he saw no reason to abandon on second thoughts.] We may well feel that Tolstoy took over from Dickens everything in this respect and changed nothing in essentials. There is nothing in these fundamental attitudes about men and women's relations in marriage that he has in common with Stendhal or Balzac, his other extra-Russian novelist influences.

iv

If part of Dickens's theme in *David Copperfield* is an enquiry into the Victorian assumption that in a woman a loving heart is better than wisdom, another is an investigation into the other Romantic-Victorian belief, the value of innocence—that is, moral simplicity and ignorance of what people are really like. It is David's 'innocence' that makes him a victim of the idea of love that has been inculcated along with other idealisms. The romantic tradition has given him to understand that love at first sight is right and proper, and accordingly his relations with Dora are conducted entirely in the conventional idiom of romantic courtship which is seen as ridiculous, and this point made inescapable by Miss Mills's soulful version of it, which brings out its essential absurdity by caricaturing it (not, as Cockshut asserts, to make David look sensible in comparison with Miss Mills—Dickens was not a thimble-rigger but an artist and he is not manipulating the reader here but directing him to what he himself feels to be the right position for seeing adolescent romantic passion justly). The dilemma of innocence is even more agonizing to Dickens than the question of affectionateness as an ultimate, since the idealization of innocence represented a menace to childhood; yet Innocence is what the heirs of the Romantic poets felt to be the true characteristic of the child. The child David's innocent trustfulness is constantly being taken advantage of, the paradigm being when he is made at the very beginning to drink 'Confusion to Brooks of Sheffield!' (himself) by the heartless plotters against his mother and himself. A later episode, in chapter V, with the waiter at the inn, is more involved and more painful showing not only the manifold meanness of the waiter (whose idea of humour consists of jeering at the unprotected little boy whom he has cheated and duped by exploiting his innocence) but also the stupidity and hatefulness of a variety of adults who take part against the child automatically. Dickens's comment, through the medium of grown-up David as he looks back at this episode in his moral history, brings out interestingly the dilemma I mean:

> If I had any doubt of him [the waiter], I suppose this half awakened it; but I am inclined to believe that with the simple confidence of a child, and the natural reliance of a child upon superior years (qualities I am very sorry any children should prematurely change for worldly wisdom), I had no serious mistrust of him on the whole, even then.

Ideally, Victorian adults were to be thought of as parents, natural protectors, and trustfully accepted as guides; and even if the actuality often failed to match the theory, children were still to be taught that it is true, even though this left them to be exploited, hurt and morally bewildered.[1] Yet at *some* point or other in growing up they must learn the probability of the theory's being humbug and in fact dangerous to trust in. The whole question therefore hinged on how 'prematurely' is to be interpreted. David would not be so attractive as a child if he had not had this simple confidence in his seniors and at this stage we can only remark, 'The more shame to them for abusing it!' [This is particularly painful in the journey to Dover.] But by the time he gets to Mr. Creakle's and accepts Steerforth, against a good deal of evidence, as a noble character and the father-figure he needs as protector, we should find David lacking

---

[1] Cf. *Oliver Twist*: the real horror at the corruption of innocence there is epitomized in Fagin, whom Oliver thinks a kind old gentleman fond of children, but who is really turning them into thieves, criminals and prostitutes; he teaches Oliver a game which Oliver later realizes is picking pockets, thus using the child's natural instinct for play to ruin him.

in acumen *if* Dickens had not shown that public opinion at the school supported David's supposition (except for Mr. Mell and Traddles – but both were without status); and he is still a *little* boy, at this stage. There is certainly a deliberate and delicate demonstration here as to the difficulty of an innocent's arriving at a true judgment in the face of public opinion, and David's moral bewilderment and unhappiness about the Mell episode, and the impossibility for him of understanding it, is finally conveyed to us as well as, which makes it more painful, the delicacy and decency of Mr. Mell in trying to assure David that he doesn't blame him. But the same pattern is repeated when David is introduced into the Steerforth home by his friend (to feed Mrs. Steerforth's maternal egoism): Miss Dartle with her ironic questions and sinister intimations is putting him into a position to draw the right conclusions about Steerforth, but David is again fortified by Mrs. Steerforth's unshakeable belief in her son and by what he believes to be Steerforth's affection for him (which is really only Steerforth's self-indulgent habit of patronage, and which contains a hateful element of contempt). David thus unsuspectingly introduces a seducer into the virtuous Noah's Ark on the Yarmouth beach, launching Little Em'ly into misery and disgrace. I think we are now undoubtedly meant to feel impatient with David over his failure to 'change his simple confidence for worldly wisdom', for it would now clearly not be 'premature' but timely. We surely feel at this stage that David is no longer simply very young but *very young for his age*,[1] that he is in danger of growing up to be what Miss Trotwood had described his mother as being, in summing up her disastrous second marriage: 'a most unworldly, most unfortunate baby'. We often enough have reason to echo his aunt's

[1] David himself feels at this time that he was 'aware, indeed, of being younger than I could have wished' – and Phiz, deliberately instructed thereto no doubt, makes this excessive immaturity inescapable visually, by stressing David's extremely unformed and innocent appearance; *v.* e.g. Phiz's picture of his introduction to Dora, and the illustration entitled: 'Mr. Micawber Delivers Some Valedictory Remarks'. In the picture 'The Friendly Waiter and I' David's smallness and innocence are even exaggerated, and the waiter's grossness made appropriately evident. The illustration entitled 'I make the acquaintance of Miss Mowcher', quite the best in the novel, brings out most intelligently all aspects of Dickens's theme as to the disabilities of innocence in a corrupt world. David's and Steerforth's contrasted faces deserve studying under a magnifying glass for subtlety of expression. On the wall among other suitable pictures we see one showing Mephistopheles looking on at the meeting of Faust and Marguerite, and another of Gulliver as a smirking and subservient mannikin amusing the hideous society of Brobdignag, David's rôle here in relation to Steerforth and Miss Mowcher.

'Blind! blind! blind!' and are clearly meant to.[1] We are also meant to reflect that his sheltered life and idealistic education at Dr. Strong's have put him in blinkers, for the period when his life was *not* sheltered, at the warehouse, occurred too early to do more for him than make him wretched and did not last long enough to turn him into an Artful Dodger. Here, in a variety of scenes and situations deliberately created for the purpose, Dickens must be recognized as consciously, persistently and with great subtlety, intimating a radical criticism of the theory of the Victorian moral code with its Romantic heritage. Dickens is no more than anyone else able to decide what is the right point of balance between being a grown-up Baby and a hardened young Artful Dodger (or in this case, a Steerforth with his sophistication derived from the 'Varsity world instead of from the gutter), but Dickens certainly feels that while the good young man is handicapped by his innocence, it is better to be a David than a James Steerforth, the proof being that Steerforth at moments felt it too. One indication we are given of Dickens's personal bias is that he likes to show that the intuitions of the innocent mind are a safer guide where feelings are concerned than worldly wisdom: the solicitor's suspicions of Annie prove to be unjust and Dr. Strong's guileless trust in her justified; Jack Maldon's attitude of sneering at the delightful simplicity of the old Doctor is not only ugly in its ingratitude but stupid, since it prevents him from understanding his cousin Annie's feelings, and we register here the truth of Dickens's argument that it is better to be even ridiculously unworldly than base, since moral stupidity (as George Eliot called it) defeats itself. [The parallel playing off of Mr. Micawber against Littimer as an argument in favour of a spontaneity that ignores some virtues as against hypocritical respectability, is a different matter and has to be established in the novel dramatically.]

Here Dickens is early in the field of examining Victorian values and assumptions. Clough began his dramatic poem 'Dipsychus' the year after

[1] In this light, there is no ground for Cockshut's objection that Steerforth's obvious failings 'make David's hero-worship seem much less touching than it is supposed to be'. It is only Mrs. Steerforth who thinks it touching, and Agnes's disregarded warning against Steerforth is one further proof that Dickens meant us to be exasperated with David's simple-minded credulity, and to realize that his need for affection and for an object to lavish affection and hero-worship on (accounted for by his history), are dangerous. At the beginning of chapter XXXII David explains that even when he has been disillusioned about Steerforth he could not have reproached him if brought face to face and still cherishes the old relation with him.

David Copperfield, and in a prose Epilogue to his poem makes his fictional uncle complain that the younger generation have been made dangerously high-minded by Dr. Arnold's schooling: 'as for my own nephews', says the worldly old gentleman who had grown up in a pre-Victorian England, 'they seem to me a sort of hobbadi-hoy cherub, too big to be innocent and too simple for anything else', adding that at 'about the age of 18 or 19' the poet himself was 'a great goose'. Clough therefore must have felt that this was so and that it was not an advantage. This is Dickens's point too, though he himself certainly didn't suffer like Clough from this Victorian disability.[1] Trollope, another writer formed before Victorian idealism was current orthodoxy, sensed likewise that something had gone wrong, though his contribution was confined to showing the dangers of innocence and the sheltered life to young ladies. In one of his novels (*Mr. Scarborough's Family*), he tells us that his heroine 'attempted to live by grand rules'–'Nor did she know it', and he goes on to make the interesting general point that reproduces Dickens's earlier inquiry in *David Copperfield*:

> Unselfishness may become want of character; generosity essentially unjust; confidence may be weakness, and purity insipid.

He actually devoted a whole, though short, novel (*Sir Harry Hotspur of Humblethwaite*) to dramatizing this insight, showing a family tragically ruined and their only child, a daughter, literally killed by these Victorian

---

[1]Dickens was a great deal more knowing at this age. The hint we are given of the difference David felt between himself, who had shared the life of the disreputable Micawbers, and the boys from unsullied homes, when he first went to Dr. Strong's school, is one of the more deeply-felt insights in the novel (chapter XVI)–e.g. 'How would it affect them, who were innocent of London life and the London streets', he wondered, 'to discover how knowing I was (and was ashamed to be) in some of the meanest phases of both?' David's remembrance of things past was buried by his rebirth as Miss Trotwood's Trotwood and his re-education in the honour system of Dr. Strong's school; this was not the case of Charles Dickens–at 15 he was a clerk in a lawyer's office, acquiring the cynical view of the law and lawyers evident in his writings from *Pickwick Papers* onwards, where he sponsored Sam Weller's knowingness against Mr. Pickwick's greenness. Pickwick's innocence is considered lovable but shown to be dangerous. Characteristically, Dickens goes deeper into the subject by showing the ridiculous innocence in some respects of 'knowing' characters such as old Tony Weller and his circle, when obliged to go outside their own purlieu–that is, that to be sharp is not to be wise. Mark Twain uses the same technique with Huckleberry Finn to make the same point.

idealisms, the disaster entirely due to her insistence on putting into practice the Christian and sentimental beliefs she had been taught as proper for a young lady and which she would have known to be impracticable if she had not been kept in such innocence of the nature of things. The idea is interesting, but Trollope was not the novelist to do it justice. His heroine is without individuality and makes no imaginative impact as Rosa Dartle, for instance, does, while Trollope's pedestrian style and no-nonsense mode of operation as a novelist deprive the subject of that sensitive notation and appropriately original presentation which it requires. We cannot but feel the advantage Dickens had in not being addicted to that logical-discursive use of language, and rational treatment of a theme, that characterizes the novels of Trollope, Thackeray, Mrs. Gaskell and all other Victorian writers of fiction not of the first order. In this Dickens stands apart with Charlotte and Emily Brontë and George Eliot.

I have shown in the development of the theme of David's typical relation to his mother and its effect on his emotional life, in the function of Miss Trotwood, in the delicate intimations of parallels between father and son, and in the whole elaborate structure of meanings expressed through such techniques, that in *David Copperfield* Dickens has triumphantly arrived at mastery of a new, his own, art of the novel. Of course, as Tolstoy said, Dickens was liable to be (in patches) 'a sentimental and loquacious writer', and (as is not the case with *Middlemarch* or Tolstoy's novels), areas, (insignificant generally) of many of his novels have to be written off. As *David Copperfield* is early in his progress, which started in *Dombey*, from willy-nilly entertainer to a free artist, we must admit that some of its parts exist on different levels of seriousness. Dickens was perfectly sincere when he told Miss Coutts that he wanted to make people more humane about prostitutes and 'fallen women' by his presentation of Martha and Emily, but Martha is, like the similar character in *Dombey*, Good Mrs. Brown's daughter, a figure drastically edited for the purpose from the originals he knew and had helped in real life. Emily is another matter. Just as Tolstoy made the conditions of Anna's marriage to Karenin so demanding of sympathy that her 'fall' seems a matter for compassion, or even more positive support, so Emily is framed as orphan, childishly innocent, very young in fact, over-sheltered and indulged by her family in the boat, and moreover given to understand by Steerforth that he will 'make her a lady' and he, so to speak, vouched for as to character by being David's old friend and hero; and in addition there is her intolerable position of being about to marry her dull cousin Ham, having yielded to pressure to engage herself to him to please her uncle. All these points are piled up to amount to a demand for a verdict of Not Guilty, even from strict Victorian moralists, presumably. In consonance with this, the blame is firmly laid at Mrs. Steerforth's door, David accompanying the outraged father-uncle to Highgate who is to shame the seducer's mother with his simple working-man's nobility of soul and expose the false values of the upper classes. The theatrical demonstrations of Rosa Dartle against Emily are to show the cruelty of conventional morality even further, since—a nice touch—Miss Dartle is personally jealous of her as a successful rival, suggesting a class as well as a personal jealousy since the whole Steerforth-Emily episode is treated by Dickens as a class matter.[1]

That the whole Yarmouth affair is a moralistic exercise is given away finally by the artificial use of dialect. We have only to observe—to feel—the living nature of the dialect that plays its essential part in *Adam Bede*, *Wuthering Heights* or *The Heart of Midlothian*, for instance, to see that Dickens's use of East Anglian coastal speech is self-conscious, and irritating in its patronizing exhibition of the quaintness of the humble—a matter of vocabulary and grammar only, with none of the vitality of Sam Weller's, Mr. Guppy's or the Kenwigs' Cockney or Mrs. Gamp's vernacular that Dickens has successfully made an expression of character. We do not need to know that Dickens in fact got Suffolk dialect up from a book, *Suffolk Words and Phrases*.[2] The series of framed interiors in which Daniel and Ham Peggotty are posed make them as artificial as Victorian academy pictures; this is especially notable in the scene when Ham tells David of

[1]So is the comparable seduction of Hetty Sorrel by 'the young squire' in *Adam Bede*, but this does not prevent George Eliot from making it the centre of a really interesting moral inquiry (and providing a convincing Nemesis for the seducer) by centring the novel on the seducer's conscience. Of course the seduction of a respectable lower-class girl by an upper-class symbol was a hallowed subject of the 19th-century theatre of the poor—the melodrama—long before *David Copperfield*. A stock feature of this subject on the stage was the stand-up fight in which the girl's dastardly seducer or would-be seducer was knocked out by her brother/ father/suitor of her own class/husband. It is interesting to note a point in Dickens's favour here as against George Eliot that while she compulsively reproduces in *Adam Bede* this embarrassing piece of drama, Dickens's better judgment carefully arranged to avoid it in *David Copperfield* by sending Steerforth abroad out of Ham's and Ham's uncle's way and not bringing him back alive.

[2]*V. Times Lit. Sup.*, April 30, 1949—K. J. Fielding.

his noble feelings towards Emily after her return, David instructing us in the right admiring response. Rebelliously we ask, if Ham was so admirable why couldn't he insist on marrying Emily on her return home and emigrating with her, instead of only forgiving her like a Christian? – one mistake of a very young girl with Emily's excuses can't be supposed to entail ruin for life in the eyes of any right-minded person! Dickens knew this was so, for he helped Miss Coutts in her rescue-work, which equipped fallen women to go to Australia to start afresh and marry there, as Martha indeed is allowed to. But Emily, who has not been a prostitute like Martha, is not allowed to forgive herself for her one false step, but must hang her head in guilt eternally. Mr. Peggotty is brought home from the colony in order to assure us, in nauseating detail, that Emily has been polluted once for all:

'She might have married well a mort of times, "but, uncle" she says to me, "that's gone for ever". Cheerful along with me; retired when others is by; fond of going any distance fur to teach a child, or fur to tend a sick person, or fur to do some kindness tow'rds a young girl's wedding (and she's done a many, but has never seen one); patient; sowt out by all that has any trouble. That's Em'ly!'

One would like to be able to believe that Dickens here is satirizing the unco' guid by holding up in caricature the doom of the fallen woman, and there does seem to me at bottom a trace of such a state of mind. Yet it seems inescapable that he was apparently endorsing the prejudices of his reading-public at this point, for though so humane a man could not at heart endorse such an attitude, and we know that in fact he did not, he is scarcely challenging it effectively. Here writing at two levels at once has muddled the message.

But the artist – the truthteller, the psychological realist – is visible without any possibility of denial or conjecture in another aspect of the Emily episode – in the morbidity Dickens shows as powering the intense affection Daniel Peggotty has for his niece – another critical comment on what could pass as 'affection' and thus as admirable – though that might be acceptable to the Victorian reader as the touching devotion of one who stood in the relation of adopted father to Little Em'ly. But while Mr. Peggotty seems at first sight to offer the pattern of disinterested devotion to the winning child he had fostered, what emerges is a horribly possessive love that is expressed characteristically in heat, violence and fantasies, impressing us as maniacal. And Dickens doesn't attempt to disguise this;

on the contrary, it is hammered home. Mr. Peggotty had no objection to his niece's marrying her cousin Ham, whom she doesn't love as much as her uncle and who, while not being a rival in her affections, will keep her in the family; but her elopement with Steerforth, even though marriage is what she intended, makes him aware of what he cannot face, that she loves Steerforth enough to leave home and uncle for him. Daniel Peggotty is shown driven by uncontrollable passion through Europe on foot to search for Emily, though without any clue as to her whereabouts, determined to find Emily and bring her home, ignoring the very relevant fact that she had preferred to give up that home in order to share Steerforth's life because she can do without her uncle. The Victorian reader understood that he was acting in the interests of Morality in rescuing Emily from a life of shame, but Dickens's attention is elsewhere, on putting into Daniel Peggotty's mouth words of a truly astonishing import:

'I'm a-going to seek my niece through the wureld. I'm a-going to find my poor niece in her shame and bring her back. . . . I'm a-going to seek her, fur and wide. . . . I began to think within my own self "What shall I do when I see her?" I never doubted her. On'y let her see my face—on'y let her heer my voice—on'y let my stanning afore her bring to her thoughts the home she had fled away from, and the child she had been—and if she had growed to be a royal lady, she'd have fell down at my feet. I know'd it well! Many a time in my sleep had I heerd her cry out, "Uncle!" and seen her fall like death afore me. Many a time in my sleep had I raised her up and whispered to her "Em'ly, my dear, I am come fur to bring forgiveness, and to take you home!" *He* was nowt to me now, Em'ly was all. I bought a country dress to put upon her; and I know'd that, once found, she would walk beside me over them stony roads, go wheer I would, and never, never, leave me more.'

It is this genius, which cannot stop at the moralistic and sentimental but which burrows down below the superficial to find an underlying psychological veracity, that is characteristic of Dickens's development as a novelist. We may ask, How does Dickens know these truths? The awful conviction, the terrifying possessive passion Daniel Peggotty's words reveal, could hardly have been expected to pass even with unsophisticated readers as natural feelings creditable to a worthy uncle. Dickens's interest in morbid states and the strange self-deceptions of human nature, shown here in the compulsive fantasying, can never before have been so nakedly displayed. And Daniel Peggotty's dream is actually realized—the artist has caught the spirit of the episode in the illustration called, like the chapter, 'Mr. Peggotty's dream comes true'—and after this Daniel Peggotty tells David of the aftermath: ' "All night long we have been together, Em'ly and me. All night long, her arms has been about my neck; and her head has laid heer; and we knows full well, as we can put our trust in one another ever more." '

There is no need to say: Perhaps Dickens did not see the purport of all this, for there is not merely the remarkable consistency to point to, but in the same novel he has deliberately embarked on, though not in the end done more than outline, another morbid father-love, in Mr. Wickfield's substitution of his daughter Agnes for the beloved wife who died soon after Agnes's birth. ' "My love for my dear child" ', said Mr. Wickfield to David, at the end, "was a diseased love, but my mind was all unhealthy then." ' The fear that his Agnes would tire of him or leave him drove him to drink and professional ruin: this, like Mr. Peggotty's relation to Emily and Miss Dartle's to Steerforth and Uriah Heep's lust to possess Agnes against her will (not only in order to keep her father in his power, for he has trapped the father in order to be able to blackmail Agnes into marrying him) are some of the more sombre undercurrents in the novel that has been described by Mr. Edmund Wilson as Dickens's 'holiday'. The scene where Uriah Heep, compensating himself for compulsory 'umbleness in his youth, parades his power over Mr. Wickfield, who is degraded into his puppet, is more unpleasant than his plots against Agnes, which the reader doesn't mind as much as David does because Agnes is too good to be true.

The submerged drama of Steerforth and Rosa Dartle is more interesting and we may well complain that Dickens has not given it more prominence and fuller attention. Its positive phase is already over when we first see them together, when we learn that there had been some kind of love relation between them that had been so stormy that he had flung a hammer at her, ruining her looks for life and her prospects of marriage— the sinister implications are recognizable in spite of the devious symbolism imposed on a Victorian novelist. [We meet a comparable instance in *Middlemarch* in the superb prolonged and involved metaphor composed to register Dorothea's moral shock at encountering on her honeymoon the unimagined spectacle of the concrete history of Rome and its alien civilizations, a projection of her shock at finding out what marriage is, and marriage to a Casaubon.]

Early on we hear the ambiguous statement Steerforth makes in reply to 'Daisy's' innocent question about his relation to the alarming Miss Dartle:

> 'And I have no doubt she loves you like a brother?' said I.
> 'Humph!' retorted Steerforth, looking at the fire. 'Some brothers are not loved over much; and some love–.'

We must finish the sentence for ourselves, but even the implications of 'looking at the fire' move us in the right direction. Rosa's version to David later is that Steerforth's interest in her proved to be of a kind she could not tolerate: ' "I descended into a doll" ' for him, she says, and therefore broke with him without herself ceasing to love him resentfully. The refusal to be his 'doll' puts her in opposition to the Clara-Dora-Emily 'wax doll' notion of the rôle of woman in love that the David Copperfields and Steerforths equally look for or impose on women,[1] but Dickens didn't develop this interesting idea. Rosa Dartle is not, except in connection with Emily, melodramatic like Edith Dombey and shows an immense advance on such a characterization. Rosa's personality and behaviour are exceptionally interesting in a Victorian novel. The total situation between them surfaces in the remarkable scene detailed in chapter XXIX, where we are shown Steerforth with cruel perversity ('with a curious smile' is all that David notices) placating and charming her against her will in order to subdue her. He seduces her into playing the harp she had long laid aside and singing him a love-song to its accompaniment:

> She stood beside it for some little while, in a curious way, going through the motion of playing it with her right hand, but not sounding it. At length she sat down and drew it to her with one sudden action, and played and sang.
> I don't know what it was, in her touch or voice, that made that song the most unearthly I have ever heard in my life, or can imagine. There was something fearful in the reality of it. It was as if it had never been written, or set to music, but sprung out of the passion within her; which found imperfect utterance in the low sounds of her voice, and crouched again when all was still. I was dumb when she

[1]David and Steerforth, representing the innocently good and the selfishly vicious forms of young manhood of the age, combine to cover the possibilities here, and are in this respect identical, hence the importance of Rosa Dartle's testimony, that she 'descended into a doll' for him–and hence we see why Dickens did not take the trouble to fill in Rosa and Steerforth's joint past: all Dickens needed was to establish this fact from it.

leaned beside the harp again, playing it, but not sounding it, with her right hand.

Steerforth makes a laughing gesture of affection by way of thanking her, 'And she had struck him, and had thrown him off with the fury of a wild cat'.

Realizing he is only playing with her and that she has again 'descended into a doll' for him in spite of her will not to, she strikes him (such a violent action, in a drawing-room, and from a lady, would be excessively shocking to the reader of the day). The painfulness of the scene is enhanced by being conveyed to us through the medium of the blind and stupidly innocent David who thinks that Rosa is 'jaundiced and perverse' for struggling – as he notes she does – against Steerforth's 'delightful art' and 'delightful nature'.

Now this is not melodrama, nor, though it is distinctly enacted, is it at all theatrical. It is memorable because it has the stamp of comprehended truth, like Rosa's habit of undermining people by ironical questioning which allows her, a dependant, the relief of expressing her contempt for them indirectly. This and the other passages of arms between Steerforth and Rosa cannot be dismissed or relegated as theatrical and rhetorical: if such scenes, thus written, had appeared in a tale by D. H. Lawrence, who would have failed to recognize them as in the genuine mode and style of Lawrence, and as exhibiting his characteristic insight into the relations between a man and a woman in such a case? It is Dickens who is the pioneer here – himself accompanied in such insights and their uses by Charlotte and Emily Brontë – and it is he who is to be seen in so much of *Dombey* and *Copperfield* taking the novel in conception and idiom out of melodrama and the language of stage rhetoric, just as in these two novels he takes the novel constructively out of the two inherited traditions of composing it (the picaresque and the sentimental moralistic), takes it in fact into the realm of psychological truth in depth that was demanded by Charlotte Brontë in a letter to her publisher, where she rejects the novel of Jane Austen, saying:

The passions are perfectly unknown to her; she rejects even a speaking acquaintance with that stormy sisterhood. . . . What sees keenly, speaks aptly, moves flexibly, it suits her to study; but what throbs fast and full, though hidden, what the blood rushes through, what is the unseen seat of life and the sentient target of death – this Miss Austen ignores. She no more, with her mind's eye, beholds the heart of her race, than each man, with bodily vision, sees the heart in his heaving breast.

As this was written in 1850, and *David Copperfield* was published in parts from 1849–50, she is recognizing a change in the conception of the novelist's function and the possibilities of the novel that had already taken place and been actualized by Dickens as well as by herself and her sister in writing *Jane Eyre* and *Wuthering Heights*.

Steerforth himself though not sufficiently explored is potentially more interesting than any other specimen of his class in Dickens until we get to Eugene in *Our Mutual Friend*. Steerforth's momentary regrets for not having David's clear conscience and his awareness that if David understood him he would lose David's admiring affection, feelings which are yet not sufficient to prevent him indulging his passing fancy for a little Em'ly,—and his sense of guilt about ruining Rosa Dartle's looks and her chances of marriage, seem to require the fuller treatment that Tolstoy gives to his similar types, such as Anatole Kuragin and Dolokhov. But Taine's complaint, that in the seduction of Emily we are shown only the consequences and not the passion, is hardly relevant, since Steerforth's feelings, such as they are in this respect, are of no interest, while Emily's can be deduced and to enlarge on them would be to expose her folly and lose our sympathy for her (as George Eliot does for her seduced maiden by showing us the inside of Hetty Sorrel's feather head). As it is, we get the benefit of sharing David's shock on learning of the elopement. The scene in chapter XXIX showing Steerforth's irresistible effect on Miss Dartle, being set immediately preceding the elopement with little Em'ly (and, as we then reflect, the imminent triumph over the one woman being the stimulus and prompting for Steerforth's 'curious' impulse to prove he retains his seductive powers over a previous victim too), this makes any demonstration by Dickens of Steerforth's similar effect on the altogether inferior Little Em'ly quite unnecessary. Dickens had actually cut out of his proofs a piece he had originally written to show Steerforth beguiling Mrs Gummidge into cheerfulness in spite of herself, but this was inevitably a poor thing and Dickens showed his judgment in excising it.[1]

[1]The assumption made by John Butt that Dickens cut it out only because he had over-written the Number, going with the claim that the passage was a success and its sacrifice a pity, ignores the fact that Dickens could have restored it when re-publishing in book form. Dickens might be given credit for good taste here, as in excising the reference to the song Rosa Dartle sings in chapter XXIX which was

Thus from such strikingly forceful and absolutely original episodes in *Copperfield* alone as I have been examining here, and those comparable in the case of *Dombey* (such as Mr Carker's sinister relations with Edith Dombey, as well as wholly other aspects of the originality there which are given critical exposition in the essay devoted to *Dombey* above), we can see that to Dickens it was the *meanings* of his mature novels which were important to him and the reason for his undertakings. The force of the language and the originality of conception and execution of such parts (in characterization, action and technique) prove that they were infinitely more the concern of the creative writer than the parts of these novels emanating from his concern (genuine though it was) for social welfare and ordinary morality. And *Copperfield* in addition discovers and explores psychological truths which are to bear fruit in *Little Dorrit* and *Great Expectations*. We have Agnes as victimized daughter shown mothering her consciously disgraced father who is morally dependent on her, and mutely aware that reproach or criticism would make her services in sustaining him useless – the first sketch for the function of the Little Dorrit who in the masterly scene in Book the First, chapter XIX is shown as not merely the embodiment of Christian virtue but as comprehending instinctively the psychological truth behind its conception, in the silent delicacy and forbearance which she brings to bear on the painful situation her father places her in, making it possible, while defending her own integrity, for him to hold up his head and survive in the only rôle open to him ('Father of the Marshalsea'). This is what we understand by the term 'Tolstoyan', while the episodes of Daniel Peggotty in his relation with his niece, and Steerforth's with Rosa Dartle, make the transference from the 'Tolstoyan' core of *Copperfield* to the Dostoievskian *Bleak House* comprehensible, just as the history of Paul and Florence Dombey's childhood, though embedded in Hogarthian satiric scenes as to the adult world, took us out of the Hogarthian mode into the Tolstoyan conception of the whole novel *Copperfield*.

This makes my point, that cannot too strongly be insisted on, that Dickens was writing about real life in the sense that 'real' means essential experience, what Charlotte Brontë called 'the unseen seat of life and the sentient target of death', 'what the blood rushes through'. Dickens above all in *Copperfield* gives proof of his understanding that Love as a

originally given as 'The Last Rose of Summer', where, as Butt admits, he had not over-written (*v.* John Butt, '*David Copperfield*: From Manuscripts to Print', *R.E.S.*, 1950).

reality, not a Victorian convention, did inevitably exist; and that it could not be ignored, suppressed or channelled into the decorous forms the age conventionally considered acceptable, without peril to the psyche, thus fulfilling the challenge, not in Charlotte Brontë's opinion met by Jane Austen or Fielding, to understand 'the heart of her race'.

Miss Mowcher is disappointing. The specimen of *her* in action (chapter XXII) is superb in its suggestions and undertones of a depravity shared with Steerforth from which David the Daisy is excluded, in which his being an amusement to both meanwhile, and still more an additional source of secret amusement to Steerforth since he is using David to mislead Miss Mowcher about which of them is after Emily, plays its part. But Dickens had made too free with the recognizable characteristics of a real woman in endowing Miss Mowcher with a suitable physical deformity; to avoid threatened trouble from the indignant original he had to turn Mowcher suddenly into a 'good' character, thus depriving her of further usefulness in any serious sense. A less forgivable thing, is to have kept the reader on edge throughout most of the novel by intimations that Annie is going to elope with, or will be found to have been seduced by, her cousin Jack Maldon, merely as a means of retaining the readership, the Strong marriage being evidently so unsuitable that an expectation of Annie's 'fall' is plausible. It was evidently very difficult for Dickens, with so disparate a reading-public, to manage to hold it–or believe he could–without some such interest (hence his care to know the sales of each number–and *David Copperfield*'s were disappointing compared with *Dombey*'s at first). Tolstoy could write for an audience of peers, that is, for himself. But Dickens was already in *David Copperfield* discovering tactics for saying what he meant or felt indirectly or beneath a surface less likely to arouse hostility in a readership of Meagleses, Podsnaps, Chillips and Agneses.[1] A successful piece of such delicacy is represented by the scenes in chapter XVI, reported by the schoolboy David who, as was inevitable, could not interpret them. The appearance is that Annie is distraught and faints either merely at the departure of her cousin (loss of her old playmate) or because she is in love with him; the deduction, made not by David but the reader, that Maldon may have already become her lover, is supported by the loss David reports of one of the cherry-coloured ribbons from her white gown (the

---

[1] The novel shows David somewhat embarrassed at finding Mr. Chillip and Mr. Omer are admirers of his books–he seems uncomfortable at having to face the fact that his readership is made up of such as these, that is.

symbolism is stressed) which her mother officiously makes public, and which the artist has confirmed by showing her afterwards at the Doctor's feet with a face full of remorse and shame and her dress, only described by David as 'disordered from the loss of the bow', open, showing her breasts. The reality, which we can deduce when the *éclaircissement* comes, is that Jack Maldon had snatched the bow when making his dishonourable intentions clear to his cousin, obviously in a physical assault, that though resisted by her filled her with horror and humiliation. What could only have been melodramatic if enacted straight, and would then have struck a note of violence out of keeping with the tone of the novel, is success-fully left to the reader's imagination, and leaves him with no way of coming to any certainty of interpretation for a good while. The credit side of this drama is that subsequently the painful nature of Annie's awareness of her false position, an innocence agonizably unable to defend itself (against her mother's use of her, her cousin's ill intentions and the insulting conclusions of Mr. Wickfield) adds very notably to the points made elsewhere in the novel about the vulnerability of Victorian youth.

Though it is easily seen that Mr. Micawber has really no place in the plot or in the action (he is perfunctorily worked in first as David's land-lord and then Traddles's, and sent to Canterbury to be employed most improbably by Heep, still more improbably made the agent of Heep's downfall), the fact that everyone remembers him as a leading feature of the novel is proof of his importance in it: we all feel that somehow he is a major contributor to the meaning of the book. Whenever he is present, even in prison or miserably in debt in mean lodgings, there is life, joy, and a defiance of the rules of Victorian good citizenship. When, as in the little party in David's rooms at Mrs. Crupp's, he is for once deflated, it is not by his real troubles but by the ethos surrounding the 'respectable' Littimer who makes everyone uncomfortable by his high standards of behaviour and ultimately turns out, ironically, to be a villainous hypo-crite, thus making plain the kind of meaning Dickens had in mind. We know that once David's boyhood got mixed up temporarily with Dickens's, through the warehouse phase of it, Mr. Micawber had to be there, for Micawber is Dickens's tribute to the life-style of his father: no doubt Dickens was aware that he had inherited some of the Micawber qualities himself and was grateful for it. [Another set of John Dickens's characteristics contributed a good deal later to William Dorrit, and Dickens took another–a disenchanted–look at even some of the Mic-awber features in his next novel, in Mr. Skimpole]. But Dickens created

Micawber to register the reasons for his affection for his father rather than his grievances, which time had softened in his memory as Dickens, as he wrote, grew to value increasingly his father's disposition and to appreciate, as a comic artist himself, John Dickens's high-handed treatment of reality.[1] It is therefore irrelevant to complain, as an undergraduate pupil of mine did, that Dickens ought to have shown realistically the misery of a family with such an improvident father and husband, as Dostoievsky does with the Marmaladov household. Dickens was not writing *Crime and Punishment* or a tract or even a naturalistic novel. The significance of Micawber is his Micawberism – he represents an essential truth of experience and one that a creative artist in such a society as mid-19th century England needed to point to and maintain. Had Dickens made Micawber a writer or artist he would not only have been completely plausible but even recognizable as an archetype: Joyce, for instance, had the swagger, the shameless assurance in drawing on the resources of others, and the eternal impecuniosity, as well as the gift for language,[2] and Oliver Goldsmith was another of the Micawber tribe. Contempt for the morrow, faith in the future and enjoyment of the present are essential attributes of the creative mind.

By an association we can easily make out, Mr. Micawber bears witness to a pre-Victorian enjoyment of living that Dickens indignantly saw being destroyed by the Murdstones and Littimers. [No one hates Micawber, not even his creditors,[3] as in fact no one seems to have objected to being bled by James Joyce, and everyone but Boswell loved Goldsmith.] Most of the responsible Victorian novelists (not just the irresponsible like

[1]Dickens went on noting his father's Micawberisms in his letters until John Dickens's death, having started to do so long before Micawber was conceived, Forster tells us.

[2]Not merely what Forster characterizes as his 'rhetorical exuberance'. There is real wit in John Dickens's snub to a Nonconformist asserting the superiority of Dissenters: 'The Supreme Being must be an entirely different individual from what I have every reason to believe Him to be, if He would care in the least for the society of your relations.'

[3]Dickens himself, though always paying his way, and sharp with publishers for his rights, was extremely open-handed with the money he earned by incredibly hard toil, and paid out largely to settle the debts of his relatives and even in-laws. Georgina Hogarth wrote that 'he *had greatly suffered* from almost every member of his own family. And *most especially from his father* . . . not only debts and difficulties, but most discreditable and dishonest dealing on the part of the father towards the son'. Dickens could justly claim that no one cared less for money as money than he did.

Wilkie Collins), who had of course been formed before the Victorian ethos was established, testify in their novels to their sense of what had been lost in human enjoyment by the advent of 'respectability', Evangelical domination, a stifling conventionality, and tastes imposed by a purse-proud and Philistine middle-class; but none does it so tellingly as Dickens.[1] Micawber is so successful that I can't help believing that he is ultimately responsible for the presence in *Anna Karenina* of Anna's brother Steve, a more reprehensible Micawber to whom everything is forgiven, even by the serious and high-minded Levin, because he increased every-

---

[1]George Eliot in *Middlemarch* makes Dickens's point in remarking that the Vincy household, with its whist-table, musical daughter and unrefined mother keeping open house, was an attraction because 'The Vincys had the readiness to enjoy, the rejection of all anxiety, and the belief in life as a merry lot, which made a house exceptional in most county towns at that time, when Evangelicalism had cast a certain suspicion as of plague-infection over the few amusements which survived in the provinces'. Correspondingly, Trollope's soft spot for scamps, even gamblers (or especially gamblers) is to be explained by his resentment of the dull propriety, restraint and hypocrisy which he saw had closed in in his lifetime. Men like Burgo Fitzgerald and Mountjoy Scarborough–dashing, generous, loved by women, running through fortunes and living shamelessly on other people–are preferable, he feels, to the drearily virtuous Mr. Pallisers and Barchester Close (Mr. Palliser, with a lively young bride, regularly sits up over blue-books till the small hours so that neglect and boredom nearly drive his wife to elope with her old flame and cousin–another angle on such a marriage as Annie Strong's). Similarly, Lady Dedlock is shown languishing in boredom, cherishing her secret past with her ne'er-do-well lover Captain Hawden in imagination. Hence Trollope's mischievous delight in bringing back the Italianized Stanhope family to set Barchester and the County by the ears. In the same decade as *David Copperfield*, in *The Warden* (1855) he had taken the reader on a visit to Plumstead Rectory (chapter VIII) in order to ask why well-off people should deliberately make themselves now such a dismal environment: 'considering the money that had been spent there, the eye and taste might have been better served; there was an air of heaviness about the rooms . . . it was not without ample consideration that those thick, dark, costly carpets were put down; those embossed but sombre papers hung up; those heavy curtains draped so as to half exclude the light of the sun . . . . The apparent object had been to spend money without obtaining brilliancy or splendour . . . . The silver forks were so heavy as to be disagreeable to the hand', etc. Then follows a catalogue of the food and drink on the lavishly-supplied breakfast-table, overflowing oppressively on to the sideboard, ending: 'And yet I have never found the rectory a pleasant house. The fact that men shall not live by bread alone seemed to be somewhat forgotten.' That man cannot live by bread alone is the message equally of Mrs. Gaskell, Dickens, Kingsley, Charlotte Brontë, George Eliot and Trollope, as much as of Ruskin, Carlyle and Mathew Arnold, and that message is communicated more persuasively and incontestably by the novelists, it seems to me.

one's enjoyment of life and was lovable. Would Steve have borne such improbable witness to the triumph of the debonaire in the face of morality if Tolstoy had not absorbed *David Copperfield* into his being? Tolstoy had comprehended and assented to Dickens's meaning, so that while we always await the Nemesis we expect Steve to receive at the moral novelist's hand, it never occurs: though Steve doesn't, like the Micawber family, actually figure in a pantomime transformation scene at the end, he is last seen successful in winning over the new head of his office by a gift, like Mr. Micawber's, for making something like punch, and still floating buoyantly over his financial and family difficulties. It is interesting that the gloomy, conscience-ridden Levin thirsts for his society and sides with him in sympathy against poor Dolly, Steve's virtuous and victimized wife, like Mrs. Micawber too in being the mother of too many children and always in debt. Just as Tolstoy appreciated a Steve, Dickens registered enjoyment from an Artful Dodger, who though led off to prison at the end of *Oliver Twist* is quite unsubdued, still impudently talking down the magistrate as he swaggers out of the court.

Undeniably, though *David Copperfield*'s true end, at David's vision in chapter LXII of the miracle his life had been, is perfect and logical, there is a twofold transformation scene tacked on, two scenes that are not, like the glimpses of the Traddles' married life, necessary to the scheme of the novel. But together they serve splendidly the purpose of the closing satiric comedy of classical tradition. The bad are shown imprisoned in a hell of solitary confinement under Mr. Creakle's supervision–ironically, while as a headmaster he was a sadistic bully to little boys, as a magistrate and theorist on the punishment of criminals he is a bullying idealist. This is truly comic and yet not so improbable a combination as some critics seem to think. The good, who have been unsuccessful in this unjust world, are reported to have been transported to a comic paradise of success and happiness in the Antipodes. I don't think this Classical ending is an argument for not taking seriously the serious parts of this novel or for relegating it as a whole to the category of fairy-tale, as is increasingly the tendency in Dickens criticism. 'Everyone has noticed, I suppose, how close *David Copperfield* is to the traditional fairy story. Much of it is a day-dream, where pieces of gigantic good or evil fortune happen without cause or consequence, where each incident seems detached from every other', etc. (*The Imagination of Charles Dickens*, A. O. J. Cockshut, 1961); 'In *David Copperfield*, Aunt Betsey Trotwood is clearly the good fairy godmother, and Uriah Heep the wicked genie'

(Edgar Johnson in *Dickens Criticism: A Symposium*, 1962) etc. By relegating some of the characters to fairy-tale types and failing to see that the
novel has a theme, by alleging that the incidents in *David Copperfield* are
'detached' and are 'without cause or consequence', Cockshut—a biassed
as well as a singularly impercipient reader—tries to deprive this novel of
any claim to be taken seriously. [He also says that the book's worst aspect
is that it is a 'fake autobiography'; if we could wipe out our perhaps unfortunate knowledge of Dickens's life there would be fewer stumbling-
blocks for critics.]

That *David Copperfield* can be, in any respect, described in outline as
what is vulgarly called a fairy-tale is surely due to the fact that the story
of Dickens's life by 1850 did actually correspond to the idea of a fairy-
tale rather than to an everyday success-story where rags to riches is
achieved by climbing the industrial or commercial ladder; David's life
in this respect paralleled Dickens's. So did Hans Andersen's, and it is
highly suggestive that these two men so greatly admired each other's
work, as also that Hans Andersen invented an art form of the fairy-tale
to express his poignantly tragic and satiric insights.[1] Both had gone from
childhood misery to comfort and fame, as the Ugly Duckling who became a swan, solely through the fairy-tale gift of genius, and both had
shameful memories in connexion with family and childhood.[2] Dickens's

[1] Andersen's Tales cover a very wide range of forms, in which the fairy-tale
counts for less than the satire, the fable, the folk-tale, and the record of childhood
experience through a child's consciousness—it was this last that made Andersen's
work of most interest to Dickens, I conjecture from his rapture at, and confessed
constant re-reading of, Andersen's tale 'The Old House' which is wholly concerned
with recapturing a child's way of seeing and feeling his encounter with old age,
and is very much in the style of the early chapters of *Copperfield*. Dickens's own
interest in what could be done by seeing life and society reflected in the eyes of
childhood never ceased, and as late as 1868 he wrote *Holiday Romance* in four parts
(two girls and two small boys serve as the authors) containing the delightful tales
of 'The Magic Fish-bone' and of 'Mrs. Orange and Mrs Lemon' which, like
Andersen's, have a serious aspect too.

[2] The details of Dickens's actual contacts with Hans Andersen and his disillusion
with him personally on sustaining an excessively long visit from Andersen in
1857, have been told by the authority on the subject, E. Bredsdorf in his 'Hans
Christian Andersen and Charles Dickens'. Dickens's courtesy was such that
Andersen never realized that he had been a bore and a burden to the Dickens
family. Andersen was delighted with them all and noted—and this is really interesting—that Mrs. Dickens seemed to him the original of Agnes ("exactly like
Agnes") in *David Copperfield*, though the Dickens ménage was on the verge of
breakdown at the time, unknown to him.

account of how he was saved, unlike and yet like Oliver Twist, from falling into the abyss of crime that seemed inevitably the fate of an un-protected child in London, is stamped with his wonder and thankfulness knowing as he did that it was not his own efforts but Providence alone that saved him. No wonder he believed that for all its dangers innocence had a considerable survival value. He wrote: 'I know that, but for the mercy of God, I might have been, for any care that was taken of me, a little robber or a little vagabond. . . . I prayed when I went to bed to be lifted out of the humiliation and neglect in which I was. . . . I do not write resentfully or angrily: for I know how all these things have worked together to make me what I am. . . . The deep remembrance of the sense I had of being utterly neglected and hopeless . . . cannot be written. My whole nature was so penetrated with the grief and humiliation of such considerations, that even now, famous and caressed and happy, I often forget in my dreams that I have a dear wife and children; even that I am a man; and wander desolately back to that time of my life' [Forster, Bk. I, §5 II]. This deeply-felt sense of the miracle that his life represented to him is the source of the passage that, I have suggested, really and very appropriately ends the novel, when having won Agnes David looks back in mind over 'Long miles of road', 'and toiling on, I saw a ragged way-worn boy forsaken and neglected . . . '–a passage not by any means sentimental but a sincere expression of the wonder Dickens felt at his own position, though he was strictly a self-made man, made by hard work, by 'toiling on'. We might also reflect that 'fairy-tales' of this type are really folk-tales, embodying the folk's experience of the truths of existence in allegoric forms. Dickens is not alone in his age with Hans Andersen. The folk-tale and fairy-story were very generally brought in-to the use of the novelist's art, owing to the new life felt to rest in these forms once attention had been called to them as something else than diversions for children, by the translation early in the 19th century first of the collections of the Brothers Grimm and later of Hans Andersen's tales. In *Silas Marner*, *Wuthering Heights* and *Jane Eyre*,[1] as much as, or more than, in the moralistic use of the fairy-tale for children that Vic-torian writers tried their hands at (such as *The Water Babies*), elements of the fairy-tale were used for wholly serious purposes. They showed a basic indebtedness to the fairy-tale, but this does not entail escapism, only

[1] *V*. my introductions and Notes to the Penguin English Library editions of *Jane Eyre* and *Silas Marner* and my essay on *Wuthering Heights* in *Lectures in America* (Chatto & Windus).

a recognition of a new vehicle for the novelist of 19th-century society. One of Hans Andersen's best tales, 'The Shadow', works entirely by using traditional motifs of folk- and fairy-tale but is nonetheless a deeply serious and valid criticism of contemporary life, with a tragic end; the truths it enforces are a matter of experience.

What stylization of life – the typicality of Dickens's experience in his age – Dickens makes in *David Copperfield* as a whole is not the fairy-tale but the myth. In the beginning of Dickens's art, in *Oliver Twist* – whose hero is in many respects the prototype of David but is left at the point where David is being reared by his great-aunt – we have the essentials of a myth existing semi-consciously in Dickens's mind, where was secreted, as we have seen, the truths he had learnt of experience in his own boy-hood about the human family and society. The bastard orphan Oliver is cruelly used by circumstances in being born fatherless and unprotected by the adults in his world who should stand in a parental relation to him, and by society which has relegated him, rightfully a gentleman by birth and entitled to a fortune by his father's will, to pauperhood and set him to degrading work in low company. Thrown on his own in London, he is set to work at underworld activities he cannot understand, and is in the greatest danger of being turned into a criminal and so lost forever to the upper world; but providentially he finds himself cast up on the threshold of relations who give him a fresh start under a new name, putting him in possession of respectability, education and love, the gifts he desires most. Yet two symbols of the horrors that had nearly engulfed him lurk outside his window and on the threshold of his consciousness – his elder brother, a heartless reprobate, and Fagin, an inexplicable mon-ster of social and moral evil, who are working against him together. But now sustained by new hopes and moral courage, he is able to brace him-self against them and so maintain his moral freedom and social respect-ability. The wholly impossible interview between Oliver and Fagin in the death-cell is to prove Oliver's moral emancipation and show that his goodness of heart (e.g. in his being able to forgive Fagin and be sorry for him) has survived his ordeals.[1] There is nothing of the fairy-tale in *Oliver Twist* and no one accuses Dickens of escapism in framing it. Perhaps the episode that most convincingly symbolizes the anguish of the child's

---

[1]*David Copperfield* is more realistic in fact, for David never forgives the Murd-stones, or Creakle, or Uriah Heep or Littimer; his goodness of heart is shown by his praying, when his ordeal is over and he is safe under Miss Trotwood's roof, 'that I never might be houseless any more, and never might forget the houseless'.

helplessness and horror is Oliver's experience when he finds that, though he has been rescued, as he thinks, by kind middle-class Mr. Brownlow, this cannot protect him: he is trapped by Nancy the prostitute, who passes herself off as his sister on the crowd of good citizens Oliver appeals to to save him, and forces him back with the aid of Bill Sikes (feminine guile plus brute force and savagery) into Fagin's underground establishment for turning children into social and moral outcasts.

David's history is more realistic, less nakedly symbolic that is, than Oliver's; for instance, he is not passive and left by coincidence on the doorstep of his only though unknown relatives, but takes the initiative of running away from his dangers and making his own way to his great-aunt though penniless. Oliver's experience of the unfeeling hostility and treachery in ordinary people and of evil lurking to drag him down are repeated in the adventures David has on the road: the young man to whom he has confided his trunk steals it and robs him of his money, then threatens him to his terror with the police so that, paradoxically, David has to run away from justice instead of getting redress from it. He then has to pawn his waistcoat as he is penniless, but the pawnbroker cheats him, and this is repeated in a nightmare variation with another pawnbroker, who is a drunken madman in addition. He registers the 'vicious looks' of the tramps, who stone him when he runs away from them, and he is attacked and robbed by a tinker who is on the way to murdering his woman companion (another Bill Sikes and Nancy) and who asserts the underworld's anti-morality:

'What lay are you upon?' asked the tinker. 'Are you a prig?'
'N-no,' I said.
'Ain't you, by G–? If you make a brag of your honesty to me,' said the tinker, 'I'll knock your brains out.'

Even when he arrives at Dover the ordinary decent people torment instead of assisting him when he asks to be directed to his aunt's house. Arrived there, his old clothes burnt and himself newly bathed, he lies motionless on the sofa and is then swaddled like a new-born babe in a suggestive representation of re-birth. He is indeed reborn, as Trotwood Copperfield, with a new pair of guardians as parents, Miss Trotwood representing inflexible rationality and Mr. Dick, who lets David help him fly his home-made kites up into the skies, bearing his mind with them 'out of its confusion. As he wound the string in, and it came lower and lower down out of the beautiful light, until it fluttered to the ground, and lay there like a dead thing, he seemed to wake gradually out of a dream; and I remember to have seen him take it up, and look about him in a lost way, as if they had both come down together'. We don't need any more direct hint that Mr. Dick, whose sensitive feelings are not emanations from Reason, represents the supplementary fostering to Miss Trotwood's common sense that Dickens believed essential to a healthy childhood–play, fantasy and poetic imagination; Mr. Dick moreover lives intuitively by a better sense than common and, as Miss Trotwood liked to say with unconscious double meaning: 'Mr. Dick sets us all right'. The kite-flier relates to the novelist in more than name. There is a Blake-like feeling and intention about all this part of David's history which shows also Dickens's inexhaustible originality of inventiveness, since though quite different it relates to Walter Gay's imaginative fostering in the home of the scientific instrument-dealer Sol Gills, who is supplemented by the simple-minded Captain Cuttle, unlearned like Old Glubb except in knowing the mysterious lore of the oceans which reason cannot compass.

Then can the Murdstones really be said, as they have been, to belong to a fairy-tale–are they ogre and Baba Yaga and defeated magically by Miss Betsey, an all-powerful fairy godmother? Surely this is a pre-posterous falsification. The facts are that the Murdstones, who go on existing throughout the book and are last seen doing very nicely in their own line, are merely discomfited in an impressively novelistic scene whose social drama is founded on psychological truth to life. We note that in it the elements of comedy–the boy David trussed up like a baby in shawls and Mr. Dick's trousers, and hemmed in by chairs, Mr. Dick having to be kept up to company behaviour by Miss Trotwood's awful eye, the ever-present anticipation of donkey-boys intruding again on the sacred green–keep under control the painful elements, notably David's agonized fear that he will be delivered up to the Murdstones and the warehouse, Miss Trotwood's own horror at the fate, only recently made known to her by David, of Poor Baby and at David's experiences (horror that is heightened by some remorse at having abandoned Clara and David), and the sense we have conveyed to us that Mr. Murdstone, un-like his sister, has enough feeling to have a bad conscience and to be made to wince at unpleasant memories ('he seemed to breathe as if he had been running, though still with a smile on his face'). The duel that develops between Miss Trotwood and Mr. Murdstone is not lessened in serious-ness by Miss Murdstone's 'perfect agony at not being able to turn the current' of Miss Trotwood's address towards herself, but this is one further indication of the novelist's full consciousness of the living nature of the material he works in, material that he is shaping with the responsibility of a great artist possessed by a theme he must develop.

Another denial of Dickens's functioning as an artist in composing *David Copperfield* is represented by the amateur psychologizing of the school of Edmund Wilson. His wild travesties of Dickens's novels and character in his crudely journalistic essay called 'Dickens: The Two Scrooges', has been one of the disastrous obstacles to getting Dickens's novels read responsibly ever since; (his characterization of Dickens's creative achievement as 'the eternal masquerade of his fiction' has been expanded by Garis into a theory that virtually relegates Dickens's work as a whole.) Thus it is asserted that Miss Murdstone was invented 'to bear the weight of the childish resentment Dickens undoubtedly felt against his own mother', though Dickens himself saw his mother as Mrs. Nickleby (and was amused at her not being able to believe in such a woman) who is so like Mrs. Micawber in her mental processes and other respects that we should be justified in claiming that it is Mrs. Micawber who was created out of his feelings about his mother when she was actually in Mrs. Micawber's circumstances. Wherever we can check Dickens's use as fictional characters of people who impinged on him in real life, even if his most painful phase, we have, it seems to me, to give him the credit on being an artist, a free creator, and not a victim of blind drives of passion he can neither control nor even recognize, as this line of critics assume.

Forster's account of the relation between the autobiographical fragment and the novel *David Copperfield* corresponds much more convincingly to the account of the novel which, as I've suggested, a sensitive and unprejudiced reader finds himself to have in his possession after reading the book. He claims that the autobiographical manuscript and the conversations he had with Dickens about it 'enable me to separate the fact from the fiction' of *David Copperfield*; he concluded that Dickens had started to write an account of the blacking-factory period of his childhood but gave it up when the novel 'began to take shape in his mind' because 'Those warehouse experiences fell then so aptly into the subject he had chosen, that he could not resist the temptation of immediately using them'. Dickens had already used other appropriate parts of his memories of this period of his childhood in his novels, with the firm objectivity of the creative mind in control of its material: Mrs. Pipchin and her home in which little Paul Dombey lodged Dickens said was drawn from 'a reduced old lady who took children in to board, and had once done so at Brighton and who, with a few alterations and embellishments, unconsciously began to sit for Mrs. Pipchin in *Dombey* when she took in me', at the time John Dickens went to prison for debt. David was no more Dickens than was Paul Dombey, and Miss Murdstone no more a creation to bear his resentment against his mother than was Mrs. Pipchin. After a while the boy Charles Dickens was transferred to a back-attic in the home of a kind family who were the originals for the Garlands in *The Old Curiosity Shop*, and Forster also tells us that the orphan servant-girl who was employed by the Dickens family in their Micawber phase was translated into the Marchioness in the same novel. All these characters have their roots equally in this unhappy period of his boyhood, yet they bear witness to an effortless impersonality – and so, it seems to me, does his use of his amatory experiences (where Maria Beadnell and Catherine Hogarth amalgamate to provide the essence of a Dora). There is, equally, no question of Dickens having undertaken *David Copperfield* to excuse himself or deceive the reading public as to his history, as some critics have amiably alleged; nor was it a piece of self-therapy. Dickens, it seems to me, gave up the idea of writing an autobiography, whether for publication or his own use, because he was a novelist and had a more satisfactory way of telling the truth (the essential truth) about his experience of life (he knew that what mattered in it was what was representative). He follows Coleridge's rule instinctively, that there should be a wide difference between his own circumstances and that of his subject, and David, the typical boy-child in his relation to a mother, is the very opposite in this respect to Charles Dickens. Since, as I have said, it is Mrs. Micawber who has a good deal in common with Mrs. Nickleby, it is more likely that she is the figure in *David Copperfield* to whom he transferred his feelings about his mother in boyhood – one notices that in her multiple troubles poor Mrs. Micawber forgot David was a boy and took him into her confidence as an adult, but that at parting 'a mist cleared from her eyes and . . . with quite a new and motherly expression in her face, put her arm round my neck and gave me just such a kiss as she might have given to her own boy'. There is a touching truth to life but no sentimentality here.

In fact, any reader of Dickens who has comprehended the way his creative thinking develops, will have noted that the Murdstones represent forces both religious and psychological, which were powerful in his society and by which his parents were untouched – the will to dominate, justified as religious righteousness, and the Evangelical and Methodist animus against the nature of childhood, together with the Puritan acquisitiveness; Dickens had already realized that these were the enemies of life as he valued it, and they coalesce and culminate in Mrs. Clennam, the doom-maker of *Little Dorrit*, who combines in herself both Mr. and Miss Murdstone. But whereas David the orphan had escaped from these forces, Arthur Clennam did not but was crushed by the Murdstone-type upbringing of his step-mother, with her gloomy religion, her sense of guilt, and her fear of love and art; in this respect Dickens evidently became less and less hopeful about the progress of the Victorian Age.

v

David Copperfield differs from *Oliver Twist* and *Dombey*, from both of which it follows on, in carrying the child who, in the case of Oliver and little Paul, is a victim merely, into a boy who is ultimately successful in conflict with the world. The innovation of the autobiographical method meant that a domestic and not directly satiric tone was required; it also demanded more subtlety of narration which allows the reader both to identify with the narrator for the most part and yet see that he is to be viewed in a way he can't of course see or understand himself. And as Dickens is not now, as in *Oliver Twist* or *Dombey*, indicting his culture but only questioning it, irony and satire are not suitable techniques. One of the less obvious advantages of the autobiographical medium is that seeing David's past from his present height of achieved happiness allows him to make out a pattern in it and show us the relatedness of events, as well as to recreate in all their poignancy his feelings at any given time. Thus the follow-through from his mother's two marriages to his own first and second marriages is divided into smaller units, from his own birth to his own virtual death as the babe in her arms in the coffin, then his fresh start in another character as the warehouse boy with the Micawbers in London, which itself ends with his reception into his great-aunt's home and is the beginning of his adolescence (not the real end of the novel, as John Bayley seemed to think when he declared that 'the novel *David Copperfield* really finishes at this point; all the rest is another novel'); after, in his new existence as 'Trotwood', he has gone through the cycle of marriage to Dora which ends with her death and Steerforth's, there follows yet another phase, of wandering through Europe to live out his mistakes, which brings him back to Agnes and the due culmination of the whole novel when, with Agnes in his arms, he looks up at the moon ('Peaceful! Ain't she!' Uriah had said, identifying the unattainable moon with 'his' Agnes) and the miraculous nature of David's life comes home to him:

> Long miles of road then opened out before my mind; and toiling on, I saw a ragged way-worn boy forsaken and neglected, who should come to call even the heart now beating against mine, his own.

Life has consisted of fresh starts, but each phase is penetrated by characters from his pasts or related to the others by parallels in incident. Dickens wrote 'Trotwood Copperfield' underlined, in his Plan for chapter XIV, showing he meant the new name to be significant. But Dr. Strong's school replaces Mr. Creakle's, and Mr. Micawber and Traddles come back into his life–it is now Traddles who lodges with the Micawbers, who is confided in and is the innocent victimized–and as soon as David starts out from Dover to find his feet Steerforth turns up in the old relation to him. Steerforth's ruining Mr. Mell in wanton cruelty, in the former phase, forecasts his heartless ruining of Little Em'ly in the later one; Mr. Murdstone's manœuvring to exercise power over David's mother and David is replaced by Uriah's machinations to secure Agnes and crush David, and so on. David himself notices this effect and stresses the cyclical nature of life when having been to Covent Garden Theatre he says: 'it was in a manner, like a shining transparency, through which I saw my earlier life moving along'–though what he had been seeing was *Julius Caesar* and the new Pantomime' and the particular relevance of this is obscure until he runs into Steerforth again in consequence.

A final evidence of the careful thinking-out of the ideas incarnated and the human truths explored in *David Copperfield* is that in chapter LVIII when David has gone abroad to recover from the two blows he has suffered–the loss of Dora his child-wife and the loss of Steerforth his father-friend–he realizes that the two blows are but one 'wound' with which he has to 'strive': they're inextricably associated not only because they are the loss of first love and first friendship, but that he now faces the fact that he was misguided in both. The sequel, a Childe Harold wandering through Europe and a Wordsworthian healing at the hand of Great Nature, is only a prolonged cliché. David has really to come to terms with his two disillusions, which he apparently does by writing a story about them; a neat way of reminding us that David is a novelist, for, as Dickens knew, this is what novelists do. The return to the England of Gray's Inn in the character of the old David is quite refreshing, his reunion with the real friend, Traddles, and the right wife, Agnes, round off the theme.

Yet except in the obviously moralistic episodes there is no obstrusive schematic intention. Dickens's creativeness did not work at the level of full consciousness that Henry James or Conrad show in their letters and introductions (though I shall not be at all surprised if the complete edition of Dickens's letters gives us plenty of interesting insights into his methods of composition). The notes we have of his plans for numbers of *Copperfield* look like random jottings until, having read the novel *as a whole* in the way I have suggested, we can see that most of them are keys to his profounder meanings–'Why Rookery' 'Brooks of Sheffield' and such were shorthand notes to keep himself in touch with his themes, though no doubt he could not have written, or even provided the material for, an essay on his art and craft as a novelist. I have elsewhere[1] cited as an example of the way the creative mind works Charlotte Brontë's indecisions about the name of her heroine in *Villette*. After naming her Lucy Snowe she changed the name to Frost, but subsequently wrote to her publisher to change it back, saying 'As to the name of the heroine, I can hardly express what subtlety of thought made me decide upon giving her a cold name, but a cold name she must have'. The conscious choice was between hard and soft cold (frost and snow) but the feeling of rightness in the necessity of a cold name was spontaneous and never analysed. The Freudian puns I have noted below in the choice of names like Dora and Doady and Murdstone were not fully conscious either, I imagine, but they are only slighter signs of the wonderful genius that produced the end of chapter IX.

Do we feel that the actual writing of *David Copperfield* is less interesting than the prose of *Dombey*? There is here nothing comparable to the wonderful passage of time passing in the desolate Dombey home, or the description of the broker's warehouse, or of the flow of the populace from the country into the city registered in the consciousness of Harriet Carker; nor scenes so fertile in satiric purpose as Mr. Dombey's second wedding or little Paul's christening or the scene in Warwick Castle among the pictures, not even in the poignant episodes in David's childhood is there any so strangely moving as Paul's introduction into Dr.

[1] In the Penguin English Library edition of *Jane Eyre*.

Blimber's establishment. Even the death-bed scene of Clara is inferior in imaginative impact to those of Paul or Paul's mother. But granted that *David Copperfield* doesn't offer us the richly impressive rewards of *Dombey*, there is, I claim, a verbal interest in the later novel that shows Dickens's Shakespearian use of the language. Dickens is a master of words because they are more than mere words to him, they are feelings and associations and dark implications. For instance, the conflicting relations of Rosa Dartle and Steerforth tell us more about Steerforth than they do about her, and that Dickens meant this is seen in another insight into Steerforth's attitude to others shown when David tells Steerforth, who has dropped in on him in London, that Traddles has been there:

'Oh! That fellow!' said Steerforth, beating a lump of coal on the top of the fire, with the poker. 'Is he as soft as ever? And where the deuce did you pick *him* up?'

David is just sensitive enough to feel from this that 'Steerforth rather slighted' Traddles, but *we* recognize something more in the brutal 'beating' of the lump of coal with the poker to break it up and the accompanying description of Traddles as 'soft' (easily broken, and only fuel for his fire to Steerforth), together with the characteristic of Steerforth's in behaving in David's room as though it were his own, in managing the fire — we have conveyed to us, without having to analyse or intellectualize it, the selfish and arrogant and even cruel traits in Steerforth, such as his ready contempt of others, that point to his subsequent brutal treatment of Emily. We see Dickens evolving this habit of making symbolic actions convey character-traits yet which are so natural that we hardly notice the symbolism, though it affects us as much more meaningful somehow than an ordinary action. A similar but distinct example is when Henry Gowan, a stranger watched from behind by Arthur Clennam, is seen to be idly tossing stones into the water with his foot. 'There was something in his way of spurning them out of their places with his heel, and getting them into the required position, that Clennam thought had an air of cruelty in it'. In due course Clennam is 'heeled' like a stone out of Gowan's path in their rivalry for Pet, cruelly, insolently and effectively. This loading of words is sometimes really witty in *David Copperfield* and reveals Dickens's understanding of how the mind works by associations it could not consciously explain. As in the sequence when Miss Trotwood discusses with David Emily's folly in eloping with Steerforth, ending: ' "I am sorry for your early experience" ' (she had therefore sensed he had been in love with Emily as a child) and immediately continues: ' "And so you fancy yourself in love! Do you?" "Fancy, aunt!" I exclaimed, as red as I could be. "I adore her with my whole soul!" "Dora, indeed!" returned my aunt'—thus making the typicality of Dora's name for the novel's purpose apparent, and apparent at the same time that Miss Trotwood has deduced she will be another Little Em'ly. So Miss Trotwood adds that ' "the little thing is very fascinating, I suppose?" "And not silly?" said my aunt. "Silly, aunt!" "Not light-headed?" said my aunt'. David says he was struck with these ideas as both new and absurd to him, but we see, without being told, that Miss Trotwood, who then mentions his likeness to his mother ('poor Baby') has realized that he is bound to fall in love with someone like his mother and that this will be a misfortune for him. She suggests that what his mother's child ought to look for is 'earnestness "to sustain and improve him" ', hinting delicately at Agnes of course, but without effect. Earnestness, the Victorian model virtue, was not what David wanted even if he needed it in an object for love. We pick up this train of thought again during the engagement, notably when David has begun to notice uneasily that everyone treats Dora as a child and that she expects to be petted. He suggests she 'might be very happy, and yet be treated rationally', but rightly sensing this is dissatisfaction with her as she is, she begins to sob.

> What could I do but . . . tell her how I doted on her, after that!
> 'I am sure I am very affectionate,' said Dora; 'you oughtn't to be cruel to me, Doady!'

We now see, by its association in the previous line with 'doted', the point of her inventing 'Doady' as her pet name for him, which he has innocently explained as 'a corruption of David'. It is her way of forcing him into sustaining the character of a doting lover towards her. There is a great deal of this kind of suggestive word-play in the novel, less obvious than the self-evident 'Murdstone' implying a stony-hearted murderer ('their gloom and their austerity destroyed her'). But of course it is not only the associations revealed by words, but the similar underground currents that determine our actions, that the novelist traces for us and shows as decisive.[1] I have always admired the train of psychological

[1] I might cite here two interesting examples from *Our Mutual Friend*. Bella Wilfer complains that she has been 'left to him in a will, like a dozen of spoons with everything cut and dried beforehand, like orange chips. Talk of orange flowers indeed!'—where the metaphorical 'cut and dried', to express the unromantic nature of the matrimonial arrangement that willed her to John Harman,

events that bring Steerforth back so fatally into David's life. After his sheltered youth at Canterbury, Miss Trotwood sends him out to see the world in order 'to have a reliance upon yourself and act for yourself', she tells him, little knowing the tragic irony this contains. What more appropriate than that he should, as soon as he gets to London, go to the theatre to see Shakespeare (*Julius Caesar*) and feel it to be a romantic experience?

> To have all those noble Romans alive before me, and walking in and out for my entertainment, instead of being the stern taskmasters they had been at school, was a most novel and delightful effect. But the mingled reality and mystery of the whole show, the influence upon me of the poetry, the light, the music, the company, the smooth stupendous changes of glittering and brilliant scenery, were so dazzling and opened up such illimitable regions of delight, that when I came out into the rainy street, at twelve o'clock at night, I felt as if I had come from the clouds, where I had been leading a romantic life for ages, to a bawling, splashing, link-lighted, umbrella-struggling,

suggests 'like orange chips', and this brings up another reference to the fate prepared for her in the will, the orange flowers being traditionally worn by a bride, their sweetness and beauty symbolizing the accepted idea of a wedding as a love-match. What Dickens is interested in is the way the mind works, with its own logic; as again in the same novel, when old Lady Tippins, seeing the butler, a freezingly correct character, offer Lightwood a note and Lightwood being affected by her to be a lover of hers, she says to him; 'Falser man than Don Juan; why don't you take the note from the Commendatore?'–moreover the note announces the death of the hero, John Harmon, making a dramatic point at the same time as suggesting that the Veneering's dinner-table is a society of the damned. [Note also that Dickens is inward with *Don Giovanni*.] The mention of Mrs. Sparsit's Roman nose which is immediately followed by the reference to her 'Coriolanian' eyebrows, when she is taking up a preposterously Coriolanian attitude about the strike, is a witty and literary use of the suggestiveness of language such as is frequently made by Dickens. Flora Finching's conversation is a dazzling and inexhaustibly entertaining demonstration of Dickens's understanding of what speech is for us; his advantage over James Joyce is that this interest is never with him pedantic and so does not become self-stultifying. Examples from the early novels are Mrs Nickleby's mental habits and conversation, Dick Swiveller's and Mrs. Gamp's. Owing to the unique nature and infinite possibilities of the English language, there was of course an English tradition of such a literary interest, going back through Sheridan's Mrs. Malaprop, Swift and others to Shakespeare the great forerunner and exemplar. A spontaneous popular tradition of delight in exploiting the nature of the language, to which Dickens also had access like all other English children, is enshrined in our rich collection of nursery rhymes and the words of children's games with their astonishing imaginative coinages and nonsense-fantasies.

hackney-coach-jostling, patten-clinking, muddy, miserable world.

I had emerged by another door, and stood in the street for a little while, as if I really were a stranger upon earth; but the unceremonious pushing and hustling that I received, soon recalled me to myself, and put me in the road back to the hotel; whither I went, revolving the glorious vision all the way . . . I was so filled with the play, and with the past–for it was in a manner, like a shining transparency, through which I saw my earlier life moving along–that I don't know when the figure of a handsome, well-formed young man, dressed with a tasteful easy negligence which I have reason to remember very well, became a real presence to me. . . . In going towards the door, I passed the person who had come in, and saw him plainly. He did not know me, but I knew him in a moment.

At another time I might have wanted the confidence or the decision to speak to him, and might have lost him. But, in the then condition of my mind, where the play was still running high, his former protection of me appeared so deserving of my gratitude, and my old love for him overflowed my breast so freshly and spontaneously, that I went up to him at once, with a fast-beating heart, and said:

'Steerforth! won't you speak to me?'

This is as remarkably imagined as it is utterly convincing. To David, Steerforth was a heroic character in his unhappy schooldays, someone larger and nobler than life, seeming to belong with the historical Classical characters in the Shakespeare play by which he has just been so aroused–without the stimulus of which he would have been too timid to claim acquaintance with his former patron. The play is then used for another purpose: David is dashed by Steerforth's expression of contempt for the performance which has so enchanted David, for by now Steerforth is at Oxford with the appropriate arrogant sophistication. In accordance with this he nicknames David 'Daisy', and uses him.

Dickens, I suggest, had a far better idea of how speech occurs and of the laws of association which direct thought than either George Eliot or Tolstoy, whose novels for the most part, though they are masterly in their understanding of behaviour, show over-rationalization in representing speech (though they never, admittedly, suffer from the attraction of the melodrama of the popular English stage which Dickens so often yields to before *Bleak House*, and which is seen forcing his conception of Martha into its mode of rhetorical utterance). Dickens is therefore particularly good at rendering the speech-habits of the illiterate and of the half-educated, and this is not a matter of masquerading himself and thus producing fat acting rôles, as is alleged by one modern school of Dickens criticism; Dickens shows a sensitive and intelligent insight into the mysterious nature of speech as one expression of the unique idiom of each of us.

It is not then Dickens who is sometimes Tolstoyan but Tolstoy who is in origin Dickensian. As we have seen, brilliantly and feelingly as Tolstoy can present the facts of Andrew Bolkonski married to a Lisa, it remains a mere episode, however moving, whereas to Dickens his view of such a marriage is that it must be considered in a wider context altogether and with the assumption that it can be explained, accounted for, and therefore understood. The assumption made by so many recent critics that Dickens is concerned to excuse David, or that we can accuse David, or even thereby accuse Dickens, is to miss the achievement of the novel completely; it goes along with the fallacy of identifying Dickens with David, Dora with either his wife or his first sweetheart or both, of denying Dickens impersonality and wisdom as a novelist in this case. George Eliot made Mr. Casaubon in quite a *Copperfield* way feel bewilderment and indignation at finding himself unhappy when married, for in choosing a beautiful young lady for a wife he had only done what his society sanctioned or even enjoined on a man, he knew. David might have argued the same, for this is Dickens's point. David could not help being a child of his age, of his age's best intentions indeed; and even more Nature's victim of the archetypal situation in being his mother's son. Steerforth is provided to show another fatherless son formed by a loving mother who differs from David in not being innocent and sensitive nor having had, what saved David, the discipline of having had to make his own way in the world—a part of the Victorian theory of life that Dickens thoroughly assented to, and which did not come within Tolstoy's knowledge.

I hope I have at any rate made out a case for Tolstoy's high opinion of *David Copperfield* and thereby of Dickens, and in doing so shown that the relation between them is not that of pigmy to giant or precursor to supercessor or entertainer to artist, but that they are two similar geniuses of the art of the novel of whom the earlier has the additional prestige of being the great original. And I have also, I hope, shown that there were grounds for Dickens's feeling of injury that Forster indicates at the end of his *Life* by writing that Dickens 'believed himself to be entitled to a higher tribute than he was always in the habit of receiving'. One thinks immediately of Henry James's parable of 'The Figure in the Carpet'.

Dora ' from a woman's point of view '

Dickens has been scolded by critics for 'not seeing David's first marriage from the woman's (Dora's) point of view', but, instead, solving David's problem by the easy expedient of removing her by death and, even worse, exonerating David from guilt for it by representing her as willing to die in order not to be a burden. 'It is better as it is', she says, which is indeed more realistic and less selfish than anything that could have been expected from Dora – which are not however the grounds on which Dickens is blamed for her death-bed admissions. Tolstoy, who also frees the husband by the death of the wife, does seem to have a moral advantage in showing his Prince Andrew harrowed by a sense of guilt towards Lisa, but this is surely because Andrew had been as a husband singularly lacking in forbearance, imagination and tenderness, of which David cannot be accused. In view of all this it is interesting that we *have* the woman's point of view on the same situation and that it rather surprisingly turns out to be essentially identical with Dickens's, though the possibility of nowadays ending an unsuitable marriage by divorce has made it unnecessary for the wife to die in the flesh; yet she too volunteers to die in effect, to free her husband. In *The Tortoise and the Hare* (1954) an able woman novelist, Miss Elizabeth Jenkins, shows a romantic, incompetent and self-centred young wife, an acknowledged beauty and charmer, who is thoroughly in love with her much older husband and who has moreover a schoolboy son. She is oriented towards the arts, poetry and sentiment instead of turning outwards to play a part in the social life her barrister-husband now needs, for his earlier sympathy with his wife's tastes, values and temperament (attractions for which he had originally fallen in love with her) has been replaced by desire for worldly success, money and what it will buy, and the gratifications of social life. A neighbour, neither young nor beautiful, who can provide these things, supersedes the increasingly unsatisfactory wife, Imogen, who gradually comes to realize this and that her inadequacies are irritating to her husband, that she is no longer a solace for and relief to his professional grind, that she can no longer charm him. She has always been out of sympathy with their boy, who prefers the other woman as a mother.

Recognizing all this, though still loving her husband, she feels obliged to yield her place to the neighbour, the Tortoise of the title, who corresponds to Agnes in being the woman the husband now realizes is the wife he needs and loves. Imogen doesn't die but she suffers extinction as far as husband, home and child are concerned, and that voluntarily. This is in spite of the novelist's sympathy with the heroine and refusal to endorse the domineering but adored husband. Imogen is last seen in a London flat (she is a country-lover) pining away on her own, though, unlike Dora, able to conceive turning herself into a useful woman: the novel ends with Imogen wiping away her tears as 'She looked about the uncared-for room. ' "I must improve", she said half aloud. "There is a very great deal to be done" '.

Another woman's point of view of a similar marriage is George Eliot's of Lydgate's. Rosamund Vincy is not loving, even in the sense that Dora may be said to be, but is like her in being extravagant, vain, unreasonable and a selfish egoist–all this being shown us through the unsympathetic woman novelist's eyes. Though George Eliot makes Rosamund kill her husband, instead of freeing him by dying herself–which is shown as being the least likely step she would ever take–this is because the woman novelist feels that Lydgate should be punished for his mistake in accepting a drawing-room ornament as a wife. Dorothea, the Agnes of *Middlemarch*, makes a parallel mistake to Lydgate's in her first choice of a partner but George Eliot finds her pardonable and arranges for her to be set free by death and find happiness in another mate.

Yet another woman's attitude to the David-Dora situation is to be found in *Jane Eyre*, and that really is surprising. St John Rivers, who has decided to go to India as a missionary, also loves a Rosamond, a gay, frivolous, 'child-like' beauty who lets him see she is anxious to marry him, and is moreover an heiress. But the poor clergyman is an intellectual, a scholar and has a religious vocation; on all these grounds he sees that the undoubted sensuous and worldly happiness he would gain by letting his taste for a Rosamond conquer him would be followed by self-disgust and repentance. He refrains, and goes off to convert the heathen. But Charlotte Brontë makes Jane Eyre thoroughly scold her cousin for his perversity in rejecting a normal happy marriage. It has always seemed to me probable that George Eliot, who was greatly impressed by *Jane Eyre* (and *Villette*), arrived at the Lydgate-Rosamund marriage out of interest in what would have happened if a man with a vocation for a profession did thoughtlessly take the course rejected by the clear-sighted St John Rivers.

APPENDIX B

Oliver Twist, Jane Eyre and *David Copperfield*

Though the underlying myth, the orphan's tale, in *David Copperfield* is, as I have said, comparable with that of *Oliver Twist*, there is one great difference which must strike everyone. Oliver is almost entirely an object used for satiric diatribe against the Poor Laws (old and new) and the society that produced them, against a society that tolerated the underworld of Fagin and Bill Sikes and did nothing to protect children against being exploited by them as thieves and prostitutes, against a society which let justice be administered by a Mr. Fang, and which ascribed to an illegitimate child inherited guilt; Oliver hardly exists as more than an innocent anonymous consciousness to register suffering and bewilderment engendered by these conditions. But David is recognizably a 'real' child and boy, with specific sufferings, in a realistic and not merely symbolic ambience; we have the impression of being taken into his confidence, that we understand his unique and not merely predictable feelings. It is true that Dickens produced little Paul Dombey in between Oliver and David, not to mention Little Nell and Smike, but Paul, like the rest of these until David, is also an object to look at from outside except for our less wholly external view of his desolation at being parted from Florence and entered into Dr. Blimber's forcing-house. It seems more to the point that *Jane Eyre* had intervened. Whatever it turns out that Dickens may or may not have said in his surviving letters about Currer Bell's first novel, which rivalled *Vanity Fair* in the reception it received from both reviewers and reading-public, he, like everyone else in the literary world, must have read it with the kind of respect we know was accorded it by novelists as different as George Eliot, Thackeray and Lockhart. Dickens no doubt unconsciously noted its relevance to his own use of the child as recording consciousness and critic of adult attitudes.

I have elsewhere[1] shown that the outlines of the orphan's myth as created by Dickens in *Oliver Twist* are repeated in *Jane Eyre*, and that, while we have no other evidence for Charlotte Brontë's having read Dickens's first serious novel, it seems very probable that it would have got to Keighley, where the Brontë sisters used the lending library, in the nine years between the appearance of Oliver and the conception of Jane.

[1] In the Note to my edition of *Jane Eyre* in the Penguin English Library.

But Charlotte Brontë invested that myth with a very different detail and ethos, and it is this detail which we find distinguishing the myth of *David Copperfield* from the form it had taken originally in *Oliver Twist*. Jane represents an immense advance on Oliver, Little Nell, Smike, or even Paul and Florence Dombey, being neither a typical nor idealized nor sentimentalized child and never used as a stalking-horse. She develops by the laws of her own being and in accordance with the pressures brought to bear on her, as David Copperfield does later (the first of Dickens's children so to do); she has a child's literal-mindedness, a child's logic, a child's pathetic cunning in self-protection and a child's intuitions about the adults who arbitrate her fate; she is always passionate, violent and fierce if oppressed intolerably, and above all resentful of injustice and craving to be loved; she has a child's terrors, as when, alone in the night after recovering from the 'fit' in the Red Room, she reports 'ear, eye and mind were alike strained by dread: such dread as children only can feel'. We recognize most of these characteristics in the child David, and later in the child Pip too, though in none of Dickens's earlier children. Jane's virtual step-mother Mrs. Reed, with 'her stony eye, opaque to tenderness', whose cruelty and injustice torture Jane, is clearly related to David's step-father and Miss Murdstone. When Jane goes to Mr. Brocklehurst's boarding-school she finds she is saddled with the character of being a vicious child thanks to Mrs. Reed, as David arriving at Mr. Creakle's finds Mr. Murdstone has arranged for him to be. There David's innocent and excellent friend Traddles is habitually discriminated against and punished unfairly by Mr. Creakle, as Jane's admirable school-friend Helen Burns had been by the sadistic teacher Miss Scatcherd. Under intolerable pressure later in life Jane runs away, losing her luggage and money at the outset, to wander penniless, starving and having to sleep on the ground in all weathers, rebuffed agonizingly by all she meets whose assistance she asks, until she collapses at the threshold of relatives who take her in out of charity and wash, tend and feed her, whereupon she is reborn as it were under a new name (Jane Elliott) and starts a new existence in family life. The same events in every detail take place in David's life, who similarly becomes Trotwood Copperfield. It seems hard to reject the conclusion that David Copperfield inherits from Jane Eyre in these respects.

It might be mentioned here that Jane Eyre, like her creator, had the customary class feelings of her age, which Dickens has in ours been accused of snobbery for showing to exist in *David Copperfield* (e.g. for making David habitually called 'Master David' by Barkis the carrier and the fisherfolk of Yarmouth, and 'Master Copperfield' by Uriah Heep). No one accuses Charlotte Brontë of snobbery or social insecurity, so I will merely remark that Jane always reports herself as being called 'Miss Jane' by Bessie the nurse, by Abbott the lady's-maid and by the apothecary, while she is still in the nursery (and a resented poor relation there at that), and that when she leaves Lowood School to go into a situation, as it was called, Bessie is called in (now a matron) solely to testify for us that 'Miss Jane' is 'quite a lady'. This is the ethos in which David Copperfield was reared in rural Suffolk, and those critics who complain of Dickens for registering it correctly are simply showing their ignorance of the facts of social life in the England of the 19th century (and some of the twentieth), before the attitudes engendered by the democratic theory of equality had made an appearance. In her autobiography *Lark Rise to Candleford* (1943) Flora Thompson, writing of her childhood in an Oxfordshire village from the cottager's angle, records as phenomenal the coming of a new type of Vicar when she grew up, who made it known that his children were to be called by their plain christian names 'at a time when other quality children were "Master" or "Miss" in their cradles'. The term 'quality' implies that deference to class distinctions was not servility but something subtler and not inherently undesirable. Those of us well read in writers of reminiscences of pre-1914 days will have noticed how frequently these illustrate this consciously or unconsciously – that manners and right attitudes for the 'quality' were instilled into them as children by the family servants and people on the estates, and a code of behaviour to be lived up to made plain; privilege implied responsibility. Cockshut ridiculing Dickens for class consciousness says that everyone in the novel 'is a little too conscious that David is a gentleman and confers honour by paying a visit', but the same holds true of all comparable Victorian novels. George Eliot, a safe guide, amusingly illustrates these traditional attitudes in showing that Mrs. Poyser, combative by nature and equal when goaded to telling off her own landlord the Squire, was yet respectful to the gentry in general and felt honoured by their notice and visits. Class distinction in the form of deference to ladies and gentlemen and their children was on the whole a tribute to birth, education and breeding (not recognized by mere income, smart clothes or pretensions unsupported by manners, which villagers were quite prepared to criticize). Comparable with this is the deference shown to craftsmen by villagers in the days when every village had resident craftsmen: traditionally accorded the honourable title of 'Master' in recognition of their superior abilities, no servility being involved. Mrs. Gaskell in her novel *North and South* (exactly contemporary with *Hard Times*) takes great care to show that her heroine, Margaret Hale a parson's daughter from Hampshire, was accustomed to having her visits to the cottagers received with pleasure, and gets a shock on moving to Manchester to find a new, Industrial Age, proletariat, without manners and aggressively egalitarian, hostile equally to mill-owners and to educated professional people, who having no standards except 'brass' despise the Hales for being poor and therefore having no right to gentility. Whether this implies real progress or only Progress depends on one's definition of civilization.

APPENDIX C

Dickens's Exposure Scenes

The exposure and denunciation, accompanied by bodily injury, of Uriah Heep in *David Copperfield*, following on the very similar exposure, denunciation and knocking down of Pecksniff by Martin Chuzzlewit in the earlier novel, has given rise to generalizations suggesting that these scenes are a characteristic of a Dickens novel and are psychologically revelatory as to their author, one recent Dickens critic observing not only that this is so but that he agrees with the self-evident conclusion drawn by someone else that these scenes are in the nature of sexual orgasms. Perhaps it would be as well therefore to take a closer look at them, to see whether they are as suggested, involuntary, or merely conventional and traditional, and how and why Dickens uses them.

The first form of such a scene is to be found in *Pickwick Papers* where Mr. Pickwick does indeed discharge his bottled-up wrath, very naturally, at having to pay the costs in an action in which he has been victimized by the rascally lawyers Dodson and Fogg; the scene is brief and kept in a mildly comic context, and is without excitement except on the part of Mr. Pickwick; it is obtrusively staged, so to speak, so that we are aware we are witnessing something comparable to a stage comedy, by the stage directions, and it is mixed in with other things proper to the conclusion of traditional comedy which have been continuously maintained from

E

Classical comedy to the Victorian pantomime, that is, marriages and comic business. Even in *Martin Chuzzlewit* this is so, where old Martin's pent-up indignation and his revelation to the company that he has only been affecting senility to entrap Pecksniff and test the others, gives the scene much more force than in the other cases I mention; the ridiculous side of Pecksniff is stressed, his intermixed speeches let down the tension, along with the barely-concealed amusement of the young men present, and the sense of our being not in a realistic novel but in the audience witnessing a traditional scene enacted on the boards is very strong. In *David Copperfield* Dickens can be felt to be staging this scene on similar lines, since Micawber is the agent through whom the exposure is made and his absurdities of behaviour and literary Micawberisms dominate the business and set the tone, the humour being underlined by Miss Trotwood's attacking Uriah bodily to make him restore her fortune that he has embezzled. In each of these two later novels there is only one scene of this type, whereas we may note in the first novel, that was written only as entertainment, the exposure scene is recurrent, where the easily-roused Mr. Pickwick exposes Mr. Jingle to the magistrate and has another such scene when he and Wardle catch the eloping couple in the inn and Mr. Pickwick denounces Mr. Jingle.

Of course in all these cases such a scene is necessary to achieve a peripeteia, and in a manner indispensable to the loose form of the picaresque novel, whose only tension results from recurrent surprises or alarms in the plot. In the picaresque novel, a form which Dickens took over for the production of his early fictions, resolution was traditionally achieved by assembling most of the characters in prison, a destination most of them would very naturally find themselves at, and the rest by mischance or the machinations of the wicked; there an opportunity arose naturally for the *éclaircissements* that would clear up the plot and prepare for the happy ending with the vindication of the innocent, and we can see this occurs in *Pickwick* too. Dickens inherited this from his models and admired predecessors, Smollett, *The Vicar of Wakefield* and all the rest. But after *Oliver Twist* and *Barnaby Rudge* prison did not come naturally to the class of characters now employed. And as Dickens turned away from the picaresque novel as unsatisfactory for his now more serious purposes, he found the mode and techniques of the serious drama (not melodrama) could be adapted to the novelist's needs. Here he could draw on Shakespeare, Molière and Ben Jonson, all of whom he admired and had seen performed, and assisted in producing or had acted in. His ambition to write an English *Tartuffe* which had produced Mr. Pecksniff, the exponent of our national hypocrisy in its Early Victorian form, gave him also the scene of Tartuffe's exposure, a scene inevitable with a dominant evil character of this type as we may see in the construction of *Measure for Measure*, *Volpone*, *The School for Scandal* and other such plays, all well known to Dickens, where the exposure of such a hypocrite as Volpone, Angelo or Joseph Surface necessitates the tense winding-up of expectation to a very dramatic and public exposure, before poetic justice can be achieved. Dickens made several versions of Tartuffe: Sampson Brass in *The Old Curiosity Shop*, Pecksniff himself, and two in *David Copperfield* – the 'umble Uriah and the respectable Littimer, where though Uriah gets the classical stage exposure Littimer is revealed, along with Uriah for a second exposure, (but this time purely satiric) in the picaresque novel's prison set-up – an interesting mixture, while the villain who is not a hypocrite, Steerforth, doesn't get 'exposed' at all. His punishment takes place off-stage, thus making very effectively the point that Dickens uses the stage exposure-scene only in connection with hypocrisy, where his models virtually imposed it on him. The scene in *Copperfield* which it genuinely excited Dickens to write, be it noted, was the storm scene with the shipwreck of Steerforth and the death of the heroic Ham. And the serious scene that balances the mainly comic one of Uriah's exposure is the exposure scene in reverse where Annie vindicates her character to her husband and to the reader too, with a staged scene and supporting cast.

Dickens did always feel the need for a strong staged scene towards the end of his novel, but it is not necessarily or even generally the one where excitement on the author's part is felt to inhere. In *Dombey and Son* the 'strong' scene is the exposure scene of a more complex kind, which has no supporting cast but is indisputably acted on the boards, being seen and directed as such by the novelist. This is the meeting at Dijon of Edith Dombey and Carker, where she denounces him as a villain and, like Annie Strong, vindicates her own character to the reader, which gives us the necessary surprise that makes the scene, since we know all about Carker's villainy already. But the excitement in the novel is all attached to Mr. Dombey's pursuit and hunting down of Carker, who is finally killed by the engine of Nemesis (and his blood, like Jezebel's, licked up by the dogs, a nice implied Biblical reference). Florence Dombey's return in the nick of time to stop her father from committing suicide is in comparison not in the least forceful or interesting.

So also in the later novels: Dickens's increasing powers as an artist incline him away from the melodramatic and even the theatrical, so that in *Bleak House* the only excitement is Mr. Bucket's (played off against the stony absence of sympathetic reaction by Sir Leicester Dedlock) when he unfolds before Sir Leicester, and later before the French maid too, the true story behind Mr. Tulkinghorn's murder. This has involved the exposure of the truth about both the lawyer and Lady Dedlock to the unsuspecting husband and the thrilling incrimination and arrest of Hortense in front of our eyes—altogether a mode of winding up a mystery story which subsequently became a stock feature of the detective novel, in which Dickens was a pioneer. But the real excitement for the reader, and what shows the art of the novelist, is in what corresponds to Mr. Dombey's hunting down Carker—Mr. Bucket's and Esther's chase up and down between St Alban's and London after her fugitive mother, in the hope of saving, not punishing, her. The true surprise in the novel is a wholly novelistic one (not in the least theatrical or stagey but psychological and truly human), to which the scene of the murderess's arrest is necessary but incidental: Sir Leicester's unpredictable reaction to what affects his honour and his family's standing. Here we have the opposite of an exposure and denunciation scene as the climax of the novel since Sir Leicester steadily continues, throughout the chase that is going on outside, to demand our mounting sympathy, admiration and compassion, reversing the usual climax that we have been assured is characteristic of Dickens. Dickens has got way from his dramatic model again.

The next novel, *Hard Times*, shows a comic exposure of both Bounderby and Mrs. Sparsit, with the disappointment and frustration of both, but these are perfectly controlled and nothing compared with the main scene with which the excitement is achieved, that of the pathetic and yet comic interview between Tom Gradgrind and his father in the circus ring and the concurrent exposure of Bitzer as the human machine constructed on the self-interest principle—and Bitzer's frustration and defeat is also entirely and appropriately comedy, as reported by the ring-master. Mr. Gradgrind's crowning self-exposure in his admission of his fatal mistakes is painful and not theatrical in the least, nor, as we had known that he was mistaken all along, is it stimulating. Louisa's escape from her lover and from the pursuing Mrs. Sparsit is truly exciting too, and has clearly excited the novelist in the writing.

With *Little Dorrit* Dickens has found a wholly unexceptionable use of the exposure scene which, while retaining the original elements of dramatic surprise and *élaircissement*, makes use of the psychological (nontheatrical) self-exposure and apologia shown in Mr. Gradgrind's case that lay at the root of *Hard Times*. The mysteries of the plot, of the Clennam house and of the household are all explained by Mrs. Clennam herself, the prime mover, in the chapter, 'Closing In', when she takes the words out of the mouth of Blandois who is about to 'expose' her, on the grounds that she cannot bear to see herself 'in such a glass as *that*'. Sitting in the wheel-chair to which she has doomed herself ('like Fate in a go-cart' as Flora had said with her usual aptness) she is driven to make her own apologia, and having confessed she is freed from her guilt-induced paralysis to stand on her feet and take steps to retrieve herself. An earlier opportunity for an exposure of the guilty, Miss Wade's case, is similarly avoided as a theatrical occasion, this time by being delivered in manuscript to Arthur Clennam to read, not in the least improbably since Dickens makes us see that it is part of her case that she should find communication with others impossible and yet needs to explain herself to make manifest her grievances. In Arthur Clennam, unlike his kind ordinary friend Mr. Meagles who is insufferable to her, she senses the appropriate person to whom to confide her apologia. The only traditional dramatic exposure in this novel is that of Mr. Casby, when Pancks exposes him to his victims in Bleeding Heart Yard as no Patriarch but a heartless slum landlord and, by shearing his locks, shows him as not venerable but a figure of fun. Pancks then runs away from the shocking spectacle he has created, pursued by waves of laughter from the witnesses, in a staged scene that is wholly comedy and almost farce.

So that in the next novel, *Great Expectations*, where Dickens achieved the greatest mastery of his medium, the exposure scenes are, as we might anticipate, much more interesting than in any other of his novels. The only exposure in a serious sense can be of Pip the protagonist – of himself to himself, as with Mr. Gradgrind and Mrs. Clennam – and of the mysterious Orlick. Pip has to realize that his expectations were fallacious and to see himself for the first time squarely as contemptible (he has long suspected this, of course, as his recurrent uneasiness betrayed), and the two are made to follow inevitably on the return of Magwitch when he reveals himself to Pip. This occurs not towards the end, as a prelude to a happy ending, but exactly in the middle of the novel and is integral to the whole conception, not contrived for a scene, nor staged as one with witnesses. The scene is nonetheless dramatic and exciting on account of the peripeteia it achieves by the explanations of Magwitch which strip, layer by layer, all the illusions from Pip of what he is and where he stands now. This is to use the conventional exposure scene for the finest purposes of a novelist. Moreover it is completed by an even more remarkable exposure scene, also with two only present, which takes place not on any human stage but in a realm which is at once non-realistic and yet touches reality. Pip is lured to it and made to endure Orlick's exposure of himself which is also an accusation of Pip, making Pip admit even more damaging truths about himself than he had found when reunited with Magwitch, and this scene is finally ended with Pip's acceptance of his rôle of criminal. The chase that we have noted as also a feature of Dickens's compositions is this time not, like Esther's in the company of the detective, to rescue the guilty, but to help the guilty and yet innocent criminal Magwitch to escape the law by Pip's aid. The public staged scene is when Pip stands trial along with Magwitch to be denounced by the Judge at the Assizes, and this is the finale of the denunciation and exposure – not of Pip but of his society by itself; and the reader of the novel finds himself automatically accused as part of the society that sanctions the Judge's mass sentence of executions, a powerful and disturbing corollary.

Our Mutual Friend, which seems to me to show very decidedly the breaking-down of Dickens's powers, has therefore as might be expected a reversion to the early type of exposure scene. Bella denounces Mr. Boffin in the regular stage setting and this is followed by the appropriate features wedding and comedy; but we have all been taken in, for another finale is needed to show us that Bella like the reader has been kept in the dark: not only about her husband's identity but that Mr. Boffin has been only a *sham* miser, a piece of theatrical nonsense resolved with disgusting sentimentality and whimsicality. There is yet another exposure scene, dull and mechanical, where Silas Wegg, a poor apology for a villain, is exposed to his own circle with unnecessary seriousness by John Harmon and undergoes a comic Nemesis by the hand of Sloppy. None of all this can be taken as anything but deplorable – tired writing and trivial moralizing that are totally out of keeping with the serious parts of the novel and are (like Mr. Venus) too dreary to be the comic relief they may be supposed to have been intended for.

Thus the last novel, *Edwin Drood*, shows that though unfinished it was working up to a merely melodramatic exposure scene, possibly in Jasper's prison, after a chase through the cathedral at night, where the intricate plot would be explained and the choirmaster exposed in his true colours, that is, as hypocrite and murderer (or, some think, only would-be murderer). There is certainly an undercurrent of heightened feeling in every part of the novel concerned with Jasper. This is associated partly with his creepy powers of an abnormal kind (something more than hypnotism seems needed to account for it) but mainly with the tension set up between his public rôle of respectable choirmaster in the cathedral, and his secret life in the underworld of opium-addiction and his privately fostered murderous enmity to his nephew, his unconscious rival in love. The suggestion of moral interest here is minimal but what possibilities it had are not explored in the novel as it develops, we can see. Such a set-up can be only melodramatic in its working out and *dénouement*, and there is no reason to suppose that we have lost anything of value by *The Mystery of Edwin Drood*'s not having been revealed to us.

CHAPTER THREE

'BLEAK HOUSE':
A CHANCERY WORLD

THERE have been two main grounds for dismissing Dickens altogether as a novelist—that is, from serious consideration as a novelist, as something other than a successful entertainer (at which no one disputes his eminence). One, which includes charges that take some such form as 'Dickens was incapable of thought', is represented by G. H. Lewes's contemporary critical attack where he complained that with Dickens 'sensations never pass into ideas'. The opposite charge is there in a recent relegation of Dickens: in denying that Dickens is more than a theatrical performer on the whole, Mr. R. Garis (in *The Dickens Theatre*, 1965—one of the few candid Dickens critiques of the modern phase and therefore most worth consideration) asserts, as a general truth, that:

> We feel a gap between conception and performance, and sometimes we virtually ignore the performance, we almost wish it away, in our full concentration on Dickens's idea. Much recent criticism adopts this attitude regularly.

and he sees 'the over-emphatic and misleading excitement about Dickens's symbolic structures not as a way of defending the success of the late novels but rather as a means of evading the issue: in Mr. J. Hillis Miller's book evasion of judgment is almost total, and Mr. Trilling raises the issue only to condescend to it'. These last observations are perfectly true, and in defending *Bleak House* against both Lewes's and Garis's charges I do not wish to be taken as evading judgment of Dickens's performance. On the contrary, I select *Bleak House* for close examination as a way of demonstrating both that Dickens was not satisfied with making fiction out of 'sensations' but had a well-grasped and deeply-felt argument, that he worked through fiction to make manifest his ideas, not as a set of ideas, but as a complex theme; and also that the ideas are not compulsive or simple-minded, nor inadequately presented as such, but are completely incarnated, dissolved into action and dialogue and feelings of representative forms of life that constitute a whole which is meaningful when (and only when) it is read with the necessary sensitiveness to the text and when the detail is related to the whole in ways implied in their context.

Some co-operation is demanded of the reader; some understanding too of what was imposed by the form of publication in parts and for a very diverse readership; and a certain amount of charity. We really should not, like Mr. Garis, make an anthology of the weaker passages and points in the plots (passages which are mostly expendable) as if they were representative, on the principle, apparently, that the chain is only as strong as its weakest link (not a criterion that applies to any novel or many great fictions would be sunk). As an example of what can be achieved by doing just this, I would like to cite Mr. Garis's use of the exhortation delivered to Tattycoram by Mr. Meagles at the end of *Little Dorrit* as they look down into the Marshalsea at Amy Dorrit passing below. Garis says:

> This is worse than inept. We have no alternative but to take the sermon as the official moral of Tattycoram's story, sponsored by the management. . . . Yet the sermon is inappropriate in several ways. Since Tattycoram has already fully and convincingly described her conversion, Mr. Meagles's sermon about duty seems a work of pharisaical supererogation worthy of Mrs. Pardiggle herself–it is hard to see how the generous Dickens could have been guilty of such tactlessness. . . . Tattycoram's promise to 'count five-and-twenty thousand' expresses well enough her pleasure in returning from Miss Wade's imprisoning system to the world, and the vocabulary, of Mr. Meagles; but it is also an unwelcome reminder of earlier doubts about Mr. Meagles's practicality. As a good audience we may have reluctantly obeyed the theatrical artist's clear instructions to forget these doubts and to co-operate in this happy reconcilation scene, but with Mr. Meagles's sermon on duty Dickens has gone too far. We don't want the sermon anyway. . . . Our sense that Dickens himself is sponsoring Mr. Meagles's sermon is confirmed also by the fact that Mr. Meagles points to the heroine of the novel as an example of right behaviour.

There are several points to make here in reply. The outstanding one is that Dickens isn't as simple a case as this writer assumes–he is very often less simple-minded than his critics, especially those outside the English tradition and in such a brutally crude one as the modern American. Even assuming that the 'sermon' is in relation to Dickens himself what Garis thinks it is, at the worst, it wouldn't constitute an annulment of the whole of the novel that has gone before, or even affect the success of Dickens's use of the Meagleses: Dickens has made a convincing demonstration (as Garis admits) of Tattycoram's feelings and behaviour.

What he implies is that Dickens has failed to do so (as regards convincing Mr. Garis, that is) with respect to what the Meagleses are and represent, and this is simply a failure in him of the reading ability that I have posited as essential. To any able reader Dickens has surely made it plain that of the Meagleses he is both appreciative and yet radically and ultimately critical. The bulk of Dickens's readers were *affreux bourgeois*, more or less Meagleses, and the tact with which Dickens offers the couple, their home and their daughter as the best specimens of their kind but with disqualifying limitations that cannot be ignored or forgiven, must be admired and respected. They have enough 'warm feeling' as parents to be hurt by the sight of the churchful of orphans and as 'practical people' (this term, which is stressed, means that they are doers as opposed to sentimentalists, but also constitutes as we are shown an essential limitation) they accordingly take an orphan girl into their home, by way of doing their share; they are even able to foresee that she might be jealous of Pet, but when they see this taking the form of bursts of rage they are unable to cope except by tactless exhortations. They are also demonstrated to be insular, thoroughly philistine, snobbish in an innocent but not harmless way, and to have done their truly beloved daughter harm by bringing her up to be a Pet. [The pet name is significant: Dickens had originally intended her to be known as 'Baby', but having already exhausted this idea in *Copperfield* made a characteristic development of his thinking on the same lines: Pet has been wronged by her parents because she has greater capabilities and could have been spared misery if she had not been made into a vehicle only for their love and for loving, at the mercy of the first determined suitor therefore–she has 'chosen' Gowan before Clennam appears and is distressed at not being able to return Clennam's love.]

Dickens shows exactly how he values them by playing them off to their advantage against the worldling Mrs. Gowan but showing Meagles at a loss and offensively patronising in his attitude to the inventor Doyce. Dickens gives them their meed of praise for their loving Pet unselfishly enough to be able to realise that they had better resign her after marriage so that Gowan will not have a grievance to use against her. All this is done with consummate art and creative fertility: some of the scenes of painful comedy Jane Austen couldn't have done better, And Dickens also leaves us in no doubt of the strength of his case *against* their kind: for instance, their simple moralising habits which have been shown as driving Tattycoram to run away and which, when–the alternative represented by Miss

Wade proving even more intolerable–she is driven to return, are still forced on her, thus showing that a Meagles can learn nothing. In exactly the same way Mr. Meagles talked English very loudly to foreigners with the conviction that they must ultimately understand it. We are also shown him self-defeating in being always moved to say the wrong thing to Miss Wade because he can't conceive that she is fundamentally not a nice well-meaning woman like his wife–a fatal absence of imagination. I simply can't agree in the face of all this (and much more could be cited) that, as Mr. Garis asserts, 'Dickens's grasp of the whole Meagles family and what they represent is always uncertain and often distinctly inept'– that would be truer to say of Matthew Arnold's ironic attacks on the Meagles class. Dickens saw that while their virtues were needed their limitations were dangerous and in some respects wholly disabling; he is tactful in making nearly all the criticism fall on the head of Mr. Meagles, leaving 'Mother' to be a good soul totally lacking comprehension. Compare Jane Austen's treatment and presentation of her equivalents, the Musgroves of Uppercross Hall in *Persuasion*, where there is a similar cultural gap between parents and children and a similar divided attitude on the part of the author to them all (I pick Jane Austen because Mr. Garis takes her as a comparison by which to fault Dickens generally); we can't help seeing that Dickens has an overwhelming advantage in inwardness, understanding, complexity and truly novelistic use of his couple.

Hence it is quite unjust to assume that Dickens 'endorses' simple-mindedly Mr. Meagles's sermon to Tattycoram, that we have been given 'clear instructions to forget these doubts ['about Mr. Meagles's practicality'] and to co-operate in this happy reconciliation scene'; there is no happy ending either to the novel as a whole or to Tattycoram's share in it, any more than there is for Mr. and Mrs. Meagles and Pet, or anyone else in *Little Dorrit* except possibly Arthur Clennam. The 'sermon' is what Mr. Meagles (not Dickens) would think appropriate, he would certainly utter it 'gently', and his approval of Amy would take the form (Dickens's doesn't) of praising her for 'doing her duty'. 'We don't want the sermon anyway', Mr. Garis complains. Well, it depends who 'we' are! Not if 'we' are present-day readers; but Dickens's readers were a different matter. With the strategy I have shown him habitually using from *Copperfield* onwards, Dickens wrote to be read in two ways. He saw that such a harmless sop to the Meagles section of his reading-public would give them the moral they could understand while allowing the rest of the novel's meaning to sink in perhaps (I am not positing such a process of reasoning as deliberate, it would be instinctive in a man who worked as Dickens did, with such continuous experience as editor and novelist of the Victorian readership). At another level, that at which he wrote to satisfy himself, the 'sermon' is seen to be what I have described.

This may justly lead us to ask questions about the degree to which Dickens was a critic of Victorianism and the extent to which he may be said, as he grew older, to have come to terms with or even succumbed to, some Victorian attitudes, but not to write off *Little Dorrit* on that and similar grounds. The Meagleses were at the heart of a Victorian problem for Dickens and he shows himself impartial, sensitive and intelligent in presenting it. He knew only too well that his public even when not Meagleses probably mostly admired a Mr. Meagles in all innocence, and that it would need critical tact to manœuvre them out of this position. At one level therefore there is the desired sermon on duty and a heroine who seems to endorse it; on another, for Mr. Garis, if he could see it, a less attractive, extremely complex case of the blindness and mistakes human beings are prone to when they are nice ordinary John Bulls, and a much more sensitive and difficult and character-demanding rôle for the heroine than following the strait path of Duty. If Dickens could have afforded to write for Mr. Garis's 'we'—assuming it existed to any extent at all then—if Dickens had been able in the later half of his career to ignore the Meagleses even more than he did,[1] literary history would have been very different; but social history would have had to be different first. George Eliot, writing *Middlemarch* a generation after, was able to profit by Dickens's achievement in ultimately knitting together a large reading public at least willing if not eager to tackle a long novel demanding serious and sustained attention; without his work she could not have made a fortune by writing novels to please herself only.

The scenes with Tattycoram and the scenes where the Gowans and Meagleses and Arthur or any of them, meet, are all splendidly realized dramatically and in no respect can they be dismissed as theatrical. I can't

[1]Dickens wrote to Wills in 1858: 'I particularly wish you to look well to Wilkie's article . . . and not to leave anything in it that may be sweeping and unnecessarily offensive to the middle class. He always has a tendency to overdo that.' Note the 'unnecessarily' and the 'overdo' which show the presence of integrity with the desire not to alienate, in Dickens's attitude to the question I have been discussing. Wilkie Collins was agressively Bohemian in his habits and enjoyed sniping at the virtuous, which Dickens had more sense than to encourage.

think of any novelist except perhaps Tolstoy who could have done as well here, certainly not Jane Austen, for there is a kind of imaginative sympathy Dickens had that she lacked. When we have been shown that Mr. Meagles's middle-class snobbery has made him finally agree to handing over his Pet to a Gowan, to be miserable for life, a spectacle neither he nor we are later spared, Dickens finishes with him in this way:

> '. . . but she's very fond of him, and hides his faults, and thinks that no one sees them—and he certainly is well connected, and of a very good family!'
> It was the only comfort he had in the loss of his daughter, and if he made the most of it, who could blame him?

Certainly not Dickens; but this is very far from being an *endorsement*.

i
The Theme

The Dickens who wrote his excellent journalistic pieces and made admirable speeches appropriate to public functions or suitable speeches at public dinners, was not the Dickens who wrote the novels or those parts (the most) of them which make them works of art. When he created as a novelist—and it is significant that he said that he could not till he had 'got up steam'—it was to express a deeper level of self than the journalist, actor, social friend or even, on the whole, the letter-writer, drew upon. This should be axiomatic, and prevent the Holloways of Eng. Lit. from citing the non-novelist to 'demolish' triumphantly interpretations of the novels drawn from the text of the novels themselves by that method of intelligent and sensitive disciplined reading which literary criticism makes possible. This applies to other novels than *Hard Times*, and perhaps above all others to *Bleak House*, which has been so generally accepted as a characteristically muddled piece of indignation (an attack on the law's delays) on the dubious evidence of Dickens's remarks about his attitude to the laws of England elsewhere and his preface to the novel itself. This has led to arguments about whether the Lord Chancellor of the novel was Lord Lyndhurst and shakings of the head over the confusions of characters and events that could not be contemporaneous and a general belief that Dickens's object in writing *Bleak House* was to get the Chancery Court reformed. Instead of an irrelevant, and indeed misleading, preface[1] devoted to justifying the doing away with Krook by Spontaneous Combustion and the factual truth of the Jarndyce case, Dickens would have done better simply to have printed on the title-page: 'These things are parables'. The nature of the theme, of his treatment of it, and the structure of the novel, would then have been made apparent.

But anyway the whole novel is set out so as to make this point inescapable for a sensitive reader. The nature of the fog that emanates from and is concentrated in the heart of London's Chancery Court is indicated in the opening chapter by the fact that the ruined suitors (Miss Flite and the Man from Shropshire) are figures of fun to the lawyers' clerks and merely nuisances to the lawyers and the judge, and by the description of the Jarndyce case itself:

> Innumerable children have been born into the cause . . . whole families have inherited legendary hatreds with the suit . . . no man's nature has been made better by it. In trickery, evasion, procrastination, spoliation, botheration, under false pretences of all sorts, there are influences that can never come to good. . . . The receiver in the cause has acquired a goodly sum of money by it, but has acquired too a distrust of his own mother, and a contempt for his own kind. . . . Shirking and sharking, in all their varieties, have been sown broadcast by the ill-fated cause; and even those who have contemplated its history from the outermost circle of such evil, have been insensibly tempted into a loose way of letting bad things alone to take their own bad course, and a loose belief that if the world go wrong, it was, in some off-hand manner, never meant to go right.
>
> Thus, in the midst of the mud and at the heart of the fog,[2] sits the Lord High Chancellor in his Court of Chancery.

Remembering that 'jarndyce' was the old-fashioned pronunciation of 'jaundice', we see that the Jarndyce Case is the case of man in the state of Victorian society. The kind of law that is the metaphor here is Equity (which can imprison for contempt of court) and is concerned with the concept of and search for true Justice; it is not the kind of law featured

---

[1] Dickens is not the only novelist whose prefaces are liable to mislead. Henry James often seems, by the time he came to write a Preface, to have forgotten why he wrote the novel (this is particularly evident in the preface to *The Awkward Age*). Dickens did in fact disapprove of prefaces on principle: 'a book should speak for and explain itself', he wrote.

[2] The association of legal processes with fog is already present in *Pickwick Papers* where the rascally lawyers are called 'Dodson and Fogg' and are denounced eventually by their victim Mr. Pickwick as 'mean, rascally, *pettifogging* robbers'. 'It is all summed up in that', he repeats.

in *Pickwick* and *Copperfield* as imprisoning for debt and which is later to be used in *Little Dorrit* as the very type of absurdity in administering injustice; nor is it the symbol of the society represented by Newgate, that Dickens finally arrived at for *Great Expectations*, a society, criminal and criminal-making, that executes men. The bearing of Justice and Equity on religion, morals and ethics, and on social sanctions and institutions, is a matter explored by Dickens throughout *Bleak House*.

We are confirmed in our reading of the overtones in the first chapter by the more direct expositions of the theme that follow. It should be noted that the prose here (in the first chapter) is quite different from the rhetoric of indignation and satire that has appeared in earlier novels. This first chapter needs to be read in its entirety, when it will be seen as tightly controlled (not dependent on either Swift or Carlyle as so often previously) and characteristically witty in operation. Though behind *Bleak House* is that characterization of his age that Carlyle, in the 'Present' part of *Past and Present*[1], made available to the novelists of Early Victorian England and by which they so richly profited, yet this style owes nothing to Carlyle's excited pulpit-pounding rhetoric, infectious as that was and particularly so for Dickens. [The contemporary parts of *Past and Present* seem to me to have been second only to Shakespeare in influencing Dickens.] What has seized Dickens's imagination is Carlyle's exposure of his culture as the *laissez-faire*, Devil-take-the-hindmost, cut-throat competitive society and the sense that they were part of it, willy-nilly: the novel is to demonstrate its heartlessness, its tragedies, its moral repulsiveness, its self-defeating wastefulness, its absurdities and contradictions, to enquire into the possibilities of goodness in such an environment, and whether anything in the nature of free-will is possible for those born into it.

Thus institutions and professions are necessarily examined. The second chapter undertakes to show that the world of high society was governed by the same laws–a self-defeating ritual of fashion–at its peak being the Dedlock family (to be in a deadlock is to be at a standstill). It contains the remarkable description of the 'place' in Lincolnshire, again unlike any earlier prose in Dickens's novels, delicate, forceful, beautiful and moving and again telling its message in suggestive and inescapable overtones:

> The waters are out in Lincolnshire. An arch of the bridge in the park has been sapped and sopped away. The adjacent low-lying

[1] Though *Past and Present* was not published till 1843, the gist of the 'Present' section appeared in 1840, as 'Chartism'.

ground, for half a mile in breadth, is a stagnant river, with melancholy islands in it, and a surface punctured all over, all day long, with falling rain. The weather, for many a day and night, has been so wet that the trees seem wet through, and the soft loppings and prunings of the woodman's axe can make no crash or crackle as they fall. The deer, looking soaked, leave quagmires, where they pass. The shot of a rifle loses its sharpness in the moist air, and its smoke moves in a tardy little cloud towards the green rise, coppice-topped, that makes a background for the falling rain. The view from my Lady Dedlock's own windows is alternately a lead-coloured view, and a view in Indian ink. The vases on the stone terrace in the foreground catch the rain all day; and the heavy drops fall, drip, drip, drip, upon the broad flagged pavement, called, from old time, the Ghost's Walk, all night. On Sundays, the little church in the park is mouldy; and the oaken pulpit breaks out into a cold sweat; and there is a general smell and taste as of the ancient Dedlocks in their graves. . . .

Boredom, depression, the absence of health, vitality and the colour of life, are irresistibly imparted here by the use of language. We note that the 'shirking and sharking' of the previous passage is not exceptional, but illustrates a vital and poetic use of language characteristic of *Bleak House*, as in the 'sapped and sopped away' here.

The plot, not altogether identical with the theme though not, as in *Oliver Twist, Nicholas Nickleby* and *The Old Curiosity Shop*, simply irrelevant to it and a nuisance, is launched in the second chapter. High Society being also In Chancery is in effect controlled by a legal mind too, Mr. Tulkinghorn, who is a solicitor to the Court of Chancery as well as being Sir Leicester's legal advisor. In fact, while the Dedlock class think they are autonomous, and employ and patronize him (' "He is, of course, handsomely paid, and he associates almost on a footing of equality with the highest society" says Sir Leicester', magnificently blind), Mr. Tulkinghorn, an interesting case, manipulates his employers, manages all their affairs – which he alone understands – while despising them, and gets his real payment by feeding and exercising his desire for power. Accordingly he is one of the agents of destruction, destroying himself in the process. Lady Dedlock is, like nearly everyone in the novel, involved somehow in the Jarndyce case, and she involuntarily betrays an interest in the handwriting of the papers Tulkinghorn is showing them. As this is an impulsive movement alien to her usual manner Tulkinghorn, being what he is, naturally follows up this clue, thus unearthing Lady Dedlock's guilty secret. The novel's *plot* is simply a touching off of a chain of cause and effect that exposes a dead past, a classical form that Dickens had never hitherto used. His next major work, *Little Dorrit*, follows the same principle of classical tragedy, all the action having taken place before the novel starts and as before it is a piece of uncharacteristic behaviour, Mrs. Clennam's (of showing regard for the girl Little Dorrit), that causes her son Arthur to follow Little Dorrit's trail and thus unearth a dead tragedy, his own origins (which are like Esther Summerson's here) and his step-mother's guilt. The plot of *Little Dorrit* therefore is only a variant on the plot of *Bleak House*, which, as they're utterly different novels, shows that by now 'plot' was recognized by Dickens to be irrelevant and *theme* the decisive factor in giving a novel its character. Lady Dedlock's 'guilt', unlike Mrs. Clennam's, is only guilt in the eyes of a morally misguided (jaundiced) society, it is implied, and this view is endorsed by the novelist, by Sir Leicester Dedlock who is a survival from a different age, and by the consensus of civilized opinion in the Chesney Wold drawing-room—also a doomed survival from an aristocratic society–when canvassed by Mr. Tulkinghorn in chapter XL ('Domestic'). Lady Dedlock's sister Miss Barbary (= 'barbarous', the name she has adopted to hide her connexion with her fallen sister) is in the position of Mrs. Clennam, of having deprived the 'guilty' mother of her child and deprived that child of a mother's love and cherishing.

The third chapter is another complete change, the first instalment of Esther Summerson's autobiography, taking her in one superb, unbroken sweep from her first memories to her introduction at the age of twenty into the court of Chancery and into Chancery London–it is in 'a London particular', as Mr. Guppy classifies the fog for her, that she arrives. The procedure being over, Esther and the wards in Chancery confer:

'And where do we go next?'

None of them knows: 'We looked at one another, half laughing at our being like the children in the wood'–the Babes in the Wood of course wandered about lost until they died of it. Miss Flite, to show them where they are likely to end, appears on this cue–' "It's a good omen for youth, and hope, and beauty" ', she says, ' "when they find themselves in this place, and don't know what's to come of it. . . . I was a ward myself. I was not mad at that time", curtseying low, and smiling between every little sentence. "I had youth and hope. I believe, beauty. It matters very little now. Neither of the three served, or saved me. . . . I expect a judgment. On the Day of Judgement. . . . Pray accept my blessing" '. We note again the Shakespearean use of language–the 'served, or saved'. It is surely evident how we are to take this. We are being told something about the human condition, and in a Shakespearean mode, as we find when this section is completed by chapter V. Miss Flite is a much more painful Ophelia, wholly conceived in terms of her environment in time and place–for instance, she has the lower-middle-class clinging to gentility, as we are shown when our three representatives of youth, hope and beauty[1] (Esther, Richard and Ada), like the Three Kings of mediaeval wall-paintings encountering Death in their path when riding out in the pride of life, go out to explore London ('A Morning Adventure') and meet Miss Flite again, with her 'mincing' manner: she takes them to her room and they realize whey she looks 'pinched': there are no coals or ashes in her grate, no spare clothing in her room and no food, and she says:

> 'I am sorry I cannot offer chocolate. I expect a judgement shortly, and shall then place my establishment on a superior footing. At present, I don't mind confessing to the wards in Jarndyce (in strict confidence), that I sometimes find it difficult to keep up a genteel appearance. I have felt the cold here. I have felt something sharper than cold. It matters very little. Pray excuse the introduction of such mean topics.'

The pathos of gentility in such circumstances, which represents a truly heroic clinging to self-respect and as such an achievement of the human spirit that Dickens has no desire to ridicule, is extraordinarily touching, and comes from the imaginative centre of a true novelist. But it is only one element in the tragedy Miss Flite incarnates. There are her birds, with their significant names, by which we are told something more painful still about the human condition in a Chancery world and with a deadly irony:

[1] Miss Flite's reiterated 'youth, hope and beauty' is echoed by Mr. George in describing his abiding devotion to his officer Captain Hawdon, who, he says, 'had been young, hopeful and handsome in the days gone by' and 'went to ruin' like Miss Flite and Richard; and, it is implied, this is the fate of mankind in general 'in Chancery'. In the novel's present Captain Hawdon is the wretched, degraded, Nemo, the law-writer, who kills himself with opium and is thrust into a pauper's mass grave, having become nobody. The elegiac note that characterizes *Bleak House* is sounded at the announcement of Richard and Ada's engagement: 'So young, so beautiful, so full of hope and promise, they went lightly on through the sunlight, as their own happy thoughts might then be traversing the years to come, and making them all years of brightness. So they passed away into the shadow, and were gone.'

'I began to keep the little creatures,' she said, 'with an object that the wards will readily comprehend. With the intention of restoring them to liberty. When my judgement should be given. Ye-es! They die in prison, though. Their lives, poor silly things, are so short in comparison with Chancery proceedings, that, one by one, the whole collection has died, over and over again. I doubt, do you know, whether one of these, though they are all young, will live to be free! Ve-ry mortifying, is it not?'

This is spine-chilling. Yet Miss Flite's peculiar tone, idiom and speech-habits are never forgotten. The Shakespearean poetic—for if this is prose it is prose which serves the purposes of poetry—continues throughout the chapter. Miss Flite explains that she ' "can't allow them to sing much for (you'll think this curious) I find my mind confused by the idea that they are singing, while I am following the argument in Court. And my mind requires to be so very clear, you know!" '. This is self-explanatory (though not allegorical but having a more subtle suggestiveness of another level of meaning). More sinister aspects of the Chancery society are then introduced to us:

'I cannot admit the air freely,' said the little old lady; the room was close, and would have been the better for it; 'because the cat you saw downstairs—called Lady Jane—is greedy for their lives. She crouches on the parapet outside for hours and hours. I have discovered' whispering mysteriously, 'that her natural cruelty is sharpened by a jealous fear of their regaining their liberty. She is sly and full of malice. I half believe that she is no cat, but the wolf of the old saying. It is so very difficult to keep her from the door.'

The last touch of horror is added when Krook himself (nicknamed the Lord Chancellor and his rag-and-bone shop the Court of Chancery) adds:

'When my noble and learned brother gives his judgement they're to be let go free,' winking at us again. 'And then,' he added, whispering and grinning, 'if that ever was to happen—which it won't—the birds that have never been caged would kill 'em.'

This casts a meaningful light back on Richard's 'cheerful' voice just previously saying to Ada: 'So, cousin, we are never to get out of Chancery!' when they found themselves by accident back at their meeting-place of the day before. Krook's pleasure ('grinning') at the idea that the wild birds would kill the caged ones if they ever got out, proves that this is true of the human species too: this seems to rule out any hope in Nature or human nature–Dickens was not at all inclined to take comfort in the belief that savagery may have something to teach civilization, he had no weakness for man in a state of nature. His hope for mankind is intimated in the novel, and is his faith in the human spirit which can show such other traits pitifully struggling for survival in those as battered by existence as Miss Flite, Jenny and Liz, and Jo of Tom-all-Alone's who though he don't know nothink can feel gratitude and so is 'not quite in outer darkness'. We may reflect that Miss Flite's name doesn't merely suggest madness ('flighty') but is related to the 'flight'-of birds.[1] Flying is after all what characterizes birds, and the bird is an ancient symbol for the soul. The devoted enemy of the birds, the cat of the twin Lord Chancellor, is of course the Law, and we are confirmed in, or reminded of, this identification when we get to Mr. Vholes who, when preying on Richard 'glances at the official cat who is patiently watching a mouse's hole' with his (Vholes's)'hungry eyes'–'official' is good!

The purpose of these experiences of Chancery London is that the three young novices shall ponder them. They are all orphans, and Esther something more forlorn, illegitimate; so they are appropriate material for Dickens to choose for exposing to the mercies of life in his time (succeed-

[1]Dickens constantly uses the symbol of the caged bird, and in such a Blakean context that one would be inclined to believe that he must have been acquainted with Blake's lyrics. Particularly 'The Schoolboy' in *Songs of Experience*, which is so close to the Blimber section of *Dombey and Son*–which has a Blake-like lyric in prose as a separate ending to the novel, summarizing the theme: the new generation of Dombey children are wandering 'free and stirring' on the beach. Blake' enquiry: 'How can the bird that is born for joy sit in the cage and sing?' is repeated in the history of little Paul who is described pining in his room at Dr. Blimber's as 'breasting the window of his solitary cage when birds flew by, as if he would have emulated them, and soared away'–probably the first form in which the idea of Miss Flite's birds was conceived by Dickens. However, I notice one even earlier when the wretched boys, released by Squeers's imprisonment, escape from Dotheboys Hall, some young children who have no homes to go to are in even worse plight at being loose, 'frightened by the solitude' (cage birds indeed!) of whom 'One had a dead bird in a little cage; he had wandered nearly twenty miles, and when his poor favourite died, lost courage, and lay down beside him'. More explicitly, when the grown-up David Copperfield passes Salem House, his old school: 'I would have given all I had, for lawful permission to get down and thrash him (the headmaster), and let all the boys out like so many caged sparrows' Esther, after the break-up of the only home she has known, goes off to school in a stage-coach with her bird-cage at her feet, having buried her doll as a sign that her childhood is ended.

ng Oliver Twist, Paul Dombey, David Copperfield but–no longer *children*). An important part of these new experiences has been Krook's account of the sufferings in Chancery and the consequent suicide of Tom Jarndyce, Ada and Richard's grandfather, to which, says Esther, ' "We listened with horror . . . to hearts so fresh and untried, it was a shock to come into the inheritance of a protracted misery" '–to realize, in short, the human lot. The cousins' summing up in this dialogue is central to the theme of the novel:

> 'Quite an adventure for a morning in London!' said Richard, with a sigh. 'Ah, cousin, cousin, it's a weary word, this Chancery!'
>
> 'It is to me, and has been ever since I can remember,' returned Ada. 'I am grieved that I should be the enemy–as I suppose I am–of a great number of relations and others; and that they should be my enemies– as I suppose they are; and that we should all be ruining one another, without knowing how or why, and be in constant doubt and discord all our lives. It seems very strange, as there must be right somewhere, that an honest judge in real earnest has not been able to find out through all these years where it is.'
>
> 'Ah, cousin!' said Richard. 'Strange, indeed! all this wasteful wanton chess-playing *is* very strange. To see that composed Court yesterday jogging on so serenely, and to think of the wretchedness of the pieces on the board gave me the headache and the heartache both together. My head ached with wondering how it happened, if men were neither fools nor rascals; and my heart ached to think they could possibly be either. But . . . at all events, Chancery will work none of its bad influences on *us*.'

It is not therefore the Law as such, but the laws of human nature and the society that man's nature has produced as the expression of our impulses, that constitute what John Jarndyce calls 'the family misfortune'. What rightly distresses Ada is the realization that merely by being born they are enemies in the struggle for existence–which the *laissez-faire* society of course did nothing to mitigate; hence the stress laid on the fact that the wide variety of people concerned in the Jarndyce case have been born into it willy-nilly, and, like Miss Flite's symbolic birds, 'die in prison'. When Richard dies on learning that the Jarndyce case has collapsed because the costs have absorbed the whole estate (this is Equity!) Miss Flite, 'weeping', 'gives her birds their liberty'. The point presumably is that she has given up expecting a Judgment in her favour–the occasion on which she had intended to release the birds–realizing now that she will have to wait for that till the Day of Judgment (which she has hitherto confused, being mad, with the court judgment) because there is no justice obtainable in this world.

The idea of Justice in this higher than legal sense of Equity is seen in *Bleak House* as the overwhelming desire of all men who are not base and which transcends all other considerations – Miss Flite has been driven mad by it and Gridley is killed by his frantic determination to have justice in this world, instead of resigning himself to suffering injustice but practising charity like the wiser John Jarndyce. Gridley's demands for justice had led to his being imprisoned for contempt of court. He seems 'a mad bull' to the ordinary man and to the lawyers a joke, but he is presented in heroic terms by Dickens: he is given a dying testament which sounds like that of the heroes of *Pilgrim's Progress* because he would not accept that injustice is the law of the land and has worn himself out in fighting the inertia that maintains injustice:

> 'But you know I made a good fight for it, you know I stood up with my single hand against them all, you know I told them the truth to the last, and told them what they were, and what they had done to me.'

He had explained earlier:

> 'It is only by resenting them, and by revenging them in my mind, and by angrily demanding the justice I never get, that I am able to keep my wits together. . . . If I did restrain myself, I should have become imbecile.'

This is akin to the later statement by Daniel Doyce explaining why he does not give up the invention he can't get the government to take up

> 'It's not put into a man's head to be buried. It's put into his head to be made useful. You hold your life on the condition that to the last you shall struggle hard for it. Every man holds a discovery on the same terms.'

Dickens was also an angry man in the face of the system, and while he recognizes, by way of Gridley's case, that his anger and heat may be looked askance at, he knows that like Gridley it keeps him from being an 'imbecile' in the sense that a Skimpole or a Conversation Kenge is one, and that to struggle hard to defend your knowledge of what is valuable is not the litigating spirit but its opposite, the defence of values. Richard goes on repeating that 'there *must* be truth and justice some where', but his mistake is in expecting to find it in the company of lawyers, who instigate litigation. Nevertheless, Richard also is a kind of tragic hero, for Dickens is saying that it is only by keeping alive the belief in justice that we can be fully human (that there *is* 'such a thing as principle'). Hence Miss Flite's anguished cry: ' "There's a cruel attraction in the place. You *can't* leave it. And you *must* expect" '. Man lives in the 'expectation' of justice and his desire for it has created the law, but human nature being what it is, this has in practice produced (typically) lawyers with their (inevitable) vested interests and Wiglomeration, represented by the Lord High Chancellor 'in the midst of the mud and at the heart of the fog'.

The conception of England in *Dombey and Son* as mercantile London and Commercial Man, or of Utility England and Economic Man in *Hard Times*, is altogether less sinister than Dickens's vision of the Bleak House that man the litigating animal has built himself and must live in ('Bleak House has an exposed sound'). For litigating is shown to be the primary instinct, leading us, as Ada saw, to 'our all ruining one another without knowing how or why' since everyone's interests place him in enmity to everyone else, even though we are all relations. Thus it will be seen that practically everyone in the novel (down to the wretched inhabitants of Tom-all-Alone's – which is in Chancery and can't be knocked down and rebuilt because of the Jarndyce Case) is in some way involved in it through no fault of his own, apart from the lawyers who *are* involved in it willingly because they make their living by keeping the system going and so are more completely of it than anyone else. But an important point in Dickens's parable is that those who are not involved willy-nilly in the Jarndyce case are gratuitously involved in litigation, either literal or metaphorical, of their own making.

Hence 'The Boythorn and Dedlock Wars' – two neighbours, Mr. Boythorn and Sir Leicester Dedlock, each of whom has ample means to live happily at peace with mankind, are engaged in private litigation over a trifling piece of land that neither wants, on principle since it is a right of way; that is, merely as an expression of their instinct of antagonism. And not only will neither yield to reason nor allow arbitration, both are determined to fight it out regardless of expense and the fact that they are as neighbours habitually put to social embarrassment and to un-Christian encounters in Church. In chapter XVIII Esther describes in detail Mr. Boythorn's delectable home ('formerly the Parsonage-house') and Paradisal garden alongside which is, we are told, 'the terrible piece of ground

in dispute where Mr. Boythorn maintained a sentry', also a fierce bull
dog, man-traps and spring-guns; he threatens trespassers with personal
chastisement and legal prosecution. [What in the last novel was invented
to endow Miss Trotwood with an amusing eccentricity has, by a char
acteristic development of Dickens's process of working out ideas, become
part of a serious and central argument.]

Mr. Boythorn, though chivalrous, high-minded and personally gentle
is given to a ferocious mode of talking. This appears when he first comes
on the scene as not inappropriate in expressing his detestation of Chan
cery, yet

> 'But how do you and your neighbour get on about the disputed right
> of way?' said Mr. Jarndyce. 'You are not free from the toils of the law
> yourself.'
> 'The fellow has brought actions against *me* for trespass, and I have
> brought actions against *him* for trespass, returned Mr. Boythorn. 'By
> Heavens! . . .'

Each of the antagonists, with all his virtues, prides himself on his strength
of character, a form of egotism which Dickens identifies in the course of
the novel as the mainspring of the litigating impulse. Thus we see that
litigation is the essential characteristic of fallen mankind (the legal system
is as old established as England itself, says Conversation Kenge), the form
that Original Sin may be said to take in the condition of mankind described by Malthus and later to be elaborated and extended by Darwin
as the struggle for existence.

Richard has concluded that they are like pieces on a chess-board, helpless and moved about in 'wretchedness', though, he says, that would be
understandable only if men were either fools or rascals and he cannot
bear to believe that they are either. But this is in his generous and hopeful youth—he is straight from school when the novel opens; his own
history is to show how of his own free will (Dickens believes we have
some measure of free will and therefore moral responsibility) he is involved in Chancery toils—degraded to its nature, thinking in accordance
with its perverted logic, allowing its system which denies disinterestedness in any man to determine his conduct ('Don't you see he is an
interested party? . . . I must maintain my rights', he says of John Jarndyce) and to alter 'all the colours of his mind'—merely as the inevitable
process of growing older and going out into the world. Esther recognizes
the change in him by asking sadly: 'Are division and animosity your

natural terms, Richard?' when he has explained that in the days when he was friendly with John Jarndyce 'we were not on natural terms'. He becomes one of Miss Flite's birds that ('poor silly things') die in prison. Even Esther is involved: she observes that Krook's cat 'looked so wickedly at me, as if I were a blood-relation of the birds upstairs'–she is indeed, for Nemo the law-writer who lodges upstairs is one of them and her unknown father.[1] The plot is almost identifiable with the theme in *Bleak House*, though it is not till *Great Expectations* that we see Dickens has made an elaborate plot become the complete and wholly necessary exemplification of a theme.

There are other gratuitous warfares going on in the novel beside the Boythorn-Dedlock affair. Marriage is seen as one form of it as often as not: worthy Mr. Snagsby's prosperous life is made almost intolerable by a suspicious domineering wife (whom he tries to placate, and to persuade into her proper rôle, by calling her 'my little woman'), while in the lower orders the men ('our masters', the brickmakers' wives call them) brutalize their wives. At the bottom of society is Jo who expects to be, and is, 'chivvied' by everyone. The Smallweed family all hate each other even more than they hate everyone else. Charley and Guster, servants, are victimized by their employers (unlike Dedlock menials) until Charley is rescued by Mr. Jarndyce. Lady Dedlock and her sister have been separated by pride; little Esther's childhood has been made wretched by moral prejudice ('Morality, Heavenly link!' as W. S. Gilbert wrote ironically of the spirit of the age); the snobbery of Pedigree makes old Mrs. Woodcourt try to stop her son's love-match with Esther; Mr. Tulkinghorn hates women, and all the philanthropists are at loggerheads. The refusal to sentimentalize is a distinctive feature of *Bleak House* and most remarkably so in an area where Dickens has hitherto been most liable to this weakness: Mrs. Blinder of Bell Yard, interviewed by Mr. Jarndyce enquiring after Neckett's orphans, admits that the other lodgers and neighbours (poor and socially sensitive) objected to him, on the grounds that ' "It is *not* a genteel calling" ', so that when he died his children didn't get as kind treatment as they otherwise might have had. ' "Similarly with Charlotte. Some people won't employ her because she was a follerer's child; some people that do employ her cast it at her; some make a merit

[1]Dickens has dispensed with the diabolical; all evil in *Bleak House* is in certain human instincts that his form of society sanctions and instutionalizes. The Devil is an unnecessary concept. Krook remarks to Mr. Tulkinghorn of Nemo: 'They say he has sold himself to the enemy; but you and I know better–he don't buy'.

of having her to work for them, with that and all her drawbacks upon her, and perhaps pay her less and put upon her more" '. Here is human nature not merely as the struggle for existence has formed it but with an added meanness and where the poor and uneducated show the same odious traits as the genteel. [This social unit of Mrs. Blinder's Bell Yard, which appears only once, is the prototype of Mrs. Plornish's Bleeding Heart Yard, with its fatal hankering after the genteel, and which plays an important part in *Little Dorrit*, another instance of Dickens's creative habit of rethinking some casual or minor invention and making it significant in a later context.]

This is how we are inducted into the theme and mode of what I find the most impressive and rewarding of all Dickens's novels, the most various and consistently lively in style of writing and composition. *Bleak House* has very little indeed to be written off as below the level of the bulk of it or incompatible with the best of it. What seems to me most remarkable of all, the greatest tribute to Dickens's creative powers— something more than fertility can account for–is that the Tolstoyan *David Copperfield* should in a couple of years be succeeded by the Dostoievskian *Bleak House*. But it was the success of *David Copperfield* in a new mode that, after the initial drop in sales, made Dickens able to take another and yet higher flight with confidence; it had given him status as well as greater financial reward, and he carried his public upward with him each time. Thus he wrote to a friend: 'It [*Bleak House*] is an enormous success; all the prestige of *Copperfield* (which is very great) falling upon it, and raising its circulation above all my other books. I am very much interested, having just written No. IV–and look forward to good things whereof the foundations are built'.

ii

Opting Out

Having established his theme in the first five chapters and begun to show its working out, Dickens then logically proceeds to enquire whether it is possible to opt out of the system or in any other way to vanquish it. How can we preserve ourselves from its corrupting influences? It is pretty obvious that Dickens didn't think that organized religion in his time offered much help and is anxious to show why (useless I'm afraid for Mr. Cockshut to scold him for not being an Anglo-Catholic). Miss Barbary was a devout church-goer of the Evangelical type, sternly puritanical and cruelly misguided (Dickens clearly held) in attributing hereditary guilt to a child, in which she was representative – there are plenty other such religious characters in Victorian fiction, and the Rev. Mr. Brocklehurst in *Jane Eyre* was identified with his real-life original by many readers. Mr. Chadband represents the inner light and Chapel culture,[1] Mrs. Pardiggle High Anglicanism and the class superiority that went with it; the Society for the Propagation of the Gospel, like Mrs. Jellyby, can see nothing nearer than Africa, and Allan Woodcourt's well-meant attempt at instructing Jo on his death-bed to repeat as a talisman a prayer Jo can't possibly understand is not sentimental but ironical in effect and, I think, in intention, since it is followed by the indignant and generous outburst with which Dickens ends the chapter (XLVII). The village church can't reconcile Mr. Boythorn and Sir Leicester who are at war all the week. Dickens, a gospel Christian rather like Tolstoy, as witness his will, looked upon religious institutions as separating men and as hostile to the spirit of Christianity.[2]

Mr. Jarndyce who has himself successfully opted out from the Jarndyce case, steadfastly practising a generous disinterestedness, has tried various idealisms to circumvent the system for others. One attempt had been to put his money to the use of the philanthropists, but he has learnt the hopelessness of that – they are only fostering their own egos, however they lay out the money. He has been more successful in using his money

---

[1] Those who would write off Mr. Chadband as a slanderous fiction and his idiom as too grossly nonsensical even for a caricature, must remember that Leonard Woolf, disgusted with the verbiage of Middleton Murry's spiritual utterances in *The Adelphi*, once mixed sentences or phrases of Chadband's with passages from Murry's unctuous prose and defied the reader (successfully) to distinguish the two. Moreover, research has shown that Chadband's is only a slight caricature of the customary idiom of purveyors of improving and spiritual ideas at that date.

[2] Dickens's Will as printed by Forster in an appendix to the *Life* ends:

'I rest my claims to the remembrance of my country upon my published works, and to my friends upon their experience of me in addition thereto. I commit my soul to the mercy of God through our Lord and Saviour Jesus Christ, and I exhort my dear children humbly to try to guide themselves by the teaching of the New Testament in its broad spirit, and to put no faith in any man's narrow construction of its letter here or there.'

Dickens himself was considered as a valuable unifying Christian influence through his novels, by many of his contemporaries, since he operated a highest common factor of Christian attitudes and implied values without activating the aggressive forces that resided in the different practices of worship.

to save Esther and to make a home for her and the other orphans, his cousins Richard and Ada: but he cannot for all his good heart and wisdom save either of these last from misery and blight. We are not told where the money comes from, that enables him to stand *au-dessus-de la mêlée*; this would be a weakness in the novel if it were not shown that his money has not availed except in Esther's case.

Like Conrad, Dickens does believe in the discipline of a profession that demands disinterested service (the opposite of the profession of the law). Mr. George and the Bagnets are admirable if simple-minded people formed by army discipline. But the detective, Mr. Bucket, who hunts out the truth of things, is nevertheless in the service of a bad system, which he cannot afford to question or think about. Though shrewd, kindly and all-knowing, he is also morally simple-minded, as witness his concern for the dying Gridley whom he has come to arrest and whom he can only try to help by offering as consolation encouragement to go on braving the law; thus Dickens shows very neatly and with some humour (of the wry kind that characterizes *Bleak House*) that the good feelings Mr. Bucket exercises whenever possible are merely paradoxical in his position and are constantly being disconcerted by the nature of the material he has to work in. Faced with the hopelessness of the system he is helpless, as we see in the dialogue arranged for this purpose with the brickmaker's wife in Tom-all-Alone's who thinks her baby would be better dead:

'Why, you ain't such an unnatural woman, I hope,' returns Bucket, sternly, 'as to wish your own child dead?'
'God knows you are right, master,' she returns. 'I am not.'
'Then don't talk in that wrong manner,' says Mr. Bucket, mollified again. 'Why do you do it?'

She explains that the sight of the children round her and their inevitable fate is the cause:

'Think of the children that your business lays with often and often, and that *you* see grow up!'
'Well, well,' says Mr. Bucket, 'you train him respectable, and he'll be a comfort to you, and look after you in your old age.'

The irony of offering this prescription to anyone living in such conditions and such a world needs (and gets from Dickens here) no comment.[1] Mr. Bucket's 'Well, well!' is an admission of the uselessness of

[1] If we remember the comparable dialogue in *The Old Curiosity Shop* between the magistrate and the two mothers, one of them of a deaf-and-dumb boy, which is

his simple morality in the face of the undeniable facts that the woman has forced him to recognize for once, of which he never voluntarily accepts the implications. Mr. Bucket with his domestic felicity, his fondness for children (when respectable) and the strict separation of his everyday good-heartedness from his bloodhound professionalism, is the precursor of the concept of the Split Man that Dickens is feeling his way towards with Mr. Bucket. It is to be deliberately launched with Pancks in *Little Dorrit*, and elaborated as Wemmick in *Great Expectations* (nothing to do with Jekyll-and-Hyde morally dual man, whom Dickens originated in Edwin Drood's uncle, the cathedral choirmaster and haunter of opium-dens).

The medical profession, which it may be remembered came well out of the first chapter of *Dombey and Son*, is here put forward by Dickens as the type of disinterested service to humanity that is needed[1] to counteract the Chancery fog. Allan Woodcourt therefore, who is shown as full of humanitarian classless feeling in his treatment of the brickmakers' wives, Miss Flite and Jo, and at Nemo's death-bed possessed of a humanity conspicuously lacking in Mr. Tulkinghorn and Krook who are there too, as well as lacking in the beadle, coroner and others at the inquest, is even shown as one to whom heroism comes natural in a shipwreck. His sense of vocation and persistence in it against poverty are held up (explicitly by Mrs. Bayham Badger) as a contrast to Richard's lack of such necessary qualities. It is therefore proper that the novel should end with Allan's appointment as a public health doctor—medical service in the public interest and not for private gain—and should marry Esther who exemplifies (and convincingly incarnates) selfless love and fully human sympathy. This is the limited hope for a future that may bring the defeat of the litigating spirit which has its roots in the claims of egotism, Dickens has shown—Esther's marriage offsets the defeat of Ada's. There is something more on the credit side and more of optimism in the

conducted in rhetorical stage terms and is merely an unconnected episode dropped into the novel arbitrarily and inserted as something overheard by accident, but not comprehended by, Little Nell, and then forgotten, we can see both how much more of an artist Dickens now is and also how he trusts the reader—or how far he can now afford to ignore the limitations as readers of much of his public. Dickens in 1860 wrote to Wilkie Collins: 'You know that I always contest your disposition to give an audience credit for nothing, which necessarily involves the forcing of points on their attention'.

[1]For the Victorian novelists' use of the idea of the doctor and medical science *v*. Appendix A.

marriage of Esther and Allan Woodcourt even though still in a (new) Bleak House than in Little Dorrit's marriage with Arthur Clennam of the firm of Doyce, Clennam and Pancks in Bleeding Heart Yard; though Arthur and his wife are blessed in each other, they have no hope of making any impact on their world of 'the arrogant, the froward and the vain' who will continue to make 'their usual uproar'. *Bleak House* is fortunate in coming mid-way in Dickens's development before his scene darkens and thins.

Woodcourt is not the only representative of medicine, the healing art, in the novel. There is also the surgeon for whom he works, Mr. Bayham Badger, whom we may take as a ludicrous figure because of his sub-servience to the innocent vanity of his wife; but we should be wrong, for even she can serve as mouthpiece for some serious considerations. Dickens thus continues the technique he practised so successfully in *David Copperfield* of appearing to write merely to divert the reader while really pursuing a serious end. Thus Mrs. Badger notices Richard's lack of the sense of vocation for medicine because, as her husband points out, ' "her mind has had the rare advantage of being formed by two such very distinguished public men as Captain Swosser and Professor Dingo" ', her two previous husbands. She is therefore able to point to the Captain's maxim, 'that if you only have to swab a plank, you should swab it as if Davy Jones were after you' (a maxim which, Mr. Badger says, applies to all professions) and to Professor Dingo's reply when accused of disfiguring buildings with his geological hammer, 'that he knew of no building save the Temple of Science'. No doubt Dickens felt that literature as he himself practised it was like the navy, science and medicine in requiring to be pursued in the spirit of these maxims, which he undoubtedly personally endorsed, and that all are citadels of disinterested service to humanity[1] in their different ways. He sees them as combating

[1]Dickens approves as a class of soldiers, sailors, and doctors, who are all protectors, whereas he sees lawyers, most schoolmasters and officers of the then local government (especially beadles) and of Victorian religion (especially self-appointed chapel ministers) as preying on society or the psyche. In *Bleak House* we note Esther, the sensitive and enquiring consciousness, speculating that Richard's having been eight years at Winchester and spending them largely in making Latin verses as an end in itself and learning nothing much besides, may be responsible for his unsatisfactoriness—because 'having never had much chance of finding out what he was fit for'—'I wondered whether Latin verses often ended in this'. Dickens however took pains to follow Dr. Blimber's cramming academy by the favourable picture of a Dr. Strong's and in *Our Mutual Friend* pays tribute to

the claims of the assertive ego that has produced the litigating or competitive society. 'Public men' in this sense are the very opposite of public women like Mrs. Pardiggle, Mrs. Jellyby and the betrothed of Mr. Quale.

Associated with the idea of doctor, scientist and naval officer is the idea of the gentleman, to which Dickens devotes a good deal of systematic attention in *Bleak House*, clearing the ground for *Great Expectations* where the idea is shown to have fallen on evil days and to be, as in the Marshalsea in *Little Dorrit*, a source of corruption. Dickens created the figure of Sir Leicester Dedlock deliberately to embody the qualities he believed, as a Radical, objectionable, but at a deeper level, and in spite of himself, what as an artist he could not help feeling to be valuable. Sir Leicester therefore inevitably exhibits Dickens's ambivalence, which is conveniently visible in the initial introduction of him in chapter II:

> Sir Leicester Dedlock is only a baronet, but there is no mightier baronet than he. His family is as old as the hills, and infinitely more respectable. He has a general opinion that the world might get on without hills, but would be done up without Dedlocks. He would on the whole admit Nature to be a good idea (a little low, perhaps, when not enclosed with a park-fence), but an idea dependent for its execution on your great county families. He is a gentleman of strict conscience, disdainful of all littleness and meanness, and ready, on the shortest notice, to die any death you may please to mention rather than give occasion for the least impeachment of his integrity. He is an honourable, obstinate, truthful, high-spirited, intensely prejudiced, perfectly unreasonable man.

the function of the parish clergyman and his wife. Dickens has a well-thought-out selective criticism of his society and does not use his remarkable powers of ridicule and satire irresponsibly–perhaps the true sign of great art. It would in any other age than ours be unnecessary to point this out, but in the world of Kingsley Amis–he is a portent, since reviewers in serious quarters and academic critics are visibly unwilling or afraid to make adverse judgments on his productions–this is not axiomatic. It is worth pointing out here, as throwing into relief Dickens's achievement, that all that now constitutes what Coleridge described as the clerisy, our only bastions against barbarism, are the consistent and systematic objects of Amis's animus: in turn his fictions have taken as targets for denigration the university lecturer, the librarian, the man of letters, the serious novelist, the grammarschoolmaster, the learned societies, the social worker; I used to remark that he would in time get to the parson, and I gather from the reviews that his last novel does. Dickens, besides making the careful discriminations that I've noted, also took care to dissociate himself from two kinds of writers–the amateur and aesthete (Skimpole) and the man occupying Amis's position–Henry Gowan.

Sir Leicester Dedlock is seen as ridiculous as regards his false idea of his importance and that of his class in a world that has no longer any use for an aristocracy as such—we see in due course that he has been quietly superseded, without his being able to recognize it, by Mr. Rouncewell, the mill-owner and banker and inventor of industrial machinery, in every sphere but 'the world of fashion';[1] the parable is wittily completed by making Rouncewell the son of Sir Leicester's housekeeper (who is not proud of him but apologetic). Sir Leicester is also obsessively undemocratic and doesn't even think much of Nature when natural, preferring it to be landscaped in a gentleman's park when, of course, it is fenced off from the public. Here Dickens's tone and style noticeably change slightly. The confident humour expressed in the robust alliteration and slang ('done up without Dedlocks') gives way to a more sensitive and complex sentence which ends seriously, and we see in the various accounts in the novel of Chesney Wold that Dickens was aesthetically very sensible of the man-made beauty of the estates of the 'great county families', to which his own powerful feeling for order and the beauty of utility must have made him partial. And we are therefore not surprised that Dickens

[1]Disraeli in *Coningsby* (1844) provided Dickens, I feel sure, with the situation represented by Sir Leicester and the ironmaster with his private bank, in his similar antagonists the superb elderly Marquess of Monmouth and the wealthy Lancashire manufacturer Mr. Millbank. Though they have no personal confrontation Millbank wins an election for his candidate against the Marquess's similarly, by his energy and speeches, also sets up his family in an estate neighbouring the Marquess's. Millbank has similar ambitions to Rouncewell's for his children: his 'opinions were of a very democratic bent' so he 'sent his son to Eton, though he disapproved of the system of education pursued there, to show that he had as much right to do so as any duke in the land. He had, however, brought up his only boy with a due prejudice against every sentiment or institution of an aristocratic character.' Disraeli presents Millbank with the same mixture of respect and a little amusement as Dickens does Rouncewell, but his attitude to Monmouth is much more one of firm rejection than Dickens's to Sir Leicester Dedlock, for Disraeli while appreciating the grand style and the high development of individuality that the old aristocracy achieved, understood that its basis was amoral and heartlessly selfish, and this he exhibits with wit, subtlety and controlled disgust, in a quite Stendhalian way. Disraeli in this novel also as Dickens does, attacks 'the idolatry of Respectability', and there is a gentleman who feels the east wind when made morally uncomfortable, like John Jarndyce. Basic to *Coningsby* even more than to *Bleak House* is the idea of playing off the still-wealthy and proud landowner who has lost his political power with the passing of pocket-boroughs, against the new-rich manufacturer-banker, equally class-conscious and proud of a superiority of achievement which determines him to usurp the privileges of the effete aristocracy, their battle-ground being inevitably the elections for Parliament.

shows he is weakening in the attitude he has taken up so blithely at first to the great landowner, whom it was evidently his intention at the outset to treat as something in a museum in a glass case, or a waxwork figure to be pointed at, and characterized as extinct. But now, with 'a gentleman of strict conscience, disdainful of all littleness and meanness' the figure comes alive and must be respected. Dickens, the artist now, is veracious and generous in admitting that the gentleman ideally stood for values that the industrial England of Mr. Rouncewell (who is allowed his own business virtues of punctuality and keeping his word, which are not however the same thing as 'integrity' and 'strict conscience') can't afford, and that the law-courts and lawyers are shown simply to despise. Nevertheless, Dickens recollects that an aristocrat is committed to a code of honour which in the modern world is a ridiculously inappropriate way of settling disputes: he is touchy and fights duels, therefore he is not the ideal enemy of the litigating society. [We are presently told that her part in the Jarndyce case 'was the only property my Lady brought him' and far from objecting, he approves of the institution of the Court of Chancery, holding that to listen to complaints about the system 'would be to encourage some persons in the lower classes to rise up somewhere like Wat Tyler'.] The chivalrous Mr. Boythorn expresses his willingness to decide his right to the disputed land by single combat with Sir Leicester 'with any weapon known to mankind in any age or country'. Thus it is demonstrated that the gentleman is an anachronism, though Dickens stresses the delicacy of feeling and chivalry to women shown by both Sir Leicester and Mr. Boythorn which is foreign to a Rouncewell. In the alternately arranged adjectives in the last sentence of this introductory description of Sir Leicester we see the Dickens scale oscillating and ending by registering rejection: a gentleman has his virtues—a pity we can't any longer afford them—but his drawbacks render him impossible. An aristocrat is ultimately one who won't compromise ('perfectly unreasonable man') and can't therefore be fitted into the world of middle-class enterprise and institutions. This is recognized perhaps by the consistent and intentionally irritating use of 'my Lady' in naming Lady Dedlock throughout the novel, an address demanding subservience.

Yet Dickens, as regards Sir Leicester, carries on this debate, and in the same open-minded manner: Sir Leicester and his set are retrograde politically, we are shown, and want to run the country in the interest of their own class and by personal influence. Pocket boroughs having been abolished, they bribe the electorate (Sir Leicester's embarrassment when

Volumnia innocently elicits this fact is revealing)–yet Mr. Rouncewell's candidate gets into Parliament largely through Mr. Rouncewell's influence and speeches. Chesney Wold and the country-house way of life, alleged to be insufferably boring, is Lady Dedlock's punishment for having married a man twenty years older than herself when she had previously had a lover, the father of her child, who still filled her thoughts, we gather. Yet Chesney Wold is beautifully ordered with contented servants and retainers and seems comparatively idyllic when measured against all the other places in the novel–even Mr. Jarndyce's home has the brickmakers' country slum at its doors. We have only to accompany Jane Austen on the trip to Sotherton (in *Mansfield Park*) to get the real feel of a way of living that is a dead conventionality with its empty pride and an air that suffocates with boredom. Jane Austen of course knew a great deal more of country houses and the old aristocracy than Dickens, but in over-formal Mansfield Park and its owner the pompous, kindly Sir Thomas Bertram, we get something like that blend of the insufferable and the invaluable that Dickens incarnates almost in spite of himself in Chesney Wold and Sir Leicester Dedlock; and for the same reason. [Probably Dickens had read Jane Austen by now–he hadn't, we know, at the time he wrote *Nicholas Nickleby*–and he may have got inspiration there. If not, it is interesting that he had made an identical analysis.] Dickens is aware of this complexity enough to try to investigate it, and finds it fascinating; this occasions some of his loveliest and most unusual prose descriptions where, in an effort to express adequately what he feels, his imagination is fired to a poetic intensity by the beauty, dignity, decorum and continuity that the great house represented.[1] The earlier Dickens novels show in several ways the prevailing influence on Dickens of the 18th century of Hogarth, Swift, Gay and Smollett; in *David Copperfield* and *Bleak House* these are seen to have lost their ascendancy and more sophisticated influences are felt to be present–Shakespeare, Jane Austen, Disraeli, and incontestably here, also, it seems to me, Pope–the Pope of the *Moral Epistles*, and particularly of *Epistle IV*, 'On the use of Riches'. [We know Dickens read and admired Pope.]

[1]It is noticeable that Dickens makes up for this inconsistency by stressing the defects of the Dedlock caste – satirizing poor harmless Volumnia, the dandy cousins, the Coodle and Doodle factions, and by providing a comic caricature of the gentleman in his great days (George IV's) in old Mr. Turveydrop, the bogus representative of Deportment who throws a satiric light on the genuine Grand Style of Sir Leicester himself.

Though the second chapter is given up to the Dedlocks and a verbal view of Chesney Wold in the rain, it is not till chapter VII that we get there, the family being still absent. Dickens's first criticism is that there is a want of imagination in the Dedlock class, that there is not 'any super-abundant life of imagination on the spot' and that Sir Leicester even when present 'would not do much for it in that particular'–this is very interesting since it is also Jane Austen's implicit criticism of the life at Mansfield and Sotherton. Dickens goes on to enquire into the possibility of a superior life of the imagination in the domestic animals, poultry and wild life, entering into their possible feelings and suggesting that they are no more limited than the people who tend them and work on the estate, a feudal entity, whose thinking is done for them by their master. The house itself is really the housekeeper's, who shows visitors over it, treasures the family traditions, and lives solely in her devotion to the idea of the Dedlock family (she is never ridiculed):

> She sits in her room (in a side passage on the ground floor, with an arched window commanding a smooth quadrangle, adorned at regular intervals with smooth round blocks of stone, as if the trees were going to play at bowls with the stones), and the whole house reposes on her mind. She can open it on occasion, and be busy and fluttered; but it is shut up now, and lies on the breadth of Mrs. Rouncewell's iron-bound bosom, in a majestic sleep.

This is a surprising kind of writing of which there is a great deal in *Bleak House*, and recognizable as characterizing the novel, yet it is hard to describe its unique effect, poetic, non-rational without being whimsical, alive with humour without being arch or playful, suggestive of metaphorical implications, and with moving overtones. Mrs. Rouncewell's limitations are not avoided: she sees everything, as in duty bound, through Dedlock eyes; her discomfort at having produced a son who, as a mechanical genius, is felt to be inimical by Sir Leicester and banished to 'the iron country farther north', and who, having become a rich iron-master, holds anti-Dedlock political views, is communicated with wit and a light touch. The presence of Sir Leicester at Chesney Wold brings out his virtues: an excellent master, though proud and lofty in his ideas he is more than courteous and always shakes hands with Mrs. Rouncewell as a mark of his genuine attachment to her, a personal relation that Dickens shows later is impossible between the self-made mill-owner and his 'hands'. [Later we learn Sir Leicester feels a personal bond with George, her younger son, too.] Dickens, however, grudges crediting the Dedlock

class with having created or supported a real civilization and shows Sir
Leicester in his study as habitually contemplating the *backs* of his books
(Dickens had the library of Timon's villa in mind, I imagine).

One of the most telling points in favour of the Dedlocks is scored in one
of the best scenes of social comdey in the novel (chapter XXVIII) when
the iron-master, his own housekeeper's son, beards Sir Leicester in his own
drawing-room, over the question of removing Lady Dedlock's maid
Rosa for a quick course in higher education to fit her for becoming Mr.
Rouncewell's daughter-in-law. Mr. Rouncewell, it then appears, though
self-educated, and his wife likewise, is proud of having risen socially and
expected his children to rise by marriage higher still (in the new fluid
society which Dickens in general backs against the caste system); he explains that these are the usual ambitions and feelings of the new class to
which he belongs. Dickens does not actually comment on this–he is not
one to make even a hero say, as George Eliot's Felix Holt does, that a
man owes something to the class he was born into and should help it to
rise too if he is lucky himself–but there is an unspoken reflection; Dickens
certainly leaves the impression that a society represented by a Mr.
Rouncewell's ideals is open to serious criticism. And this is borne out
by the great scene, a set piece, in chapter XL, when Mr. Tulkinghorn
tells the story designed to let Lady Dedlock know that he has found out
her secrets. The alleged 'fellow-townsman' of Mr. Rouncewell's (who is
described as being in the position Mr. Rouncewell would be in if he had
known of Lady Dedlock's past) takes the girl, his daughter, who is a
great lady's protégée, away 'as if from reproach and disgrace' when the
discovery is made: like Little Em'ly Lady Dedlock would be considered
a source of contamination to young girls by the Rouncewell class. But
Mr. Tulkinghorn's insolent fiction is more than a notification to Lady
Dedlock, it serves to sound the company's moral reaction, which turns
out to be wholly opposed to the automatic response based on the bourgeois theory that women can be divided into the pure and the fallen.
Volumnia refuses to entertain the possibility of such a history at all, Sir
Leicester 'generally refers back in his mind to Wat Tyler' (thus forecasting his indignant reaction when Mr. Bucket tells him that the late Mr.
Tulkinghorn had entertained suspicions of Lady Dedlock), while 'The
majority incline to the debilitated cousin's sentiment, which is in few
words–"No business–Rouncewell's fernal townsman"'. As so often,
the throw-away line disguises, without detracting from, the intended
seriousness of the content, and is here made more effective by the con-

tempt conveyed by the languid cousin's drawl. Thus we see that Dickens saw in the Great House class an alternative moral code to the cruel blanket morality of Victorian public opinion, made by the new dominant middle-class; the upper class were capable of personal judgment and would stand by their own, refusing to allow the bourgeoisie to apply their rules to its members. We are invited to admire the moral courage and independence shown here explicitly when (in chapter LIV and subsequently) Sir Leicester does behave accordingly when the scandal about his wife reaches him and she, mistakenly, takes flight. Ironically, this was unnecessary, we learn. When the disclosure of her 'guilty' past is made to him, he declares unequivocally that he has nothing to forgive and thinks no less of his wife than before (as she did not belong to his class by birth she could not know this, but took her line from her religious sister who had cast her off for her 'sin'). Dickens ends the chapter of the disclosure by three paragraphs of plain, unrhetorical prose which enter with the most delicate imaginative insight into the feelings of the unhappy elderly gentleman who has suffered a series of shocks to all he believed in and felt most deeply, and is succumbing to a stroke and paralysis from it. He sees his privacy and family pride exposed to vulgar scandal, but he feels only for his wife as the sufferer, since he is capable of real, personal, unselfish feeling:

> It is she who, at the core of all the constrained formalities and conventionalities of his life, has been a stock of living tenderness and love. susceptible as nothing else is of being struck with the agony he feels. He sees her, almost to the exclusion of himself; and cannot bear to look upon her cast down from the high place she graces so well.
>
> And even to the point of his sinking down on the ground, oblivious of his sufferings, he can yet pronounce her name with something like distinctness in the midst of those intrusive sounds, and in a tone of mourning and compassion rather than reproach.

It is in keeping with this use of Chesney Wold that the penultimate chapter of the book is given up to an elegy on the passing of the great house in the Victorian Age, which Dickens sees as the victory of the iron-master over the gentry ('the great old Dedlock family is breaking up')–a lament for the human loss this means:

> The greater part of the house is shut up, and it is a show-house no longer. . . . Closed in by night with broad screens, and illuminated only in that part, the light of the drawing-room seems gradually contracting and dwindling until it shall be no more. . . . Thus Chesney

Wold. With so much of itself abandoned to darkness and vacancy . . . with no family to come and go, no visitors to be the souls of pale, cold shapes of rooms, no stir of life about it;—passion and pride, even to the stranger's eye, have died away from the place in Lincolnshire, and yielded it to dull repose.

It is Dickens the artist, the poet, who mourns the loss of 'passion and pride', which only can be nourished by such a cultural context,[1] and who sees that 'dull repose' is the death of the spirit which the light of the drawing-room had formerly kept alive. A parallel tribute to this is that George Rouncewell rejects his brother's offer of a post in his works, preferring personal service to Sir Leicester who needs him and whom he also needs. Sir Leicester, who started as a butt, ends in pathos and dignity and is like Gridley in representing that moral courage which in our Chancery world is heroism. However, he is still at war with Boythorn–'the quarrel goes on to the satisfaction of both' to the last, reaffirming Dickens's original point that the idea of the gentleman cannot lead us out of Chancery, perhaps led us in.

But, Dickens has asked himself, there is yet another professional man, the artist. What does the practice of the arts imply? Skimpole, unnecessary to the plot but essential to the theme, was created as a means of testing the popular idea of the practitioner of the arts (any of them–he composes a little, paints and draws, sings and plays, writes verse and is a man of sensibility, also a gifted talker). After the theme has been systematically advanced in the first five chapters, Dickens takes the three children of this world away from Chancery London into the country, through what seems to be idyllic countryside and to a paradise of a home (chapter VI, 'Quite at Home'). There is however a serpent in this paradise. As soon as they are installed the theme is taken up again with the worthy John Jarndyce's opening: ' "There's no one here but the finest creature upon earth–a child" '.

> 'I don't mean literally a child,' pursued Mr. Jarndyce; 'not a child in years. He is grown up–he is at least as old as I am–but in simplicity, and freshness, and enthusiasm, and a fine guileless inaptitude for all worldly affairs, he is a perfect child.'
> We all felt that he must be very interesting.'

[1]Dickens's view of the nature and function of an aristocracy is here remarkably like Yeats's, who saw the great house as the creation and home of proud, passionate, violent, men who thereby nourished the arts and inspired artists to creativity.

The formulation is ironic. What has hitherto been for Dickens an uncritically accepted Romantic image of childhood is now exposed to criticism (as I noted its being uneasily reconsidered in the form of David Copperfield's dangerous innocence)–the criticism being intimated through the 'innocent' enthusiasm of Mr. Jarndyce. It is thus suggested that the idea of a grown-up child–an adult who has never matured–is the reverse of valuable.

> 'He is a musical man; an Amateur, but might have been a Professional. He is an Artist, too; an Amateur, but might have been a Professional. He is a man of attainments and of captivating manners....'

Dickens is particular to specify at the outset that Skimpole is essentially a dilettante–no professional musician or artist could be a Skimpole; Dickens of course was, and prided himself on being, thoroughly professional in all his undertakings. And by now Dickens, the author of *Dombey* and *Copperfield*, had ceased to find satisfaction solely in his 'inimitable' powers as entertainer, humourist and so forth, realizing that his self-respect depended on his being an Artist, his status that of serious novelist with a responsibility to his art ('the art that he holds in trust' as his own noble formulation ran when in his obituary notice on Thackeray he rebuked him for irresponsibility). How, he must now have been asking himself, how to justify the profession of writing novels in this Bleak House, a world bursting with sin and sorrow, where men are in Chancery? While Dickens is not ready with an answer, he is clear about what he is not: as a novelist he is *not* a Skimpole, who is an Amateur, a dilettante, and something even worse. Skimpole, essentially an entertainer in private life, is also an actor and nothing else; singing for his supper, always acting a part, he has no real self; a parasite, he has no sense of responsibility either as an artist, a husband or parent. Skimpole is not of course, as used to be claimed, Leigh Hunt, except in the conveniently happy temperament which Dickens borrowed and the appropriate appearance (which had to be toned down by the artist to avoid trouble). Except in his claims to be childlike Skimpole is a recognizable later Victorian type, an aesthete, who systematically substitutes aesthetic reactions for human ones. Henry James's Gabriel Nash (in *The Tragic Muse*) might be Skimpole's brother, and he like Skimpole is something of an Oscar Wilde without the vice. Skimpole already uses the paradox as a means of explaining the principles he follows in his practices.

What is truly remarkable about the conception of Skimpole is not merely that Dickens predicted the aesthetic movement through him—the signs were there already to be read by an acute observer of the literary and social scene—but that Dickens who, we are so frequently assured by Dickens specialists, had no powers of thought, should have gone straight to the centre of the Skimpole case and exposed its philosophical basis—not as such but by the novelist's true art of dramatizing it. Skimpole's style of amusing, playful fantasy which refuses to be serious and therefore cannot be easily reprehended since only a prig would be hostile to such a butterfly, is maintained throughout, as in his opening apologia, which even flutters from idea to idea in a butterfly movement:

> 'I covet nothing,' said Mr. Skimpole in the same light way. 'Possession is nothing to me. Here is my friend Jarndyce's excellent house. I feel obliged to him for possessing it. I can sketch it and alter it. I can set it to music, When I am here, I have sufficient possession of it, and have neither trouble, cost, nor responsibility.'

This subjectivism seems harmless and delightful, but on it Skimpole erects a technique of flattery: he is necessary to society as an exponent of beauty, he argues, and therefore those practical worldly people who can't of course feel exquisitely like himself are indebted to him and are in the enviable position of owing him a living:

> 'I envy you your power of doing what you do. . . . I almost feel as if *you* ought to be grateful to *me*, for giving you the opportunity of enjoying the luxury of generosity. I know you like it. For anything I can tell, I may have come into the world expressly for the purpose of increasing your stock of happiness,' etc.

Esther, the truly sensitive recording consciousness of the book, notes that 'Of all his playful speeches (playful, yet always fully meaning what they expressed) none seemed to be more to the taste of Mr. Jarndyce than this. . . . We were all enchanted'. Skimpole is more plausible as an object for Jarndyce to lay out his money on than the philanthropists. Esther soon realizes that Jarndyce blinds himself to the ugly truth about Skimpole because he needs to believe that it is possible to beat the system, that Skimpole has successfully opted out of it. 'I thought I could understand', writes Esther, 'how such a nature as my guardian's, experienced in the world, and forced to contemplate the miserable evasions and contentions of the family misfortune, found an immense relief in Mr. Skimpole's avowal of his weaknesses and display of guileless candour', 'to find one perfectly undesigning and candid man . . . could not fail to give him pleasure'. Keeping to his principles, on his first meeting with the young people Skimpole fleeces them; taken with them to Bell Yard to see the desolate orphan children, Skimpole's 'usual gay strain' grates on us as outrageously inappropriate to the occasion (chapter XV.) This has been brought about partly by Esther's natural sympathy for the heroically self-reliant little creatures and partly by bringing in Gridley who in spite of his own genuine and deeply-felt grievances against life has shown active helpfulness to the children. All Skimpole can produce is an affectation of sympathy, a display of egotism:

> 'He said . . . he had been a benefactor to Coavinses; that he had actually been enabling Coavinses to bring up these charming children in this agreeable way developing these social virtues! Insomuch that his heart had just now swelled, and the tears had come into his eyes, when he had looked round the room, and thought, 'I was the great patron of Coavinses, and his little comforts were *my* work!'

We are therefore ready on Skimpole's next appearance for a complete exposure of his theory of life, his philosophy and his apologia. This is managed wholly dramatically in chapter XVIII by taking them all down to the Chesney Wold neighbourhood and bringing Skimpole up against his opposite, Boythorn, a man of convictions that he is always ready to put into practice energetically, and whose excessive energies are always channelled into violent expressions of principle, a man proud of the fact that he is always in deadly earnest. As Skimpole points out, this is liable to make him disagreeable, and for Skimpole it is axiomatic that 'everybody's business in the social system is to be agreeable. It's a system of harmony, in short.' To which Boythorn makes the very relevant objection: ' "Is there such a thing as principle, Mr. Harold Skimpole?" ', Skimpole's reply is that he doesn't know what such a thing is.

Dickens has been a good deal accused by academic and literary Skimpoles of being characteristically (that is, self-indulgently) angry, but it seems not to have been noticed that in comparing the angry men Gridley and Boythorn with Skimpole in the setting of their Chancery world he has defended himself adequately, by showing the contemptible nature of the man who plays for safety and comfort. Skimpole ends this protracted argument with Boythorn by a full and candid statement of the aesthetic and solipsistic position which he systematically adopts. He has candour here, in not shrinking from the conclusions that will strike the average man as morally objectionable:

DICKENS

'Enterprise and effort,' he would say to us (on his back), are delightful to me. I believe I am truly cosmopolitan. I have the deepest
sympathy with them. I lie in a shady place like this, and think of the
adventurous spirits going to the North Pole, of penetrating to the
heart of the Torrid Zone, with admiration. Mercenary creatures ask,
'What is the use of a man's going to the North Pole! What good does
it do?' I can't say; but, for anything I *can* say, he may go for the purpose – though he don't know it – of employing my thoughts as I lie
here. Take an extreme case. Take the case of the Slaves on the American plantations. I daresay they are worked hard, I dare say they don't
altogether like it, I dare say theirs is an unpleasant experience on the
whole; but they people the landscape for me, they give it a poetry for
me, and perhaps that is one of the pleasanter objects of their existence.
I am very sensible of it, if it be, and I shouldn't wonder if it were!'

This is surely as brilliant an intellectual exercise for the purpose as a novel
could show, something we are more accustomed to thinking of as Pea-
cock's forte. The explanation exposes itself. Other people don't exist for
Skimpole in their own right, and yet he demands their services since he
can't, being a social parasite, exist without them. Skimpole's claim to pre-
ferential treatment is that as an artist he *has* sensibility, and he needs to feed
it, we see, but at the cost of excluding human considerations (the Southern
slave issue was then very much in the public eye as well as the ground for
taking it as 'an extreme case' which Skimpole agrees he is willing to face
as the test of his position). He is therefore committed by his theory of
non-involvement, in order to live agreeably, either to the most callous
heartlessness, as to such issues as the slavery question, taking a purely
picturesque view of them, or to an equally vicious self-indulgent sentimentality, as we see the next time he is brought on the scene (in chapter
XXXI). There Jo, with the fever on him, is brought home by Esther and
Charley to be helped; Skimpole with his basic selfishness instantly objects
to Jo's being brought in to infect them all: ' "He's not safe, you know" '.
Skimpole has in fact had a training in medicine[1] but couldn't be bothered
to practise: he is an anti-doctor (we must remember the symbolic part
played by the medical man in this novel), refusing to operate the medical
code of obligation to the sick. He advises turning Jo out – after all, other
people don't really exist for him – and subsequently assists Mr. Bucket in

[1]This is very neat: Skimpole is tied into the thematic structure of the novel as a
renegade doctor. Cf. Kingsley's Romantic poetaster in *Two Years Ago* who deserted
his medical apprenticeship for poetry and comes to a bad end, discussed in Appendix A.

surreptitiously putting Jo out into the night.[1] When Esther returns from seeing Jo looked after she finds Skimpole 'playing snatches of pathetic airs, and sometimes singing to them with great expression and feeling. When we rejoined him in the drawing-room he said he would give us a little ballad, which had come into his head, "apropos of our young friend"; and he sang one about a Peasant boy,

"Thrown on the wide world, doom'd to wander and roam,
  Bereft of his parents, bereft of a home",

–quite exquisitely. It was a song that always made him cry, he told us.' It would hardly be possible to give a better illustration of sentimentality.

We see him adapting his form of candour to flattering Sir Leicester Dedlock:

Sir Leicester seemed to approve of this sentiment highly. 'An artist, sir?'

'No,' returned Mr. Skimpole. 'A perfectly idle man. A mere amateur.'

Sir Leicester seemed to approve of this even more.

Here we have a fresh budding-off of Dickens's thinking, which is going to throw up Henry Gowan in a later novel. Like Taine, in his *Notes sur l'Angleterre*, Dickens had noted that in England, unlike France, artists had no accepted social position based on recognition of their value to the community. In a utilitarian, puritanical society they were looked at askance for various reasons and Dickens was sensitive to status. The essential sign of a gentleman in the vulgar mind was that he didn't work for a living, and in rejecting the title of artist in favour of being an amateur, Skimpole is showing that he is a gentleman, to Sir Leicester's approval; Dickens notes this against both of them. In due course one sign of Mr. Dorrit's contemptible snobbery is that he has doubts about letting the apparently Bohemian Henry Gowan paint his portrait until he is assured Gowan is not really an artist but a gentleman of good family. Dickens has taken the case further with Gowan who is seen as the enemy of all disinterestedness and hating the real thing, the artist. Skimpole has talent and abilities but *never finishes anything*–having no real belief in the value of what he is doing or any sense of serving something outside himself. Skimpole, his charm gradually dispelled for us, fades out of the novel leaving a bad taste behind him (exactly like Henry James's Gabriel Nash,

[1] If this is thought too much to believe of even a Skimpole, we may remember Wilde shows in *The Picture of Dorian Gray* that the aesthete does not, quite logically, shrink even from murder if his comfort demands it.

who is played off in *The Tragic Muse* against the man who has a real vocation as painter). Skimpole's epitaph is given to Esther by the experienced Bucket: ' "Whenever a person proclaims to you 'In worldly matters I'm a child', you consider that that person is only a-crying off from being held accountable, and that you've got that person's number, and it's Number One." ' Skimpole then is in one aspect Dickens's reconsidering in the context of social responsibility the habits of Micawber (though Micawber of course is not offered as an artist); in another, he is one stage in Dickens's attempt to prove himself something other than an entertainer, a demonstration that the writer is not less concerned than others for his fellow-slaves but more, not irresponsible and self-indulgent but peculiarly responsible in his understanding of 'the family misfortune'. Dickens is saying that the artist must be 'held accountable' in life and art, that these two are inseparable; sensibility and taste can't exist in a void; indifference to one's fellows means paying the penalty as an artist of sterility; refusal to make a stand on principle is to commit an artist to parasitism; to have no concern for justice is to be condemned to triviality. Dickens shows himself now ready to assent to Lawrence's 'I write for the race', and writing *Dombey and Son, David Copperfield* and *Bleak House* were his path to it.

iii

Case-Histories of Life in Chancery

There is another feature of the Skimpole conception that is important: his assumption of the character of the child. He is thus, with his mock-innocence, a pseudo-child, yet in so far as he is a child at all, the only one in the novel. This is a significant departure for Dickens, to whom the image of the child has hitherto been a necessary conception and the child's sensibility that records criticism of the adult world a necessary technical mode. Here half the novel is Esther's autobiographical narrative and yet Esther grows up early in her first chapter, indeed she can hardly be said ever to have had much childhood at all, and the same applies to such other children as figure in the novel: Charley, Tom and little Emma are prematurely forced to be little adults, responsible, stoical and sobered by extreme hardship, just as Esther had been cheated out of happy trusting childhood by the knowledge forced on her that she had no right to exist and was unloved. The wholly characteristic children of the Chancery world are the Smallweeds who were 'little old men and women' from birth because the family 'strengthened itself in its practical character' and therefore 'discarded all amusements, discountenanced all story-books, fairy-tales, fictions and fables, and banished all levities whatsoever. Hence the gratifying fact, that it has had no little child born to it, and that the complete little men and women whom it has produced have been observed to bear a likeness to old monkeys with something depressing on their minds. . . . Judy never owned a doll, never played at any game', etc. They are thus the idea of the child in a utilitarian society –that society which indeed 'strengthened itself in its practical character'– that Dickens next projected into the central theme of a novel as the Gradgrind children and Bitzer in *Hard Times*, who were disasters because likewise robbed of their natural inheritance of imaginative literature, play, fun and make-believe, all of which Dickens rightly saw to be essential to a healthy childhood. The Smallweeds, justly so named, are brought up to unenlightened self-interest only, and figure as puppets in a Punch-and-Judy show kind of entertainment, as awful warnings on the margin of the novel. That Dickens had already the whole of the anti-Utilitarian case crystallizing in his mind ready for *Hard Times* is shown by the development of the Smallweed characteristics in the Bitzer direction too:

'Been along with your friend again, Bart?'
Small nods.
'Dining at his expense, Bart?'
Small nods again.
'That's right. Live at his expense as much as you can, and take warning by his foolish example. That's the use of such a friend. The only use you can put him to,' says the venerable sage.

Esther however is fully human and framed to be a very carefully complete study of what a sensitive child is made into in such circumstances as are posited for her. Her aunt is a very moderate version of a Murdstone; Esther understood her to be 'a good, good woman' and that it was Esther's own fault that she was illegitimate. On her aunt's death she feels obliged to bury her doll, her only friend, with tears–in a grave in the garden; it is left to us to deduce, since Esther doesn't understand her action herself, that she was showing herself obedient to the rule laid down for her of 'submission, self-denial, diligent work'. Esther, like Little Dorrit the child with the stigma of prison birth, accepts her lot without complaint or self-pity and is even excessively docile, though

Esther nonetheless suffers from the 'wound' she knew she had received in childhood, 'the fault I had been born with (of which I confessedly felt guilty and yet innocent)'–the child's confusion between what it is told it should feel, and what it feels instinctively, could hardly be better put. She undertakes to atone by being useful and trying to win love. Thus is explained her constantly noting down compliments paid her and marks of affection shown her, which are to her necessary proofs that she has won the right to be alive. Yet, ignoring the care and the wonderful imaginative insight it has taken to build up and maintain Esther's case, criticism habitually complains of her for showing the traits that are proof of Dickens's indignant and compassionate understanding of an aspect of the life of his time that only a great novelist could demonstrate. Esther can hardly believe people when they tell her how useful, pretty and lovable she is and writes it all down to be able to. Esther has never been Pet or Baby to anyone and even in Mr. Jarndyce's circle her excessive maturity is recognized by nicknames like 'Dame Durden' and 'Little Old Woman'.

Esther has an interesting psychological consistency, and is the more remarkable for being Dickens's first successful attempt at creating a girl from the inside–Florence Dombey is convincing only in childhood and Agnes never at any time. Esther is even a young lady too, so that to have established her through autobiography is a real triumph for such a thoroughly masculine writer. We know more about Esther than any other young woman in Dickens's novels and she has more reality than any except Bella Wilfer (before Bella's marriage). Esther is always true to her own peculiarities but they are not mannerisms; her individual sensibility is shown in her unusual sensitiveness to her surroundings anywhere and her quite personal descriptions of natural scenery. Chapter III, Esther's first, is as a chapter one of the very best Dickens ever wrote in a mode not committed to satire (as the remarkable first chapter of *Dombey* is). Her submissiveness makes her blame herself whenever as a child she is unsuccessful in winning the affection she craves, but she never criticizes the others, so that her submissiveness becomes painful to us, as it was meant to. The psychology of an illegitimate child of her time can never have been caught with greater fidelity.[1] She is intelligent through the

[1]About ten years ago one of our most responsible newspapers printed an article enquiring about illegitimacy in these post-Victorian times when no one believes in Miss Barbary's religious horror of it, and published an interesting correspondence that ensued from many wishing to give their own experience. This bore out

intensity of her sensibility but, unlike Pip, not morally timid or weak. On the contrary, she demands respect by her strength of character and resourcefulness, which comes out in all her contacts with Mr. Guppy, in her sympathy with Miss Flite, Caddy, Jenny, Jo and any other unfortunates she meets, and in her very natural self-compensation in instinctively mothering younger girls like Charley, Caddy and Ada. It is in keeping too that she doesn't allow herself to entertain the idea that Allan Woodcourt is attracted by herself or that she is entitled to love and marry him, and that she should persuade herself it is her duty to refuse him in order to marry her guardian out of gratitude–this looks like Dickens reconsidering the idea of the Strong marriage and admitting his mistake there, for Jarndyce himself sees such a marriage would be wrong and resigns Esther to a more appropriate husband. Esther has forced herself to burn the treasured posy Woodcourt had left for her exactly as she had buried the beloved doll in her younger phase. [One is constantly surprised by Dickens's persistence in 'filling in' Esther when he has so much else on his hands in this demanding novel.] What is even more remarkable is Dickens's imaginative insight into her reactions to exceptional situations, as when, her looks having been ruined by the smallpox, she cannot bear to meet Ada in case she sees signs in Ada's face of being shocked or repelled; after steeling herself to the meeting she hides behind the door at the last minute. When she learns from her mother the secret of her birth her second reaction–the first having been to reassure and comfort her mother–is to relapse into the feelings of her childhood and wish she had never been born. While it is Dickens who had treasured the anecdote of the village girl who, though literate, follows her illiterate bridegroom in making a cross instead of signing the marriage register, in order not to 'shame him', it is appropriate that the novelist should give it to Esther to tell and comfort herself with because it represents the delicacy of feeling[1] which she desires to find in others at this point, to support her in

surprisingly Dickens's insights. One started: 'I am illegitimate, and have been in social work for 20 years, so I have had ample opportunity to study the problem. I have noticed one point above all: whatever their background or experience, illegitimates seem to feel the need to apologize for their existence. . . .'

[1] That there is delicacy of feeling forms a considerable part of Dickens's reasons for any optimism being possible in the face of the litigating nature of man, since sympathy and imagination are the counter-agents. In our Kingsley-Amis type civilization 'delicacy' has become a term of contempt with the intellectual guardians of our culture–I note a school of Anglo-American reviewers, for instance, who sneer at 'delicacy' as 'a prototype *Scrutiny* word of praise'.

her distress, against her fear of being shamed by those she loves. All this and much more in Esther's history is proof that Dickens had the true creative artist's power of feeling himself into and sustaining a character who is as far as possible from being himself. But there is even more striking testimony, in demonstrating that Dickens also understood that such a nature under such strains must develop signs of psychic stress, and though Esther is not driven to the borders of mania like Miss Wade, Dickens gives remarkably convincing glimpses of her difficulties. When Esther has learnt that Lady Dedlock is her mother:

> Knowing that my mere existence as a living creature was an unfore-seen danger in her way, I could not always conquer that terror of myself which had seized me when I first knew the secret. At no time did I dare to utter her name. I felt as if I did not even dare to hear it. If the conversation anywhere, when I was present, took that direction, as it sometimes naturally did, I tried not to hear it—I mentally counted, repeated something that I knew, or went out of the room. I am con-scious, now, that I often did these things when there can have been no danger of her being spoken of; but I did them in the dread I had of hearing anything that might lead to her betrayal through me.

Again, Dickens's understanding of the relation between dreams and the hidden truths of experience is shown in Esther's noting, without being able to say why, that she always dreamt of the period of her life when she lived with her aunt, and in her delirious dreams during her fever:

> Everything else seemed to have retired into a remote distance, where there was little or no separation between the various stages of my life which had really been divided by years. In falling ill, I seemed to have crossed a dark lake, and to have left all my experiences, mingled to-gether by the great distance, on the healthy shore. . . . While I was very ill, the way in which these divisions of time became confused with one another, distressed my mind exceedingly. At once a child, an elder girl, and the little woman I had been so happy as, I was not only oppressed by cares and difficulties adapted to each station, but by the great perplexity of endlessly trying to reconcile them. . . . I laboured up colossal staircases, ever striving to reach the top, and ever turned, as I have seen a worm in a garden path, by some obstruction, and labouring again . . . that worse time when, strung together somewhere in great black space, there was a flaming necklace, or ring, or starry circle of some kind, of which *I* was one of the beads! And when my only prayer was to be taken off from the rest, and when it was such an inexplicable agony and misery to be a part of the dreadful thing.

This last dream is the one that is representative of the theme of the novel, a nightmare version of what Ada and Richard had debated at the beginning of the novel when they had been inducted into the Chancery world where there is no freewill except in moral decisions. Esther can pray 'to be taken off' and not to be a 'part of the dreadful thing' but it is only by her love and sympathy that she can get off. We are in *Bleak House* well on the way to the prison world of *Little Dorrit* where each is locked into his own appointed or self-made cell, and to the still worse state of Pip in *Great Expectations* who, wholly passive, has not even moral choice until his world falls into ruins around him and he sees that he is tied hand and foot to the Newgate society by a contract he never knowingly entered into. Esther's sensibility is unique in Dickens's novels not only in being essentially feminine but in being different from the sensitiveness shown by other unhappy Dickens children, even Little Dorrit, who is a working-girl and not a lady and whose experience is limited to the society of the poor, and her possibilities of action very circumscribed. And Esther is mature, not innocent with David Copperfield's disabilities, her early experiences having given her a precocious understanding of the painfulness of life and the cruelty of circumstance which enables her to understand John Jarndyce's kind of innocent goodness and appreciate it and *yet* see that it was as to Skimpole self-indulgent and that Skimpoles need firm treatment (which she can and does provide). Yet she has womanly tact and, like the Ibsen of *The Wild Duck*, she sees that in some circumstances it is better to let well alone, in accordance with which she hopes that Caddy and Prince will never see through Mr. Turveydrop but go on believing in him happily since they will have to put up with him anyway. Esther is not sentimentalized and as a good angel is altogether more acceptable than Agnes, showing an advance on that part of the previous novel. For Dickens is also prepared to show us Esther's limitations—her shrinking from criticism of mothers (psychologically this is right, from her), as in her attempt to stop Caddy from judging her mother to have failed in her duty—Dickens is clearly on Caddy's side here—and her own effort to deny her dislike of Mrs. Woodcourt who is anxious her son should not be recognized by Esther as a suitor.

It is necessary to insist on the success Esther represents for the novelist since she is so important to the novel as the registering consciousness and has been consistently under-rated by critics; it is she through whom we apprehend the truth about Mr. Vholes who is thus brought into the mode of the book as not merely a legal shark, like Conversation Kenge and

Guppy, but a thematic presence. We might not rejoice in Esther's society ourselves but she is impressive as a similar character, Fanny Price, is in *Mansfield Park* (another link with that novel, and there is something incipiently Victorian about both Fanny herself and Jane Austen's attitude to her). Through Esther, as through Fanny, we get a just apprehension of the other performers in her world.

Esther is not the only case-history in *Bleak House*, since it seems that Dickens had the intention of showing that such a society warps its products (we are on the way to the disappearance of the Romantic image of childhood and its replacement by the sociologically realistic child produced by our Bleak House, the Dolls Dressmaker). Mr. Tulkinghorn is another masterly study in abnormality, though completely a human being—Dickens has outgrown the stage of throwing up inexplicable monsters like Fagin, Quilp, Squeers and Pecksniff. Yet Tulkinghorn, though all of a piece and thoroughly accounted for, is commonly seen as a mystery or an engine of melodrama. Actually, the only extraordinary thing about him is the contrast between his public self and his private self, that inner self which drives him; and while his innocuous public self makes him seem negligible to his employers, the revelation of his private self is terrifying to those who like Lady Dedlock stand in his way or arouse his antipathies. He lives only in his sense of power, hating Lady Dedlock for having more influence with her husband than himself, and all women for their rôle in life and that irrational nature of theirs which he can't control. He has of necessity to suppress both his pleasure in dominating and his distaste for women, when with his employers, but relieves himself when it is safe to exhibit these passions openly as in bullying and torturing poor innocent George (because he has dared to withhold his specimen of Captain Hawdon's handwriting—this chapter is called 'The Turn of the Screw' and George describes Mr. Tulkinghorn as 'a slow-torturing kind of man'), torturing Lady Dedlock with his knowledge of her past and his threats of exposing her to her husband (though this is a bluff which she should have known he would never dare to bring off since his position depended on keeping the secrets of the aristocracy—'as it were, the steward of the legal mysteries, the butler of the legal cellar, of the Dedlocks'). He cheats and coarsely abuses the French maid to the point of goading her into murdering him—if she hadn't, someone else eventually would have done, as Dickens intimates by showing the fateful Roman on the ceiling pointing eternally to Tulkinghorn's predestined end. It is only Dickens (before Dostoievski) who would comprehend that such a case as Mr. Tulkinghorn invites murder. Content to move in the world in rusty black and never conversing, he rests on his sense of power and if possible exercises it discreetly even there, as when he enjoys telling Sir Leicester that Rouncewell has beaten him in the election, and in letting Lady Dedlock know in public that he has discovered her past, with the hint: 'I leave you to imagine, Sir Leicester, the husband's grief'.

There are other family lawyers or lawyer-surrogates in Victorian novels who have some of Mr. Tulkinghorn's traits in a milder form—one thinks of, among others, Mr. Forrester the agent of Trollope's Duke of Omnium, Mathew Jermyn the family lawyer of the Transomes in *Felix Holt*, with his own knowledge of the lady's guilty past, and Disraeli's Baptist Hatton, in *Sybil*—all secretive men of power who manage their clients' affairs to their own satisfaction—but none has the dreadful consistency and desire to torture of Dickens's creation here. Dickens's characters such as Bounderby and Tulkinghorn impinge uniquely on the reader because they represent an essence, containing the essential truth about some aspect of their society without being diluted by all the inessentials that make the characters of other novelists more acceptably 'lifelike'. Thus Mrs. Gaskell's mill-owner Mr. Thornton in *North and South* (co-eval with *Hard Times*) though first presented as rebarbative is carefully composed of both good qualities and obnoxious views about his 'hands' and the manufacturing ethos; eventually he is shown reclaimed by the heroine and circumstances, and fit for her to marry. He has in fact all the attitudes and principles and most of the traits of the bad Victorian mill-owner out of which Dickens has composed his Bounderby, but Mr. Thornton's significant characteristics have been so diluted and so counter-balanced by better qualities, to achieve authorial fairness, that their real viciousness can hardly be apprehended. Dickens, by selecting the essence of the type, his unique characteristics, and then activating the character so formed in a context which brings out their significance with a startling degree of vividness, lit up by sardonic humour, achieves a more important kind of success as art and criticism of life. [From instances in Francis Place's *Life* it seems there were far more brutal masters in the earlier period.]

Turn to Mr. Vholes and one realizes the *inclusiveness* of the mode of *Bleak House*, which is followed by a triumph of *exclusive* art in *Hard*

Times, for Vholes represents a feat of creative brilliance in complexity, and in neither of the conventions that determine Esther and Tulkinghorn; he is not limited by psychological consistency or uniform presentation. He starts by being little more than a rhetorical conception to expose the true nature of the new Victorian middle-class ideal, respectability (in chapter XXXIX 'Attorney and Client'), but just previously, in Esther's first encounter with him, we get an intimation of his meaning in the general purpose of the novel:

> Dressed in black, black-gloved, and buttoned to the chin, there was nothing so remarkable in him as a lifeless manner, and a slow fixed way he had of looking at Richard . . . and now I observed that he was further remarkable for an inward manner of speaking. . . . I never shall forget those two seated side by side in the lantern's light; Richard, all flush and fire and laughter, with the reins in his hand; Mr. Vholes, quite still, black-gloved and buttoned up, looking at him as if he were looking at his prey and charming it. I have before me the whole picture of the warm dark night, the summer lightning, the dusty track of road closed in by hedgrows and high trees, the gaunt pale horse with his ears pricked up, and the driving away at speed to Jarndyce and Jarndyce.

Vholes has entangled Richard in the Jarndyce case and is to assist at his ruin; he is now come to take him back to London to watch the action in court. We hardly need the evocation of Death's pale horse to identify the nature of the black figure with his lifelessness and inward manner of speaking and gaze riveted on his prey, to identify who is driving with Richard and to where.

In the second appearance, which is in the third-person narrative, we first get an account of Vholes's chambers in Symond's Inn, remarkably like the allegorical description of Barnard's Inn later in *Great Expectations* only here sinister and not humorous in tone. All the imagery associated with Vholes is sinister – e.g. his blue bags of legal documents are 'hastily stuffed, out of all regularity of form, as the larger sorts of serpents are in their first gorged state'; he is identified with 'the official cat'; he looks at Richard 'never winking his hungry eyes'. Thus we come to Vholes himself. The name describes a rodent who undermines river-banks, the vole, but this was also used throughout the Victorian Age as a well-known term meaning 'to win all the tricks' in such card-games as écarté and other gambling-games of skill, and it would be quite like the Dickens of *Bleak House* to intend such a pun. We may compare Sir Leicester Dedlock's attributing anything democratic that comes to his notice to an outbreak of Wat Tylerism and his Wat Tylerish adversary the 'new man' Mr. Rouncewell having named his son Watt (after the inventor who launched the industrial age with steam power); this is a pun that Dickens undoubtedly intended, and I have noted others already.

Thus prepared, we approach Vholes as a representative figure in his age:

> Mr. Vholes is a very respectable man. He has not a large business, but he is a very respectable man. He is allowed by the greater attorneys who have made good fortunes, or are making them, to be a most respectable man. He never misses a chance in his practice; which is a mark of respectability. He never takes any pleasure; which is another mark of respectability. He is reserved and serious; which is another mark of respectability. His digestion is impaired, which is highly respectable. And he is making hay of the grass which is flesh, for his three daughters. And his father is dependent on him in the Vale of Taunton.

Mr. Vholes is cited by the forces of reaction, on account of his respectability, as reason for blocking all attempts at reform of the English law:

> ... Take a few more steps in this direction, say they, and what is to become of Vholes's father? Is he to perish? And of Vholes's daughters? Are they to be shirt-makers or governesses? As though, Mr. Vholes and his relations being minor cannibal chiefs, and it being proposed to abolish cannibalism, indignant champions were to put the case thus: Make man-eating unlawful, and you starve the Vholeses!

Evidently Dickens had a Shakespearean model in mind here, as so often in *Bleak House*,[1] in this case the ironic technique of Mark Antony in his

---

[1] e.g. in chapter XL, when Lady Dedlock awaits Mr. Tulkinghorn's arrival at Chesney Wold in an agony of apprehension and undecided how to deal with him. Volumnia, who pretends to be pining for him, says, 'I had almost made up my mind that he was dead'.
'Everybody starts. For a gun is fired close by.
"Good gracious, what's that?" cries Volumnia, with her little withered scream.
"A rat", says my Lady. "And they have shot him."
Enter Mr, Tulkinghorn, followed by Mercuries with lamps and candles.'
Perhaps the use of *Hamlet* and its dramatic irony is too blatant here, but it shows how Dickens's imagination was working. The intention is to forecast the murder of Tulkinghorn who will later be shot, and to put the reader on a false trail of suspecting Lady Dedlock as the murderess, for which the *Hamlet* references were unnecessary. But that it *is* a dramatic technique and one used in the play within the play

funeral oration on Caesar, the shifting implications of 'honourable man' being paralleled by the gradual undermining of the concept of 'respectable man'. Thus we learn successively that a respectable man is expected to have a large business, that a reliable testimony to respectability is that of attorneys who have made large fortunes out of the law 'or are making them'—we know how, having sat in on Chancery procedure for over half the novel—and now (coming into the open) that a mark of respectability is to be unscrupulous. This, Dickens was telling his readers, is what your ideal of respectability is worth! Then we get another glimpse of respectability as conceived by a society that is in Chancery: 'He never takes any pleasure'—to do so would be a waste of time and a reprehensible desire to enjoy oneself (hits at the Evangelical and the business outlooks, which are seen to converge here). The sense of how ridiculous all this is has for the moment replaced Dickens's indignation and contempt and the author of *Pickwick* emerges to pillory the notion that to enjoy food and conviviality should be now held to be reprehensible. The joking parody of piety follows in the finale: 'And he is making hay of the grass which is flesh, for his three daughters'. The last thrust and its repetitions in the following paragraphs of the rhetoric are like the irony of Mathew Arnold in *Culture and Anarchy* and have a similar target—Puritanism and middle-class morality in the Victorian Age. The argument about the nature of English institutions in general is developed with wit as well as high spirits from the fact that Mr. Vholes is too respectable to be sacrificed—'As though, Mr. Vholes and his relations being minor cannibal chiefs, and it being proposed to abolish cannibalism, indignant champions were to put the case thus: Make man-eating unlawful, and you starve the Vholeses!' In fact, the Vholeses *do* live by man-eating and the joke reminds us of the actuality.

So that we then see Mr. Vholes in his personally sinister aspect again:

> Mr. Vholes, quiet and unmoved, as a man of so much respectability ought to be, takes off his close black gloves as if he were skinning his hands, lifts off his tight black hat as if he were scalping himself, and sits down at his desk . . . and proceeds in his buttoned-up half-audible voice, as if there were an unclean spirit in him that will neither come out nor speak out.

in *Hamlet* has brought in the imitation of and reference to the close of that with the call for lights, and the identification of the inquisitive solicitor with the rat in the arras, who was Polonius and, as Lady Dedlock is evidently thinking, was killed for his curiosity and meddling, as she at least wishes Tulkinghorn may be.

–where the sinister implications of their being nothing under the gloves but a skeletal hand and nothing under the hat but a skull is capped by the concluding suggestion that this corpse is animated by an evil spirit. Urging Richard then to put his trust in Vholes's zeal for his cause, he says: ' "This desk is your rock, sir!" Mr. Vholes gives it a rap, and it sounds as hollow as a coffin.'

The final impression of Vholes comes from Esther and has therefore her peculiar perceptiveness:

> I happened to turn my eyes towards the house, and I saw a long thin shadow going in which looked like Mr. Vholes. . . . Mr. Vholes who had looked at me while speaking, here emerged into the silence he could hardly be said to have broken, so stifled was his tone . . . gauntly stalked to the fire, and warmed his funeral gloves. . . . Mr. Vholes put his dead glove, which scarcely seemed to have any hand in it, on my fingers, and took his long thin shadow away. I thought of it on the outside of the coach, passing over all the sunny landscape between us and London, chilling the seed in the ground as it glided along.

Thus Vholes, by the sensitive Esther, is perceived to be nothing but his shadow–a shadow without a man–an 'it', no hand in the glove, no voice to break the silence; we don't need to speculate what Esther feels the shadow is of as she imagines it, in that blood-curdling image, 'chilling the seed in the ground' wherever it passed between Jarndyce's Bleak House and that other Bleak House made by Chancery. The macabre effect of Mr. Vholes is free from any touch of the theatrical or the melo-dramatic in its creation in simple and unrhetorical words; he weaves in and out of the other characters' lives, fixing on Richard as his prey whom no one–wife or friend–can save, intimating that life in the Chancery world is a Dance of Death. In any novel before *Copperfield* Dickens would have presented Vholes in a Hogarthian satiric mode, but there is nothing of the eighteenth-century satiric or of Hogarth's moral commentary on his age in these images.

Bleak House thus has an extraordinary imaginative richness which is not just a matter of length or of showing a complete social world from the pinnacle of fashion to the London slum and from the High Court of Chancery to Chesney Wold. Its greatness lies in its genuine complexity, variety that is fully controlled in the interest of a deeply-felt theme without thereby being impoverished as *Our Mutual Friend* may be felt to have been. And yet the path Dickens followed from *Dombey* to *Hard Times* and *Little Dorrit* passes, as I've shown, through *David Copperfield* and

Bleak House necessarily, and without these two experiments he would not have got there. There is a more profound and sober understanding in *Bleak House* than in any previous Dickens novel of the nature of living and the interaction of members of a society, though I can't agree that the chain of cause and effect that brings Lady Dedlock to her death in the clothes of the brickmaker's wife at the threshhold of the paupers' burial-ground is convincing: it is, however, felt to be *right* in the context of the novel, which is perhaps sufficient–reason may baulk at it afterwards but the whole mode of the novel undercuts a merely rational reading. Is it made sufficiently clear that Lady Dedlock is being punished not for a 'guilty' past but for being the pinnacle of an irresponsible society? I think so, for no one in the novel except the contemptible characters or the unco' guid has anything but compassion towards her and Captain Hawdon, and her relation with him is shown as the only real life she had had. Two genuine lovers were doomed to misery and disgrace, a tragedy forecasting Ada and Richard's. Quite unambiguous and a more subtle moral point is that Esther has to lose her looks for her charity and humanity in taking in Jo and nursing Charley–good intentions are irrelevant if one is part of a society based on injustice and irresponsibility, making the point that society is one and indivisible as regards infectious diseases at least. Carlyle had pointed this out by declaring in *Past and Present* that in the *laissez-faire* state there was one sole link between high and low: typhus fever. Kingsley two years earlier in *Alton Locke* had found a novelistic form for Carlyle's idea by showing in his terrible account of the tailors' sweat-shops how typhus and other diseases due to the disgusting conditions in which the tailors worked and lived were transmitted to the well-to-do via the clothes made for them there, and no doubt Dickens adapted this for his own purpose in *Bleak House*. It is impossible to read nineteenth-century novels in bulk without coming to the conclusion, I find, that the Victorian novelists read and used each other's work quite as freely as Elizabethan and Jacobean dramatists did theirs. This was more or less recognized, the Early Victorian novelists being inevitably the main source of ideas and techniques. Thus Dickens wrote resignedly in a letter in 1852 about *Uncle Tom's Cabin*: 'She (I mean Mrs. Stowe) is a leetle unscrupulous in the appropriatin' way. I seem to see a writer with whom I am very intimate (and whom nobody can possibly admire more than myself) peeping very often through the thinness of the paper. Further I descry the ghost of Mary Barton, and the very palpable mirage of a scene in The Children of the Mist; but in spite of this, I consider the book a fine one.' We may also remember Thack-eray's feeling – of satisfaction, not resentment – that he thought Dickens with *David Copperfield* had improved by turning to domestic life and the history of a young man's difficulties and progress, by taking a leaf out of his book (*Pendennis*, 1848–1850). I have argued in my introductory essay to *Miss Marjoribanks* by Mrs. Oliphant (Chatto & Windus) that George Eliot was indebted to it for the new tone and attitude to her heroine of *Middlemarch*, while Mrs. Oliphant had herself evidently arrived at the idea of her 'Chronicles of Carlingford' series, of which *Miss Marjoribanks* formed part, by the success in the previous decade that novelists had had with Cranford, Barchester and Milby (the scene of the last of George Eliot's 'Scenes from Clerical Life'). The complicated inter-relatedness of *Oliver Twist*, *Jane Eyre* and *Copperfield* I have already illustrated. A great deal of the Victorian novelists' achievement is due to such cross-fertiliza-tion, illustrated still more by Henry James's debt to them for themes, characters, settings, ideas, symbols and imagery – above all those of Dickens and George Eliot.

iv

I would like to illustrate what I meant by saying that there is a new Dickens mode in *Bleak House* over and above the numerous points of growth that I have pointed to in *David Copperfield* which are seen developed here. There is this extraordinary combination of the painfully serious that tends towards the macabre even, which yet consorts with a high-spirited, witty and sometimes humorous apprehension of life with-out discordance, and runs to a finer awareness of the quality of personality and human relations – I think of Dickens's writing of the trooper George: 'from his superfluity of life and strength seeming to shed down tem-porary vigour upon' the dying Jo, or of the Bleak House of the poor's existence in the country as seen in this bird's eye view:

> On the waste, where the brick-kilns are burning with a pale blue flare; where the straw-roofs of the wretched huts in which the bricks are made, are being scattered to the wind; where the clay and water are hard frozen, and the mill in which the gaunt blind horse goes round all day, look like an instrument of torture. . . .

and which yet exist without incongruity in the same novel as this grimly funny account of a Victorian funeral (Mr. Tulkinghorn's), recording a ridiculous ritual of the age; too high-spirited for a Hogarth or a Gillray satire, it is characteristically Dickensian in tone:

> . . . strictly speaking, there are only three other human followers, but the amount of inconsolable carriages is immense. The peerage contributes more four-wheeled affliction than has ever been seen in that neighbourhood. Such is the assemblage of armorial bearings on coach panels, that the Heralds' College might be supposed to have lost its father and mother at a blow. The Duke of Foodle sends a splendid pile of dust and ashes, with silver wheel-boxes, patent axles, all the last improvements, and three bereaved worms, six feet high, holding on behind, in a bunch of woe. All the state coachmen in London seem plunged into mourning; and if that dead old man of the rusty garb . . .

The absurdity of the parade of mourning without any real mourners is not only a macabre joke, it is presented as another instance of the Chancery way of life. Thus Dickens is also able to let us savour the humours relevant to Sir Leicester–who 'repeats in a killing voice: "The young man of the name of Guppy?" ' or (a hit at a Victorian characteristic) is 'not so much shocked by the fact, as the fact of the fact being mentioned', those brought out by the colloquies between Sir Leicester and Mr. Bucket with his new classless familiarity which is without deference but is willing to humour: 'If there's a blow to be inflicted on you, you naturally think of your family. You ask yourself, how would all them ancestors of yours, away to Julius Caesar–not to go beyond him at the present–have borne that blow?' and the debilitated cousin's 'Haven't a doubt–zample–far better hang wrong fler than no fler'. The presentation of Mrs. Pardiggle is of the same order, with her voice that impressed Esther's fancy 'as if it had a sort of spectacles on too', who 'pulled out a good book as if it were a constable's staff, and took the whole family into custody' but who is still less of a joke, for it is clear that it is she and her kind who erected the 'iron barrier' which Esther was 'painfully sensible' existed 'between us and those people' (the brickmakers whose homes Mrs. Pardiggle is shown invading).

Mr. Guppy has only to be compared to Dickens's earlier examples of the Cockney-clerk model, such as Dick Swiveller, to see that he is at least as entertaining but also a great deal more than a joke; he is further illustration of the theme of the novel, and the amusing and the serious aspects of him are quite inseparable, from his first introducing himself into Chesney Wold (when it is not open to the public) in that idiom Dickens handles so expertly: 'Us London lawyers don't often get an out', and his forcing himself on Lady Dedlock to prise her secrets out of her to assist him in marrying Esther, in order to advance himself in the world, throughout his proposals and retractions of his proposal to Esther in his characteristic mixture of legal jargon and romantic clichés. Dickens is a master of the use of the clichés of Romanticism (and unlike Mark Twain he sees that they represent something more than an absurdity). The Romantic and its idiom had indeed fallen on evil days and into vulgar minds by mid-Victorian times. Mostly a blend of the tricks and sentimentality of Byron at his worst, Tom Moore and Victorian drawing-room ballads, the language of feeling and sentiment is used to amuse by Dickens with a full appreciation of its ludicrous inappropriateness to his Dick Swivellers, Young John Chiveries, Mr. Moddles and so forth of lowish life, and to sentimental young ladies like Julia Mills. But in William Guppy's use it sharpens a satire: the sentimental idiom and professions never for a moment prevent Mr. Guppy from putting his business interests first. The lifelessness and artificiality of this jargon bring out the remoteness of such sentiments from anything Guppy really feels and is actuated by; the fact of such a meaningless idiom being in use to express alleged feeling is proof that such a society has no real feelings to express of this kind, but that it has a desire to lay claim to a language of the heart, because it is somehow aware that self-interest is not enough, an unconscious recognition of a fact on which Dickens's optimism is based. Only a Bitzer, constructed by the novelist for the purpose of showing the impossibility of a human machine actuated solely by self-interest, can exist without the idealism and feelings that make us human, and Mr. Guppy is far from being a Bitzer. The human complexity is registered in his 'going with one leg and staying with the other' when he is torn between what his decent instincts tell him is mean behaviour to Esther and what his self-interest tells him is expedient, when in spite of his 'witness-box face' he can't help showing he is ashamed, and is therefore a pitiable human being; his discomfort is heightened when he discovers that Esther has in fact come to let him off, making a scene essentially humorous but not simply comic. Setting off the absurdity of his sentimental idiom is the fact that his genuine affection for his very trying mother is always expressed in restrained exasperation – the Guppys are a great advance on the Heep mother and son. Thus though Mr. Guppy is an agent of Chancery and so trained that sharp practice is second nature to him (he is the precursor of Mr. Jaggers in carrying over to private life the habit of cross-examination as a form of conversation) he has another nature too, the first nature of all human beings (Dickens thinks), if only it were given a chance. A pathetic example of this need for an idealism, the consciousness that something is needed outside Chancery practice to make life worth living, is shown in Guppy's and his friends' passion for connoisseuring fashionable British Beauty and covering their walls with the Galaxy Gallery collection of engravings of it; even the Bitzer-like Bart Smallweed has *his* ideal and models himself on Guppy, in spite of his grandfather's admonitions.

But the best way of illustrating the variety of *Bleak House* and its progress towards a finer art is by juxtaposing the old and the new prose techniques which exist in it side by side, as here:

> Into a beastly scrap of ground which a Turk would reject as a savage abomination, and a Caffre would shudder at, they bring our dear brother here departed, to receive Christian burial.
>
> With houses looking on, on every side, save where a reeking little tunnel of a court gives access to the iron gate – with every villainy of life in action close on death, and every poisonous element of death in action close on life – here, they lower our dear brother down a foot or two: here, sow him in corruption, to be raised in corruption: an avenging ghost at many a sick bedside: a shameful testimony to future ages, how civilization and barbarism walked this boastful island together.
>
> Come night, come darkness, for you cannot come too soon, or stay too long, by such a place as this! Come straggling lights into the windows of the ugly houses; and you who do iniquity therein, do it at least with this dread scene shut out! Come, flame of gas, burning so sullenly above the iron gate, on which the poisoned air deposits its witch-ointment slimy to the touch! It is well that you should call to every passer-by, 'Look here!'

> 'He was put there,' says Jo, holding to the bars and looking in.
> 'Where? O, what a scene of horrors!'
> 'There!' says Jo, pointing. 'Over yinder. Among them piles of bones, and close to that there kitchen winder! They put him wery nigh the top. They was obliged to stamp upon it to git it in. I could unkiver it for you with my broom, if the gate was open. That's why they locks it, I s'pose,' giving it a shake. 'It's always locked. Look at the rat!' cries Jo, excited. 'Hi! Look! There he goes! Ho! Into the ground.'
> The servant sinks into a corner – into a corner of that hideous archway, with its deadly stains contaminating her dress; and putting out her two hands, and passionately telling him to keep away from

her, for he is loathsome to her, so remains for some moments. Jo stands
staring, and is still staring when she recovers herself.
    'Is this place of abomination, consecrated ground?'
    'I don't know nothink of consequential ground,' says Jo, still staring.
    'Is it blessed?'
    'WHICH?' says Jo, in the last degree amazed.
    'Is it blessed?'
    'I'm blest if I know,' says Jo, staring more than ever; 'but I shouldn't
think it warn't. Blest?' repeats Jo, something troubled in his mind.
'It an't done it much good if it is. Blest? I should think it was t'othered
myself. But I don't know nothink!'

It will be seen at once that the dialogue between the disguised Lady Dedlock and Jo at the gate of the public burial-ground for paupers makes the
laboured irony of the previous description of the funeral unnecessary,
since the dialogue effects, by purely novelistic means without intrusive
authorial comment, what the rhetorical passage tries to do, but does it
much more effectively and economically (besides avoiding an adverse
reaction from any who may object to being preached at–though it is
true that the Victorians were avid listeners to and purchasers of sermons).
Dickens in the course of writing this novel must have come to realize
that it is more satisfactory for the novelist to act out rather than to tell,
however long he may have held this view in theory, as we know he did.
As we can see from the second of my extracts, Dickens could perfectly
well dissolve what he wanted to communicate into dialogue and action
without any 'telling', but he seems unable to trust to that alone, or else,
as in the first of my extracts, he cannot control altogether his indignation
at some monstrous feature of the life of his time. We may hazard that the
reason for the form the first extract takes is the unfortunate influence of
Carlyle's excitable prose on him (as can be seen even more clearly in *Tale
of Two Cities*, where the inspiration is Carlyle's *History of the French
Revolution* and the only interest the novel has is Dickens's case-history
of Dr. Manette); Carlyle's ideas irresistibly led to Dickens's employing
his tricks of prose rhetoric too. The sad thing is that Dickens without
Carlyle, free to create from his own powerful and much more sensitive
and lively imagination, is so much better a writer. There is nothing so
telling in the earlier passage as the horror achieved by the casual statement: 'They was obliged to stamp on it to git it in. I could unkiver it for
you with my broom, if the gate was open.' It is Jo's taking such things
for granted–the rat is the only feature of the case that interests him, but

not even the rat is shocking to him – that make the horrors really sickening, and this is finally intensified by our realization that the impact of the situation is not only on us but on Lady Dedlock, who is bound to the dead man – 'it' – by her former passionate love and by having borne his child, and has proved her abiding concern for him by having had Jo show her all the places connected with his last days, of which this burial-ground is the climax. We note the sense of its all happening in our presence by its being written in the present tense and by Jo's 'giving it [the gate] a shake', and his staring at her unable to understand why she is upset at what is, for him, an everyday matter of course. Even the dreadful irony secured in the first extract by deploying the phrases from the Christian burial-service and showing that they here have a literal truth, is surpassed by the irony in the dialogue that questions its being consecrated ground. The characteristic use in this novel of the Dickensian pun that I have noted is here seen in the play on 'blessed': 'Is it blessed?' 'I'm blest if I know' which underlines Jo's unblessed state and takes us without a jolt into the bitter humour of 'It an't done it much good if it is. Blest? I should think it t'othered myself.' There is no need for Dickens here to accuse his readers explicitly of tolerating a society which throws the bodies of the poor into such a mockery of consecrated ground and has no more sense of responsibility than to bury corpses under kitchen windows, and we have here intimated the additional irony of a so-called Christian country allowing the children of the poor to be brought up in Jo's condition of spiritual darkness.

The interest of the first extract is the way it moves in and out of automatic writing, tending towards blank verse[1] (Dickens's greatest weakness and always associated with his vague reaching for what Shakespeare would have done in his place). Thus we get:

> Come night, come darkness, for you cannot come too soon
> Or stay too long, by such a place as this! . . .
> And you who do iniquity therein,
> Do it at least with this dread scene shut out!
> Come flame of gas. . . .

and at this point Dickens ceases to write blank verse but instead becomes Shakespearean in a real sense because the gas-jet recalls him to an actual

---

[1] 'If in going over the parts you find the tendency to blank verse (I *cannot* help it, when I am very much in earnest) too strong, knock out a word's brains here and there' – *Letters*, Nov. 13th 1846.

scene where he must have remembered it 'burning so sullenly' because of the 'poisoned air', and that the metal of the gate felt slimy from the horrible deposits–fumes from the decaying bodies and therefore 'witch-ointment' since it was with human grease and extracts from corpses that witches made their ointments. And he sees that the arresting light is a signal to every passer-by to stop and witness this outrage, thus *calling* 'Look here!'. The real poetry in Dickens's prose is always in some detail of a concrete experience which has lodged in and therefore touched off his imagination.

And *Bleak House* is full of this poetry. Braque said that the quality he valued above all else in art was what he called '*poésie*', a mysterious quality which an artist achieves 'when he transcends his talent and exceeds himself' and which each artist 'can discover for himself only through his intuitions'. It is in *Bleak House*, as in *Dombey and Son*, that we see Dickens taking a great leap forward and consistently transcending his talent, to use Braque's fine phrase. In *Bleak House* we are constantly being surprised by signs of this. Krook is described like someone in a Wordsworth poem: 'His throat, chin and eyebrows were so frosted with white hairs, so gnarled with veins and puckered skin, that he looked from his breast upwards like some old root in a fall of snow'. Esther watches Charley from Bell Yard run back to her work 'and melt into the city's strife and sound, like a dewdrop in an ocean'. One could make an anthology. But I would dwell most on the extraordinary feat of showing with such variety and imaginative power Skimpole's attitudes to everything and every one as wholly aesthetic, without being monotonous or predictable. I have already quoted him on the orphans (on both Jo and 'the little Coavinses') and on his logical refusal to feel he should feel gratitude. Dickens doesn't take the easy line of making Skimpole stupid or gross–no, he is surprisingly intelligent, if to be merely quick, clever, observant and witty is; it's only feeling that he lacks, though feeling for the Arts and Nature is his stock-in-trade (what he would call sensibility). Of his opposite and adversary Boythorn, the man of principles: ' "Nature forgot to shade him off a little, I think?" observed Mr. Skimpole. "A little too boisterous, like the sea? A little too vehement–like a bull, who has made up his mind to consider every colour scarlet? But I grant a sledge-hammering sort of merit in him!" ' And on the angry Man from Shropshire:

He said, Well, it was really very pleasant to see how things lazily adapted themselves to purposes. Here was this Mr. Gridley, a man of robust will, and surprising energy–intellectually speaking, a sort of inharmonious blacksmith–and he could easily imagine that there Gridley was, years ago, wandering about in life for something to expend his superfluous combativeness upon–a sort of Young Love among the thorns–when the Court of Chancery came in his way, and accommodated him with the exact thing he wanted. There they were, matched, ever afterwards! Otherwise he might have been a great general, blowing up all sorts of towns, or he might have been a great politician, dealing in all sorts of parliamentary rhetoric; but, as it was, he and the Court of Chancery had fallen upon each other in the pleasantest way, and nobody was much the worse, and Gridley was, so to speak, from that hour provided for.

On Jo:

'It seems to me that it would be wiser, as well as in a certain kind of way more respectable, if he showed some misdirected energy that got him into prison. There would be more of an adventurous spirit in it, and consequently more of a certain sort of poetry. I don't see why our young friend, in his degree, should not seek to invest himself with such poetry as is open to him . . . and I don't know but what I should be more interested in our young friend, as an illustration of such a case, than merely as a poor vagabond–which anyone can be.'

What Dickens succeeds in demonstrating is the inhumanity of the aesthetic attitude to life, though Skimpole is allowed all the playfulness, paradoxes and fancifulness that disguise this. Skimpole's callousness and dialectic are more remarkable than the looking-glass logic of Mr. and Mrs. Micawber, even. For diverting as Skimpole is, Dickens makes us recognize each time that Skimpole lacks something–that the aesthete's selfishness is more than the ordinary self-centred man's, it is a systematic refusal to be involved as a human being, except sentimentally which commits him to nothing and is therefore self-indulgent. Skimpole is really one of Dickens's monsters and quite the finest–what is Pecksniff's hypocrisy or Quilp's malice in comparison, for they are coarse and re-petitive whereas Skimpole has inexhaustible resources of sophistry? He is the link between Disraeli's dandies and the *fin-de-siècle* aesthetes, and I have often wondered whether Oscar Wilde plagiarized him.

Clough, one of the most intelligent contemporary critics of Vic-torianism, reviewing 'Recent English Poetry', which included Arnold's first two volumes, complained that whereas such poetry might be claimed to have 'great literary value' it was merely academic so that poetry had ceased to matter as a force in the life of his time. Why, he asked, did people prefer *Bleak House*, as they plainly did, he said: 'Is it, that to be widely popular, to gain the ear of multitudes, to shake the hearts of men, poetry should deal more than at present it usually does, with general wants, ordinary feelings, the obvious rather than the rare facts of human nature?' The novelist, Clough argues, deals now with 'the actual, palpable things with which our everyday life is concerned' and to emulate the novelist poetry 'must be in all points tempted as we are; exclude nothing, least of all guilt and distress, from its wide fraternization'. 'The modern novel', he says, giving as examples *Bleak House* and *Vanity Fair*, 'is preferred to the modern poem, because we do here feel an attempt to include these phenomena which, if we forget on Sunday, we must remember on Monday. . . . The novelist does try to build us a real house to live in; and this common builder, with no notion of orders, is more to our purpose than the student of ancient art who proposes to lodge us under an Ionic portico.' 'The true and lawful haunts of the poetic powers', he says, are 'no more upon Pindus or Parnassus' but 'in the blank and desolate streets, and upon the solitary bridges of the midnight city, where Guilt is, and wild Temptation, and the dire compulsion of what has once been done . . . there walks the discrowned Apollo, with unstrung lyre'.

That it is *Bleak House* and Dickens that Clough has in mind is clear from the last sentence. Clough shows himself, like Dickens, refusing to be a Skimpole in his refusal to accept the rôle of Romantic poet in the new conditions of man's life in his age and in insisting that the poet, as the novelist has chosen to do, must live in the everyday world and not only 'include these phenomena' but see his function as bringing order into it and meaning. And it is very much to Clough's credit, 'himself a poet' and the friend of Mathew Arnold, that he was able to see that the true and best Victorian poetry was written by the novelist, that is, that the novel had in his time superseded the poem as the vehicle of art-speech. In this review Clough was also strongly rebutting Arnold's Classicaldon's prescription for modern poetry, as described in Arnold's preface to his *Poems* of 1853; Arnold himself never realized that the predominance of the novelist was now a fact, and smugly assigned *Little Dorrit* (and by implication all of Dickens) to the Temple of Philistia.

It has been my object to show that *Bleak House* disproves both Lewes's complaint, that 'Dickens's sensations never pass into ideas' and a modern reaction against those Dickens appreciators who have confined themselves to pointing out that Dickens worked through ideas and symbols, a reaction seen in Mr. Garis's charge that Dickens's ideas are executed in

DICKENS

clumsy melodrama or are crudely theatrical performances either mainly or fatally. While the mature Dickens, from *Dombey* onwards that is, investigates and constates the life of his time through an intelligent apprehension of its social, moral and psychological nature, it is strictly as a novelist, not a philosopher, not a didactic moralist; nor as a mere performer (entertainer even) – to be which implies some degree of deception. Nor, though Dickens's best novels are schematic, a novelist of the kind academics like to discuss diagrammatically; the systematic world of Thomas Mann's novels, for instance, is peopled by characters who have minimal characterization of expression, gesture, mode of feeling and apprehension, who talk and argue but hardly ever act, boring shadows–compared to these Dickens's characters enjoy a rich life of idiom and emotion though still, as in Mann's novels, each plays a part in a complex whole and stands in relation to a total theme. Moreover each mature Dickens novel is a unique whole and it is an error to suppose –as is sometimes alleged–that any character from one of those could have appeared in a different novel from the one in which it functions– for one thing, the stylization differs, and each novel has its own *timbre*. No one well read in the non-fictional as well as the fictional literature of the early and mid-nineteenth century can question the truth of Dickens's understanding of the nature of the age he lived in, particularly in its tendency to produce children and adults of an exceptional kind and in the extraordinary psychological traits, due to its special pressures, they present. Mayhew's *London Labour and the London Poor* (published in 1851 with a final volume in 1862) confirms many of Dickens's insights,[1] but a more interesting kind of confirmation is to be found in the biographies of the later nineteenth century, the lives of the children of those formed by the earlier Dickens phase; these confirm the remarkable insight into the deeper truths of life that Dickens, like Lawrence, saw as the material of the novelist.

Through the various children such as Esther Summerson Dickens was working towards Arthur Clennam who really includes the earlier ones (he would even have married a Dora if both their parents had not intervened–and his realization that if he had been able to fulfil his youthful romantic dream he would have made a great mistake which the apparent cruelty of the parents had prevented, shows that Dickens no longer sees parents as simply the cause of their children's frustrations). Arthur's childhood is shown only retrospectively since it is on the adult thus produced,

[1]*V.* Appendix B: 'Mayhew and Dickens'.

176

and his problems as an adult, that the mature novelist focuses now – we have seen that this was true of Esther too. Arthur had been ham-strung by his parents' marital hostility, by the pressures of his (step-)mother's Calvinism and by her not unrelated self-righteousness in forcing him against his inclinations into the family business of money-dealing – when he, now a man of forty, nerves himself after his father's death to tell her he wishes to leave the firm she solemnly curses him. Having been treated always as a child naturally prone to evil who must be kept in the right path, he has no will-power, no capacity for happiness, and no belief in himself. That this combination and his circumstances were widely representative of the deep-seated ills of Dickens's culture is of course why Arthur Clennam was chosen as the hero of the novel. There are Little Dorrits in Mayhew and such, their actuality is easily proved, but for Arthur Clennams we have better sources than social historians.

For instance, Matthew Smith the well-known painter showed a comparable case-history (one among many such). He was born in industrial Yorkshire in 1879 – I take the facts from the Biographical Note supplied by his friends to the volume of reproductions, published by Allen & Unwin. 'His childhood and boyhood', it tells us, were dominated by the personality of his father, who was a man of great force of character and hard-headed business vision. A strict Noncomformist, who went to chapel twice every Sunday and also taught in Sunday School, Frederick Smith was a cultured example of the successful industrialist of his day, but 'he had no sympathy with Matthew's growing awareness of his vocation as a painter. Frederic Smith ruled his family, as he ruled his business, absolutely. . . . Matthew was haunted as a boy and as a youth by the fear of his father's displeasure.' Taken from school and put into the family works in Manchester, Matthew was 'a complete failure' and his health suffered seriously, yet his father would not consider letting him become an artist because the proper way of life was to be a business man and the arts, besides being a leisure activity rightly, were in the case of painting dubiously moral since the nudity of models was involved. The father's significance is that he was widely representative, and so was the psychological strain on his family. Matthew was twenty-one before he could make his wishes known effectively: 'Such was his frustration and despair that at last he nerved himself to stand up to his father, choosing the solemn occasion of Sunday tea. The family sat silent, heads bowed, while Matthew and his father fought it out.' In the end, Matthew won (by threatening to leave home) and was allowed to attend the Manchester

School of Art, 'but applied design, not painting, was to be his main subject, and his father gave instructions that his son was on no account to be allowed near any class-room where women were posing in a state of undress'. The combination Dickens had diagnosed, and represents in Mrs. Clennam as typical, are all represented here (except for her sexual jealousy as a wronged wife – her marriage was never consummated since Arthur's mother, a professional singer, had been her husband's choice until his uncle forced him into a loveless marriage). Frederic Smith exhibits the self-righteousness, the inflexible prejudices of Noncomformity, the Puritan acquisitiveness and materialism, fear of pleasure and of the sensuous (Mrs. Clennam's 'those accursed snares of Satan, the arts'), the belief in the absolute right of the parent to decide the lives of the children, even when adult, the painful effects of the domineering over the whole family, and the control of economic power to secure this[1] – though Matthew was allowed for the next four years to attend art school and afterwards one in London even, 'he had little or no pocket-money and was kept strictly under his father's control'.

The inevitable consequences were to turn him into an Arthur Clennam, as Dickens had foreseen: his health troubles developed into breakdowns, he had no self-confidence even when he at last got abroad to Brittany which enchanted him (his father, when the doctor sent him abroad for his health, stipulated he should not go to wicked Paris; this was in his thirtieth year). It is surprising that he was able to marry at thirty-three, two years before his father's death which at last gave him financial freedom though never freedom from the despair, and 'nervous and emotional strains', from which he continued to suffer even when, at forty-four, he found the voluptuous model who enabled him to produce his characteristic nudes and vivid sensual paintings of flowers and fruit, paintings flooded with rich colour and painted with the vigour of a young man. Though he was now free as an artist he never overcame the sense of isolation and self-distrust caused by his family history, and he could never settle into family life.

The difficulty of being an artist of any kind in such a culture is manifest,

[1]Arnold Bennett, born and bred in the industrial Non-conformist Victorian society, constantly makes the situation described here the centre of his better novels and tales about his native Five Towns. In his most ambitious work, *Clayhanger*, the father, an uncultivated version of a Frederic Smith, is shown in impressive detail forcing his son, who wished to be an artist and architect, into the family works and economic dependence, thus turning him into an Arthur Clennam – frustrated, depressed and celibate till a marriage late in life.

and perhaps Dickens's increasing appreciation of his father owed a good deal to the son's realization that he had been spared the respectable middle-class upbringing and conventional schooling of the time which were, as he shows in many of his novels he believed them to be, the enemy of the creative spirit. The tension in the family of Matthew Smith I've cited is feelingly presented by Dickens in the remembered childhood of chapter III of *Little Dorrit*, called 'Home' to make the point clear, and in Mrs. Clennam's account in her apologia at the end of the novel of her own life and her reasons for her persecution of the Dorrits (she had caused their rotting away in a long imprisonment for debt by withholding a legacy due to Frederick Dorrit, a patron of the arts – if the fact is not very plausible the motivation is and essential to Dickens's case, and we can now see that it was symbolically right). Yet Dickens was himself spared these psychological conditions of Victorian family life, and to create them so successfully, having diagnosed and comprehended their causes, re-presents a very considerable feat. One understands why Dickens filled his own children's lives with acting, jokes, dancing, singing, parties, travel, seaside spells, and all kinds of happy nonsense (Edmund Wilson of course finds a sinister explanation for such things), and why he liked to describe scenes of joviality as well as to show the horrors of such family life as that of the Clennams, the Wilfers, the Snagsbys, the Grad-grinds and the Murdstones, among others such as Esther's childhood home.

APPENDIX A

The Symbolic Function of the Doctor in Victorian Novels

Victorian novelists of the unoriginating kind go on using the doctor as physician in his traditional aspect of either wise family friend or humor-ously as a self-important old humbug, but in either case his chief asset is the bedside manner – as it inevitably was, of course, before medical science had been developed on modern lines. Encouraging the patient and his family to pin their faith on him and Nature's healing power was prob-ably most of what the doctor could do without harm, outside elementary surgery. Just as a science of nursing and hospital management resulted from the Crimean War so the necessity for sanitary reforms and public health services resulted in England from the epidemics produced by crowded cities and the new industrial slums, and from the advent of cholera. The doctor had thus to be thought of as filling quite a new rôle, a modern figure concerned not for private practice among the well-to-do but for public health and the scientific advancement of medicine, a figure as disinterested as the cleric and visibly more important in the new social conditions. Thus he became an evident symbol and available as such to the novelist as a central character instead of a stock background-filler.[1]

Dickens in *Bleak House* (1852) is early in the field in using the doctor in this way. I have pointed out Allan Woodcourt's part in the novel's theme, Dickens's use of the surgeon who cites naval officer and academic scientist to state his professional theory, and that the aesthete is there re-presented as a renegade doctor–all interesting ideas for that date, and particularly in that the grounds for optimism of the novel consist in the marriage of the doctor, now become a public health official, to Esther Summerson[2]–love and charity wedded to disinterested service and scientific knowledge. But it is Kingsley, generally in the lead as to ideas, however wildly and patchily he developed them in his novels, who in *Two Years Ago* (1857) produced the doctor as hero and as the genuinely modern figure required for the rôle–'two years ago' being when the cholera epidemic hit England. Tom Thurnall, son of a doctor and with a vocation for medical practice as well as a generally scientific bent, has also a strong social conscience, though tough-minded and a rolling stone. Wrecked on the Cornish coast, he stays on in the fishing village mainly in order to see it through the cholera which he knows is on the way. He fights disease in the same spirit as earlier heroes fought sin and the pursuit of science is his religion, he being a sceptic as regards Christianity. Rather surprisingly he cuts a better figure than the good young High Church curate who is simply ineffective in spite of his idealism and good-will, having antagonized the fishermen as a gentleman and, they believe, a crypto-Papist, while the widely-experienced doctor is shown tactfully managing them, and the reactionary, the vicious and the foolish, fighting vested interests, winning respect all round and completely indifferent to

[1]He is still useful as such in similar conditions of political and social disorder in our own age, witness Camus's heroic doctor, the protagonist in *La Peste*, and Pasternak's doctor-poet in *Dr. Zhivago*, who endures and is martyred in the course of the Russian revolution.

[2]The suggestive surname is explained in the tribute paid Esther by Ada and Jarndyce: 'They said that wherever Dame Durden went, there was sunshine and summer air'.

class considerations, as well as physically courageous. Kingsley has put much more into him than Dickens has into Allan Woodcourt, and the great speech Tom is given to explain to the curate his obsessive sense of vocation is really convincing:

> 'I do it because I like it. It's a sort of sporting with your true doctor. He blazes away at a disease where he sees one, as he would at a bear or a lion; the very sight of it excites his organ of destructiveness. Don't you understand me? You hate sin, you know. Well, I hate disease. Moral evil is your devil, and physical evil is mine. I hate it, little or big; I hate to see a fellow sick; I hate to see a child rickety and pale; I hate to see a speck of dirt in the street; I hate to see a woman's gown torn; I hate to see her stockings down at heel; I hate to see anything wasted, anything awry, anything going wrong; I hate to see water-power wasted, manure wasted, land wasted, muscle wasted, pluck wasted, brains wasted; I hate neglect, incapacity, idleness, ignorance, and all the disease and misery which spring out of that. There's my devil; and I can't help, for the life of me, going right at his throat, wheresoever I meet him!'

Kingsley's novel, like its predecessor *Bleak House*, is deliberately schematic and the doctor is in the centre of a system of representative characters – an aristocratic landlord and an objectionable squire; the curate for whom the villagers have no use till the cholera epidemic shows his moral stamina and he finds his function; a Romantic poet who 'had been apprenticed to Tom's father but had run away from medicine to literature', and comes to a bad end generally as, like Skimpole, an aesthete, one who 'had also (and prided himself too, on having) all Goethe's dislike of anything terrible or horrible, of sickness, disease, wounds, death, anything which jarred with that "beautiful" which was his idol'; and a contrasting character who is the true artist. A painter who, seeing that the invention of photography is a science that must have sooner or later an impact on art, he has given up painting when the novel starts in order to experiment with the camera for a spell to find out what it can do as well as or better than the painter and what it can't do, so that he can rethink the question of the function of the artist in a new scientific age – whereas the Romantic poet had rejected Tom's suggestion that the poets ought to 'take to the microscope' and write poems about the new realities thus made manifest. The heroine is a Methodistical Cornish girl called Grace who thus symbolically provides Tom with the faith he has rejected hitherto since he ultimately marries her, as his only salvation, after a long resistance, for she is a village girl, though beautiful, saintly and gifted–this shows a characteristic collapse into hysterical emotionalism that seems the only way Kingsley could bring a novel to an end.

We can see that George Eliot, in supplying Dr. Lydgate with a central rôle in *Middlemarch* in 1872, was therefore not particularly original, except in putting him back into an earlier age of unscientific medicine in the English provincial scene (as we see from Trollope whose Barsetshire doctors are of the thoroughly old-fashioned type, even his hero Dr. Thorne of the novel of that name a year later than *Two Years Ago*). But Mrs. Oliphant, like George Eliot a thoroughly up-to-date intellectual, had published in 1865 her best novel, *Miss Marjoribanks*, where a leading figure, the heroine's father, is a Scotch doctor who is hard, sardonic of tongue and outlook, and takes a wholly scientific view of people; his life is centred on the scientific advancement of medicine and he is shown as having considerable contempt for the drawing-room where his daughter reigns, slipping away to his study to write up his cases for *The Lancet*. Like Lydgate too he is very conscious of being of good family. I have argued in my introduction to the Zodiac edition of *Miss Marjoribanks* (Chatto & Windus, 1969) that George Eliot probably took from this novel the tone of her original attitude to her heroine in *Middlemarch* and that the presence of Dr. Lydgate there owes much to the scientific–oriented doctor who dominates Carlingford in the earlier novel. Possibly also to the whole tradition going back to *Bleak House*, which had provided the form of a social microcosm which George Eliot uses in *Middlemarch*, except that she replaces London by a provincial town in the Midlands and that instead of Chesney Wold we have two contrasted estates and landlords, one the good old Tory landlord (Sir James Chettam who is her Sir Leicester Dedlock, and even shows himself willing to fight a duel) and the other as a source of humour, a bad landlord, Mr. Brooke, who has Radical views though not to the extent of doing his duty by his tenants. The idea of putting a modern scientific medical man into such an unpromising context had already been suggested by Kingsley, as I've shown. Lydgate, who in *Bleak House* or *Two Years Ago* would have been allowed to marry the symbolically fitting character Dorothea Brooke, and so fulfilled and provided with a field of action suited to his qualities and talents, touches her life only ideally, so to speak, and comes to grief partly through defeat by the reactionary elements in the town but mainly through marrying the wrong woman who deflects him from public service to private practice among the rich to satisfy her social ambitions;

he dies in the bitterness of self-contempt, and his widow then marries a physician of the old school who can provide her with a carriage. It is thus George Eliot the 'meliorist', as she considered herself (neither an optimist nor a pessimist) who follows the comparatively hopeful uses of the new doctor-figure by a thoroughly defeatist one.

Another reason for the usefulness of the doctor as a symbol for Victorian novelists was that he was necessarily outside class, privileged to tell the truth to the upper classes and handle them impartially, frequently having to be let into secrets not even revealed to the family lawyer. Dickens in *Little Dorrit* makes a very marked distinction between Physician, who is straightforward, self-respecting and immune to the snobbery and Mammon-worship practised by all around him and representatives of the other professions such as Bar and Bishop. Trollope's Dr. Thorne is habitually shown snubbing ladies of noble birth who try unsuccessfully to put him down, and maintaining a position of moral superiority to the aristocracy and the new rich alike; Dr. Lydgate, Dr. Marjoribanks and Dr. Tom Thurnall are of the same pattern–all happily born gentlemen, but despising the drawing-room and its values and refusing to bow the neck to Mammon (except for Lydgate's defeat by his wife eventually.) But 'Physician' in *Little Dorrit*, named generically like a character in a morality-play–which the scenes in the Merdles' house would seem to suggest–is much loftier in conception than any of these actual physicians. 'Where he was, something real was': he causes everyone, even Mrs. Merdle, to speak the truth to him, he is shown practising charity and, imperturbable, looking on the just and the unjust alike, 'his equality of compassion no more disturbed than the Divine Master's of all healing was'. In fact, he is the truly wise man as well as truly good. Thus for Dickens the physician in essence is virtually sanctified, but as we have seen, by the time Dickens was ending *Little Dorrit*, where Physician appears in the late chapters, (snubbing 'Bishop' incidentally), the character had been evolving in this direction. Henry James merely follows on the Dickens of *Little Dorrit* in this, as so often, when in *The Wings of the Dove* he makes his physician, Sir Luke Strett, all-knowing and apostolic.

APPENDIX B

Mayhew and Dickens

Mayhew's *London Labour and the London Poor* was published in three volumes in 1851 and followed by a fourth in 1862. While confirmation for Dickens's material accounts of the nature and sufferings of the lives of poor and submerged classes of Londoners, and country boys and girls attracted to London, are provided by Mayhew, the main interest for readers of Dickens's novels is that he incidentally furnishes collateral evidence about the effects on children of having to support themselves and younger brother and sisters, which bear out what in Dickens's novels might be disbelieved otherwise. Dickens, in his constant patrolling of the streets of London – his 'magic lantern' – for exercise and inspiration, and in his considerable charities, had plenty of opportunities of making his own observations, but Mayhew, being factual, escapes the possible charge of romanticizing or sentimentalizing his evidence, though evidently he must in the cases of his underworld characters have frequently bowdlerized what he was told for publication.

As to the truth to life of Charley and her family in *Bleak House*, Amy Dorrit in *Little Dorrit* and Jenny Wren in *Our Mutual Friend*, Mayhew in some of his characters, such as the Orphan Flower Girl and the Water Cress Girl, gives confirmation of the unchildlike nature, the respectability maintained under the most unlikely circumstances, the fortitude, and the touching depth of affection and unselfishness of such children, as well as their (and many old people too) having Betty Higden's pride in not taking charity and in escaping the workhouse (or 'Union').

He tells of 'The little watercress girl, who, although only eight years of age, had entirely lost all childish ways, and was, indeed, in thoughts and manner, a woman. There was something cruelly pathetic in hearing this infant, so young that her features had scarcely formed themselves, talking of the bitterest struggles of her life, with the calm earnestness of one who had endured them all. I did not know how to talk with her. . . . Her little face, pale and thin with privation, was wrinkled where the dimples ought to have been, and she would sigh frequently.' She had already been a twelvemonth in the streets selling cresses and before that had taken care of a young baby with real pleasure. When she got home she scrubbed the floor ' "and put the room to rights . . . All my money

I earns I puts in a club and draws out to buy clothes with. It's better than spending it in sweet-stuff, for them as has a living to earn. Besides it's like a child to care for sugar-sticks, and not like one who's got a living and vittals to earn. I ain't a child but I'm past eight, I am." ' etc.

The orphan flower-girl supported her younger sister and brother with what help they could give, sharing one room with a married couple, the woman (their landlady) giving the children friendly services like Mrs. Blinder. The eldest, now fifteen, told Mayhew: ' "Mother died seven years ago last Guy Faux day. I've got myself, and my brother and sister, a bit o 'bread ever since, and never had any help but from the neighbours. I never troubled the parish. . . . We can all read. I put myself and I put my brother and sister to a Roman Catholic school—and to Ragged schools. My brother can write, and I pray to God that he'll do well with it" ', etc.

Hence we can trust Dickens in his presentation of such characteristics—to us of the Welfare State Society unbelievable—as he attributes to his Dolls' Dressmaker and to young sister-mothers like Lizzie Hexham, Little Dorrit and Charley, while we may note that their impressive qualities, as well as their sufferings and sacrifices and stunted physique, were brought into being and operation by that social system which Dickens criticizes so radically. Self-help, one of its by-products, is after all the best kind of help. [Dickens's findings on what the Welfare State ethos has done in altering the character, mentality and outlook of the English working-class—that is, on the Trade Union state of mind thus engendered—would also have been worth having.] From his observation of the London streets alone Dickens must clearly have been struck by the difference between the premature gravity, the precocity and the excessive responsibilities of the children of the poor, in contrast to what he saw to be the arrested development, particularly of the girls, of the petted children of the well-off, so much so as to make this a recurrent and ultimately a leading idea in his novels.

Mayhew also frees Dickens from charges of sentimentalizing the poor, for he documents Dickens's belief that it was the poor who showed sympathy and charity for the destitute, that aged husbands and wives in extreme poverty and illness could show themselves, in Mayhew's own words, 'heroic' in their devoted attachment and loyalty to each other, and he illustrates the touching affection of the shockingly poor in their human relations, as well as the liveliness of language in idiom and capabilities of self-expression in the illiterate and ignorant of all ages then. His interviews with what he called 'the humbler classes' in their homes and in the streets of London furnish evidence of the actuality of Artful Dodgers and Noah Claypoles, Fagins, Orlicks and Magwitches, Martha Endells, Betty Higdens, Lizzie Hexhams and Little Dorrits. We have his evidence of the truth of Dickens's observation of the clinging to respectability, or the still more astonishing yearning for it, in those almost or quite at the bottom of the social and moral ladder, as a Victorian characteristic. What we might dismiss as the improbable fantasy-dreams related by Jenny Wren are realized in the case of the Crippled Street Bird-Seller ('I've never seemed to myself to be a cripple in my dreams. Well, I can't explain how, but I feel as if my limbs was all free like–so beautiful' etc.)

Dickens of course was quite capable of doing his own Mayhewing, and from his letters, and articles in periodicals, as well as his early (pre-Mayhew) novels, can be seen to have done so.

CHAPTER FOUR

'HARD TIMES':
THE WORLD OF BENTHAM

HARD TIMES is not a difficult work; its intention and nature are pretty obvious. If, then, it is the masterpiece I take it for, why has it not had general recognition? To judge by the critical record, it has had none at all. If there exists anywhere an appreciation, or even an acclaiming reference, I have missed it. In the books and essays on Dickens, so far as I know them, it is passed over as a very minor thing; too slight and insignificant to distract us for more than a sentence or two from the works worth critical attention. Yet, if I am right, of all Dickens's works it is the one that, having the distinctive strength that makes him a major artist, has it in so compact a way, and with a concentrated significance so immediately clear and penetrating, as, one would have thought, to preclude the reader's failing to recognize that he had before him a completely serious, and, in its originality, a triumphantly successful, work of art.

The answer to the question asked above seems to me to bear on the traditional approach to 'the English novel'. For all the more sophisticated critical currency of the last decade or two, that approach still prevails, at any rate in the appreciation of the Victorian novelists. The business of the novelist, you gather, is to 'create a world', and the mark of the master is external abundance—he gives you lots of 'life'. The test of life in his characters (he must above all create 'living' characters) is that they go on living outside the book. Expectations as unexacting as these are not, when they encounter significance, grateful for it, and when it meets them in that insistent form where nothing is very engaging as 'life' unless its relevance is fully taken, miss it altogether. This is the only way in which I can account for the neglect suffered by Henry James's *The Europeans*, which may be classed with *Hard Times* as a moral fable—though one might have supposed that James would enjoy the advantage of being approached with expectations of subtlety and closely calculated relevance. Fashion, however, has not recommended his earlier work, and this (whatever appreciation may be enjoyed by *The Ambassadors*) still suffers from the prevailing expectation of redundant[1] and irrelevant 'life'.

[1]In relation to 'redundant' and 'abundant', see (e.g.) page 225 below.

187

I need say no more by way of defining the moral fable than that in it the intention is peculiarly insistent, so that the representative significance of everything in the fable–character, episode, and so on–is immediately apparent as we read. Intention might seem to be insistent enough in the opening of *Hard Times*, in that scene in Mr. Gradgrind's school. But then, intention is in some well-known places in Dickens's work–and this has been generally thought of as a Dickensian characteristic–notably insistent without its being taken up in any inclusive significance that informs and organizes a coherent whole; and, for lack of any expectation of an organized whole, it has no doubt been supposed that in *Hard Times* the satiric irony of the first two chapters is merely, in the large and genial Dickensian way, thrown together with melodrama, pathos and humour– and that we are given these ingredients more abundantly and exuberantly elsewhere. Actually, the Dickensian vitality is there in its varied characteristic modes, which should–surely–here be the more immediately and perceptively responded to as the agents of a felt compelling significance because they are free of anything that might be seen as redundance: the creative exuberance is controlled by a profound inspiration that informs, directs and limits.

The inspiration is what is given in the grim clinch of the title, *Hard Times*. Ordinarily what are recognized as Dickens's judgments about the world he lives in ('Dickens's social criticism') are casual and incidental–a matter of including among the ingredients of a book some indignant treatment of a particular abuse. But in *Hard Times* he is unmistakably possessed by a comprehensive vision, one in which the inhumanities of Victorian civilization are seen as fostered and sanctioned by a hard philosophy, the aggressive formulation of an inhumane spirit. The philosophy is represented by Thomas Gradgrind, Esquire, Member of Parliament for Coketown, who has brought up his children on the lines of the experiment recorded by John Stuart Mill as carried out on himself. What Gradgrind stands for is, though repellent, nevertheless respectable; his Utilitarianism is a theory sincerely held and there is intellectual disinterestedness in its application. But Gradgrind marries his eldest daughter to Josiah Bounderby, 'banker, merchant, manufacturer', about whom there is no disinterestedness whatever, and nothing to be respected. Bounderby is Victorian 'rugged individualism' in its grossest and most intransigent form. Concerned with nothing but self-assertion and power and material success, he has no interest in ideals or ideas–except the idea of being the completely self-made man (since, for all his brag, he is not that in fact). Dickens here makes a just observation about the affinities and practical tendency of Utilitarianism, as, in his presentment of the Gradgrind home and the Gradgrind elementary school, he does about the Utilitarian spirit in Victorian education.

All this is obvious enough. But Dickens's art, while remaining that of the great popular entertainer, has in *Hard Times*, as he renders his full critical vision, a stamina, a flexibility combined with consistency, and a depth that he seems to have had little credit for. Take that opening scene in the school-room:

'Girl number twenty,' said Mr. Gradgrind, squarely pointing with his square forefinger, 'I don't know that girl. Who is that girl?'

'Sissy Jupe, sir,' explained number twenty, blushing, standing up, and curtsying.

'Sissy is not a name,' said Mr. Gradgrind. 'Don't call yourself Sissy. Call yourself Cecilia.'

'It's father as call me Sissy, sir,' returned the young girl in a trembling voice, and with another curtsy.

'Then he has no business to do it,' said Mr. Gradgrind. 'Tell him he mustn't. Cecilia Jupe. Let me see. What is your father?'

'He belongs to the horse-riding, if you please, sir.'

Mr. Gradgrind frowned, and waved off the objectionable calling with his hand.

'We don't want to know anything about that here. You mustn't tell us about that here. Your father breaks horses, don't he?'

'If you please, sir, when they can get any to break, they do break horses in the ring, sir.'

'You mustn't tell us about the ring here. Very well, then, Describe your father as a horse-breaker. He doctors sick horses, I dare say?'

'Oh, yes, sir!'

'Very well, then. He is a veterinary surgeon, a farrier, and horse-breaker. Give me your definition of a horse.'

(Sissy Jupe thrown into the greatest alarm by this demand.)

'Girl number twenty unable to define a horse!' said Mr. Gradgrind, for the benefit of all the little pitchers. 'Girl number twenty possessed of no facts in reference to one of the commonest animals! Some boy's definition of a horse. Bitzer, yours.'

· · · · ·

'Quadruped. Graminivorous. Forty teeth, namely twenty-four grinders, four eye-teeth, and twelve incisive. Sheds coat in the spring;

in marshy countries, sheds hoofs too. Hoofs hard, but requiring to be shod with iron. Age known by marks in mouth.' Thus (and much more) Bitzer.

Lawrence himself, protesting against harmful tendencies in education, never made the point more tellingly. Sissy has been brought up among horses, and among people whose livelihood depends upon understanding horses, but 'we don't want to know anything about that here'. Such knowledge isn't real knowledge. Bitzer, the model pupil, on the button's being pressed, promptly vomits up the genuine article, 'Quadruped. Graminivorous', etc.; and 'Now, girl number twenty, you know what a horse is'. The irony, pungent enough locally, is richly developed in the subsequent action. Bitzer's aptness has its evaluative comment in his career. Sissy's incapacity to acquire this kind of 'fact' or formula, her un-aptness for education, is manifested to us, on the other hand, as part and parcel of her sovereign and indefeasible humanity: it is the virtue that makes it impossible for her to understand, or acquiesce in, an ethos for which she is 'girl number twenty', or to think of any other human being as a unit for arithmetic.

This kind of ironic method might seem to commit the author to very limited kinds of effect. In *Hard Times*, however, it associates quite con-gruously, such is the flexibility of Dickens's art, with very different methods; it co-operates in a truly dramatic and profoundly poetic whole. Sissy Jupe, who might be taken here for a merely conventional *persona*, has already, as a matter of fact, been established in a potently symbolic rôle: she is part of the poetically-creative operation of Dickens's genius in *Hard Times*. Here is a passage I omitted from the middle of the excerpt quoted above:

The square finger, moving here and there, lighted suddenly on Bitzer, perhaps because he chanced to sit in the same ray of sunlight which, darting in at one of the bare windows of the intensely white-washed room, irradiated Sissy. For the boys and girls sat on the face of an inclined plane in two compact bodies, divided up the centre by a narrow interval; and Sissy, being at the corner of a row on the sunny side, came in for the beginning of a sunbeam, of which Bitzer, being at the corner of a row on the other side, a few rows in advance, caught the end. But, whereas the girl was so dark-eyed and dark-haired that she seemed to receive a deeper and more lustrous colour from the sun when it shone upon her, the boy was so light-eyed and light-haired that the self-same rays appeared to draw out of him what little colour he ever possessed. His cold eyes would hardly have been eyes, but for the short ends of lashes which, by bringing them into immediate contrast with something paler than themselves, expressed their form. His short-cropped hair might have been a mere continuation of the sandy freckles on his forehead and face. His skin was so unwholesomely deficient in the natural tinge, that he looked as though, if he were cut, he would bleed white.

There is no need to insist on the force–representative of Dickens's art in general in *Hard Times*–with which the moral and spiritual differences are rendered here in terms of sensation, so that the symbolic intention emerges out of metaphor and the vivid evocation of the concrete. What may, perhaps, be emphasized is that Sissy stands for vitality as well as goodness–they are seen, in fact, as one; she is generous, impulsive life, finding self-fulfilment in self-forgetfulness–all that is the antithesis of calculating self-interest. There is an essentially Laurentian suggestion about the way in which 'the dark-eyed and dark-haired' girl, contrasting with Bitzer, seemed to receive a 'deeper and more lustrous colour from the sun', so opposing the life that is lived freely and richly from the deep instinctive and emotional springs to the thin-blooded, quasi-mechanical product of Gradgrindery.

Sissy's symbolic significance is bound up with that of Sleary's Horse-riding where human kindness is very insistently associated with vitality.

The way in which the Horse-riding takes on its significance illustrates felicitously the poetic-dramatic nature of Dickens's art. From the utilitarian schoolroom Mr. Gradgrind walks towards his utilitarian abode, Stone Lodge, which, as Dickens evokes it, brings home to us concretely the model régime that for the little Gradgrinds (among whom are Malthus and Adam Smith) is an inescapable prison. But before he gets there he passes the back of a circus booth, and is pulled up by the sight of two palpable offenders. Looking more closely, 'what did he behold but his own metallurgical Louisa peeping through a hole in a deal board, and his own mathematical Thomas abasing himself on the ground to catch but a hoof of the graceful equestrian Tyrolean flower act!' The chapter is called 'A Loophole', and Thomas 'gave himself up to be taken home like a machine'.

Representing human spontaneity, the circus-athletes represent at the same time highly-developed skill and deftness of kinds that bring poise, pride and confident ease–they are always buoyant, and, ballet-dancer-like, in training:

> There were two or three handsome young women among them, with two or three husbands, and their two or three mothers, and their eight or nine children, who did the fairy business when required. The father of one of the families was in the habit of balancing the father of another of the families on the top of a great pole; the father of the third family often made a pyramid of both those fathers, with Master Kidderminster for the apex, and himself for the base; all the fathers could dance upon rolling casks, stand upon bottles, catch knives and balls, twirl hand-basins, ride upon anything, jump over everything, and stick at nothing. All the mothers could (and did) dance upon the slack wire and the tight-rope, and perform rapid acts on bare-backed steeds; none of them were at all particular in respect of showing their legs; and one of them, alone in a Greek chariot, drove six-in-hand into every town they came to. They all assumed to be mighty rakish and knowing, they were not very tidy in their private dresses, they were not at all orderly in their domestic arrangements, and the combined literature of the whole company would have produced but a poor letter on any subject. Yet there was a remarkable gentleness and child-ishness about these people, a special inaptitude for any kind of sharp practice, and an untiring readiness to help and pity one another, deserving often of as much respect, and always of as much generous construction, as the every-day virtues of any class of people in the world.

Their skills have no value for the Utilitarian calculus, but they express vital human impulse, and they minister to vital human needs. The Horse-riding, frowned upon as frivolous and wasteful by Gradgrind and malig-nantly scorned by Bounderby, brings the machine-hands of Coketown (the spirit-quenching hideousness of which is hauntingly evoked) what they are starved of. It brings to them, not merely amusement, but art, and the spectacle of triumphant activity that, seeming to contain its end within itself, is, in its easy mastery, joyously self-justified. In investing a travelling circus with this kind of symbolic value Dickens expresses a profounder reaction to industrialism than might have been expected of him. It is not only pleasure and relaxation the Coketowners stand in need of; he feels the dreadful degradation of life that would remain even if they were to be given a forty-hour week, comfort, security and fun. We recall a characteristic passage from D. H. Lawrence.

The car ploughed uphill through the long squalid straggle of Tevershall, the blackened brick dwellings, the black slate roofs, glistening their sharp edges, the mud black with coal-dust, the pavements wet and black. It was as if dismalness had soaked through and through everything. The utter negation of natural beauty, the utter negation of the gladness of life, the utter absence of the instinct for shapely beauty which every bird and beast has, the utter death of the human intuitive faculty was appalling. The stacks of soap in the grocers' shops, the rhubarb and lemons in the greengrocers'! the awful hats in the milliners all went by ugly, ugly, ugly, followed by the plaster and gilt horror of the cinema with its wet picture announcements, 'A Woman's Love,' and the new big Primitive chapel, primitive enough in its stark brick and big panes of greenish and raspberry glass in the windows. The Wesleyan chapel, higher up, was of blackened brick and stood behind iron railings and blackened shrubs. The Congregational chapel, which thought itself superior, was built of rusticated sandstone and had a steeple, but not a very high one. Just beyond were the new school buildings, expensive pink brick, and gravelled playground inside iron railings, all very imposing, and mixing the suggestion of a chapel and a prison. Standard Five girls were having a singing lesson, just finishing the la-me-do-la exercises and beginning a 'sweet children's song.' Anything more unlike song, spontaneous song, would be impossible to imagine: a strange bawling yell followed the outlines of a tune. It was not like animals: animals *mean* something when they yell. It was like nothing on earth, and it was called singing. Connie sat and listened with her heart in her boots, as Field was filling petrol. What could possibly become of such a people, a people in whom the living intuitive faculty was dead as nails, and only queer mechanical yells and uncanny will-power remained?'

Dickens couldn't have put it in just those terms, but the way in which his vision of the Horse-riders insists on their gracious vitality implies that reaction.

Here an objection may be anticipated—as a way of making a point. Coketown, like Gradgrind and Bounderby, is real enough; but it can't be contended that the Horse-riding is real in the same sense. There would have been some athletic skill and perhaps some bodily grace among the people of a Victorian travelling circus, but surely so much squalor, grossness and vulgarity that we must find Dickens's symbolism sentimentally false? And 'there was a remarkable gentleness and childishness about these people, a special inaptitude for any kind of sharp practice'—that, surely, is going ludicrously too far?

If Dickens, intent on an emotional effect, or drunk with moral enthusiasm, had been deceiving himself (it couldn't have been innocently) about the nature of the actuality, he would then indeed have been guilty of sentimental falsity, and the adverse criticism would have held. But the Horse-riding presents no such case. The virtues and qualities that Dickens prizes do indeed exist, and it is necessary for his critique of Utilitarianism and industrialism, and for (what is the same thing) his creative purpose, to evoke them vividly. The book can't, in my judgment, be fairly charged with giving a misleading representation of human nature. And it would plainly not be intelligent criticism to suggest that anyone could be misled about the nature of circuses by *Hard Times*. The critical question is merely one of tact: was it well-judged of Dickens to try to do *that*–which had to be done somehow–with a travelling circus?

Or, rather, the question is: by what means has he succeeded? For the success is complete. It is conditioned partly by the fact that, from the opening chapters, we have been tuned for the reception of a highly conventional art–though it is a tuning that has no narrowly limiting effect. To describe at all cogently the means by which this responsiveness is set up would take a good deal of 'practical criticism' analysis–analysis that would reveal an extraordinary flexibility in the art of *Hard Times*. This can be seen very obviously in the dialogue. Some passages might come from an ordinary novel. Others have the ironic pointedness of the schoolroom scene in so insistent a form that we might be reading a work as stylized as Jonsonian comedy: Gradgrind's final exchange with Bitzer (quoted below) is a supreme instance. Others again are 'literary', like the conversation between Gradgrind and Louisa on her flight home for refuge from Mr. James Harthouse's attentions.

To the question how the reconciling is done–there is much more diversity in *Hard Times* than these references to dialogue suggest–the answer can be given by pointing to the astonishing and irresistible richness of life that characterizes the book everywhere. It meets us everywhere, unstrained and natural, in the prose. Out of such prose a great variety of presentations can arise congenially with equal vividness. There they are, unquestionably 'real'. It goes back to an extraordinary energy of perception and registration in Dickens. 'When people say that Dickens exaggerates', says Santayana, 'it seems to me that they can have no eyes and no ears. They probably only have *notions* of what things and people are; they accept them conventionally, at their diplomatic value.' Settling down as we read to an implicit recognition of this truth, we don't readily and confidently apply any criterion we suppose ourselves to hold for distinguishing varieties of relation between what Dickens gives us and a normal 'real'. His flexibility is that of a richly poetic art of the word. He doesn't write 'poetic prose'; he writes with a poetic force of evocation, registering with the responsiveness of a genius of verbal expression what he so sharply sees and feels. In fact, by texture, imaginative mode, symbolic method, and the resulting concentration, *Hard Times* affects us as belonging with formally poetic works.

There is, however, more to be said about the success that attends Dickens's symbolic intention in the Horse-riding; there is an essential quality of his genius to be emphasized. There is no Hamlet in him, and he is quite unlike T. S. Eliot.

> *The red-eyed scavengers are creeping*
> *From Kentish Town and Golders Green*

–there is nothing of that in Dickens's reaction to life. He observes with gusto the humanness of humanity as exhibited in the urban (and suburban) scene. When he sees, as he sees so readily, the common manifestations of human kindness, and the essential virtues, asserting themselves in the midst of ugliness, squalor and banality, his warmly sympathetic response has no disgust to overcome. There is no suggestion, for instance, of recoil–or of distance-keeping–from the game-eyed, brandy-soaked, flabby-surfaced Mr. Sleary, who is successfully made to figure for us a humane, anti-Utilitarian positive. This is not sentimentality in Dickens, but genius, and a genius that should be found peculiarly worth attention in an age when, as D. H. Lawrence (with, as I remember, Wyndham Lewis immediately in view) says, 'My God! they stink' tends to be an insuperable and final reaction.

Sentimentality, as everyone knows, is to be found in Dickens's *œuvre*. We have it in *Hard Times* (though not to any seriously damaging effect) in Stephen Blackpool, the good, victimized working-man, whose perfect patience under infliction we are expected to find supremely edifying and irresistibly touching as the agonies are piled on for his martyrdom. But Sissy Jupe is another matter. A general description of her part in the fable might suggest the worst, but actually she has nothing in common with Little Nell: she shares in the strength of the Horse-riding. She is wholly convincing in the function Dickens assigns to her. The working of her influence in the Utilitarian home is conveyed with a fine tact, and we do really feel her as a growing potency. Dickens can even, with sufficient success, give her the stage for a victorious *tête-à-tête* with the well-bred and languid elegant, Mr. James Harthouse, in which she tells him that his duty is to leave Coketown and cease troubling Louisa with his attentions:

> She was not afraid of him, or in any way disconcerted; she seemed to have her mind entirely preoccupied with the occasion of her visit, and to have substituted that consideration for herself.

The victory of disinterestedness is convincing enough as one reads.

At the opening of the book Sissy establishes the essential distinction between Gradgrind and Bounderby. Gradgrind, by taking her home, however ungraciously, shows himself capable of humane feeling, however unacknowledged. We are reminded, in the previous school-room scene, of the Jonsonian affinities of Dickens's art, and Bounderby turns out to be consistently a Jonsonian character in the sense that he is incapable of change. He remains the blustering egotist and braggart, and responds in character to the collapse of his marriage:

> 'I'll give *you* to understand, in reply to that, that there unquestionably is an incompatibility of the first magnitude – to be summed up in this – that your daughter don't properly know her husband's merits, and is not impressed with such a sense as would become her, by George! of the honour of his alliance. That's plain speaking, I hope.'

He remains Jonsonianly consistent in his last testament and death. But Gradgrind, in the nature of the fable, has to *experience* the confutation of his philosophy, and to be capable of the change involved in admitting that life has proved him wrong. (Dickens's art in *Hard Times* differs from Ben Jonson's not in being inconsistent, but in being so very much more flexible and inclusive – a point that seemed to be worth making because the relation between Dickens and Jonson has been stressed of late, and I have known unfair conclusions to be drawn from the comparison, notably in respect of *Hard Times*.)

The confutation of Utilitarianism by life is conducted with great subtlety. That the conditions for it are there in Mr. Gradgrind he betrays by his initial kindness, ungenial enough, but properly rebuked by Bounderby, to Sissy. 'Mr. Gradgrind', we are told, 'though hard enough, was by no means so rough a man as Mr. Bounderby. His character was not unkind, all things considered; it might have been very kind indeed if only he had made some mistake in the arithmetic that balanced it years ago.' The inadequacy of the calculus is starkly exposed when he brings it to bear on the problem of marriage in the consummate scene with his eldest daughter:

> He waited, as if he would have been glad that she said something. But she said never a word.
>
> 'Louisa, my dear, you are the subject of a proposal of marriage that has been made to me.'
>
> Again he waited, and again she answered not one word. This so far surprised him as to induce him gently to repeat, 'A proposal of marriage, my dear.' To which she returned, without any visible emotion whatever:
>
> 'I hear you, father. I am attending, I assure you.'
>
> 'Well!' said Mr. Gradgrind, breaking into a smile, after being for the moment at a loss, 'you are even more dispassionate than I expected, Louisa. Or, perhaps, you are not unprepared for the announcement I have it in charge to make?'
>
> 'I cannot say that, father, until I hear it. Prepared or unprepared, I wish to hear it all from you. I wish to hear you state it to me, father.'
>
> Strange to relate, Mr. Gradgrind was not so collected at this moment as his daughter was. He took a paper knife in his hand, turned it over, laid it down, took it up again, and even then had to look along the blade of it, considering how to go on.
>
> 'What you say, my dear Louisa, is perfectly reasonable. I have undertaken, then, to let you know that–in short, that Mr. Bounderby...'

His embarrassment–by his own avowal–is caused by the perfect rationality with which she receives his overture. He is still more disconcerted when, with a completely dispassionate matter-of-fact-ness that does credit to his *régime*, she gives him the opportunity to state in plain terms precisely what marriage should mean for the young Houyhnhnm:

> Silence between them. The deadly statistical clock very hollow. The distant smoke very black and heavy.
>
> 'Father,' said Louisa, 'do you think I love Mr. Bounderby?'
>
> 'Mr. Gradgrind was extremely discomforted by this unexpected question. 'Well, my child,' he returned, 'I –really–cannot take upon myself to say.'
>
> 'Father,' pursued Louisa in exactly the same voice as before, 'do you ask me to love Mr. Bounderby?'
>
> 'My dear Louisa, no. I ask nothing.'
>
> 'Father,' she still pursued, 'does Mr. Bounderby ask me to love him?'
>
> 'Really, my dear,' said Mr. Gradgrind, 'it is difficult to answer your question–'

'Difficult to answer it, Yes or No, father?'

'Certainly, my dear. Because'–here was something to demonstrate, and to set him up again–'because the reply depends so materially, Louisa, on the sense in which we use the expression. Now, Mr. Bounderby does not do you the injustice, and does not do himeslf the injustice, of pretending to anything fanciful, fantastic, or (I am using synonymous terms) sentimental. Mr. Bounderby would have seen you grow up under his eye to very little purpose, if he could so far forget what is due to your good sense, not to say to his, as to address you from such ground. Therefore, perhaps, the expression itself–I merely suggest this to you, my dear–may be a little misplaced.'

'What would you advise me to use in its stead, father?'

'Why, my dear Louisa,' said Mr. Gradgrind, completely recovered by this time. 'I would advise you (since you ask me) to consider the question, as you have been accustomed to consider every other question, simply as one of tangible Fact. The ignorant and the giddy may embarrass such subjects with irrelevant fancies, and other absurdities that have no existence, properly viewed–really no existence–but it is no compliment to say that you know better. Now, what are the Facts of this case? You are, we will say in round numbers, twenty years of age; Mr. Bounderby is, we will say in round numbers, fifty. There is some disparity in your respective years, but . . .'

–And at this point Mr. Gradgrind seizes the chance for a happy escape into statistics. But Louisa brings him firmly back:

'What do you recommend, father?' asked Louisa, her reserved composure not in the least affected by these gratifying results, 'that I should substitute for the term I used just now? For the misplaced expression?'

'Louisa,' returned her father, 'it appears to me that nothing can be plainer. Confining yourself rigidly to Fact, the question of Fact you state to yourself is: Does Mr. Bounderby ask me to marry him? Yes, he does. The sole remaining question then is: Shall I marry him? I think nothing can be plainer than that.'

'Shall I marry him?' repeated Louisa with great deliberation.

'Precisely.'

It is a triumph of ironic art. No logical analysis could dispose of the philosophy of fact and calculus with such neat finality. As the issues are reduced to algebraic formulation they are patently emptied of all real meaning. The instinct-free rationality of the emotionless Houyhnhnm is a void. Louisa proceeds to try and make him understand that she is a living creature and therefore no Houyhnhnm, but in vain ('to see it, he must have overleaped at a bound the artificial barriers he had for many years been erecting between himself and all those subtle essences of humanity which will elude the utmost cunning of algebra, until the last trumpet ever to be sounded will blow even algebra to wreck').

Removing her eyes from him, she sat so long looking silently towards the town, that he said at length: 'Are you consulting the chimneys of the Coketown works, Louisa?'

'There seems to be nothing there but languid and monotonous smoke. Yet, when the night comes, Fire bursts out, father!' she answered, turning quickly.

'Of course I know that, Louisa. I do not see the application of the remark.' To do him justice, he did not at all.

She passed it away with a slight motion of her hand, and concentrating her attention upon him again, said, 'Father, I have often thought that life is very short.'–This was so distinctly one of his subjects that he interposed:

'It is short, no doubt, my dear. Still, the average duration of human life is proved to have increased of late years. The calculations of various life assurance and annuity offices, among other figures which cannot go wrong, have established the fact.'

'I speak of my own life, father.'

'Oh, indeed! Still,' said Mr. Gradgrind, 'I need not point out to you, Louisa, that it is governed by the laws which govern lives in the aggregate.'

'While it lasts, I would wish to do the little I can, and the little I am fit for. What does it matter?'

'Mr. Gradgrind seemed rather at a loss to understand the last four words; replying, 'How, matter? What matter, my dear?'

'Mr. Bounderby,' she went on in a steady, straight way, without regarding this, 'asks me to marry him. The question I have to ask myself is, shall I marry him? That is so, father, is it not? You have told me so, father. Have you not?'

'Certainly, my dear.'

'Let is be so.'

The psychology of Louisa's development and of her brother Tom's is sound. Having no outlet for her emotional life except in her love for her brother, she lives for him, and marries Bounderby–under pressure from Tom–for Tom's sake ('What does it matter?'). Thus, by the constrictions and starvations of the Gradgrind *régime*, are natural affection and capacity for disinterested devotion turned to ill. As for Tom, the *régime* has made of him a bored and sullen whelp, and 'he was becoming that not unprecedented triumph of calculation which is usually at work on number one'–the Utilitarian philsophy has done that for him. He declares that when he goes to live with Bounderby as having a post in the bank, 'he'll have his revenge'.–'I mean, I'll enjoy myself a little, and go about and see something and hear something. I'll recompense myself for the way in which I've been brought up.' His descent into debt and bank-robbery is natural. And it is natural that Louisa, having sacrificed herself for this unrepaying object of affection, should be found not altogether unresponsive when Mr. James Harthouse, having sized up the situation, pursues his opportunity with well-bred and calculating tact. His apologia for genteel cynicism is a shrewd thrust at the Gradgrind philosophy:

> 'The only difference between us and the professors of virtue or benevolence, or philanthropy–never mind the name–is, that we know it is all meaningless, and say so; while they know it equally, and will never say so.'

Why should she be shocked or warned by this reiteration? It was not so unlike her father's principles, and her early training, that it need startle her.

When, fleeing from temptation, she arrives back at her father's house, tells him her plight, and, crying, 'All I know is, your philosophy and your teaching will not save me', collapses, he sees 'the pride of his heart and the triumph of his system lying an insensible heap at his feet'. The fallacy now calamitously demonstrated can be seen focused in that 'pride', which brings together in an illusory oneness the pride of his system and his love for his child. What that love is Gradgrind now knows, and he knows that it matters to him more than the system, which is thus confuted (the educational failure as such being a lesser matter). There is nothing sentimental here; the demonstration is impressive, because we are convinced of the love, and because Gradgrind has been made to exist for us as a man who has 'meant to do right':

> He said it earnestly, and, to do him justice, he had. In gauging fathomless deeps with his little mean excise rod, and in staggering over the universe with his rusty stiff-legged compasses, he had meant to do great things. Within the limits of his short tether he had tumbled about, annihilating the flowers of existence with greater singleness of purpose than many of the blatant personages whose company he kept.

The demonstration still to come, that of which the other 'triumph of his system', Tom, is the centre, is sardonic comedy, imagined with great intensity and done with the sure touch of genius. There is the pregnant scene in which Mr. Gradgrind, in the deserted ring of a third-rate travelling circus, has to recognize his son in a comic negro servant; and has to recognize that his son owes his escape from Justice to a peculiarly disinterested gratitude–to the opportunity given him to assume such a disguise by the non-Utilitarian Mr. Sleary, grateful for Sissy's sake:

> In a preposterous coat, like a beadle's, with cuffs and flaps exaggerated to an unspeakable extent; in an immense waistcoat, knee breeches, buckled shoes, and a mad cocked-hat; with nothing fitting him and everything of coarse material, moth-eaten, and full of holes; with seams in his black face, where fear and heat had started through the greasy composition daubed all over it; anything so grimly, detestably, ridiculously shameful as the whelp in his comic livery, Mr. Gradgrind never could by any other means have believed in, weighable and measurable fact though it was. And one of his model children had come to this!
>
> At first the whelp would not draw any nearer but persisted in remaining up there by himself. Yielding at length, if any concession so sullenly made can be called yielding, to the entreaties of Sissy–for Louisa he disowned altogether–he came down, bench by bench, until he stood in the sawdust, on the verge of the circle, as far as possible, within its limits, from where his father sat.
>
> 'How was this done?' asked the father.
>
> 'How was what done?' moodily answered the son.
>
> 'This robbery,' said the father, raising his voice upon the word.
>
> 'I forced the safe myself overnight, and shut it up ajar before I went away. I had had the key that was found long before. I dropped it that morning, that it might be supposed to have been used. I didn't take the money all at once, I pretended to put my balance away every night, but I didn't. Now you know all about it.'
>
> 'If a thunderbolt had fallen on me,' said the father, 'it would have shocked me less than this!'
>
> 'I don't see why,' grumbled the son. 'So many people are employed in situations of trust; so many people, out of so many, will be dishonest. I have heard you talk, a hundred times, of its being a law. How can *I* help laws? You have comforted others with such things, father. Comfort yourself!'
>
> The father buried his face in his hands, and the son stood in his disgraceful grotesqueness, biting straw: his hands, with the black partly

worn away inside, looking like the hands of a monkey. The evening was fast closing in; and, from time to time, he turned the whites of his eyes restlessly and impatiently towards his father. They were the only parts of his face that showed any life or expression, the pigment upon it was so thick.

Something of the rich complexity of Dickens's art may be seen in this passage. No simple formula can take account of the various elements in the whole effect, a sardonic-tragic in which satire consorts with pathos. The excerpt itself suggests the justification for saying that *Hard Times* is a poetic work. It suggests that the genius of the writer may fairly be described as that of a poetic dramatist, and that, in our preconceptions about 'the novel', we may miss, within the field of fictional prose, possibilities of concentration and flexibility in the interpretation of life such as we associate with Shakespearean drama.

The note, as we have it above in Tom's retort, of ironic-satiric discomfiture of the Utilitarian philosopher by the rebound of his formulae upon himself is developed in the ensuing scene with Bitzer, the truly successful pupil, the real triumph of the system. He arrives to intercept Tom's flight:

Bitzer, still holding the paralysed culprit by the collar, stood in the Ring, blinking at his old patron through the darkness of the twilight.

"Bitzer," said Mr. Gradgrind, broken down and miserably submissive to him, 'have you a heart?'

'The circulation, sir', returned Bitzer, smiling at the oddity of the question, 'couldn't be carried on without one. No man, sir, acquainted with the facts established by Harvey relating to the circulation of the blood, can doubt that I have a heart.'

'Is it accessible,' cried Mr. Gradgrind, 'to any compassionate influence?'

'It is accessible to Reason, sir,' returned the excellent young man. 'And to nothing else.'

They stood looking at each other; Mr. Gradgrind's face as white as the pursuer's.

'What motive – even what motive in reason – can you have for preventing the escape of this wretched youth,' said Mr. Gradgrind, 'and crushing his miserable father? See his sister here. Pity us!'

'Sir,' returned Bitzer in a very business-like and logical manner, 'since you ask me what motive I have in reason for taking young Mr. Tom back to Coketown, it is only reasonable to let you know ... I am going to take young Mr. Tom back to Coketown, in order to deliver him over to Mr. Bounderby. Sir, I have no doubt whatever that Mr. Bounderby will then promote me to young Mr. Tom's situation. And I wish to have this situation, sir, for it will be a rise to me, and will do me good.'

'If this is solely a question of self-interest with you–' Mr. Gradgrind began.

'I beg your pardon for interrupting you, sir,' returned Bitzer, "but I am sure you know that the whole social system is a question of self-interest. What you must always appeal to is a person's self-interest. It's your only hold. We are so constituted. I was brought up in that catechism when I was very young, sir, as you are aware."

'What sum of money,' said Mr. Gradgrind, 'will you set against your expected promotion?'

'Thank you, sir,' returned Bitzer, 'for hinting at the proposal; but I will not set any sum against it. Knowing that your clear head would propose that alternative, I have gone over the calculations in my mind; and I find that to compound a felony, even on very high terms indeed, would not be as safe and good for me as my improved prospects in the Bank.'

'Bitzer,' said Mr. Gradgrind, stretching out his hands as though he would have said, See how miserable I am! 'Bitzer, I have but one chance left to soften you. You were many years at my school. If, in remembrance of the pains bestowed upon you there, you can persuade yourself in any degree to disregard your present interest and release my son, I entreat and pray you to give him the benefit of that remembrance.'

'I really wonder, sir,' rejoined the old pupil in an argumentative manner, 'to find you taking a position so untenable. My schooling was paid for; it was a bargain; and when I came away, the bargain ended.'

It was a fundamental principle of the Gradgrind philosophy, that everything was to be paid for. Nobody was ever on any account to give anybody anything, or render anybody help without purchase. Gratitude was to be abolished, and the virtues springing from it were not to be. Every inch of the existence of mankind, from birth to death, was to be a bargain across the counter. And if we didn't get to Heaven that way, it was not a politico-economical place, and we had no business there.

'I don't deny,' added Bitzer, "that my schooling was cheap. But that comes right, sir. I was made in the cheapest market, and have to dispose of myself in the dearest.'

Tom's escape is contrived, successfully in every sense, by means belonging to Dickensian high-fantastic comedy. And there follows the

solemn moral of the whole fable, put with the rightness of genius into
Mr. Sleary's asthmatic mouth. He, agent of the artist's marvellous tact,
acquits himself of it characteristically:

'Thquire, you don't need to be told that dogth ith wonderful
animalth.'
'Their instinct,' said Mr. Gradgrind, 'is surprising'.
'Whatever you call it–and I'm bletht if I know what to call it'–
said Sleary, 'it ith athtonithing. The way in which a dog'll find you–
the dithtanthe he'll come!'
'His scent,' said Mr. Gradgrind, 'being so fine.'
'I'm bletht if I know what to call it,' repeated Sleary, shaking his
head, 'but I have had dogth find me, Thquire . . .'

– And Mr. Sleary proceeds to explain that Sissy's truant father is certainly
dead because his performing dog, who would never have deserted him
living, has come back to the Horse-riding:

'he wath lame, and pretty well blind. He went to our children, one
after another, ath if he wath a theeking for a child he knowed; and
then he come to me, and throwed hithelf up behind, and thtood on
hith two fore-legth, weak ath he wath, and then he wagged hith tail
and died. Thquire, that dog wath Merrylegth.'

The whole passage has to be read as it stands in the text (Book the
Third, chapter VIII). Reading it there we have to stand off and reflect at
a distance to recognize the potentialities that might have been realized
elsewhere as Dickensian sentimentality. There is nothing sentimental
in the actual effect. The profoundly serious intention is in control, the
touch sure, and the structure that ensures the poise unassertively complex.
Here is the formal moral:

'Tho, whether her father bathely detherted her; or whether he
broke hith own heart alone, rather than pull her down along with
him; never will be known now, Thquire, till–no, not till we know
how the dogth findth uth out!'
'She keeps the bottle that he sent her for, to this hour; and she
will believe in his affection to the last moment of her life,' said Mr.
Gradgrind.
'It theemth to prethent two thingth to a perthon, don't it, Thquire?'
said Mr. Sleary, musing as he looked down into the depths of his
brandy-and-water: 'one, that there ith a love in the world, not all
Thelf-interetht after all, but thomething very different; t'other, that
it hath a way of ith own of calculating or not calculating, whith

thomehow or another ith at leatht ath hard to give a name to, ath the wayth of the dogth ith!'

'Mr. Gradgrind looked out of the window, and made no reply. Mr. Sleary emptied his glass and recalled the ladies.

It will be seen that the effect (I repeat, the whole passage must be read), apparently so simple and easily right, depends upon a subtle interplay of diverse elements, a multiplicity in unison of timbre and tone. Dickens, we know, was a popular entertainer, but Flaubert never wrote anything approaching this in subtlety of achieved art. Dickens, of course, has a vitality that we don't look for in Flaubert. Shakespeare was a popular entertainer, we reflect—not too extravagantly, we can surely tell ourselves, as we ponder passages of this characteristic quality in their relation, a closely organized one, to the poetic whole.

Criticism, of course, has its points to make against *Hard Times*. It can be said of Stephen Blackpool, not only that he is too good and qualifies too consistently for the martyr's halo, but that he invites an adaptation of the objection brought, from the negro point of view, against Uncle Tom, which was to the effect that he was a white man's good nigger. And certainly it doesn't need a working-class bias to produce the comment that when Dickens comes to the Trade Unions his understanding of the world he offers to deal with betrays a marked limitation. There were undoubtedly professional agitators, and Trade Union solidarity was undoubtedly often asserted at the expense of the individual's rights, but it is a score against a work so insistently typical in intention that it should give the representative rôle to the agitator, Slackbridge, and make Trade Unionism nothing better than the pardonable error of the misguided and oppressed, and, as such, an agent in the martyrdom of the good working man. (But to be fair we must remember the conversation between Bitzer and Mrs. Sparsit:

'It is much to be regretted,' said Mrs. Sparsit, making her nose more Roman and her eyebrows more Coriolanian in the strength of her severity, 'that the united masters allow of any such class combination.'

'Yes, ma'am,' said Bitzer.

'Being united themselves, they ought one and all to set their faces against employing any man who is united with any other man,' said Mrs. Sparsit.

'They have done that, ma'am,' returned Bitzer; 'but it rather fell through, ma'am.'

'I do not pretend to understand these things,' said Mrs. Sparsit with dignity. '. . . I only know that those people must be conquered, and that it's high time it was done, once and for all.')

Just as Dickens has no glimpse of the part to be played by Trade Unionism in bettering the conditions he deplores, so, though he sees there are many places of worship in Coketown, of various kinds of ugliness, he has no notion of the part played by the chapel in the life of nineteenth-century industrial England. The kind of self-respecting steadiness and conscientious restraint that he represents in Stephen did certainly exist on a large scale among the working-classes, and this is an important historical fact. But there would have been no such fact if those chapels described by Dickens had had no more relation to the life of Coketown than he shows them to have.

Again, his attitude to Trade Unionism is not the only expression of a lack of political understanding. Parliament for him is merely the 'national dust-yard', where the 'national dustmen' entertain one another 'with a great many noisy little fights among themselves', and appoint commissions which fill blue-books with dreary facts and futile statistics – of a kind that helps Gradgrind to 'prove that the Good Samaritan was a bad economist'.

Yet Dickens's understanding of Victorian civilization is adequate for his purpose; the justice and penetration of his criticism are unaffected. And his moral perception works in alliance with a clear insight into the English social structure. Mr. James Harthouse is necessary for the plot; but he too has his representative function. He has come to Coketown as a prospective parliamentary candidate, for 'the Gradgrind party wanted assistance in cutting the throats of the Graces', and they 'liked fine gentlemen; they pretended that they did not, but they did'. And so the alliance between the old ruling class and the 'hard' men figures duly in the fable. This economy is typical. There is Mrs. Sparsit, for instance, who might seem to be there merely for the plot. But her 'husband was a Powler', a fact she reverts to as often as Bounderby to his mythical birth in a ditch; and the two complementary opposites, when Mr. James Harthouse, who in his languid assurance of class-superiority doesn't need to boast, is added, form a trio that suggests the whole system of British snobbery.

But the packed richness of *Hard Times* is almost incredibly varied, and not all the quoting I have indulged in suggests it adequately. The final stress may fall on Dickens's command of word, phrase, rhythm and image: in ease and range there is surely no greater master of English except Shakespeare. This comes back to saying that Dickens is a great poet: his endless resource in felicitously varied expression is an extraordinary responsiveness to life. His senses are charged with emotional energy, and his intelligence plays and flashes in the quickest and sharpest perception. That is, his mastery of 'style' is of the only kind that matters – which is not to say that he hasn't a conscious interest in what can be done with words; many of his felicities could plainly not have come if there had not been, in the background, a habit of such interest. Take this, for instance:

> He had reached the neutral ground upon the outskirts of the town, which was neither town nor country, but either spoiled... '

But he is no more a stylist than Shakespeare; and his mastery of expression is most fairly suggested by stressing, not his descriptive evocations (there are some magnificent ones in *Hard Times* – the varied *décor* of the action is made vividly present, you can feel the velvety dust trodden by Mrs. Sparsit in her stealth, and feel the imminent storm), but his strictly dramatic felicities. Perhaps, however, 'strictly' is not altogether a good pointer, since Dickens is a master of his chosen art, and his mastery shows itself in the way in which he moves between less direct forms of the dramatic and the direct rendering of speech. Here is Mrs. Gradgrind dying (a cipher in the Gradgrind system, the poor creature has never really been alive):

> Her feeble voice sounded so far away in her bundle of shawls, and the sound of another voice addressing her seemed to take such a long time in getting down to her ears, that she might have been lying at the bottom of a well. The poor lady was nearer Truth than she had ever been: which had much to do with it.
> On being told that Mrs. Bounderby was there, she replied, at cross purposes, that she had never called him by that name since he had married Louisa; and that pending her choice of an objectionable name, she had called him J; and that she could not at present depart from that regulation, not being yet provided with a permanent substitute. Louisa had sat by her for some minutes, and had spoken to her often, before she arrived at a clear understanding who it was. She then seemed to come to it all at once.
> 'Well, my dear,' said Mrs. Gradgrind, 'and I hope you are going on satisfactorily to yourself. It was all your father's doing. He set his heart upon it. And he ought to know.'

H   207

'I want to hear of you, mother; not of myself,'

'You want to hear of me, my dear? That's something new, I am sure, when anybody wants to hear of me. Not at all well, Louisa. Very faint and giddy.'

'Are you in pain, dear mother?'

'I think there's a pain somewhere in the room,' said Mrs. Gradgrind, 'but I couldn't positively say that I have got it.'

After this strange speech, she lay silent for some time.

'But there is something—not an Ology at all—that your father has missed, or forgotten, Louisa. I don't know what it is. I have often sat with Sissy near me, and thought about it. I shall never get its name now. But your father may. It makes me restless. I want to write to him, to find out, for God's sake, what it is. Give me a pen, give me a pen.'

Even the power of restlessness was gone, except for the poor head, which could just turn from side to side.

She fancied, however, that her request had been complied with, and that the pen she could not have held was in her hand. It matters little what figures of wonderful no-meaning she began to trace upon her wrappers. The hand soon stopped in the midst of them; the light that had always been feeble and dim behind the weak transparency, went out; and even Mrs. Gradgrind, emerged from the shadow in which man walketh and disquieteth himself in vain, took upon her the dread solemnity of the sages and patriarchs.

With this kind of thing before us, we talk not of style but of dramatic creation and imaginative genius.

NOTE

The following is a pretty recent pronouncement on Dickens in general and on *Hard Times* in particular—it comes from Dr. John Holloway's contribution to *Dickens in the Twentieth Century* (edited by John Gross):

What the discussion [Dr. Holloway's of *Hard Times*] seems to issue in is a view of the novel's moral intention that accords with the quality and development of Dickens's whole mind. He was not a profound or prophetic genius with insight into the deepest levels of experience; but (leaving his immense gifts aside for a moment) a man whose outlook was amiable and generous, though it partook a little of the shallowness of the merely topical, and the defects of the bourgeois–the word is not too hard–Philistine.'

That is explicit enough; with my avowed purpose as criterion, I don't ask for better, and the deliberately emphatic 'Philistine' gives a good concluding resonance. The passage seems worth quoting because, bluntly challenging as it offers to be, the critic isn't to be charged with any brashness of originality; the view of Dickens he states doesn't quarrel with that generally held. It's my own account of *Hard Times* that he challenges–he explicitly writes with his eye on what I wrote in *Scrutiny*.

The gifts that made Dickens one of the very greatest of creative writers are not, in fact, merely 'left aside for a moment'; they are flatly denied and dismissed. I won't spend words on Dr. Holloway's offer to disprove my account of *Hard Times* by adducing what Dickens said at Birmingham in a speech after a civic dinner. It goes, that offer, with the conviction (shared with Humphrey House and others) that Dickens, unlike his critics, hadn't the intellectual capacity for understanding Bentham, and with the attempt to show that *Hard Times* (a moral fable being an essay turned into art) is not an alpha, or even a beta, essay on Utilitarianism. What reply is there to such an approach?–unless, with a finger on a place in the text: 'But take this, and ponder what it does and to what it owes its power'?

If, however, inappropriate assumptions preclude any recognition of the nature of creative expression as Dickens practises it, there will be no recognition of the power, and the reply fails. Thus Dr. Holloway dismisses my commentary on the significance of the Horse-riding with this:

> It doesn't seem to be anything even remotely Lawrentian (this was after all, a pre-Nietzsche novel).
> On the contrary, it too, like its opposite, operated (for all its obvious common sense and its genuine value) at a relatively shallow level of consciousness, one represented by the Slearies, not as vital horsemen, but as plain entertainers.
> In fact, the creed which Dickens champions in the novel against the Gradgrinds seems to be in the main that of 'all work and no play makes Jack a dull boy.' How unwilling many will be to admit this!

Unwilling! I can't but observe that the critical consciousness to which this kind of confidence belongs operates at decidedly a not-profound level. Lawrence didn't need to learn from Nietzsche that life flows from sources far below the level of will and ego-enforced idea; that it is spontaneous, unmeasurable and creative; and that men, all the same, are continually trying, in one way and another, to ignore or defeat these truths. If he had needed to find them in other writers he could have learnt them from Shakespeare and the Greek tragic poets and from all the creative writers and artists he studied with the insight of genius. My immediate point is that he could have learnt them from Dickens, with whom he has special affinities, and to whom, like the post-Dickensian novelists in general, he was immensely indebted.

The robust realism of commonsense, however, assures us that Dickens is to be thought of, not as a great artist and novelist, but as an entertainer (a genius, of course). The Horse-riding is a circus, and a circus is entertainment, and all the meaning we can reasonably take from the part it plays in *Hard Times* is that all work and no play makes Jack a dull boy. This chimes with the notion of Dickens that has been generally endorsed by the authorities on his 'social criticism'. To this day a specialist on Dickens's relation to the Victorian age will, when he holds forth publicly, pay his due tribute to the creative writer with a comic-turn rendering of some selected 'Dickens characters'.

I hadn't, in the way Dr. Holloway implies, thought of any conventional symbolic value belonging to horses; but all that we see of the Horse-riding evokes for us spontaneous and daring vitality disciplined into skill and grace. It brings together the elements and aspects of an intense, deep and embracing significance – that which animates the whole dramatic poem.

This, however, is to postulate something that doesn't exist for my critic, for whom there is no 'dramatic poem' – no conceivable significance of such a kind as could justify that description. He has, it seems, the Dickens authorities with him. And yet the insistence developed in *Hard Times* has been, explicitly and implicitly, present in Dickens's work from before *Dombey and Son*, where it plays so central a part. Dr Holloway might, I suppose, say that little Paul died of 'all work and no play' added to deprivation of a mother's love. What, then, does he make of Paul's weakness for old Glubb, which Dickens obviously intends us to see as highly significant? The fact is that 'all work and no play' in Dr Holloway's use of the phrase is – as Dickens's genius has not availed to bring home to him – grossly reductive. Years before *Hard Times*, and years before *Dombey and Son* too, Dickens was insisting that 'play' as a need is intimately bound up with 'wonder', imagination and creativity, and that any starving of the complex need is cruel, denaturing and sterilizing, and may be lethal. There is, for instance, in *The Old Curiosity*

Shop (chapter XXXI), the scene in Miss Monflathers' Boarding and Day Establishment, with the rebuke inflicted on Little Nell and elaborated for the edification of those present.

'Don't you feel how naughty it is of you,' resumed Miss Monflathers, 'to be a waxwork child, when you might have the proud consciousness of assisting, to the extent of your infant powers, the manufactures of your country; of improving your mind by the constant contemplation of the steam-engine; and of earning a comfortable and independent subsistence of from two-and-ninepence to three shillings per week?'

Immediately before *Hard Times* comes *Bleak House*, and there we have the Smallweeds.

During the whole time consumed in the slow growth of this family tree, the house of Smallweed, always early to go out and late to marry, has strengthened itself in its practical character, has discarded all amusements, discountenanced all story-books, fairy tales, fictions and fables, and banished all levities whatsoever. Hence the gratifying fact, that it has had no child born to it, and that the complete little men and women whom it has produced have been observed to bear a likeness to old monkeys with something depressing on their minds.

Of the sister-twin we are told:

Judy never owned a doll, never heard of Cinderella, never played at any game.

Her twin-brother:

couldn't wind up a top for his life. He knows no more of Jack the Giant Killer, or of Sinbad the Sailor, than he knows of the people in the stars. He could as soon play at leapfrog, or at cricket, as change into a cricket or a frog himself. But he is so much the better off than his sister that on his narrow world of fact an opening has dawned, into such broader regions as lie within the ken of Mr. Guppy. Hence, his admiration and his emulation of that shining enchanter.

The basic utilitarian principle of self-interest gets its explicit statement here:

'Aye, aye, Bart!' says Grandfather Smallweed. 'How are you, hey?'
'Here I am,' says Bart.
'Been along with your friend again, Bart?' Small nods.
'Dining at his expense, Bart?' Small nods again.
'That's right. Live at his expense as much as you can, and take

warning by his foolish example. That's the use of such a fool. The only use you can put him to,' says the venerable sage.

Bleak House leads on to *Hard Times*, and *Hard Times* leads on to *Little Dorrit.*

Those who rest complacently or resolutely on the conviction that Dickens was a Philistine will see little point in that last clause. But the tharacteristic insistence as developed in *Little Dorrit*, where, as a proud and conscious major artist, Dickens conducts a sustained and searching inquiry into contemporary civilization, entails a full overtness of pre-occupation with the place, and the human necessity, of art.

CHAPTER FIVE

DICKENS AND BLAKE:
'LITTLE DORRIT'

i

THE indisputable but misleading proposition that the Dickensian genius is the genius of a great entertainer can be, we have seen, advanced, *Hard Times* being in question, to justify a blankness to the sharply focused power–that is, to the clear significance–of that highly concentrated work, and so to its distinction as creative literature; for if you can't take the significance you will hardly see *Hard Times* as the patent classic it is. *Little Dorrit*, on the other hand, answers so obviously and abundantly to what has for so long been the prevailing notion of the essentially Dickensian that it enjoys general recognition as one of the master's major performances. Yet that it is one of the very greatest or novels–that its omission from any brief list of the great European novels would be critically indefensible–is not a commonplace. The significance focused with a sharp economy in *Hard Times*–a significance the force and bearing of which can't be too insistently impressed on an age of statistical method, social studies and the computer–is at the deep centre of *Little Dorrit*; but published commentary on Dickens doesn't encourage the recognition that any book of his *has* a deep centre. *Little Dorrit* is one that has; it exhibits a unifying and controlling life such as only the greatest kind of creative writer can command.

There seems to be a pretty general conviction among us that in recent years we have achieved, in regard to the 'art of the novel', a critical sophistication unknown in the Victorian age. Perhaps we have. But the truly portentous effect of the changes that have transformed civilization in the hundred years since Dickens died is not that he strikes the reader as antiquated, naïve and Victorian, but that the conditions of the kind or greatness represented by *Little Dorrit* have disappeared from the world and a corresponding blindness results, induced by the climate of implicit assumptions and ideas that now prevails. The firmly established cult of Shakespeare generates no effective light.

I won't offer to elaborate the parallel between Shakespeare's development and achievement as the great popular playwright of our dramatic efflorescence and Dickens's as the marvellously fertile, supremely successful and profoundly creative exploiter of the Victorian market for fiction. There is clearly, however, a need to insist that Dickens no more than Shakespeare started from nothing and created out of a cultural void. 'A waif himself, he was totally disinherited': Santayana's observation illuminates nothing except the assumptions behind it; it is stultifyingly false. Dickens belonged as a popular writer, along with his public, to a culture in which the arts of speech were intensely alive. That was a good start. Anyone concerned to enforce the truth that he wrote out of a peculiarly rich inheritance – rich in relation to the needs of an artist of his gift and destiny – would have good reason to think first of the part of Shakespeare himself in it; Shakespeare – the point is an essential one – who then really *was* a national author. The most important aspect of Dickens's notorious indebtedness to the theatre (though this is not the point usually made) is to be seen there. Not that the life and power of Shakespeare for Dickens were merely a matter of the theatre. He read immensely, with the intelligence of genius, and his inwardness with Shakespeare, the subtlety of the influence manifest, and to be divined, in his own creative originality, can't be explained except by a reader's close and pondering acquaintance. I will add, by way of enforcing this kind of comment on the view that the author of *Dombey and Son*, *Little Dorrit* and *Great Expectations* was a Philistine, the related note that he knew the Romantic poets – one can't, by the time one comes to *Little Dorrit*, fail to see it as an important enough truth to be affirmed.

He mixed freely in the cultivated company he needed: class did indeed, as his novels make us very much aware, exist in Victorian England, but class constituted no barrier that got in his way. The higher cultural world of intellect and spirit was quick to recognize his genius, and he hadn't to form any sense of finding it difficult of access. We see these as pregnantly significant points when we ask how it was that, just as Shakespeare could be both the established favourite of the groundlings in the popular theatre and the supreme poetic mind of the Renaissance, master explorer of human experience, so Dickens, pursuing indefatigably his career as bestselling producer of popular fiction, could develop into a creative writer of the first order, the superlatively original creator of his art.

He was intensely an artist, unlike as he was either to Flaubert or to Henry James, and as he develops he becomes more and more describable as a dedicated one. *Dombey and Son*, in ways I have discussed, solved only partially Dickens's problem: that of achieving the wholly significant work of art as a successful serial-writer, writing always against time and for the popular market. *Bleak House* again, rich and diverse as it is in the creative felicities of a great novelist and poet, doesn't altogether solve that problem. But in *Little Dorrit* the thing is done. There are no large qualifications to be urged, and the whole working of the plot, down to the melodramatic dénouement, is significant—that is, serves the essential communication felicitously. When the secret of Arthur Clennam's birth is revealed, it completes the presented significance of Mrs. Clennam and the Clennam house:

> ... Satan entered into that Frederick Dorrit, and counselled him that he was a man of innocent and laudable tastes who did kind actions, and that here was a poor girl with a voice for singing music with. Then he is to have her taught. Then Arthur's father, who has all along been secretly pining, in the ways of virtuous ruggedness, for those accursed snares which are called the Arts, becomes acquainted with her. And so a graceless orphan, training to be a singing girl, carries it, by that Frederick Dorrit's agency, against me, and I am humbled and deceived.

This emphasis on art at the moment of confession—Mrs. Clennam's characteristic kind of confession—has nothing gratuitous about it. What Dickens hated in the Calvinistic commercialism of the early and middle Victorian age—the repressiveness towards children, the hard righteousness, the fear of love, the armed rigour in the face of life—he sums up now in its hatred of art. That he should do so is eloquent of the place he gave to art in human life and of the conception of art that informs his practice (it seems to be essentially Blake's). He conveyed his criticism of Victorian civilization in a creative masterpiece, a great work of art, which it would be fatuous to suppose he achieved accidentally and unconsciously, without meaning it and without knowing it. What, at a religious depth, Dickens hated about the ethos figured by the Clennam house was the offence against life, the spontaneous, the real, the creative, and, at this moment preceding the collapse of the symbolic house, he represents the creative spirit of life by art.

For Arthur Clennam the ethos is that which oppressed his childhood, glowering on spontaneity, spirit and happiness and inculcating guilt, and which, in its institutional manifestation, appals him as the English Sunday, wrapping London in a pall of gloom on his first morning back, he being bound towards the old childhood home to see his 'mother' again after twenty years of exile. It is the beginning of the sustained criticism of English life that the book enacts. For Clennam himself it is the beginning of an urgently personal criticism of life in Arnold's sense – that entailed in the inescapable and unrelenting questions: 'What shall I do? What *can* I do? What are the possibilities of life – for me, and, more generally, in the very nature of life? What are the conditions of happiness? What is life for?' Despondent, muted, earnest, with an earnestness derived from the upbringing the anti-life ethos of which he intensely rejects, he can't but find himself with such a criticism of life as his insistent preoccupation.

> So here I am, in the middle way, having had twenty years –
> Twenty years largely wasted . . .

– The resonance as of a religious concern with basic criteria and ultimate issues carried by this from its context in *Four Quartets* and from the opening of the *Divina Commedia* doesn't make it inappropriate here – for the usual easy and confident denial of any profundity of thought to Dickens is absurd and shameful.

The inquest into contemporary civilization that he undertook in *Little Dorrit* might equally be called a study of the criteria implicit in an evaluative study of life. What it commits him to is an enterprise of thought; thought that it is in our time of the greatest moment to get recognized, consciously and clearly, *as* thought – an affair (that is) of the thinking intelligence directed to a grasp of the real. Dickens's capacity for effective thought about life is indistinguishable from his genius as a novelist. A great novelist is addicted to contemplating and pondering life with an intensity of interest that entails – that *is* – the thought that asks questions, seeks answers and defines. And (whatever that last verb might seem to imply) he doesn't need to be told that he must take a firm hold on the truth that life, for a mind truly intent on the real, is life in the concrete; that life is concretely 'there' only in individual lives; and that individual lives can't be aggregated, generalized or averaged.

On the other hand, he knows that the serious and developed study of the individual life can't but be a study of lives in relation, and of social conditions, conventions, pressures as they affect essential life. The really great novelist can't but find himself making an evaluative inquiry into the civilization in which he finds himself–which he more and more finds himself in and of.

I might have added a couple of sentences ago that he doesn't need to be reminded–or to remind himself–that 'life' is a necessary word and that the impossibility of arriving at any abstract definition acceptable to him is far from being evidence of an unreality about what the word portends: it is the opposite.

Dickens in the nature of his creative undertaking aims at communicating generally valid truths about what can't be defined. I point here to the importance of getting it recognized that his genius as a novelist is a capacity for profound and subtle thought. His method, with all its subtleties and complexities, is a method of tackling what is in one aspect an intellectual problem: he tackles it, beyond any doubt, consciously and calculatingly.

I have already noted how Clennam, returned after twenty years of exile, dejected and without momentum or aim, opens, out of a particular situation and the pressure of a personal history, the critique of Victorian civilization. The questioning, so largely for him a matter of self-interrogation that implicitly bears on the criteria for judgment and value-perception, starts in that reverse of theoretical way, but–or so–with great felicity. The answer implicit in *Little Dorrit* is given creatively by the book, and it is not one that could have been given by Clennam himself. Not only is it something that can't be stated; the Clennam evoked for us is obviously not adequate to its depth and range and fulness, his deficiency being among the characteristics that qualify him for his part in the process by which the inclusive communication of the book is generated. Each of the other characters also plays a contributory part, inviting us to make notes on his or her distinctive 'value' in relation to the whole.

Nevertheless, about Dickens's art there is nothing of the rigidly or insistently schematic. We find ourselves bringing together for significant association characters as unlike, for instance, as Miss Wade, Henry Gowan, William Dorrit and Mrs. Clennam, or seeing a rightness that is other than one of piquant or pleasing complementarity in the mutual attraction that manifests itself (a fact of the narrative) between Doyce, Clennam, Pancks and Cavalletto. And when we have got as far as that we are aware of already having made a note that Gowan (for instance) associates in significant relationship with characters who form a quite different grouping from that in which I have just placed him, so that, if in our diagrammatic notation we have been representing groupings by lines linking names, the lines run across one another in an untidy and undiagrammatic mess. The diagrammatic suggestion is soon transcended as the growing complexity of lines thickens; we arrive at telling ourselves explicitly what we have been implicitly realizing in immediate perception and response: 'This, brought before us for pondering contemplation, is life–life as it manifests itself variously in this, that and the other focusing individual (the only way in which it can).'

In the striking power with which the book achieves the effect I point to here Clennam plays an important part, one that entails the unique status he has among the characters. That he is very important doesn't mean that he competes for inclusion among the 'Dickens characters', for he isn't a character in that sense, though he decidedly exists for us–is felt (that is) as a real personal presence. He has in this respect a clear affinity with Pip of *Great Expectations*, who, though so centrally important in that book, is not described at all, or endowed with describable, or at any rate very distinctive, characteristics. What is required of Pip is that he shall be felt unquestionably to exist as a centre of sentience, an identity, and Dickens's art ensures that he shall, for it ensures that the reader shall implicitly identify himself with Pip and *be* his sentience–while remaining, nevertheless, as the reader, another person (sufficiently another person in many cases, it seems, not to think of protesting when an authority calls *Great Expectations* 'a snob's progress').

Little Dorrit, the equally astonishing and very different masterpiece, is very differently organized; Clennam is not 'I' in it, and not the ubiquitous immediate consciousness that registers and presents. Yet he too is felt as a pervasive presence, or something approaching it. He has been very early, with a subtlety of purpose and touch Dickens isn't as a rule credited with, established as that–established as the presence of what one may very well find oneself referring to as plain unassertive normality. And what that means is that we tend to *be* Clennam, as we obviously don't William Dorrit, Mr. Meagles, Daniel Doyce, Henry Gowan, Pancks–or any other character in the book. He is for us a person, *the* decently ordinary person among the *dramatis personae* ('ordinary' here not being used in a placing or pejorative way, but reassuringly), and he has at the same time a special status, unavowed but essential to his importance; it is implicit in his being, not a queer or unpleasant case, but the immediate focal presence of representative human sentience–ours (for ours, being our own, *is* that; it is the immediate concrete 'presence of life').

Clennam's consciousness of deprivation and disablement, avowed by him directly at the outset, in his exchange with Mr. Meagles in chapter II,[1] where the quarantine-freed travellers prepare to disperse, isn't at all a contradiction that has to be reconciled with this special status, or with the suggestions of the word 'normality'; without having suffered his childhood, we accept with ready sympathy the sense of the world represented by this earnest, intelligent and pre-eminently civilized man: we respect him as we respect ourselves. The way in which Clennam serves the effect that the intellectual-imaginative purpose of *Little Dorrit* requires has nothing of the diagrammatic or the logical about it; it works by imaginatively prompting suggestion, so that the reader sees and takes in immediate perception what logic, analysis and statement can't convey. The effect is to make us realize explicitly why we are right to pick on *Little Dorrit* as a supreme illustration of the general truth about great creative writers, that their creative genius is a potency of *thought*. We tell ourselves that in presenting the large cast of diverse characters and the interplay between them Dickens is conducting a sustained, highly conscious and subtly methodical study of the human psyche; that he is concerned to arrive at and convey certain general validities of perception and judgment about life – enforcing implicitly in the process the truth that 'life' is a necessary word; that it is not a mere word, or a word that portends nothing more than an abstraction.

It won't, perhaps, be out of place to clinch this critical insistence with a comparative reference to Blake. Blake too was a creative writer whose genius was a penetrating insight into human nature and the human condition, and whose creativity was a potency of thought. The mythical works, with the complexities, ambiguities and shifting 'symbolic' values that defy the diagrammatizing interpreter, give us Blake's method of grappling with the problem ('lives' and 'life') that Dickens tackles with

---

[1] "And now, Mr. Clennam, perhaps I may ask you, whether you have come to a decision where to go next?"
' "Indeed no, I am such a waif and stray everywhere, that I am liable to be drifted where any current may set."
' "It's extraordinary to me–if you'll excuse my freedom in saying so–that you don't go straight to London", said Mr. Meagles, in the same tone of a confidential adviser.
' "Perhaps I shall."
' "Ay! But I mean with a will."
' "I have no will. That is to say", he coloured a little, "next to none that I can put in action now." '

the innovating resources of an inspired and marvellously original novelist in *Little Dorrit*.

ii

We quite early find that we are engaged intimately and deeply in Clennam's personal life. The book, in making the Clennam theme–the necessity-impelled battle with the challenging questions–a unifying one, gives us his *éducation sentimentale*. There is the shattering disillusion of Flora, the one redeeming memory (she had been) of his childhood:

> It is no proof of an inconstant mind, but exactly the opposite, when the idea will not bear close comparison with the reality, and the contrast is a fatal shock to it. Such was Clennam's case. In his youth he had ardently loved this woman, and had heaped upon her all the locked-up wealth of his affection and imagination. That wealth had been, in his desert home, like Robinson Crusoe's money; exchangeable with no one, lying idle in the dark to rust, until he poured it out for her. Ever since that memorable time, though he had, until the night of his arrival, as completely dismissed her from any association with his Present or Past as if she had been dead (which she might easily have been for anything he knew), he had kept the old fancy of the Past unchanged in its old sacred place. And now, after all, the last of the Patriarchs coolly walked into the parlour, saying in effect, 'Be good enough to throw it down and dance upon it. This is Flora.'

There is Pet Meagles, the charming girl with whom he, at forty (inevitably, as the just-quoted passage tells us), falls in love, but whom, we can see, as Dickens clearly sees and implicitly says, he oughtn't (even though the parents favour him–even if Pet's assent could be won) to be allowed to marry. And there is Little Dorrit, and, finally, marriage, with the fittingness, not to be dismissed as romantic or sentimental, that makes it something quite other than a conventional conclusion.

In all this, which is done with delicacy and penetration, we can no doubt see some direct drawing on personal history; but Dickens himself, intimately presented as Clennam is, wasn't at all like Clennam. Clennam's past has left him discouraged in his vital spontaneity. The creative force of life in him has no confident authority; he, we can say with point, is *not* an artist. But in that set inquest into Victorian civilization which *Little Dorrit* enacts for us he is a focal agent–focal in respect of the implicit judgments and valuations and the criteria they represent. We have here, representatively manifest, the impersonalizing process of Dickens's art: the way in which he has transmuted his personal experience into something that is not personal, but felt by us as reality and truth presented, for what with intrinsic authority they are, by impersonal intelligence. His essential social criticism doesn't affect us as urged personally by the writer. It has the disinterestedness of spontaneous life, undetermined and undirected and uncontrolled by idea, will and self-insistent ego, the disinterestedness here being that which brings a perceived significance to full realization and completeness in art. The writer's labour has been to present something that speaks for itself.

That Dickens's finest work has the impersonality of great art is something I have to insist on; the fact is at the centre of my theme. Consider the Marshalsea in *Little Dorrit*, and the kind of emphasis that marks Edmund Wilson's discussion of its significance–Wilson being a critic who enjoys a very high prestige. He, in his well-known essay,[1] makes the significance mainly a matter of the psychological traumata suffered by Dickens in childhood, and invites us to see Dickens 'working the prison out of his system' in the conceiving and writing of his *œuvre*. But this is to ignore the nature of Dickens's development as an artist, and the greatness of his greatest book. And it is to misdirect the attention and to put obstacles in the way of perception and understanding. No one would wish to question that the Marshalsea was an intensely charged memory for Dickens, or that it *was* so by reason of the well-known facts of his personal history. But there is no need to know those facts in order to appreciate *Little Dorrit*; they have virtually no critical relevance, and if, as we read, we occupy ourselves with a quest for the evidence of traumata, we are disastrously misdirecting our attention.

A colleague of mine some years ago hailed, as giving us the most promising kind of clue for future criticism, the discovery that Dickens was an 'anal dandy'. I don't expect to see anyone seriously attempting that approach, yet the ostensibly more respectable substitutes for an intelligent interest in the great novelist's art are really no better.

The significance of the Marshalsea is the significance we take in a disinterested response to the text; and, as we go on taking it, it expands and subtilizes–the profound irony of the novel expressing itself in that process. The prison is the world of 'the mind-forged manacles'; it is Society with a big S, as well as the society we all have to live in; it is Mrs.

[1]In *The Wound and the Bow*.

Clennam's will and self-deception (figured also in her arthritic immobilization and her wheeled chair); it is Henry Gowan's ego; it is Pancks's 'What business have I in the present world, except to stick to business? No business'; it is for the great Merdle the Chief Butler's eye; it is life in our civilization as Clennam–as, more inclusively, the Dickens of *Little Dorrit*–registers it.

When towards the end Clennam finds himself literally imprisoned in the Marshalsea and lapses into accidie, we have no need to ponder symbolic values: the focused charge has its immediate effect. The Blakean indeterminateness of what the Marshalsea 'stands for' is a condition, in fact, of the major part the 'symbol' plays in the whole wonderfully close organic unity. In the shifting metaphorical suggestiveness there is a unifying constant; it is the implicitly evoked contrasting opposite–opposite of what the stale and squalid prison, closed in upon by the city 'where the chartered Thames doth flow', evokes directly. When we say that for Dickens, and for us, it is ego-free love, creative spontaneity, Little Dorrit's bouquet, Flora Casby, the erupting Pancks, Doyce, Cavalletto and Dickens himself, we don't unsay 'unifying constant'. And to say that the book, the created whole, justifies this last sentence seems a good way of pointing to the nature of Dickens's triumphant success.

The problem ('social problem') with which Dickens's book challenges us in the Marshalsea isn't of a kind to which discussions of Dickens's part (or the absence of it) in the abolition of imprisonment for debt has any relevance. That isn't to say that Dickens didn't in his innermost being cry out against the very idea of imprisonment for debt. The book does that. The fact that imprisonment for debt had been abolished before he wrote *Little Dorrit* only serves to make the spirit of his use of the Marshalsea the more unambiguous. All his early readers would know of the not distant actuality, and no one would for a moment suppose him ignorant of the abolition.[1] There has been no excuse at any time for any reader not to realize the nature and take the force of this 'social criticism' as the book makes it. They are those exemplified in the passage (Book the First,

---

[1] The opening phrase of the book is 'Thirty years ago', and chapter VI begins: 'Thirty years ago there stood, a few doors short of the church of Saint George, in the borough of Southwark, on the left-hand side of the way going southward, the Marshalsea Prison.' Nevertheless, it is England of the time of writing that Dickens plainly offers to examine. The 'anachronism' doesn't in the least qualify the felicity of his use of the Marshalsea; rather, it serves to emphasize the essential nature of his 'social criticism'.

chapter XXXV) in which Little Dorrit, her father's release being imminent, makes her protest against the conditions of it—though obviously
her essential protest comes to more than that:

'Mr. Clennam, will he pay all his debts before he leaves here?'
'No doubt. All.'
'All the debts for which he has been imprisoned here, all my life,
and longer?'
'No doubt.'
There was someting of uncertainty and remonstrance in her look;
something that was not all satisfaction. He wondered to detect it,
and said:
'You are glad that he should do so?'
'Are you?'
'Am I? Most heartily glad.'
'Then I know I ought to be.'
'And are you not?'
'It seems to me hard,' said Little Dorrit, 'that he should have lost
so many years and suffered so much, and at last pay all the debts as
well. It seems to me hard that he should pay in life and money both.'
'My dear child –,' Clennam was beginning.
'Yes, I know I am wrong,' she pleaded timidly 'don't think any
the worse of me; it has grown up with me here.'
The prison, which could spoil so many things, had tainted Little
Dorrit's mind no more than this. Engendered, as the confusion was,
in compassion for the poor prisoner, her father: it was the first speck
Clennam had ever seen, it was the last speck Clennam ever saw, of
the prison atmosphere upon her.

The speck, of course, is upon Clennam. I say 'of course', but I know
from questions and discussion—and there is the (to me) astonishing commentary in A. O. J. Cockshut's book[1] on 'this slight taint of irresponsibility' ('It is beyond her imagination that the creditor also might have
suffered hardship through unpaid debts')—I know that the irony can be
missed. Yet who, on reflection, can conceive Dickens to have meant any
but that judgment which is conveyed by Little Dorrit? Besides the
cruelty, the offence against life, of imprisonment for debt (and it was
society that had entailed indebtedness on the essentially innocent William
Dorrit), there is the stultifying irrationality: the debtor in prison is debarred from setting about earning the means of repayment. The im-

[1] *The Imagination of Charles Dickens*, pages 40–41.

prisoning him represents starkly the most indefensible idea of retribution. And life against money!–it is the blasphemous iniquity of that, legally and righteously enforced, that Little Dorrit can't swallow: who can suppose that it's the money she cares about? Her protest is against the whole code, and the unspeakable her father has suffered. The taint is what clings to Clennam, clings still from his upbringing; the taint of the Calvinistic commercial ethos (prison), and it manifests itself in his taking her as he does, and reproving her with that firm forbearing look. If we take Dickens's irony, *we* don't assume that look or that tone; we leave them to Clennam, and it's not for Little Dorrit that we make allowances.

It seems to me that not to be sure of this is to have missed the creative arch-intuition in Dickens, the deep imperative preoccupation that organizes the immense range of evoked life, the wealth of diverse interest, into significance–for everything in the book is significant in terms of the whole. Dickens's art in that brief exchange between Little Dorrit and Clennam is making the same affirmation it makes in the *tête-à-tête* between Louisa and her father about Bounderby's proposal of marriage. The affirmation is of life, which–this is the insistence–doesn't belong to the quantitative order, can't be averaged, gives no hold for statistics and can't be weighed against money. Little Dorrit is profoundly modest and not a person of intellectual force, and Clennam, she knows, is good, so she defers to him; but she has seen–for *her* feeling is perception–that to acquiesce in the suggestion that life *can* be weighed against money is a sin against life. Not crime, but sin; it is a word one *has* to use, even though Dickens (Cockshut's judgment) knows nothing about sanctity, and is charged with shallowness, or philistinism, in matters of religion.

'Life', it may be commented, is a large word. Certainly it is a word we can't do without and unquestionably an important one, and the importance is of a nature that makes it obviously futile to try to define abstractly, by way of achieving precision, the force or value it has as I have just used it. We feel the futility the more intensely in that, as we consider Dickens's art in *Little Dorrit*, we see very potently at work a process that it seems proper to call definition by creative means. There are other important words, so closely associated–as, prompted by *Little Dorrit*, we find we have to invoke them–with 'life' that we judge them to be equally unsusceptible of what is ordinarily meant by definition; and these we unmistakably see getting a potent definition in the concrete. And as, with reassuring effect, we inquire into the justification of this last phrase, we recognize that what the prompted words in association portend gets *its* definition as the creative work builds up. Dickens's essential 'social criticism', his inquest into Victorian civilization, is inseparable from this process. It is plain that neither the process (which is Dickens's art) nor the significance has been, or can be, appreciated by critics, scholarly or otherwise, who can tell us—with forbearance and counter-concessions—that Dickens never grew up intellectually, and that there is no reason to suppose that he could have made much of Bentham.

The points I have made about the nature and significance of *Little Dorrit* can be enforced by illustration abundantly and in many ways, as any responsive reader will easily exemplify; for the book has the abound-ingness and the inexhaustible subtlety of the greatest art. My obvious next move is to record some of the notes that one finds oneself jotting down, as one reads, regarding the criteria implicit in Dickens's critique of civilized England. When one has noted the set of indicative, or focal, words one is prompted to seize on, the words to which I have just re-ferred, and made the essential commentary on them, one has at the same time done a lot to explain the force of calling *Little Dorrit* an 'affirmation of life'. But to say that is to point to the difficulty; the words *are* focal, and the aboundingness, whatever Henry James might have thought, was not redundant. So I must make it plain at once that there can be no neat and systematic exposition, and avow that I find the directness of approach I may have seemed to promise out of place.

I will start with some reflections on the character whose name gives the book its title. Little Dorrit, the heroine (if that is not too incongruous a word), has a large and very important part in the complex whole, and unmistakably represents human qualities on which Dickens sets a high value. Of her the first thing it seems natural to say is that she is good—which is not one of the 'focal words' in my own list. But if one says she is good it must be to add that she is utterly unlike Little Nell. I have found myself insisting on this obvious enough truth because, as I know from much arguing about Dickens, that people nowadays are apt to shy away from goodness as Little Dorrit evokes it, and, when challenged, to reply by associating her with Little Nell. They may have been shifted out of House's kind of injustice, by which Dickens's 'social doctrine' is reduced to a Cheeryble benevolence, but they still baulk at taking feminine goodness seriously.

Of course, to suggest taking Little Nell seriously would be absurd: there's nothing there. She doesn't derive from any perception of the real; she's a contrived unreality, the function of which is to facilitate in the reader a gross and virtuous self-indulgence. But the Little Dorrit we know, if we read and see and respond, emerges for us out of the situation and the routine of daily life that produced her–I mean, conditioned just *that* manifestation of what she spontaneously was, in the living individuality that started its unfolding when she was born in the Marshalsea. Her genius is to be always beyond question genuine–real. She is indefectibly real, and the test of reality for the others. That is a proposition to which the dramatic poem gives the clearest meaning. The characteristic manifests itself in her power to be, for her father and brother and sister, the never-failing providence, the vital core of sincerity, the conscience, the courage of moral percipience, the saving realism, that preserves for them the necessary bare minimum of the real beneath the fantastic play of snobberies, pretences and self-deceptions that constitutes genteel life in the Marshalsea. It is done, not merely told us, with inexhaustible fulness, diversity and power.

Little Dorrit is unquestionably 'there' for us. Dickens's creativity in achieving this is a matter of appealing to our experience. We recognize in her a profoundly important human possibility–one that has a normative bearing. There seems to me point in recalling here the parallel provided by James in his Maisie. I think of James because, having once suggested, with good reason, that the prompting to that masterpiece, *What Maisie Knew*, had been a memory of little David Copperfield's situation in the Micawber household,[1] it has struck me that Little Dorrit, a child and the family's unfaltering stay, had certainly no less a part in the prompting. Incorruptibly innocent and sincere, what does she know–really know? To know would be to recognize and to judge: she judges and doesn't judge. She understands enough to be infallible in response.

I mean with these three last sentences merely to justify my 'parallel': to think of elaborating a comparison between the two works would be absurd. James's intention, perfectly executed, is, in the characteristic Jamesian way, strictly and narrowly limited, and his book is really a *nouvelle*. That the unrecognized memory could play so essential a part in the imaginative conception (my suggestion is a convinced one) can be seen as an implicit tribute to Dickens on James's part, the recall of which is immediately very much in place. He translated the Little Dorrit situation, the poignant human truth and the irony of which had clearly made a deep impression on him, into terms of a social world (or, rather, stratum) he had observed closely–and with revulsion. In saying that

[1]See the essay, 'What Maisie Knew', in *Anna Karenina and Other Essays*.

James's intention in his *nouvelle* is severely limiting (I put it this way now), I don't mean merely that there are many more things in Dickens's book than the 'Little Dorrit situation' that James responded to creatively. My point is (and in making it I challenge the Jamesian critical attitude towards Dickens) that that situation as Dickens presents it involves the whole of the book he called *Little Dorrit*, and can be appreciated for what it is only by those who are open to the force of that truth. James's assured critical bent is that of the decidedly less great artist.–My concern is not to depreciate James, but to vindicate the genius of Dickens.

Immediately it is with the inquiry into 'criteria' and 'values' as it centres upon Little Dorrit herself. The affinity between her and Maisie is that they both so obviously prompt the characterizing notes, 'ego-free love', 'disinterestedness' and 'innocence'. There is no compelling reason why the admirer of *What Maisie Knew* should feel that such notes ought to be developed further; he wouldn't, in the nature of the case, be engaged in the kind of inquiry I have avowed as my own concern–an inquiry into the criteria implicit in a critique of a civilization. It is only as involved–through all kinds of personal relations, contacts and implicit cross-references–in that civilization that Little Dorrit exists to be studied as a focus of significance, and she is a very important one.

Dickens's abundance, range and untense freedom are the conditions, not only of an inexhaustibly subtle relatedness,[1] but of depth. I will pick up at this point the side-references I have thrown out to Blake. It has long seemed to me that there is the closest essential affinity between Dickens and the author of 'London'. It was in relation to the question of 'criteria' and 'values' that the affinity was borne in on me: I found that in reading Dickens I was jotting down the same words and phrases as those prompted by Blake. As for the nature of the affinity, I will quote what I have written elsewhere.[2]

But, of course it will be asked: what influence can Blake, who was far from being a current author in his time and didn't come in with the Romantic poets, be supposed to have had? A study of the evidence may some day be written showing that Blake, his poetry and his thought were well enough known to make him an 'influence' of certainly not less importance on the literature of the Victorian age

---

[1] 'The novel is the highest example of subtle inter-relatedness that man has discovered.'–D. H. Lawrence, *Phoenix* ('Morality and the Novel'), page 528.

[2] Introduction to *The Image of Childhood* by Peter Coveney (Peregrine Books), page 19.

than Wordsworth; for *Little Dorrit*, where the characteristics that make one think of Blake belong to the essential organic structure of the dramatic poem, is a much greater creative work than any in which Wordsworth may be seen as counting in a major way, and it is representative of the art that puts Dickens among the very greatest creative writers.

But I am not intending to commit myself to the belief that Dickens had read Blake. What is plain beyond question is that he was familiar with Wordsworth and with Romantic poetry in general, and that his interest and responsiveness were those of an originating genius who was equipped by nature to be himself a great poet. Further, a man of wonderfully quick intelligence, he mixed with the *élite* that shared the finest culture of the age and, when first frequented by him, was like himself pre-Victorian. One can say that his genius, entailing a completeness of interest in human life (Dickens was not 'a solemn and unsexual man'), cities and civilization that it was Wordsworth's genius not to have, spontaneously took those promptings of the complex romantic heritage which confirmed his response to early Victorian England; confirmed the intuitions and affirmations that, present organically in the structure and significance of *Hard Times* and *Little Dorrit*, make one think of Blake.

I have in mind, of course, the way in which the irrelevance of the Benthamite calculus is exposed; the insistence that life is spontaneous and creative, so that the appeal to self-interest as the essential motive is life-defeating; the vindication, in terms of childhood, of spontaneity, disinterestedness, love and wonder; and the significant place given to Art—a place entailing a conception of Art that is pure Blake.

In *Hard Times*, with its comparative simplicity as a damning critique of the hard ethos and the life-oppressing civilization, the identity of the affirmatives, or evoked and related manifestations of life and health and human normality, by which he condemns, with those of Blake is clear. *Little Dorrit* is immensely more complex, and offers something like a comprehensive report on Victorian England—what is life, what are the possibilities of life, in this society and civilization, and what could life, in a better society, be? To elicit the convinced assent to the proposition that here too the underlying structure of value-affirmations (implicit, spontaneous, inevitable) upon which the form and significance depend is Blakean, is not so easy. But the structure is there; for the book *has* organic form and essential economy: it is all significant.

–The entailed immediate emphasis for me is that, if one's commentary is to be effective in the required way, one will be conscious of facing a challenge to one's tactical skill. And, with 'disinterestedness', 'ego-free love' and *Little Dorrit* in mind, I think that my best move is to adduce Blake's distinction between the 'identity' and the 'selfhood'. 'Identity' is the word with which he insists, in the face of the ethos of 'Locke and Newton', that what matters is life, that only in the individual is life 'there', and that the individual is unique. With the distinction he insists also that the individual is a centre of responsibility towards something that is not him- (or her-)self. The distinction points to a basic truth–and not the less because there are perhaps difficulties in the way of seeing the distinction as absolute; a truth that is made to manifest itself concretely, its force brought home to us, by the great novelist's art. In fact I know of no better way of developing an account of Blake's thought than by turning, as I do now, to *Little Dorrit*, my theme being the thought–the insight and intelligence–of Dickens.

iii

What Little Dorrit herself is as a person is established for us, i.e. 'created', by the dramatic interplay with others in which the narrative presents her; the significance we see in her is developed by a complex implicit play of contrasts and affinities that involves all the characters in the cast. Her great opposite is Mrs. Clennam, the righteously unforgiving, who in the dénouement asks her forgiveness. Immediately after the confrontation with the blackmailing Rigaud,[1] and its sequel, the nightmare passage through the streets to the Marshalsea, we are told of the proud tormented woman, as she waits for Little Dorrit to come to her:[2] 'She stood at the window, bewildered, looking down into the prison out of her own different prison, when a soft word or two of surprise made her start, and Little Dorrit stood before her'. Little Dorrit, it comes to her, is the offered–the sought–opening of escape, and she takes it. The prison out of which she looks is the selfhood: Urizen, one has found oneself calling it–as one had found oneself calling the other too. Having achieved, in appeal and confession, a measure of release from her solitary confinement, she rushes with Little Dorrit out of the Marshalsea, and arrives at the grim and stale old house just as it splits and crumbles in dust and thunder before their eyes and subsides into rubble.

[1] Part the Second, chapter XXX.
[2] Part the Second, chapter XXXI.

Mrs. Clennam too sank to the ground; from that hour she never recovered the ability 'to lift a finger or speak a word'; 'reclined in her
wheeled chair . . . she lived and died a statue'. The mechanism of will,
idea and ego had stopped; but, after the years during which the spontaneous upflow had been jealously and righteously excluded, there was
nothing that could take over; only a sad ghost of identity for a while
remained, wholly impotent. She couldn't now, in the manner of those
days of Urizenic domination, drive her wheeled chair with a thrust of
her foot from one place to another in her enclosing room.[1]

The selfhood encloses; it insulates; the closure against the creative flow
from below is at the same time a closure against surrounding lives and
life. In Mrs. Clennam and Miss Wade and Henry Gowan the identity
has become the selfhood: the thing is achieved. The word 'responsibility'
I used gives some clue to the way in which this happens—some clue to

---

[1]The suggestion of life become mechanism is used pervasively and subtly in
Little Dorrit. Here, for instance, with immediate relevance to Mrs. Clennam's case,
is the opening of chapter XXIX, Book the First:
　'The house in the city preserved its heavy dullness through all these trans-
actions, and the invalid within it turned the same unvarying round of life.
Morning, noon, and night, morning, noon, and night, each recurring with its
accompanying monotony, always the same reluctant return of the same sequences
of machinery, like a dragging piece of clockwork.
　'The wheeled chair had its associated remembrances and reveries, one may
suppose, as every place that is made the station of a human being has. Pictures
of demolished streets and altered houses as they formerly were when the occupant
of the chair was familiar with them; images of people as they used to be, with
little or no allowance for the lapse of time since they were seen; of these there
must have been many in the long routine of gloomy days. To stop the clock of
busy existence at the hour when we were personally sequestered from it; to
suppose mankind stricken motionless, when we were brought to a standstill;
to be unable to measure the changes beyond our view by any larger standard
than the shrunken one of our own uniform and contracted existence; is the
infirmity of many invalids, and the mental unhealthiness of almost all recluses.
　'What scenes and actors the stern woman most reviewed, as she sat from season
to season in her one dark room, none knew but herself. Mr. Flintwinch, with
his wry presence brought to bear upon her daily life like some eccentric mechanical force, would perhaps have screwed it out of her, if there had been less resistance
in her; but she was too strong for him.'
The potent doubleness of suggestion represented by the co-presence and combined
action of 'dragging piece of clockwork' in the first paragraph and 'stop the clock
of busy existence' in the second will have been noted. The 'symbolic' value of Mrs.
Clennam and the Clennam house has the kind of indeterminateness that makes the
Marshalsea pervade the whole novel.

the nature and significance of the process. 'Disinterestedness', and 'ego-free love' are easily said; but the responsibility in question hasn't–the effect of the whole complex work is to bring that out–its complete re-presentation, its full comprehensive paradigm, in Little Dorrit, whose goodness is innocence. The presence of Daniel Doyce, who is both short and sharp about Henry Gowan, makes that plain. Doyces are rare, but what Doyce represents in so unqualified a way can't be dispensed with. One learns, however, to expect, in general, varying degrees of qualifi-cation; the life-thwarting potentialities in the psyche being uneliminable and insidious. Doyce's indefeasible 'responsibility towards something other than himself' entails, to be effective, his being strongly conscious of it. Such a consciousness can hardly *not* entail a sense of one's identity's being important; one's identity is oneself, and, as the habit of this last word in free use intimates, the shift to a dominating sense of one's unique and unshared selfhood as the important thing is insidiously easy.

Mrs. Clennam's Calvinistic religion enables her to transmute the service of her will–of her possessiveness, pride, jealousy, vengefulness and life-hatred–into the service of God, and this gives a poised, judicially stern and quasi-rational authority to her ruthless dominance:[1] Urizen reigns. The essential nature of her disease is brought out by the simpler case of Miss Wade. Miss Wade has no need of disguised self-justification, and no need of God. In her, 'identity' *is* 'selfhood', completely, simply and without misgiving; as if, in fact, she *were* God, a jealous and vengeful one, and blameless. She has no Little Dorrit on whom to appease a sup-pressed need of tenderness and an unavowed qualm of conscience. Her righteousness is wholly a sense of being wronged (i.e. sinned against). And she *has* been wronged, how irremediably, the state expressed with mechanical invariableness in her behaviour manifests; she has been wronged by Victorian civilization, being a victim of the Victorian attitude towards illegitimacy[2]–the attitude as experienced by the sex which was the more exposed to its cruellest consequences: she *needs* to be wronged in order to keep up the intensity of her resentment, the passion which for her is life.

[1] "As well might it be charged upon me that the stings of an awakened con-science drove her mad, and that it was the will of the Disposer of all things that she should live so, many years. I devoted myself to reclaim the otherwise pre-destined and lost boy; to give him the reputation of an honest origin; to bring him up in fear and trembling, and in a life of practical contrition for the sins that were heavy on his head before his entrance into this condemned world.'" Part the Second, chapter XXX.   [2]See page 155 above.

To us the whole process presents itself as a hysterical mechanism–a mechanism which in fact is madness, and this is what she describes in the *curriculum vitae* she hands to Clennam[1] in order to convince him of the hopelessness of his quest. Her need to be wronged is a need to dominate– to be uniquely real, unconditioned and absolute; and driven by it she destroys, she herself being the victim who *can't* escape. She doesn't rescue Tattycoram in order to make her happy; she doesn't want to make herself happy–essentially she is destructive. This it didn't take Tattycoram long to discover–or, rather, she had felt the lethal fascination at the first contact, and knew at once that the fascination was fear: restored to Twickenham, she confesses that.

No one would call Henry Gowan mad, but it is not for nothing that Miss Wade, in her *compte rendu* of herself, records that he was the first person who understood her, and that he understood her at once. He knew at a glance what her resentful pride meant, because his own pride was of a kind that could express itself only in resentment, his resentment being not less destructive, but more subtly so, than hers. His pleasure is to disconcert, and he uses his gentlemanly aplomb and his skill, which is constantly in practice, to that end. An extended example of the trait and of the gratuitousness of its manifestation is his part in the conversation at the supper-table of the Great Saint Bernard convent[2] (Book the Second, chapter I). This incidental descriptive sentence sufficiently characterizes it: 'There was enough of mocking inconsistency at the bottom of this speech to make it rather discordant, though the manner was refined and the person well-favoured, and though the depreciatory part of it was so skilfully thrown off, as to be very difficult for those not perfectly acquainted with the English language to understand, or, even understanding, to take offence at: so simple and dispassionate was its tone.' But if he hadn't known that the peculiar offensiveness would be felt for what it was, there would have been no point in the adroitness. Nevertheless, the inconsistency was not calculated; it expresses something in his basic condition.

We are told of this formidably proud man that he has 'no belief in anyone, because he had no belief in himself'. His insistent consciousness of superiority is an underlying consciousness of nullity; the stultifying contradiction, sensed if not recognized, makes him sinister in his all-

[1]Book the Second, chapter XXI.

[2]The implicit, significantly sympathetic, valuation conveyed to us of the young monk who urbanely and firmly presides is unmistakable.

round destructiveness; he feels that if he doesn't assert, as something that doesn't need asserting, his intrinsic superiority–the 'reality' of which is the recognition it gets–he is nothing. His case is given in Blandois' formula: 'He is more than an artist; he is well-connected'. His Barnacle kin have earned his resentment by not jobbing him into a well-salaried sinecure (the claim on the country that is a Barnacle's right), and he has had, defiantly, to fall back on 'being an artist.' He treats them, when they come up for mention, in his destructively equivocal way, but nevertheless cherishes with challenging intensity–born a Frenchman he would have been an addicted duellist–the superiority which is nothing but a matter of being 'one of them' ('one of us', of course, in direct speech).

Brought a commission to paint Mr. William Dorrit's portrait, he insults Blandois, the insultable kept-friend who brings it; 'for he resented patronage almost as much as he resented the want of it'. Next day, he pays a call on the gentleman.

Mr. Dorrit then mentioned his proposal. 'Sir,' said Gowan, laughing, after receiving it gracefully enough, 'I am new to the trade, and not expert in its mysteries. I believe I ought to look at you in various lights, tell you you are a capital subject, and consider when I shall be sufficiently disengaged to devote myself with the necessary enthusiasm to the fine picture I mean to make of you. I assure you,' and he laughed again, 'I feel quite a traitor in the camp of those dear, gifted, noble fellows, my brother artists, by not doing the hocus-pocus better. But I have not been brought up to it, and it's too late to learn it. Now, the fact is, I am a very bad painter, but not much worse than the generality. If you are going to throw away a hundred guineas or so, I am as poor as a poor relation of great people usually is, and I shall, be very much obliged to you, if you'll throw your money away upon me. I'll do the best I can for the money; and if the best should be bad, why even then, you may probably have a bad picture with a small name to it, instead of a bad picture with a large name to it.'

This tone, though not what he had expected, on the whole suited Mr. Dorrit remarkably well. It showed that the gentleman, highly connected, and not a mere workman, would be under an obligation to him.

The mocking inconsistency that imposes itself as ironic poise is an aggressively dominating mode of Mrs. General's 'surface', with its proscription of 'wonder', 'opinions' (i.e. convictions), and reality. Gowan practices this mode, the implicit intention and force of which are destructive, because, knowing deep down that he doesn't know what, if anything, is real in himself, he is determined to eliminate all possible tests of reality: the reality of the self he prefers not to recognize for what it is had better, for others (and himself too), remain a brilliant and disconcerting equivocation. His essential nihilism, profoundly personal, and at the same time highly significant for Dickens's 'social criticism', has a poignant manifestation in the upshot, for the Meagleses, of the sacrifice of their Pet.

By this time, Mr. Gowan had made up his mind that it would be agreeable to him not to know the Meagleses ... he mentioned to Mr. Meagles that personally they did not appear to him to get on together, and that he thought it would be a good thing if–politely, without any scene, or anything of that sort–they agreed that they were the best fellows in the world, but were best apart. Poor Mr. Meagles, who was already sensible that he did not advance his daughter's happiness by being constantly slighted in her presence, said, 'Good, Henry! You are my Pet's husband; you have displaced me, in the course of nature: if you wish it, good!' This arrangement involved the contingent advantage, which perhaps Henry Gowan had not foreseen, that both Mr. and Mrs. Meagles were more liberal than before to their daughter, when their communication was only with her and her young child; and that his high spirit found itself better provided with money, without being under the degrading necessity of knowing whence it came.[1]

If it is necessary to drive home the point that 'essential nihilism' is not a rhetorical emphasis but a cool judicial constatation, a passage offers itself from the exchange (Book the First, chapter XXVI) in which Gowan tells Clennam: 'You are genuine also'.

'By Jove, he is the finest creature?' said Gowan. 'So fresh, so green, trusts in such wonderful things!'
Here was one of the many little rough points that had a tendency to grate on Clennam's hearing. He put it aside by merely repeating that he had a high regard for Mr. Doyce.
'He is charming! To see him mooning along to that time of life, laying down nothing by the way and picking up nothing by the way, is delightful! It warms a man. So unspoilt, so simple, such a good soul! Upon my life, Mr Clennam, one feels desperately worldly and wicked in comparison with such an innocent creature. I speak for myself, let me add, without including you. You are genuine also.'

[1]Book the Second, chapter XXXIII.

'Thank you for the compliment,' said Clennam: ill at ease; 'you are too, I hope?'

'So so,' rejoined the other. 'To be candid with you, tolerably. I am not a great impostor. Buy one of my pictures, and I assure you, in confidence, that it is not worth the money. Buy one of another man's—any great professor who beats me hollow—and the chances are that the more you give him, the more he'll impose upon you. They all do it.'

'All painters?'

'Painters, writers, patriots, all the rest who have stands in the market. Give almost any man I know ten pounds, and he'll impose upon you to a corresponding extent; a thousand pounds—to a corresponding extent; ten thousand—to a corresponding extent. So great the success, so great the imposition. But what a capital world it is!' cried Gowan, with warm enthusiasism. What a jolly, excellent, lovable world it is!'

'I had rather thought,' said Clennam, 'that the principle you mention was chiefly acted on by—'

'By the Barnacles?' interrupted Gowan, laughing.

'By the political gentlemen who condescend to keep the Circumlocution Office.'

'Ah! Don't be hard upon the Barnacles,' said Gowan, laughing afresh, 'they are darling fellows! Even poor little Clarence, the born idiot of the family is the most agreeable and the most endearing blockhead! And by Jupiter, with a kind of cleverness in him too, that would astonish you!'

'It would. Very much,' said Clennam, drily.

'And after all,' cried Gowan, with that characteristic balancing of his which reduced everything in the wide world to the same light weight, 'though I can't deny that the Circumlocution Office may ultimately shipwreck everybody and everything, still, that will probably not be in our time—and it's a school for gentlemen.'

We see here, neatly exemplified in these juxtaposed passages, how Dickens's analysis, presented in what is so distinctively a *novelist's* art, becomes 'social criticism'; or, to put it another way, how inseparable, in his art, the two are. William Dorrit, we note, not for the first time, but, as we read the episode of the portrait commission, with sharpened realization of what is involved, sacrifices life and reality to nullities—does it blindly, and with an unction of righteousness, in his set will to vindicate his dignity, his gentlemanly status, his 'position'. He does it, we comment now, in what is at bottom essentially Gowan's way; his resentments have the same significance as Gowan's, and he is as incapable of happiness. And he is committed to supporting, with all the power of influence and suggestion he may have, the civilization, the world of privilege, and the cultural ethos that breed the Gowans, the Mrs. Generals, the Chief Butlers and Mr. Merdle. The difference is that William Dorrit has (it is largely a further indebtedness to Amy) a claim on our sympathy, and we see him in any case as a victim; whereas Gowan, strongly individualized as a formidable person and a militant parasite (his partnership with the bully Blandois defines a trait of his own), consciously *means* to be the disconcerter and destroyer. His highly articulate utterances make that plain, and make plain also, in a less conscious way, his representative significance, so that, as a dramatic character among the others, he gives something like explicit formulation–he certainly prompts explicitness in us–to the spirit he represents. Thus he plays a major part in relation to Dickens's design to make a packed Dickensian novel a critique of English civilization.

It is obvious that he has a contrasting opposite in Little Dorrit, who, in the Marshalsea, is the centre, the test, and the generator of reality. Nevertheless, she isn't the full answer to Gowan's challenge–for it's as a challenge, provoking and enforcing Dickens's full positive answer, that Gowan has his presence in the book (which he pervades, as Little Dorrit herself, Mrs. Clennam and the Marshalsea do). It is not for nothing that the arch-nihilist is made to present himself as an artist, and that the characteristic Gowan demonstrations (I may call them) that I have just adduced make his hatred of the real artist and of art, his implicit denial that art has any importance in civilization, overt and explicit. Here again we have the affinity between Dickens and Blake–unmistakably a natural and essential affinity. Dickens lays the same kind of emphasis on the creative nature of life as Blake does, and insists in the same way that there is a continuity from the inescapable creativeness of perception to the disciplined imaginative creativeness of the skilled artist, and that where art doesn't thrive or enjoy the intelligent esteem due to it the civilization is sick. Little Dorrit, whom I have called a contrasting opposite to Gowan the nihilist, is not only *not* an artist; she hasn't the makings of an artist in her. It is in *being*–being what she is–that she is creative.

Like the other key characters, she stands in a relation of contrast to more than one of the *dramatis personae*; but her antithesis above all is Mrs. Clennam, whose value-significance is more complex and more comprehensive than Gowan's. (We have by now, I suggest, these words noted down as bearing on the theme of 'criteria': reality, courage, disinterestedness, truth, spontaneity, creativeness–life.) When we compare Little Dorrit, as we naturally do, with Sissy Jupe, we see the significance of Sissy's relation to the Horse-riding. Little Dorrit's goodness and disinterestedness go with a modesty that is withdrawingness, and it is wonderful how Dickens conveys this without presenting them as anything but positive–creative with the essential creativity of life. Their effect on Clennam (a part of whose rôle it is to be virtually the reader's immediate presence in the book) is given in that nosegay he finds by his tea-cup on waking from a fevered doze, he lying ill in the Marshalsea, the prison of this world (Book the Second, chapter XXIV). He has had an insistent dream-sense of a garden:

–a garden of flowers, with a damp warm wind gently stirring their scents. It required such a painful effort to lift his head for the purpose of inquiring into anything, that the impression appeared to have become quite an old and importunate one when he looked round. Beside the tea-cup on his table he saw, then, a blooming nosegay: a wonderful handful of the choicest and most lovely flowers.

Nothing had ever appeared so beautiful in his sight. He took them up and inhaled their fragrances, and he lifted them to his hot head, and he put them down and opened his parched hands to them, as cold hands are opened to receive the cheering of a fire.[1]

iv

But in Little Dorrit herself the disinterestedness of life–disinterested, and so implicitly creative, in being not ego-bound and not slave to a mechanism– hasn't that overt relation with the developed creativity of art which Dickens so clearly intended in Sissy. Where, then, in the book have we the clear recognition-challenging emphasis on the *creative* nature of life (the large word I may now, perhaps, give the right focal force to by adding, 'the spontaneous, the disinterested, the ego-free, the reality-creating')? Is there any better answer than to point to Henry Gowan, the poised and drifting waster of the Best Families who, being unprovided for by his Barnacle kin, is 'being an artist'[2]–to point to *him* as evoking by

[1] We note how the intense sensuous vividness of that is generated in the temperature-paradox.

[2] I have discussed the force of this phrase of Lawrence's in the note at the end of *D. H. Lawrence: Novelist*, and in the essay on *Anna Karenina* in *Anna Karenina and Other Essays*.

negation Dickens's positive conception of the artist and of art? Yes, there is Daniel Doyce. It is eloquent both of the impersonality of Dickens when creatively engaged and of the unconventional first-handness and fulness of his conception of art that, in his greatest work, he should have conveyed most explicitly his proud consciousness of the creative function by making its special representative an inventor. Dickens, we know–if we take it on the authority of Lord Snow (both a bi-cultural sage and a novelist), was a 'natural Luddite'. Nevertheless, the significance of Doyce is plain and undeniable. Dickens, in fact, insists on it; Doyce's distinctive function is to *be* it. Even when we consider his part in the plot, of which we might be tempted for a moment to say that an inventor as such wasn't necessary to it, we see that what he essentially does, by being the person Dickens made him, is to bring the becalmed and debilitated Clennam into touch with strong and intransigent creativity.

Talking with him (Part the First, chapter XVI), Clennam is struck by the force of that disinterestedness in him which is the reverse of indifference, being commitment and resolution and undeflectable courage, though not at all of the order of ego-assertive will, but its antithesis. When, having heard of the obstructing Circumlocution Office, Clennam suggests that it's a pity Doyce ever entered into so hopeless a battle and had better give it up, Doyce, 'shaking his head with a thoughtful smile', replies that 'a man can't do it':

'You hold your life on the condition that to the last you shall struggle hard for it.[1] Every man holds a discovery on the same terms.'

[1] That we have a positive Dickensian affirmation here is beyond doubt. It is an insistence on that 'upright' human posture, with its entailed hazards, which Marvell treats of in 'A Dialogue between the Soul and Body'. No one realizing how essential to the Dickensian critique the emphasis is could endorse Cockshut's reflections on the significance of the Marshalsea:

The first description (chapter VI) of the Marshalsea is curiously nostalgic; and we soon find the place possesses an attraction for its inmates. It is a place of rest, of kindness, of gentle and harmless deceits.

When Mrs. Dorrit is giving birth there, the charwoman says ,'The flies trouble you, don't they dear? But p'r'aps they'll take your mind off it, and do you good. What between the buryin' ground, the grocer's, the waggon-stables, and the paunch trade, the Marshalsea flies gets very large. P'r'aps they're sent as a consolation, if only we know'd it.' The religious sensibility revealed here may not be of a very high order, but the humanity and kindness are genuine. In the same scene the beery, disreputable doctor says: 'We are quiet here; we don't get badgered here; there's no knocker here, sir, to be hammered at by creditors

'This is to say,' said Arthur, with a growing admiration of his quiet companion, 'you are not finally discouraged even now?'

'I have no right to be, if I am,' returned the other. 'The thing is as true as ever it was.'

It is the quiet unassertive impersonality of his conviction that especially impresses Clennam. Of the effect on him of Doyce's manner on a later occasion we are told:

He had the power, often to be found in union with such a character, of explaining what he himself perceived, and meant, with the direct force and distinctness with which it struck his own mind. His manner of demonstration was so orderly and neat and simple, that it was not easy to mistake him. There was something almost ludicrous in the complete irreconcilability of a vague conventional notion that he must be a visionary man, with the precise, sagacious travelling of his eye and thumb over the plans, their patient stoppages at particular points, their careful returns to other points whence little channels of explanation had to be traced up, and his steady manner of making everything good and everything sound, at each important stage, before taking his hearer on a line's-breadth further. His dismissal of himself from his description was hardly less remarkable. He never said, I discovered this adaptation or invented that combination; but showed the whole thing as if the Divine artificer had made it, and he had happened to find it. So modest he was about it, such a pleasant touch of respect was mingled with his quiet admiration of it, and so calmly convinced he was that it was established on irrefragable laws.

Dickens himself was neither an inventor nor a scientist, but he understood that kind of conviction from the inside: he was a great artist, and familiar with the compelling impersonal authority of the real (and not the less for knowing so well that there is no grasp of the real that is not creative). It is not for nothing that Doyce is the severest critic of Henry Gowan, and that the first criticism recorded of that gentleman is what

and bring a man's heart to his mouth. Nobody comes here to ask if a man's at home, and say he'll stand on the door till he is. Nobody writes threatening letters about money to this place. It's freedom, sir, it's freedom.'

Actually, what Dickens's evocation registers is not attraction, but recoil–intense and 'placing'. It is an evocation of final human defeat as a subsidence into a callous living deadness of abject acquiescence. If we are to talk of 'religious sensibility', then what we have is Dickens's vision of the Marshalsea as Hell: 'Abandon hope all ye who enter here'.

Doyce says in reply to Clennam's questioning:

'An artist, I infer from what he says?'
'A sort of one,' said Daniel Doyce in a surly tone.
'What sort of one?' asked Clennam, with a smile.
'Why, he has sauntered into the Arts at a leisurely Pall Mall pace,'
said Doyce, 'and I doubt if they care to be taken so easily.'

On Doyce, that judgment invites implicit recognition from us which
is stated (Part the Second, chapter XXV) about Physician: 'where he was,
something real was'. With intrinsic fitness he, with Clennam, becomes
patron and employer of Cavalletto, the light-hearted, warm-hearted and
spontaneous little Italian who surprises Bleeding Heart Yard by his ability
to sit down and be happy, though poor. We note that Doyce, Clennam,
Pancks and Bleeding Heart Yard are all drawn to him.

But Doyce, all said, is not an artist. Cavalletto carves things in wood,
but that hardly makes him, either, an artist in a sense that licenses us to
set him, as an actual creative presence in the book, over against Gowan,
the anti-artist and arch-nihilist. The fact is that if a novelist sees reason
for having among his characters an artist whose *raison d'être* is to *be* an
artist all he can do is to introduce someone of whom we are told that he
is an artist, and show him behaving in a way that seems to make the
allegation plausible. Dickens's conception of art and its importance was
too serious, profound and intelligent to let him think such a solution
worth resorting to. Doyce, however, doesn't represent all that is done
in *Little Dorrit* to make creativity-as-the-artist an actual presence – a potent
presence in relation to which Gowan takes on his full value.

Dickens is a different kind of creative writer from both James and
Tolstoy, neither of whom could have produced Flora Casby. The relevance of bringing in Flora at this point is given here, as it might be in
a passage quoted from any one of her characteristic dramatic appearances
–and they are all characteristic:

Flora, uttering these words in a deep voice, enjoyed herself immensely.
'To paint,' said she, 'the emotions of that morning when all was
marble within and Mr. F's Aunt followed in a glass-coach which
it stands to reason must have been in shameful repair, or it never
could have broken down two streets from the house and Mr. F's
Aunt brought home like the fifth of November in a rush-bottomed
chair I will not attempt, suffice it to say that the hollow form of

breakfast took place in the dining-room downstairs that papa partaking too freely of pickled salmon was ill for weeks and that Mr. F and myself went upon a continental tour to Calais where people fought for us on the pier until they separated us though not for ever that was not yet to be.'

The statue bride, hardly pausing for breath, went on, with the greatest complacency, in a rambling manner, sometimes incident to flesh and blood.

'I will draw a veil over that dreamy life, Mr. F was in good spirits his appetite was good he liked the cookery he considered the wine weak but palatable and all was well, we returned to the immediate neighbourhood of Number Thirty Little Gosling Street London Docks and settled down, ere we had yet fully detected the housemaid in selling the feathers out of the spare bed Gout flying upwards soared with Mr. F to another sphere.'

His relict, with a glance at his portrait, shook her head and wiped her eyes.

'I revere the memory of Mr. F as an estimable man and most indulgent husband, only necessary to mention Asparagus and it appeared or to hint at any little delicate thing to drink and it came like magic in a pint-bottle it was not ecstasy but it was comfort, I returned to papa's roof and lived secluded if not happy during some years until one day papa came smoothly blundering in and said that Arthur Clennam awaited me below, I went below and found him ask me not what I found him except that he was still unmarried still unchanged.'

Flora obviously enjoys herself (as we are told she does) in these astonishing expressive flights. It is obvious too that Dickens enjoys them, and takes delight in imagining Flora; and what is in fact astonishing is the ease and fertility with which he conceives her copious unpredictabilities, which, with all their leaps, poetic compressions and feats of imaginative linkage and substitution, are essentially sequential and coherent. It is important, however, not to convey a false implication in thus imputing enjoyment to Dickens. The enjoyment here is not different in kind from that which we may properly see in all his creating. Flora, that is, is not a piece of gratuitous 'Dickensian' exuberance; she has a major value in relation to Dickens's comprehensive design, and needs, for a full appreciation, to be seen as part of a whole finely nerved organism.

She is talking, in the quoted passage, to Little Dorrit, towards whom from the outset she shows a warm-hearted sympathy. She has indeed a great deal in common with the 'dear little thing' – the differences serving, among other things, to emphasize that fact. She is disinterested, spontaneous and good-natured and – for all her addiction to romantic self-dramatization – 'real', with a robust basic reality that her addiction sets off. She is as incapable of snobbery as Little Dorrit herself, a truth that, with an innocent unconsciousness, she demonstrates in the interview she achieves with the embarrassed William Dorrit Esquire in his London hotel – giving proof in the whole episode of the kind of courage that doesn't recognize itself as courage (Part the Second, chapter XVII). Though we are told that 'when she worked herself into full mermaid condition, she did actually believe whatever she said in it', we are also told, correctively, that she 'had a decided tendency to be always honest when she gave herself time to think about it'. And, talking with Little Dorrit in the pie-shop at the end of the book (Part the Second, chapter XXXIV), she 'earnestly begs' her 'to let Arthur understand that I don't know after all whether it wasn't all nonsense between us though pleasant at the time'. The 'full mermaid condition' is much in the nature of the condition produced by her other indulgence, brandy. But it mustn't be suggested that her adventurous expressive flights are nothing but romantic irresponsibilities of self-indulgence. They are also poetic in a strong way, and register, in their imaginative freedom and energy, much vivid perception and an artist's grasp of the real. Thus, correcting Mr. Dorrit's impression that the Clennam of Clennam & Co. must be Arthur, she replies: 'It's a very different person indeed, with no limbs and wheels instead and the grimmest of women though his mother.'

> Mr. Dorrit looked as if he must immediately be driven out of his mind by this account. Neither was it rendered more favourable to sanity by Flora's dashing into a rapid analysis of Mr. Flintwinch's cravat, and describing him, without the lightest boundary line of separation between his identity and Mrs. Clennam's, as a rusty screw in gaiters.

The reader, however, sees the felicity. And when, in the passage I have quoted above from Flora's unbosoming eloquence to Little Dorrit, we arrive at 'until one day papa came smoothly blundering in' we note how perfectly that gives us the Patriarch. Responding appreciatively to these felicities of creative utterance – and they abound – we can't help being conscious, to the point of full and explicit recognition, that the genius here, in these inspired improvisations, is Dickens's own. But that doesn't mean that we don't take the flights as Flora, and Flora as a person who is 'there' beyond all possible doubt.

There are other characters in *Little Dorrit* who invite the description 'Dickensian'–the adjective used in this way implying that they so little fall within the expectation suggested by the word 'realism' that they could occur only in a context boldly or licentiously unrealistic. It will be sufficient for my purpose to adduce Pancks.

Pancks, who may reasonably be thought of as a stylized Dickensian figure of comedy, associates easily in personal intercourse, not only with Flora, but with Little Dorrit herself and with Clennam who, tending to be very largely the reader's own presence in the imagined drama, is for us at the centre of realistic 'normality'. His significance, half-detected by Clennam in the abrupt factual dryness (is it sardonic?), as creative life imprisoned in the tyrannical mechanisms of a business civilization, is brought out by contrast with Cavalletto.

> The foreigner . . . –they called him Mr. Baptist in the Yard–was such a chirping, easy, hopeful little fellow, that his attraction to Pancks was probably the force of contrast. Solitary, weak, and scantily acquainted with the most necessary words in the only language in which he could communicate with the people about him, he went with the stream of his fortunes, in a way that was new in those parts.[1]

This is Pancks:

> 'Yes, I have always some of 'em to look up, or something to look after. But I like business,' said Pancks, getting on a little faster. 'What's a man made for?'
> 'For nothing else?' said Clennam.
> Pancks put the counter question, 'What else?' It packed up, in the smallest compass, a weight that had rested on Clennam's life; and he made no answer.
> 'That's what I ask our weekly tenants,' said Pancks. 'Some of 'em will pull long faces to me, and say, Poor as you see us, master, we're always grinding, drudging, toiling, every minute we're awake. I say to them, What else are you made for? It shuts them up. They haven't a word to answer. What else are you made for? That clinches it.'
> 'Ah dear, dear, dear!' sighed Clennam.[2]

Pancks's briskness is that of a nippy steam-tug (he 'docks' in the office at Casby's house), snorting about mechanically on his 'proprietor's'

[1]Book the First, chapter XXV.   [2]Book the First, chapter XIII.

business. 'You oughtn't to be anybody's proprietor, Mr. Clennam', he remarks. 'You're much too delicate.' The signs of vital energy, converted by repression into dangerous potentiality, are there, however, in insistent traits:

> His little black eyes sparkled electrically. His very hair seemed to sparkle as he roughened it. He was in that highly-charged state that one might have expected to draw sparks and snaps from him by presenting a knuckle to any part of his figure.'[1]

The great eruptive discharge takes place in the scene (Book the Second, chapter XXXII), towards the end of the book, that has its climax in the cropping, with Pancks's suddenly drawn scissors, of the Patriarch's venerable locks, the shearing-off of the broad hat-brim, and the replanting of the lopped crown on the now unpatriarchal head. But what I want to emphasize in order to bring out the point of proceeding in this way from Flora Casby to Mr. Pancks is the nature of the eloquence with which Pancks accompanies his dramatic demonstrations. This excerpt from the sustained and abundantly felicitous episode will suffice for my purpose:

> Mr. Pancks and the Patriarch were instantly the centre of a press, all eyes and ears; windows were thrown open, and doorsteps were thronged.
> 'What do you pretend to be?' said Mr. Pancks. 'What's your moral game? What do you go in for? Benevolence, ain't it? YOU benevolent!' Here Mr. Pancks, apparently without the intention of hitting him, but merely to relieve his mind and expend his superfluous power in wholesome exercise, aimed a blow at the bumpy head, which the bumpy head ducked to avoid. This singular performance was repeated, to the ever-increasing admiration of the spectators, at the end of every succeeding article of Mr. Pancks's oration.
> 'I have discharged myself from your service,' said Pancks, 'that I may tell you what you are. You're one of a lot of impostors that are the worst lot of all the lots that are to be met with. Speaking as a sufferer by both, I don't know that I wouldn't as soon have the Merdle lot as your lot. You're a driver in disguise, a screwer by deputy, a wringer, a squeezer, and a shaver by substitute. You're a philanthropic sneak. You're a shabby deceiver!'

[1] Book the First, chapter XXXII. Also: 'He had suddenly checked himself. Where he got all the additional black prongs from, that now flew up all over his head, like the myriads of points that break out in the large change of a great firework, was a mystery.'

(The repetition of the performance at this point was received with a burst of laughter.)

'Ask these good people who's the hard man here. They'll tell you Pancks, I believe.'

This was confirmed by cries of 'Certainly', and 'Hear!'

'But I tell you, good people–Casby! This mound of meekness, this lump of love, this bottle-green smiler, this is your driver!' said Pancks. 'If you want to see the man who would flay you alive–here he is! Don't look for him in me, at thirty shillings a week, but look for him in Casby, at I don't know how much a year!'

'Good!' cried several voices. 'Hear Mr. Pancks!'

'Hear Mr. Pancks?' cried that gentleman (after repeating the popular performance). 'Yes, I should think so! It's almost time to hear Mr. Pancks. Mr. Pancks has come down into the Yard tonight, on purpose that you should hear him. Pancks is only the Works, but here's the Winder.'

The audience would have gone over to Mr. Pancks, as one man, woman, and child, but for the long, grey, silken locks, and the broad-brimmed hat.

'Here's the Stop,' said Pancks, 'that's the man that sets the tune to be ground. And there's but one tune, and its name is Grind, Grind, Grind! Here's the Proprietor, and here's his Grubber. Why, good people, when he comes smoothly spinning through the Yard tonight, like a slow-going benevolent Humming-Top . . .'

Dramatic utterance of that kind couldn't (nor, of course, could the accompanying kind of action) be contained in a novel by Tolstoy any more than in one by James. And as of Flora's, so of Pancks's, we can say that he enjoys his creative flights and felicities, adding that so, again, does Dickens. And, again, to say this is not to pass, or to suggest, an adverse criticism on the novelist.

When we have in this way taken conscious note of the one case after the other we realize that the presence of Dickens they represent can be pointed to in numberless manifestations; diverse, but continuous in the sense that they belong to, they have their part in building up, a unity of effect. We take them, whether or not in full consciousness, not only in characters, but in the vivid energy of descriptions and the evocations of *décor* and atmosphere (as, for instance, of the Alps, Italy, Rome, Boulogne and London–to suggest the diversity and range of function and expressive value). In short, we see that we are not playing with a fanciful idea but recording a critical observation of major critical importance when we say that, opposing and placing Henry Gowan, the real artist *is* present in *Little Dorrit*–concretely present. He is present, the only way he *could* be, as Dickens himself, the creative Dickens. It is a presence potently enough felt, and at the same time impersonal enough, to perform perfectly its function in the organic whole. It is a success that is conditioned by the astonishing flexibility of Dickens's art–its supple sureness in combining modes and conventions that might well have seemed irreconcilable.

What I have been pointing to is an emphasis (so to speak) in the total creativity of the book–it is apparent for instance when Little Dorrit is brought into close relation with Flora; an emphasis that prompts us to the recognition that Little Dorrit, though she may be the heroine, doesn't represent the whole of Dickens's answer to Henry Gowan, and, further, that her marriage with Arthur Clennam, though (solving the personal problem of each) it may be right and happy, is neither a romantically exalted 'happy ending', nor a triumphant upshot of the inquiry, the complex intensity of questioning, that the book so largely is. Dickens is neither a romantic optimist nor a pessimist (a proposition that holds of Blake too). And it isn't that Little Dorrit is being *criticized* when we are moved to wish that she weren't so docile to Mrs. General. Dickens doesn't simplify (nor does Blake). His human concern, being profound, is inescapably a concern with society and civilization, and, in face of Mrs. General, Henry Gowan, Gowan's mother, the Patriarch, the Barnacles and Merdle, he insists that qualities and energies not represented by Little Dorrit are indispensable too.

Nevertheless, there is no infelicity in the book's being called by her name. She is at its centre, and the subtlety, delicacy and penetration with which Dickens conveys her distinctive paradoxical strength are, though not what 'Dickensian' commonly suggests, profoundly characteristic of his genius. In the painful scene after the rejection of young Chivery, her father's line being to suggest, with a mastery of inexplicitness and of non-recognition in himself of what he means, that, in aid of the process by which (though a prisoner) he has succeeded heroically in preserving his self-respect as a gentleman, she should keep young John on a string, she gives us a representative instance of the way in which, by force of a complete and unquestionable disinterestedness, she can bring her father to the point of glimpsing from time to time the reality of what he is–and in so doing make him for us something of a tragic figure. Disinterestedness in her is goodness and love; she differs from Sissy in that, while manifested in scenes of this kind as a decisive presence, she can't be called a challenging one–there are no dark hair and eyes and lustrous gleams (these in *Little Dorrit* belong to Tattycoram). Yet her decisiveness, with its peculiar quality, leaves us in no doubt, it is brought so potently home to us.

Of course, the art in general of *Little Dorrit* is more complex in its subtlety than that of *Hard Times*: the large book is not merely larger; it offers something in its point-to-point treatment of life that doesn't go and couldn't, with moral-fable economy, the scale and abundance of the work being necessary to the distinctive preoccupation with significance and to the accompanying local pregnancy. This truth is illustrated by the way in which the episode (Book the First, chapter XIX) I have referred to–and it is relevant to note that, without any effect of mere repetition, there have already been a number of the kind–comes in the whole generously charged and delicately modulated chapter that contains it. For a just critical consideration one has to re-read the whole chapter.

It gives us first the two brothers, William urging the broken Frederick[1] to profit by the model in front of him:

> The Father of the Marshalsea said, with a shrug of modest self-depreciation, 'Oh! You might be like me, my dear Frederick; you might be, if you chose!' and forbore, in the magnanimity of his strength, to press his fallen brother further.

William Dorrit's possession of his rôle is complete, and magnificently confident. It carries him over the jar of the elder Chivery's surliness, which he meets by turning an enhanced sublimity of patronizing solicitude on Frederick.

> 'Be so kind as to keep the door open a moment, Chivery, that I may see him go along the passage and down the steps. Take care,

---

[1]When, in *The Princess Casamassima*, we consider Mr. Vetch (who, though once a gentleman, is reduced to earning his living as a fiddler in a low theatre) along with Millicent Henning in comparison with Frederick Dorrit and Fanny, it becomes hardly questionable, and not the more so for the differences, that memories of *Little Dorrit* were the promptings to James's characters. His dependence on Dickens is more general than that, and may fairly be called parasitic. Thus the prison, the child protagonist whose young life is intimately associated with it, and the seamstress in the squalid area of London, are plainly vague memories of *Little Dorrit*, used in *The Princess Casamassima* for atmosphere unconvincingly, since James had no corresponding first-hand knowledge. It is significant that he expressed a high admiration for Dickens's Fanny.

Frederick! (He is very infirm.) Mind the steps! (He is so very absent.) Be careful how you cross, Frederick! (I really don't like the notion of his wandering at large, he is so extremely liable to be run over.)'

With these words, and with a face expressive of many uneasy doubts and much anxious guardianship, he turned his regards upon the assembled company in the Lodge: so plainly indicating that his brother was to be pitied for not being under lock and key, that an opinion to that effect went round among the Collegians assembled.

But he did not receive it with unqualified assent; on the contrary, he said, 'No, gentlemen, no; let them not misunderstand him.'

And he proceeds to deliver his homily on the rare union of qualities needed by the man who shall be able to support existence and maintain his self-respect as a gentleman in the Marshalsea.

Was his beloved brother Frederick that man? No. They saw him, even, as it was, crushed. Misfortune crushed him. He had not power of recoil enough, not elasticity enough, to be a long time in such a place, and yet preserve his self-respect and feel conscious that he was a gentleman. Frederick had not (if he might use the expression) Power enough to see in any little attentions and–and–Testimonials that he might under such circumstances receive, the goodness of human nature, the fine spirit animating the Collegians as a community, and at the same time no degradation to himself, and no depreciation of his claims as a gentleman. Gentlemen, God bless you!

If the boldness of the stylization as seen in extracts might prompt one to recall that Dickens had much frequented Ben Jonson, one would never, reading currently through the whole page, think of finding a descriptive felicity in 'Jonsonian' for this art, which is so sensitively supple over so unlimited a human range. Indeed, reading through the whole chapter, one isn't prompted to talk of stylization: the nature of Dickens's marvellous freedom suggests too much, in the exquisite vital sensitiveness that we see the boldness to be, the analogy of Shakespeare, and there are in fact the strongest reasons for calling the art of the great Dickens Shakespearian. This is the emphasis one might very well resort to if called on to justify the observation that Dickens is not only a different kind of genius from James, but a genius of a greater kind. The creative life in him flows more freely and fully from the deep sources–the depth, the freedom and the fulness being the conditions of the Shakespearian suppleness.

I refer in this comparative way to James because there is good reason for insisting that Dickens is certainly no less a master than James of the subtleties of the inner life–the inner drama of the individual life in its relations with others. The vivid external drama in the chapter under consideration (Book the First, chapter XIX) has its meaning in the inner drama, which is so largely a matter of the essentially inexplicit; or, rather, the inner drama is conveyed, with an inevitable felicity of supple shifts, in terms of the external. William Dorrit's public demonstration of his heroically sustained rôle of Gentleman modulates into the domestic scene with his daughter.

Her arm was on his shoulder, but she did not look into his face while he spoke. Bending her head, she looked another way.

'I–hem!–can't think, Amy, what has given Chivery offence. He is generally so–so very attentive and respectful. And to-night he was quite–quite short with me. Other people there too. Why, good Heaven! if I was to lose the support of Chivery and his brother officers, I might starve to death here.' While he spoke, he was opening and shutting his hands like valves; so conscious all the time of that touch of shame that he shrunk before his own knowledge of his meaning.

'I–ha!–I can't think what it's owing to. I am sure I can't imagine what the cause of it is. There was a certain Jackson here once, a turnkey of the name of Jackson (I don't think you remember him, my dear, you were very young) and–hem!–and he had a–brother and this–young brother paid his addresses to–at least, but did not go as far as to pay his addresses to–but admired–respectfully admired–the–not the daughter, the sister–of one of us; a rather distinguished Collegian; I may say, very much so. His name was Captain Martin; and he consulted me on the question whether it was necessary that his daughter–sister–should hazard offending the turnkey's brother by being too–ha!–too plain with the other brother–Captain Martin was a gentleman and a man of honour, and I put it to him–first to give me his–his own opinion. Captain Martin (highly respected in the army) then unhesitatingly said, that it appeared to him that his–hem!–sister was not called upon to understand the young man too distinctly, and that she might lead him on–I am doubtful whether lead him on was Captain Martin's exact expression: indeed I think he said tolerate him–on his father's–I should say brother's–account. I hardly know how I strayed into this story. I suppose it has been through being unable to account for Chivery; but as to the connection between the two, I don't see–'

His voice died away, as if she could not bear the pain of hearing him, and her hand crept to his lips. For a little while, there was a dead silence and stillness, and she remained with her arm round his neck, and her head bowed down upon his shoulder.

She says nothing, turns no dark eyes upon him, but merely by continuing to be what unselfconsciously she is, brings him to a halt and an unwilling self-realization—self-realization, though tainted and fleeting. It is utterly convincing; by the close acquaintance we have been given with her, she exists for us in a way that makes it so.

> ... he began his meal. They did not, as yet, look at one another. By little and little he began; laying down his knife and fork with a noise, taking things up sharply, biting at his bread as if he were offended with it, and in other similar ways showing that he was out of sorts. At length he pushed his plate from him, and spoke aloud. With the strangest inconsistency.
>
> 'What does it matter whether I eat or starve? What does it matter whether such a blighted life as mine comes to an end, now, next week, or next year? What am I worth to anyone? A poor prisoner, fed on alms and broken victuals; a squalid and disgraced wretch!'
>
> 'Father, father!'

Where shall we find an art like this? It is astonishingly original, the art of a great poet who is essentially a novelist. We can see that without a familiarity with the theatre of the time Dickens couldn't have given William Dorrit, the Gentleman, that speech at the prison lodge, but we feel nothing infelicitously theatrical about it. And in noting that the convention Dickens actually uses is that of reported oratory we perceive at the same time what a manifestation of triumphant tact his use of it is. It makes what might otherwise have seemed too challengingly exaggerated in its absurdity, *too* stagey (for William Dorrit is essentially an actor here, playing the rôle he has cast himself for in the play, the histrionic unreality he has made of his life in the Marshalsea), wholly acceptable. Dickens in fact improvises, in a way characteristic of his art, his own convention, and does so with a perfect rightness. Our response as to a painfully disturbing actuality of life retains its full power; we don't lose our embarrassed and apprehensive sense of the emotional and moral crisis—the poignant affair of John Chivery immediately present to us in the background.

The domestic sequel, the intimate scene between father and daughter, issues with a complete naturalness out of all that has gone before, and it is horrible and tragic. The father (Father of the Marshalsea) is committed to his rôle with an alcoholic's irredeemableness; he can't face life apart from it. But, without support from her, which in this matter it is impossible for her to give–a fact that there's no saving him from having to admit to himself, he can't sustain it. The fostered unrealities collapse; for a terrible moment of humiliation he can't help seeing things as they are–what his daughter is, what he himself is, and what are their relations.

How is it possible not to recognize in the deviser of such an art, an art serving with such boldness, penetration and delicacy such an insight into the human soul, one of the very greatest of those dramatic poets whose genius has gone into the novel? The particular human situation presented in the chapter is of course central to *Little Dorrit*, and it appears recurrently in closely analogous forms, such recurrence with variation being necessarily entailed in the undertaking and the designed total effect. For another major instance, a comparable scene in which the painful comedy of the heroically preserved gentleman-status has for upshot a collapse into something like abject self-recognition, one can point to that which ensues on the Father's encountering old Nandy ('one of my pensioners') being escorted into the Marshalsea on Little Dorrit's arm (Book the First, chapter XXXI). The irony of the Chivery episode has a further development when Mr. Dorrit, no longer the Father of the Marshalsea but impeccably and opulently a gentleman on tour, and rejoicing in Fanny's marriage to Edmund Sparkler, step-son of the great Merdle, torments poor Amy with the insistent and confident admonition that it is now her turn, her duty, to make an equally good marriage.

'Amy,' he resumed; 'your dear sister, our Fanny, has contracted–ha hum–a marriage, eminently calculated to extend the basis of our–ha–connection, and to–hum–consolidate our social relations. My love, I trust that the time is not far distant when some–ha–eligible partner may be found for you.'

'Oh no! Let me stay with you. I beg and pray that I may stay with you! I want nothing but to stay and take care of you!.'

She said it like one in sudden alarm.

'Nay, Amy, Amy, Amy,' said Mr. Dorrit. 'This is weak and foolish, weak and foolish. You have a–ha–responsibility imposed on you by your position. It is to develop that position, and be–hum–worthy of that position. As to taking care of me; I can–ha–take care of myself. Or,' he added after a moment, 'if I should need to be taken care of, I–hum–can, with the–ha–blessing of Providence, *be* taken care of. I–ha–hum–I cannot, my dear child, think of engrossing, and–ha–as it were, sacrificing you.'

Reinstated in wealth and position, the Dorrit family in Italy not only don't need the practical and material services so long taken for granted; they can afford—as they desire—never to be reminded of the real: they are securely in and of Society, which is personified for us in Mrs. General—form, surface and emptiness; Papa, potatoes, prunes and prisms. Mrs. General (who may be counted on not to decline Mr. Dorrit's imminent proposal) is a companion figure to Mr. Gradgrind; they represent complementary 'social' ways of emptying the reality out of life—to note which is to recall the significance of Mr. James Harthouse's part in *Hard Times*.

But for Little Dorrit there is no challenge she can offer to meet dramatically with the counter-challenge: that kind of demonstration is not what life has cast her for. Deprived of her *raison d'être*, slighted, disciplined and neglected, she finds the beautiful and squalid world around her unreal in its strangeness, and looks back to the real reality left behind in the Marshalsea—a reality created among those familiar unrealities by love, spontaneity and habitual service of life:

> the more surprising the scenes, the more they resembled the unreality of her own inner life as she went through its vacant places all day long. The gorges of the Simplon, its enormous depths and thundering waterfalls, the wonderful road, the points of danger where a loose wheel or a faltering horse would have been disastrous, the descent into Italy, the opening of that beautiful land, as the rugged mountain-chasm widened and let them out from a gloomy and dark imprisonment—all a dream—only the old mean Marshalsea a reality. Nay, even the old mean Marshalsea was shaken to its foundations when she imagined it without her father. She could scarcely believe that the prisoners were still lingering in the close yard, that the mean rooms were still every one tenanted, and that the turnkey still stood in the Lodge letting people in and out, all just as she well knew it to be. With a remembrance of her father's old life hanging about her like the burden of a sorrowful tune, Little Dorrit would wake from a dream of her birthplace into a whole day's dream. The painted room in which she awoke, often a humbled state-chamber in a dilapidated palace, would begin it; with its wild red autumnal vineleaves overhanging the glass, its orange-trees on the cracked white terrace outside the window, a group of monks and peasants in the little street below, misery and magnificence wrestling with each other upon every rood of ground in the prospect, no matter how widely diversified, and misery throwing magnificence with the strength of fate. . . . Then

breakfast in another painted chamber, damp-stained and of desolate proportions; and then the departure, which, to her timidity and sense of not being grand enough for her place in the ceremonies, was always an uneasy thing.

V

Dickens, as in the chapter from which that comes (Book the Second, chapter III), can evoke scene and setting through long passages on successive pages, while relying with an easy confidence on a sustained attention from the reader–an attention as inevitably given as if what was being presented were a gripping narrative of events. For this evocative power that Dickens so abundantly commands is a different thing from what we admire, perhaps, in Ruskinian poetic prose (and Dickens, employing it, shows himself in an obvious way a greater poet than any of the Victorian formal poets). It is not merely that the effects in which it manifests itself present so vitally nervous a diversity; in considering this livingness we can't but observe that it belongs to an art that doesn't go in for set descriptions–products of a talent that we can think of as something additional to the gift that makes Dickens a great novelist. Dickens's evocations are always a novelist's; they are doing the novelist's essential work.

In the chapter I have been quoting from they give us in poignant immediacy–give us as an experienced or suffered state–the peculiar loneliness and hunger of Little Dorrit's situation; and the insistence, or free-flowing abundance (never felt as *longueur*), is necessary to the effect, so important an element in the total communicated significance of the novel. The family proceeds towards Venice:

> So they would be driven madly through the narrow unsavoury streets, and jerked out at the town gate. Among the day's unrealities would be, roads where the bright red vines were looped and garlanded together on trees for many miles; woods of olives; white villages and towns on hill-sides, lovely without, but frightful with their dirt and poverty within; crosses by the way; deep blue lakes with fairy islands, and clustering boats with awnings of bright colours and sails of beautiful form; vast piles of buildings mouldering to dust; hanging-gardens where the weeds had grown so strong that their stems, like wedges driven home, had split the arch and rent the wall; stone-terraced lanes, with the lizards running into and out of every chink;

253

beggars of all sorts everywhere: pitiful, picturesque, hungry, merry children-beggars and aged beggars. Often at posting-houses, and other halting-places, these miserable creatures would appear the only realities of the day . . .

In the evocation of Venice we get the obsessive sense that troubles the poor girl settling into a nostalgic hopelessness of enchantment:

> In this crowning unreality, where all the streets were paved with water, and where the death-like stillness of the days and nights was broken by no sound but the softened ringing of church-bells, the rippling of the current, and the cry of the gondoliers turning the corners of the flowing streets, Little Dorrit, quite lost by her task being done, sat alone to muse.

To the potency of this mode of the Dickensian genius George Eliot and Henry James after her, pay a tribute the more telling because unconscious (James at a remove, for he clearly derives through her). I am thinking of the passage in chapter 20 of *Middlemarch* that evokes, in terms of the effect on her of Rome, the state of fevered despair to which marriage with Casaubon has so soon brought Dorothea, and the unmistakably related passage in *The Portrait of a Lady* that gives us the disillusioned Isabel. To be sure of the derivative relation to Dickens one has only to recall Little Dorrit looking round at the grandeur and strangeness and squalour of the immemorial city. I will quote two sentences.
The family has moved on to Rome:

> Through a repetition of the former Italian scenes, growing more dirty and more haggard as they went on, and bringing them to where the very air was diseased, they passed to their destination. A fine residence had been taken for them on the Corso, and there they took up their abode, in a city where everything seemed to be trying to stand still for ever on the ruins of something else–except the water, which, following eternal laws, tumbled and rolled from its glorious multitude of fountains. (Part the Second, chapter VII.)

The peculiar poetic genius comes out here with cogent felicity in what, for a close, follows the 'except', evoking as 'eternal laws' the spontaneity and power of life–triumphant gloriously even in the eternal city; no, *not* triumphant as they ought to be (for the metaphorical potency of that close is complex). This, we say (perceiving as we say it that the Dickensian vitality of the whole passage is involved) is essential Dickens: neither George Eliot nor James is a great poet in this sense–the sense in which we find the description felicitous and potent when we acclaim this kind of effect as intensely characteristic of the writer's genius. For George Eliot, of course, as for us, the whole preceding evocation of Little Dorrit's state of malign enchantment makes its power felt in what we take as her response to Rome. Hence the profound impression associated in particular with Rome that George Eliot recalls unwittingly in her derivative passage.

But the nature of the distinctive genius as represented by the kind of poetic life I have called attention to is not fully recognized if we don't, in considering the passage last quoted, note the tone, manner and burden of the paragraph into which, illustrating one manifestation of what I have called Dickens's flexibility, it leads (the flexibility being something that has for its accompaniment pregnancy–manifestations, these, of the author's wholeness and profundity of possession by his human theme). What follows immediately is this:

> Here, it seemed to Little Dorrit that a change came over the Marshalsea spirit of their society, and that Prunes and Prisms got the upper hand. Everybody was walking about St. Peter's and the Vatican on somebody else's cork legs, and straining every visible object through somebody else's sieve. Nobody said what anything was, but everybody said what Mrs. General, Mr. Eustace, or somebody else said it was. The whole body of travellers seemed to be a collection of voluntary human sacrifices, bound hand and foot, and delivered over to Mr. Eustace and his attendants to have the entrails of their intellects arranged according to the taste of that sacred priesthood. Through the rugged remains of temples and tombs and palaces and senate halls and theatres and amphitheatres of ancient days, hosts of tongue-tied and blindfolded moderns were carefully feeling their way, incessantly repeating Prunes and Prisms, in the endeavour to set their lips according to the received form. Mrs. General was in her pure element. Nobody had an opinion. There was a formation of surface going on around her on an amazing scale, and it had not a flaw of courage or honest free speech in it.

Reality, courage, disinterestedness, truth, spontaneity, creativeness – and, summing them, life: these words, further charged with definitive value, make the appropriate marginal comment. Little Dorrit, whose desolate sense of the unreality is what we have been sharing, is the focal presence of what they stand for. But she is beaten. For her–a profound irony–the real is what, at her father's liberation, she left behind in the Marshalsea. The point implicitly made (the book makes it in many ways) is that reality is a collaborative creation: Little Dorrit, in 'chartered', mean and gloomy London, had found collaboration in the responsive human needs of her father and his other children, and in the human good-nature of the turnkeys, the Collegians and Flora—even of Mrs. Clennam. But in Italy she is wholly denied it; her love for her father is reduced to expressing itself in docility to Mrs. General, the arch-unreality. He, on the other hand (for Dickens's irony is pregnant) has *not* left the Marshalsea behind; in this genteel world of collusive unreality the old familiar Marshalsea is the concealed reality—a menacing fact, ever-present in apprehension and suspicion.

Reality for him *is* what has to be feared. The Marshalsea he now, as a courier-respected gentleman, inhabits in Italy (and, when he goes there, in London) is the collusive unreality of the genteel world. It too is a collaborative creation. The novel gives us a richly diverse view of the creating and maintaining. Here again we have the subtlety of Dickens's insight into the human psyche. Little Dorrit, like anyone else, needs collaboration in creating the reality she can grasp—more comprehensively, the reality she can implicitly believe herself to be, and that which she can feel with assurance she lives in. Her father too, as he exemplifies—with effects of both comedy and pathos—every day, can't get on without collaboration: without it he couldn't have maintained the unreality he inhabited as a gentleman in the Marshalsea (the prison that also protected —as he recognized in declining the turnkey's offer to let him step outside into the street for a glimpse of the world.) It was a system of countenanced empty pretensions. But so is that in which he proudly takes his place when he is liberated into Society; the 'real' unreality is equally un-real, and, in its own way, equally a prison. It is unreal in a way symbolized by the authority of Mrs. General, who is concerned for nothing but a conventionally approved kind of surface. Members, by observing a given code, are enabled to feel that their claims to be genteel, correct and of the 'right people' are recognized by the others who observe the code and are recognized; the recognition—a matter of externals (or 'surface')—is everything. The system of authoritative conventions that makes this Society possible is itself a perverse product of creative collaboration, collaborative creativity being so essentially in and of the human psyche that it must, one way or another, have play.

A Henry Gowan, whose social distinction is a matter of being recognized as most unquestionably one of the socially distinguished—one of the born and guaranteed *élite*, can rely on the system to give him his status and support him in it, in spite of the quasi-Bohemian habit he affects and his deliberately disconcerting articulateness (he doesn't, of course, threaten anything that matters much to Mrs. General or the Chief Butler).

Here we have the aspect of the system that particularly prompts the use of the word 'snobbery'—a word the implications of which are brought out when we say, as we might have done, that we can't do clinical justice to Tattycoram without giving full weight to the benevolent British obtuseness of Mr. Meagles, the retired banker, who *is*, as Dickens is not, a Philistine, placed as such by Dickens, and a snob as well.

No one has surpassed Dickens in the treatment of Victorian snobbery—indeed, has anyone approached him? He is clear-sighted about the social realities it portends; he sees that the successful banker's amiable weakness represents a major political fact, and may be said to give us the effective condition of the continued unchallenged power of the Barnacles—whose Circumlocution Office, even if we don't accept it as exhaustively representative of the way the country was administered, conveys so unanswerably what we know to have been a large measure of the essential truth. The Gowans are a branch of the Barnacle clan, so Mr. Meagles though he would have saved his daughter from Henry Gowan if he could, gets immense satisfaction from the wedding.[1] The irony of the situation is developed in the comedy—painful, but still comedy, marvellous in its perfection—of the various dialogues in which Mrs. Gowan imposes on Clennam, the Meagleses and the world her version of the marriage, which makes Henry the victim of designing bourgeois climbers, Pet's good looks being the bait.

These things exhibit a consummate art that is very characteristic of Dickens's genius. In the rendering of manners at the social level at which they are the essential art of living, to be practised with the assurance only a conscious state of initiation can give, Dickens is certainly not a lesser

[1]Here, at a lower social level, is Plornish on William Dorrit:

' "Ah! there's manners! There's polish! There's a gentleman to have run to seed in the Marshalsea jail! Why, perhaps you are not aware", said Plornish, lowering his voice, and speaking with a perverse admiration of what he ought to have pitied or despised, "not aware that Miss Dorrit and her sister dursn't let him know that they work for a living. No!" said Plornish, looking with a ridiculous triumph first at his wife, and then round all the room. "Dursn't let him know it, they dursn't!" '

It's in place to remember Rugg's concern that Clennam should have more respect for himself and his legal representative, and shift to the King's Bench.

master than Henry James. The dialogue, along with the rest of the notation, in the scenes of 'highly civilized' intercourse I have referred to is perfect (and it comes from the creator of Flora Finching). In those scenes, of course, Mrs. Gowan is the assured practitioner – the exploiter – of 'civilization', and Clennam and Meagles are the practised upon; the genius of the greater novelist comes out in the way the comedy is made painful for us by the quite uncomic significances that our deep sympathies respond to: we protest, in fact – the human issues are too important for us to be anything but partisan.

Fanny, in accepting the brainless Edmund Sparkler, does so as belonging with accomplished and single-minded assurance to that 'civilization', having, on the Dorrit re-emergence into Society, achieved her unquestioned position with exemplary completeness. Her ability to do so was achieved in the Marshalsea: it is the product of her upbringing, and her father can see in her the reward and vindication of his resolute stand for 'self-respect'.[1] The subtle perfection with which Dickens does her is seen in the way in which, enjoying the comedy of her unfailing success in holding her own socially, we never forget that she is the pupil of the Marshalsea and the sister of Little Dorrit, so that her value even in these scenes is felt as more than satiric. She provides, in fact, one more illustration of what, associating it with pregnancy and depth, I have called flexibility, meaning the ease with which his art moves between different tones and modes. We can't but regard her with a marked lack of sympathy, our applause being only for her spirit and skill in the heartless comedy of manners in which she triumphs; but at the same time she belongs as essentially to the sombre theme of the Marshalsea, the long drama of human disaster with its disturbing and monitory significance, as Little Dorrit and the rest of the family do.

[1]He has Mrs. General's corroboration:

'I took the liberty', said Mr. Dorrit again, with the magnificent placidity of one who was above correction, 'to solicit the favour of a little private conversation with you, because I feel rather worried respecting my – ha – my younger daughter. You will have observed a great difference of temperament, madam, between my two daughters?'

Said Mrs. General in response, crossing her gloved hands (she was never without gloves, and they never creased and always fitted) 'There is a great difference.'

'May I ask to be favoured with your view of it?' said Mr. Dorrit, with a deference not incompatible with majestic severity.

'Fanny' returned Mrs. General, 'has force of character and self-reliance, Amy, none.' Book the Second, chapter V.

And this is the moment to note a preoccupation of Dickens's that has its part in the normative impulsion and the essential positive nisus, without which his inquest into civilization in England would be something other than the great creative work it is. The 'civilization' with which Fanny, the reverse of disabled by her Marshalsea education, triumphantly identifies herself is that in terms of which Henry Gowan, so unambiguously 'more than an artist', is beyond question a gentleman. But the word 'gentleman' as used consciously by Dickens in pursuit of his artist's purpose of exploration and definition has a number of different values, the relations between which clearly seem to him a matter of great interest. Ferdinand, the pleasant young Barnacle, is a kinsman of Henry Gowan's and a member of the same privileged class. In applying the word to him, however, we find ourselves, at the prompting of Dickens's art, doing it in this way: 'Ferdinand is charming, genuinely kind, and, in short, a gentleman'. At the Circumlocution Office, where the Barnacles in general make no attempt to disguise their lack of any decent human consideration, and show not the least concern for manners, Ferdinand, with urbane friendliness, tries to dissuade Clennam from the futility of pursuing his inquiries.

This kind of thing, it will be commented, merely exemplifies the rôle that Ferdinand, who identifies himself happily with the system that maintains him, plays in it; plays in that whole complex organism of pretence, pretension, privilege, parasitic class-interest and 'civilization' – the whole social malady – that Dickens is exposing. And certainly Ferdinand's charm, in Dickens's sense of it as in Clennam's, is a matter for exasperation and diagnostic comment: we remember as characteristic the part played by Ferdinand on the occasion of the Merdle dinner in finally bringing together for a tête-à-tête – the end for which the dinner was arranged – Lord Decimus and the great Merdle (Book the Second, chapter XII). Ferdinand has charm, urbanity and tact, and here Dickens shows them functioning. Before the culminating achievement – this we remember too – they have been shown functioning in the same spirit, but to an effect that eliminates all possibility of amusement or complaisance in the reader.

> 'Pray,' asked Lord Decimus, casting his eyes around the table, 'what is this story I have heard of a gentleman long confined in a debtor's prison, proving to be of a wealthy family, and having come into the inheritance of a large sum of money? I have met with a variety of allusions to it. Do you know anything of it, Ferdinand?'

'I only know this much,' said Ferdinand, 'that he has given the Department with which I have the honour to be associated'; this sparkling young Barnacle threw off the phrase sportively, as who should say, we know all about these forms of speech, but we must keep it up, we must keep the game alive; 'no end of trouble, and has put us into innumerable fixes.'

And he gives an account of the characteristic ritual of incompetence, incuria and obstruction, protracted in complete indifference to any decent human consideration, and holding up the discharge of the Dorrit debt and Mr. Dorrit's release from prison for months, that makes 'charm' and 'urbanity', for the reader, exceedingly unpleasant words.

'It was a triumph of public business,' said this handsome young Barnacle, laughing heartily. 'You never saw such a lot of forms in your life.'

He exhibits himself, in short, as the voice of the Barnacle caste, and utterly devoid of imaginative sympathy.

We mustn't, however, simplify. The visit that Clennam in the Marshalsea receives from Ferdinand doesn't come altogether under this account. The elegant gentleman riding up and dismounting is immediately recognized as unmistakably a gentleman at the Lodge and by the prisoners. But 'gentleman' shifts its value when, defining the effect on us of the scene in Clennam's room, we say that it shows Ferdinand as charming, genuinely kind, and in short 'a gentleman'. The effect itself isn't a simple one. He makes the 'confession of his faith as the head of the rising Barnacles who were born of woman'–'A little humbug and a groove, and everything goes on admirably, if you leave it alone' (a faith 'to be followed under a variety of watchwords which they utterly repudiated and disbelieved'), and 'Nothing could be more agreeable than his frank and courteous bearing, or adapted with a more gentlemanly instinct to the circumstances of his visit'.

It is a faith, or 'civilized' philosophy, that no one to whom the questions about life and civilization preoccupying Dickens matter can have failed to meet with and to hate. And that Dickens expresses here the strong feeling with which the 'social criticism' he conveys in the Barnacles and Gowans and their Merdle is charged is quite clear. Yet we remind ourselves–or are not allowed to forget–that Ferdinand's visit *is* kind. And the favourable element in our response, an essentially evaluative one, is confirmed and enforced by the contrast with the immediately succeeding visitor, Blandois, who proclaims himself with characteristic gratuitousness 'a gentleman from the beginning and a gentleman to the end'. The contrast prompts us with the implicit judgment that Ferdinand has not only external good breeding, but, associated with it, something that distinguishes him radically from Henry Gowan, the gentlemanly 'friend' of the blackguard to whom, in calling him a blackguard, we deny the name of gentleman in any sense. If anyone should comment that the element of genuineness in Ferdinand merely adds to his plausibility, qualifying him to represent an essential constituent of the Barnacle system, and serving to make the noxious ethos of the Circumlocution Office seem amiable, Dickens's art prompts us with a reply: it won't do simply to see Ferdinand as linked back with Lord Decimus and the Gowans, ignoring the significance of his being drawn, as he unmistakably is, towards Clennam, to whom he goes out of his way to be kind. The significance lies in the implicit recognition on the part of so limited a representative of good breeding that Clennam himself is a gentleman – Clennam in whom good breeding, apparent in his bearing and manners, expresses and engages (as even Ferdinand in his way perceives) something deep within that repudiates the Barnacle philosophy.

I am insisting, then, that 'gentleman' means something important here, and that Dickens – his art is witness – values very highly certain social and cultural achievements it portends. No one more unequivocally than he has placed snobbery and the stupidities and cruelties of class-pride ('exclusiveness'), but he has the reverse of contempt for civilization manifested as manners – manners that in their refined form come under 'politeness'; he knows that they may be, in what they entail or engage, more than a mere matter of external social grace or aplomb – Mrs. General's 'form' and 'surface'. He simplifies no questions and doesn't suggest that there can be any simple answers, and the ways in which he uses the word 'gentleman' in *Little Dorrit*, the range of his related uses (on one occasion, where in our period remoteness we a little flinch he tells us that John Chivery showed the feelings of a gentleman), would repay study. By way of enforcing this suggestion, I will remark that in the world of (say) Kingsley Amis no one is a gentleman; the idea, whether as represented by Henry Gowan, Ferdinand, Clennam or John Chivery, is unknown – and the word has no use.

Before I proceed to justify the observation that Dickens clearly means us to judge Clennam a gentleman *par excellence*, I will slip in a point raised by the mention of Ferdinand. He belongs to the Circumlocution Office. Whether or not the Circumlocution Office conveys an altogether fair criticism of Government and bureaucracy at the time of the Crimean War doesn't matter. Life always has to be defended, vindicated and asserted against Government, bureaucracy and organization – against society in that sense. The defence and assertion are above all the business of the artist, which is never what those who think that the 'responsibility of the writer' is something he can be instructed in suppose.

I have observed that Ferdinand's taking to Clennam is a recognition that Clennam, though so demonstratively not of the ruling caste, but an offence to it, is a gentleman: in doing so Ferdinand, for all his un-questioning identity with the odious world of privilege and snobbery to which he belongs, implicitly recognizes that the 'civilization' of man-ners seems somehow to entail, at any rate for him, something more than Henry Gowan's assured superiority and easy social competence do for Henry Gowan. Dickens knew, in bringing in such an episode, what significances constituted its point, and I won't offer to develop them further in general terms. Ferdinand likes what we and Daniel Doyce like in Clennam, in whom the external 'civilization' that qualifies him to be dealt with as a gentleman by Mrs. Gowan expresses and engages (to his disadvantage in dealing with her, a given kind of lady) sensitiveness, modesty and sympathetic tact.[1] That is, it expresses and engages the qualities that enable him to be the intimate and wholly acceptable friend to Doyce that, with all his bourgeois geniality and good-nature, the obtuse and patronizing Meagles can't be.

These are the qualities that, when it comes to coping with Flora, put Clennam at the disadvantage that has those decidedly comic aspects – as, for example, when, having contrived that she should be shown round the dark old Clennam house so familiar to them in childhood, she makes the

---

[1] "I have been expecting him", said Mrs. Plornish, "this half-an-hour, at any minute of time. Walk in, sir."

'Arthur entered the rather dark and close parlour (though it was lofty too), and sat down in the chair she placed for him.

' "Not to deceive you, sir, I notice it," said Mrs. Plornish, "and I take it kind of you."

'He was at a loss to understand what she meant: and by expressing as much in his looks, elicited her explanation.

' "It ain't many that comes into a poor place, that deems it worth their while to move their hats", said Mrs. Plornish. "But people think more of it than people think." ' (Part the First, chapter XII).

escorting Arthur clasp her with his arm beneath her shawl. The whole comedy of Flora tends too much to be thought of as a self-justifying spontaneity of the Dickensian genius—a kind of creative largesse. It *is* comedy, and of a lively kind; but it doesn't follow that the comedy hasn't its part to play in a total significance. I have already pointed to ways in which Flora tells in the essential communication of the book. And it can now be observed with some force that a corrective emphasis is conveyed by the piquant contrast she presents with Clennam. Flora is decidedly not a lady in the sense that Clennam is a gentleman; but her exuberantly ungenteel characteristics don't blind us—the contrary—to her robust and warm good-nature and the uninhibited completeness with which she has the courage of it. In fact, in her superbly innocent spontaneity she is the great anti-snob; she is qualified to be that as Clennam obviously isn't.[1] And her creative vitality brings home to us the way in which Clennam's virtues, necessary as they are, don't represent all that is necessary—I mean, in relation to the criteria of Dickens's evaluative inquiry, which was initiated in the opening of *Little Dorrit* by the presentation of the repatriated Clennam's own predicament; criteria that are sought, elicited, and brought to conscious recognition (that is, determined) in the course of the inquiry itself.

vi

I have referred to the way in which in the sufficiently dramatic poetry of Flora's discourses we feel the presence of Dickens the creative genius himself. We know it to be impossible that any utterance of Clennam's should affect us in that way. This certainty, however, doesn't entail the conclusion that Dickens the poet, the incomparable Victorian master of poetic expression, is therefore debarred from having any direct part in the processes that make Clennam present to us. Consider the following— Blandois, belonging as he does to the melodramatic side of *Little Dorrit*, has melted into thin air, and the problem for Dickens (it might indeed have presented itself to him as one) is to make us feel in immediacy that

---

[1]What Flora and Pancks have in common is that each vindicates dramatically an essential human realness that is independent of good breeding, and that, in both, what might seem calculated to make them uncongenial to Clennam only lends emphasis to the approving constatation that the reader in due course arrives at— sharing it with Clennam himself.

the prolonged and unexplained disappearance *does* profoundly trouble
Clennam, so that he is obsessed by it:

> It was in vain that he tried to control his attention, by directing it
> to any business occupation or train of thought; it rode at anchor by
> the haunting topic, and would hold to no other idea. As though a
> criminal should be chained in a stationary boat on a clear deep river,
> condemned, whatever countless leagues of water flowed past him, to
> see the body of the fellow-creature he had drowned lying at the
> bottom, immovable and unchangeable, except as the eddies made it
> broad or long, now expanding, now contracting, its terrible linea-
> ments; so Arthur, below the shifting current of transparent thoughts
> and fancies which were gone and succeeded by others as soon as
> come, saw, steady and dark, and not to be stirred from its place, the
> one subject that he endeavoured with all his might to rid nimself of,
> and that he could not fly from. . . . It was like the oppression of a
> dream, to believe that shame and exposure were impending over
> her and his father's memory . . .

It is a developed formal simile, but a simile that has the swift directness
of effect of the most spontaneous metaphor.

To take a different kind of manifestation of the same poetic gift, this
is dramatic speech at a moment of crisis:

> Mrs. Clennam stood still for an instant, at the height of her rapid
> haste, saying in stern amazement:
> 'Kept here? She has been dead a score of years or more. Ask
> Flintwinch—ask *him*. They can both tell you that she died when
> Arthur went abroad.'
> 'So much the worse,' said Affery with a shiver, 'for she haunts the
> house, then. Who else rustles about it, making signals by dropping
> dust so softly? Who else comes, and goes, and marks the walls with
> long crooked touches, when we are all abed? Who else holds the door
> sometimes? But don't go out—don't go out! Mistress, you'll die in
> the street!'

Affery resumes here, with the attendant uncanny reverberations and
feelings and apprehensions, the warning signs (as they turn out to be) that
portend the collapse of the house. Our acquaintance with that shored-up
structure, the inmates and the inner gloom—

> At the heart of it his mother presided, inflexible of face, indomitable
> of will, and austerely opposing herself to the great final secret of all life.

–is associated with these disturbing monitions, coming to us in the force of Dickens's prose with the immediacy of actual sensations, and having in terms of the symbolic significance a charging effect (the symbolism works as immediately as metaphor) that there is no need to enlarge upon.

There had been nothing like this poetic power of the great novelist's prose since Shakespeare's blank verse. A power that has of its nature such diverse manifestations forbids any offer to do it justice by assembling examples. It is a condition–this is my point at the moment–of the flexibility of Dickens's art; of his ability to bring together in the service of one complex communication such a diversity of tones and modes. I will allow myself one more illustration.

Mr. Merdle, making an apparently bored and pointless call on the Sparklers, borrows, as he gets up to go, a penknife:

'Tortoise-shell?'

'Thank you', said Mr. Merdle; 'yes, I think I should prefer tortoise-shell.'

Edmund accordingly received instructions to open the tortoise-shell box, and give Mr. Merdle the tortoise-shell knife. On his doing so, his wife said to the master-spirit, graciously:

'I will forgive you, if you ink it!'

'I'll undertake not to ink it,' said Mr. Merdle.

The illustrious visitor then put out his coat-cuff, and for a moment entombed Mrs. Sparkler's hand: wrist, bracelet, and all. Where his own hand shrunk to was not made manifest, but it was as remote from Mrs. Sparkler's sense of touch as if he had been a highly meritorious Chelsea Veteran or Greenwich Pensioner. Thoroughly convinced, as he went out of the room, that it was the longest day that ever did come to an end at last, and that there was never a woman, not wholly devoid of personal attractions, so worn out by idiotic and lumpish people, Fanny passed into the balcony for a breath of air. Waters of vexation filled her eyes; and they had the effect of making the famous Mr. Merdle, in going down the street, appear to leap, and waltz, and gyrate, as if he were possessed by several devils.

Merdle, the stolid, coarse and commonplace, is actually going to the warm-baths to sever his jugular vein. For the victorious and bored Fanny, who–pure untroubled selfhood–is Little Dorrit's antithesis, he has no real existence, indebted to him as she is (having captured his stepson) for *her* existence in the highest stratum of Society. And *he* is an essential nullity. But the empty, credulous and conscienceless self-interest (which serves nothing real) of Society has made him a force for evil, in working which he has achieved disaster for himself. The significance of what Fanny sees is for us–who see both what *she* sees and her. That the last sentence of the passage portends something sinister and disastrous we know without reflecting. And Fanny is one among the multitude to whom the great financier's suicide will announce ruin.

It is time to say something about the aspect of Victorian civilization that Merdle stands for, the part he plays in Dickens's critique, and the bearing it has on the essential communication of *Little Dorrit*. The Merdle ethos is significantly different from the Calvinistic commercialism of the decaying Clennam house. The financier has no touch of Calvinism; he is cultivated by the best people, lives in a fashionable quarter, and has as much access to the most exclusive drawing-rooms and dining-tables as he cares to enjoy. But, for reasons that come out in an acid exchange with his wife (Book the First, chapter XXXIII), there is for him very little enjoyment. I quote from that exchange, however, with my eye primarily on the theme of nothingness, which presses itself on us yet again as we contemplate the nature of his relations with Society.

Merdle–Dickens, it seems relevant to remark, was familiar with demotic French–acquired the freedom of Society when the widowed Mrs. Sparkler became Mrs. Merdle. She, in what we take as a representative *tête-à-tête*, tells him that he is unfit for Society, and that there is a positive vulgarity in carrying his affairs about with him as he does.

'How do I carry them about, Mrs. Merdle?' asked Mr. Merdle.

'How do you carry them about?' said Mrs. Merdle. 'Look at yourself in the glass.'

Mr. Merdle involuntarily raised his eyes in the direction of the nearest mirror, and asked, with a slow determination of his turbid blood to his temples, whether a man was to be called to account for his digestion?

'You have a physician,' said Mrs. Merdle.

'He does me no good,' said Mr. Merdle.

Mrs. Merdle changed her ground.

'Besides,' said she, 'your digestion is nonsense. I don't speak of your digestion. I speak of your manner.'

'Mrs. Merdle,' returned her husband, 'I look to you for that. You supply manner, and I supply money.'

Society itself–Mrs. Merdle–couldn't quarrel with this summary, which answers to the implicit contract between itself and Merdle. The comment on it is the wonderful chapter (Book the Second, chapter XXV) that ensues on Fanny's loan of the tortoise-shell penknife. There is a dinner at Physician's, attended by the most illustrious company; and no one–not even his wife–is troubled by the fact that there is a vacancy in the place at table where Merdle should have been. The only difference the absence makes is that the guests are freer to whisper their questions and speculations about the honour–a peerage?–that is going to be conferred on the great public benefactor.

The guests depart, Physician hands Mrs. Merdle to her carriage, sends (characteristically) the servants to bed, and settles down to read in his study. A ring of the door-bell takes him down to the door, and the upshot is that he hurries round to the warm baths.

There was a bath in that corner, from which the water had been hastily drained off. Lying in it, as in a grave or sarcophagus, with a hurried drapery of sheet and blanket thrown across it, was the body of a heavily-made man, with an obtuse head, and coarse, mean, common features. A skylight had been opened to release the steam with which the room had been filled; but it hung, condensed into waterdrops, heavily upon the walls, and heavily upon the face and figure in the bath. The room was still hot, and the marble of the bath still warm; but, the face and figure were clammy to the touch. The white marble at the bottom of the bath was veined a dreadful red. On the ledge at the side, were an empty laudanum-bottle and a tortoise-shell handled penknife–soiled, but not with ink.

Physician doesn't question that it's his duty to break the news to Merdle's wife. He hurries round to Wimpole Street, and after much rousing of flunkeys succeeds in getting the Chief Butler summoned.

At last that noble creature came into the dining-room in a flannel gown and list shoes, but with his cravat on, and a Chief Butler all over. It was morning now. Physician had opened the shutters of one window while waiting, that he might see the light.

'Mrs. Merdle's maid must be called, and told to get Mrs. Merdle up, and prepare her as gently as she can to see me. I have dreadful news to break to her.'

Thus Physician to the Chief Butler. The latter, who had a candle in his hand, called his man to take it away. Then he approached the window with dignity, looking on at Physician's news exactly as he had looked on at the dinners in that very room.

'Mr. Merdle is dead.'

'I should wish,' said the Chief Butler, 'to give a month's notice.'

'Mr. Merdle has destroyed himself.'

'Sir,' said the Chief Butler, 'that is very unpleasant to the feelings of one in my position, as calculated to awaken prejudice, and I should wish to leave immediately.'

'If you are not shocked, are you not surprised, man?'

The Chief Butler, erect and calm, replied in these memorable words. 'Sir, Mr. Merdle never was the gentleman, and no ungentlemanly act on Mr. Merdle's part would surprise me. Is there anybody else I can send to you, or any other directions I can give before I leave, respecting what you would wish to be done?'

The Chief Butler is not a less apt representative of Society than Mrs. General. The difference between his attitude to Merdle and Mrs. Merdle's is that he is less directly involved in the contract, and not at all involved in the discomfort caused by the suicide. He took the post for the wages; he was appointed to maintain the standards of civilization; he has done so to perfection and is doing so in his reply to Physician.

The episode of the Chief Butler might properly be called satiric in its irony. Actually it is horrifying, and we are not permitted the detachment that 'satiric' tends to suggest. The whole chapter engages us profoundly and the dominant tone is tragic. It is not for nothing that the presiding, and (for us) determining, consciousness in the chapter is Physician's, of whom we are told–and feel: 'Where he was, something real was'. In fact, the inclusive mode in which Dickens has composed the chapter is one that engages the full profound sense of reality generated in us by what has gone before in the book. We don't, then, take pleasure of any kind in constating the Chief Butler's utter human indifference–his nullity of the pure unqualified selfhood. What we do take in, and take in with horror, is the revealed nothingness of both terms of the Merdle contract– 'manner' and 'money'. With horror, because Merdle's death is a real death, and figures for us in immediacy (whether we say so to ourselves or not) the disaster brought upon innumerable real lives by the collusive perversity that created him–a collaborative illusion, but an illusion hiding realities fraught with destruction. So what we are made to contemplate is not only little Paul Dombey's question (which is more than a question): 'What can money do?' We have the disturbing demonstration, under the head of 'money', of realities that, lightly treated, may vindicate themselves grimly at the expense of Society itself.

We may feel that we needn't worry about Society (though the complex Dorrit situation, with its sensitive filaments, puts difficulties in the way of making more than a fleeting satisfaction of that response). But the Dickensian genius leaves us vividly realizing that the red-stained bath signals a large human disaster for society with a small *s*, entailing real and immeasurable human suffering.

The chapter containing Mrs. Merdle's arch aplomb in the face of questions about her husband's imminent honour and the Chief Butler's classical replies to Physician ends with this:

> So, the talk, lashed louder and higher by confirmation on confirmation, and by edition after edition of the evening papers, settled into such a roar when night came, as might have brought one to believe that a solitary watcher on the gallery above the Dome of St. Paul's would have perceived the night air to be laden with a heavy muttering of the name of Merdle, coupled with every form of execration.
>
> For, by that time it was known that the late Mr. Merdle's complaint had been, simply, Forgery and Robbery. He, the uncouth object of such wide-spread adulation, the sitter at great men's feasts, the roc's egg of great ladies' assemblies, the subduer of exclusiveness, the leveller of pride, the patron of patrons, the bargain-driver with a Minister for Lordships of the Circumlocution Office, the recipient of more acknowledgments within ten or fifteen years, at the most, than had been bestowed in England upon all peaceful benefactors, and upon all the leaders of all the Arts and Sciences, with all their work to testify for them, during two centuries at least–he, the shining wonder, the new constellation to be followed by the wise men bringing gifts, until it stopped over certain carrion at the bottom of a bath and disappeared–was simply the greatest Forger and the greatest Thief that ever cheated the gallows.

It is impossible to discuss Amy Dorrit as disinterestedness (and the creative nisus that placed her at the centre of *Little Dorrit* is intrinsically normative) without being brought to an explicit recognition that the disinterested individual life, the creative identity, is of its nature a responsibility towards what can't be possessed. As Daniel Doyce knows, and testifies in the utterance I have quoted,[1] the creative originality in him, though it entails resolution and sustained effort, isn't *his*: he is the focus and devoted agent. And I will permit myself here to quote once again from that place in the opening of *The Rainbow* which I have found

[1]See page 238 above.

frequently an apt *locus classicus*–the place where we are told of Tom Brangwen that 'he knew he did not belong to himself'.

The implicit insistence is everywhere in *Little Dorrit*. The rise, in such a distinctively resuming and concentrating chapter as I have been adducing, to the close I have quoted is not a mere exhibition of accomplished rhetoric on the part of a practised popular writer. The reference to St. Paul's is not just convention. It invokes institutional religion, of course, but not in the spirit of satiric irony. The institutional is invoked as representing something more than institution; as representing a reality of the spirit, a testimony, a reality of experience, that, although it is a reality of the individual experience or not one at all, is more than merely personal. That the appeal is to the living cultural heritage which has its life here and now, and is kept living as a language is, becomes manifest as we move through that last paragraph of the chapter to the end. The inherited totality of the values, the promptings, the intuitions of basic human need, that both 'manner' and 'money', in their lethal way, have no use for–that is what is being evoked. The reader who really reads Dickens will hardly feel that there is anything of rhetorical indelicacy in the overtly associating reference to the New Testament theme. The effect of it is to emphasize how essentially the spiritual, in what no one could fail to recognize as a religious sense, is involved in the whole evocation. How Dickens would have replied to theologically Christian questioning who can say? And who would think that, in the context of the present discussion, there could be much point in speculating? The value of Dickens's vindication of the spirit lies in its being a great artist's–as Blake's is; and that kind of vindication has a peculiar importance for us today.

vii

The implicit insistence I have spoken of is what those who talk of Dickens's bourgeois and unspiritual conventionality clearly miss–though it is inseparable from what makes him major. It takes many forms. We can point to it again and again in his prose. The astonishing life of language that characterizes his work–the infinitely varied power of his prose, and its vividness of imaginative evocation–manifests itself in ways that anyone would call poetic in those passages which evoke *décor*. But of course it is never any more mere evocation of *décor* than what we have in the opening of *Hamlet* is that. Consider the arrival of the Dorrit family at the convent of the Great St. Bernard, with the whole dazed, awed and subdued party.

What has awed and subdued them has been almost as present to us as if we had ourselves been with the caravan. The daunting Alpine transcendence, the changing light, the known factual remoteness that is contradicted by appearance, the ethereal that is known by the evidence of the near at hand to be in fact inimically rugged, forbidding and massive, the de-realizing effect of the strange and shifting reality–the prose that evokes all this has certainly the Romantic poets behind it. But there would be no more point in calling this art 'romantic' than in calling Lawrence's that in *St. Mawr* (and the Dickensian genius in this vein is as marvellous as the comparable Laurentian).

The air had been warm and transparent through the whole of the bright day .... The snowy mountaintops had been so clear that unaccustomed eyes, cancelling the intervening country, and slighting their rugged height for something fabulous, would have measured them as within a few hours' easy reach. Mountain-tops of great celebrity in the valleys whence no trace of their existence was visible sometimes for months together, had been since morning plain and near, in the blue sky. And now, when it was dark below, though they seemed solemnly to recede, like spectres who were going to vanish, as the red dye of the sunset faded out of them and left them coldly white, they were yet distinctly defined in their loneliness, above the mists and shadows.

Seen from those solitudes, and from the Pass of the Great Saint Bernard, which was one of them, the ascending night came up the mountain like a rising water. When it at last rose to the walls of the convent of the Great Saint Bernard, it was as if that weather-beaten structure were another Ark, and floated on the shadowy waves.

. . . .

At length, a light on the summit of the rocky staircase gleamed through the snow and mist. The guides called to the mules, the mules pricked up their drooping heads, the travellers' tongues were loosened, and in a sudden burst of slipping, climbing, jingling, clinking and talking, they arrived at the convent door.

Other mules had arrived not long before, some with peasant riders and some with goods, and had trodden the snow about the door into a pool of mud. Riding-saddles and bridles, pack-saddles and strings of bells, mules and men, lanterns, torches, sacks, provender, barrels, cheeses, kegs of honey and butter, straw bundles and packages of many shapes, were crowded confusedly together in this thawed quagmire, and about the steps. Up here in the clouds, everything was seen through cloud, and seemed dissolving into cloud. The breath of the men was cloud, the breath of the mules was cloud, the lights were encircled by cloud, speakers close at hand were not seen for cloud, though their voices and all other sounds were surprisingly clear. Of the cloudy line of mules hastily tied to rings in the wall, one would bite another, or kick another, then the whole mist would be disturbed with men diving into it, and cries of men and beasts coming out of it, and no bystander discerning what was wrong. In the midst of this, the great stable of the convent, occupying the basement story, and entered by the basement door, outside which all the disorder was, poured forth its contribution of cloud, as if the whole rugged edifice were filled with nothing else, and would collapse as if it had emptied itself, leaving the snow to fall upon the bare mountain summit.

While all this noise and hurry was rife among the living travellers, there, too, silently assembled in a grated house, half-a-dozen paces removed, with the same cloud enfolding them, and the same snow-flakes drifting in upon them, were the dead travellers found upon the mountain. The mother, storm-belated many winters ago still standing in the corner with her baby at her breast; the man who had frozen with his arm raised to his mouth in fear or hunger, still pressing it with his dry lips after years and years. An awful company, mysteriously come together! A wild destiny for the mother to have foreseen! 'Surrounded by so many and such companions upon whom I have never looked, and never shall look, I and my child will dwell together inseparable on the Great Saint Bernard, outlasting generations who will come to see us, and will never know our name, or one word of our story but the end.'

The living travellers thought nothing of the dead just then.

We are very soon given them within the convent, reinstalled in their confident egos, and being absolute Society. But it is impossible (for the reader, I mean) to have forgotten the potent evocation of time, eternity, the non-human universe, the de-realizing lights and vapours, and death. The effect is to bring out with poetic force the nothingness of the Dorrit-Gowan-Barnacle human world. But it is not merely that Society, as figured in its sheltered conceit by the party enjoying warmth, wine, food and the mutual assurance of its superiority, is, for us, exposed to the irony and the challenge it ignores. We who live in the technologico-Benthamite age can hardly miss a force the episode–that is, the chapter–

has for our time; for the whole book forms an exquisitely nerved context, and Dickens's analysis is radical. 'The individual life is tragic, but there is social hope': 'society' as invoked in Snow's representative cliché-wisdom is a nothing, and it is essentially the *New Statesman*'s, and, not only Mr. Harold Wilson's, but that of politicians, statesmen, social scientists and leader-writers in general. To those troubled by the vanishing of what humanity more and more desperately needs if it is not to be deprived of all that makes it human, the 'society' of organization, social science, 'welfare', equality and statistics is as empty a nothing as the 'Society' of manner and exclusiveness.

Dickens's evocation of death, time and eternity and the non-human universe certainly plays a part in his critical irony, but he has no more bent than Blake towards conceiving life or mankind reductively. His exposure of unrealities is a vindication of human creativity, and an insistence that such a vindication, real and achieved, can (as Daniel Doyce is there to testify) have no hubris in it. *Little Dorrit* confronts the technologico-Benthamite world with a conception of man and society to which it is utterly blank, the blankness being a manifestation of its desperate sickness. I have offered my grounds for saying this in my discussion of Dickens's affinity with Blake. To insist that the psyche, the individual life, is both of its nature creative and in its individuality inherently social is to insist that all human creativity is, in one way or another, collaborative, and that a cultural tradition is a collaboratively sustained reality in the way exemplified by a living language – by the language of Shakespeare, of Blake and of Dickens (to adduce three highly individual and potently creative writers). Dickens insists to this effect both implicitly and consciously, and, having the genius that created the Dickensian novel, more manifestly than Blake does.

To make the last point, of course, is to recognize that Dickens and Blake, significant as the affinity is, are also very different. Those who object to the way in which I have emphasized the affinity may point to the radical difference in the fact that there is no Swedenborg and no Boehme in Dickens's case. That fact certainly constitutes a difference; but it is not radical in the sense that it makes the recognition of an affinity absurd. Blake's interest in Swedenborg and Boehme, and, in general, in the 'sources' that for devotees and researchers constitute the 'perennial philosophy', is relatively accidental; his protest against 'Locke and Newton' in terms of insight into the human psyche is essential. He owed more to Shakespeare than to the 'perennial philosophy', and those voluminous works of research and systematization do very little for the understanding of his importance as the great enemy of spiritual philistinism. Dickens is in the same sense as Blake a vindicator of the spirit – that is, of life. The creativity he insists on as an aspect of disinterestedness is inseparable from the 'identity's' implicitly recognized responsibility to something that (not 'belonging to itself') it doesn't, and can't, possess.

Such formulations as these by themselves are merely wordy formulations; but nothing could be more convincing than the art they point to. Dickens's communication is, in its clear validity, compelling and unanswerable. In its political bearing it represents all that can be properly asked of an artist as such – and what it contributes is basic and indispensable: to comment that Dickens had no political philosophy and no practical advice to give reformers and politicians is gratuitous, obtuse and ungrateful. But it is in the same way true that to dismiss his claim to be recognized as a vindicator of the spirit, such as we sorely need, with the remark that he gives no sign of being concerned – or equipped – to answer the probing questions that theologically religious critics are moved to put, is beside the point, and unintelligent. The great artist presents the indispensable testimony of experience, perception and intuition, he being in respect of these an adept. The difference between Dickens and Blake is not that Blake is more spiritual; rather, it can with a measure of truth be said to be that Blake's genius – which certainly suffered for lack of that essential kind of collaboration which Dickens's relations with his public gave *him* – led him to spend a vast deal of his life and effort wrestling with ultimate questions that inevitably defeated him. (That, presumably, is what Lawrence meant when he said that 'Blake was one of those filthy obscene knowers' – the implication being that, tainted with Urizenic malady, he failed to respect the force of his own insistence on essential 'wonder'.) The evidence of defeat is failure in his major creative enterprises – failure implicitly recognized by Blake himself as he makes attempt after attempt, aspiring to a possession of 'answers' that is unattainable.

It is the prophetic books that give Blake his standing as a great addict of the specifically religious quest; but actually, for all the grist he affords the research-mills and the symbol-specialists, his concern for the spirit is of the same order as Dickens's – he is, whatever the differences in emphasis and accent, religious in the same sense. The characters of the myths, in their confusing, equivocal and changing relations, are faculties, potentialities and aspects of the human psyche. But 'human' – the word becomes challenging in an un-Dickensian way when we consider the cosmic note of Blake's insistence on creativity and of his defiance in general of Newton and Locke. The emphasis, all the same, rests on 'human' to such effect that theologizing students of Blake[1] (who quite properly invoke too his aphorisms and prose commentaries) discuss whether or not, or how far, he should be pronounced heretical.

That kind of doubt has never been raised about Dickens; the placing criticism, making him a lesser creative writer than the greatest, has been that he is a Philistine–like Mr. Meagles; to be pronounced merely conventional, and, in his genial worldly way, not much concerned. I hope, nevertheless, that I have justified my contention that the psychological insight (if 'psychological' is the word) so clearly determining the organization of *Little Dorrit*, with the entailed perceptions, intuitions and evaluative criteria that make 'psychology' a word one hesitates to use, is Blakean. And the criticism to be dismissed by way of completing the case is of the order of that which remarks Dickens's failure to have a political theory or programme–it is not a creative writer's business to be a theologian or a philosopher. Dickens communicates a profound insight into human nature, the human situation and human need; we have no right to ask anything else of a great artist.

In spite of the essential affinity I have been emphasizing, the sense of the human situation conveyed so potently in the Alpine chapter is distinctively Dickens's and not Blake's. Nor, though clearly post-Romantic, is it Wordsworthian. The evocation of the Alps is associated, significantly, with the vision of the mortuary and its long-frozen dead; and the effect– not merely in relation to the touring party within the convent–is one, profoundly characteristic of the great Dickens, of solemn anti-hubristic realism. It is a realism, one must add, strongly anti-Gowan, enforcing, as it does, the dependence of the human world on the collaborative creativity that generates it, and sustains it continually as a living and authoritative reality.

I need say no more about the differences. The point of establishing affinities between two great writers is that they *are* great writers, and therefore in essential ways very different. The importance of the affinity depends on that–I mean, the peculiar importance for us now. With Blake and Dickens I associate Lawrence, so that we have a line running into the twentieth century. And when I accept the description of Dickens

[1]See, e.g., *The Theology of William Blake*, J. G. Davies.

as 'the greatest of the romantic novelists',[1] it is with the proviso that, in the complex Romantic movement, Blake in particular is the poet I take it to be invoking. For it is he pre-eminently who represents what I have in mind in saying that the Romantic movement added something – that is, enriched the human heritage in ways not as a rule given clear or full recognition even in sympathetic uses of the adjective.

The general failure to recognize Dickens's greatness is a failure to perceive the force of the truth I point to here. Something of indubitable high value the Romantic movement brought to the human heritage was a distinctive sense of responsibility towards life. Lawrence implicitly invokes this truth in the comment with which he dismisses Eliot's 'classicism': 'This classiosity is bunkum, still more cowardice.' Eliot's classicism *is* anti-romanticism – explicitly; when he identifies the 'romantic' it is always in characteristics that enforce the pejorative senses of the word.

The kind of vital strength that makes Dickens a 'romantic novelist' and relates him to Blake is what Eliot rules out from the creative process and the 'mind of the artist' in his account of 'impersonality', which has for essential purpose to deny that art expresses, or in any way involves, a responsibility towards life. That kind of denial, in Eliot and his nine-teenth-century prompters, is a new thing, and its appearance – it being a reaction (and incoherent) – is an index of the new consciousness of responsibility against which it reacts. The century of the American and the French Revolutions, of the opening Industrial Revolution, and of the inevitable reaction against 'Locke and Newton', produced changes, challenges and creative incitements enough to make the emergence of a new sense of human responsibility comprehensible, and to explain a notable development of language. Writers in the English tradition, responding to the development, had the immeasurable advantage of being able to draw – as both Blake and Dickens did – on Shakespeare.

[1]See *The Image of Childhood: The Individual and Society – A Study of the Theme in English Literature*. Peter Coveney. Peregrine Books.

CHAPTER SIX

HOW WE MUST READ
'GREAT EXPECTATIONS'

I⊤ must have been very much easier to read *Great Expectations* adequately –that is, with a sympathetic and intelligent comprehension of the spirit in which it was written and of what it was actually about–in Dickens's own day, or in any time up to the present, than it evidently is now. For not only has Dickens's society gone for ever, and with it many (though not all) of the difficulties and problems of a young man living in that age, but the young reader in ours is further handicapped by crass misdirections from contemporary Dickens specialists. Even ignoring the bright-idea merchants who are with us in all specialisms in literary studies nowadays, there are the blind-bat school of Dickens critics who make pseudo-logical objections to what they represent, often inaccurately or quite unjusti-fiably, as Dickens's ideas, and who have no real knowledge of the con-stitution and actuality of Dickens's society–in addition, too often no intuitive feeling for the implications of our language as Dickens used it, no sensitiveness to his tone of voice and to his overtones, no understand-ing of the conventions in which he wrote, and whose obstinate literal-mindedness and absence of all imaginative insight leave one in despair.[1]

---

[1]e.g. I have noted a series of recent objections to the 'implausibility' of the novel: i. We are not told why Compeyson didn't marry Miss Havisham–when in fact we are told by Magwitch that a few years after the jilting Compeyson certainly had a wife 'which Compeyson kicked mostly' (suggesting a marriage of long standing), and as though Miss Havisham's brother would have ventured on such a conspiracy with a man free to double-cross him, Arthur's declared aim being to get a share of the loot as well as to humiliate his sister! ii. That Magwitch isn't much like an old lag–as though Dickens's point weren't that he isn't a natural old lag (through low mentality or vicious instincts) but a potentially decent fellow driven to crime in childhood, and who at the first chance makes good in Australia, with a motive–to vindicate himself indirectly against the 'gentlemen', 'from the judge in his wig, to the colonist' who despised him, by setting up 'his boy' in London. iii. Pip never seems to meet any girl but Biddy and Estella–this betrays a failure to grasp the whole method of the novel which works in representative experience: Biddy is the best that village life can produce and she can gain no hold on Pip's imagination

Then there are the critics who reduce this novel to a matter of fairy god-mothers and princesses, to fairy-tale dimensions and remoteness from any actuality, or to some other-world of folk-tale elements and primitive symbolism. It is true that Pip likens Miss Havisham to a fairy godmother when he thinks she has become his patron, but she has in fact almost no part in the chain of cause and effect that binds him to his convict bene-factor. And when he thinks of Estella as the Sleeping Beauty whom he will awaken with a kiss and thus bring life back to Satis House, this is to heighten for Pip the basic irony, as Pip is later to discover, of her being the very opposite of a princess in actuality and of the fact that she was never destined for him, as also that Satis House cannot be revivified but is revisited by Pip and Estella, when they do come together ultimately, as a site cleared for rebuilding. The adjuncts of the fairy-tale are employed (or rather deployed) as a mode of thought natural to a romantic country boy, but they are not the terms in which Dickens himself worked or thought here, and he dissociates himself from Pip throughout the novel, very skilfully, though the method is subtle and easy to overlook, since the narrative is autobiographical.

What is required is to be able to substantiate the conviction one has from reading the novel that it is a great novel, seriously engaged in dis-cussing, by exemplifying, profound and basic realities of human ex-perience. Even those who sense that this novel is meaningful are not in general successful in offering a convincing and adequate account of its meanings. It is the reverse of a Victorian reader who now reads *Great Expectations*, at once too sophisticated and yet too humanly ignorant: anyone who is now engaged in reading English Literature with under-graduates even in England must feel (unless of the same generation) that he has to introduce delicately complex perceptions and a social civilization of which that literature is the flower, to a brutally callous generation as to sensibility, students who except in rare cases have lost contact with the traditional culture that could and did produce both the self-educated genius Dickens and a public to read and support him. To

because she *is* only the product of the village, while Estella, who does incarnate values that satisfy his imaginative needs, so permeates his life that no one else is necessary or possible for him. iv. Why do we not hear anything about Pip's feelings towards his sister between his childhood and Orlick's insulting her? The reason is that the novel pursues a theme and is not a total recall of Pip's memories even though Pip is the narrator, and to suppose the scenes of his life are chosen for theatrical effect or some other arbitrary or derogatory reason is to ignore the art which furnishes the right, expressive occasions for advancing that theme.

have an easily available cynicism but no reverence for life's serious issues, no aim in living otherwise than to satisfy basic instincts, is a particular disqualification for appreciating what *Great Expectations* has to offer.

The difficulty we are faced with is to find an approach, a way in, which cannot be waived away as sentimental or faulted as far-fetched. I propose to start with an irrefutable pointer to the essential nature of Dickens's dealing with men and women, which incidentally has the merit of exposing a notorious English academic contention that Dickens was primarily an irresponsible concoctor of acting parts, as though his novels were merely material for the public readings of his very last phase. In an interesting book, *Some Reflections on Genius*, published in 1960, Lord Brain reprinted a paper called *Dickensian Diagnoses* he had once given to the medical association that is of very considerable interest to the reader of Dickens and more relevant to an insight into Dickens's work than that of many of the well-known Dickens 'authorities'. As it is too long to quote from adequately, I select a few sentences which will give the gist of his conclusions, based on ample reference to the novels, the conclusions of an authority in his field:

> What is surprising is that Dickens should have given such detailed and accurate descriptions of the disorders from which his characters suffered. He was not content with vague diagnoses like brain fever, which figure in the works of some of his contemporaries, and even those who wrote later. Dickens looked on disease with the observing eye of the expert clinician, and he recorded what he saw, and what the patient told him, so that he often gives us accounts which would do credit to a trained physician. . . . Dickens's psychiatric studies are as comprehensive and as varied as his observations on organic diseases. . . . Perhaps the most remarkable example of Dickens's psychiatric insight is the case of Dr. Manette in *A Tale of Two Cities*. It is remarkable for the accuracy of his account of a case of multiple personality and loss of memory, because it is the most comprehensive of his studies of psychological abnormality, and because it includes an anticipation of psychotherapy. . . . At a time when medicine itself was only just beginning to recognize the importance of physical signs, the characters in the world of Dickens's imagination are so real that they have recognizable diseases of body and mind, described with the accuracy and insight of a great clinical observer.

Thus we have the best authority for endorsing our own perception that Dickens was neither interested in people as an actor-manager, for their theatrical possibilities, nor was he, as Edmund Wilson and others have asserted, under the compulsions of a psychological disorder he could neither understand nor control – as if he were like Kafka, able only to describe and project in fictions his own neuroses. But interesting as Russell Brain's observations on Dickens's gifts as a clinical observer are, they are only a pointer to a more important fact, that Dickens was much more than this or than an amateur psychologist fictionizing his own observations. It is not merely an interest in case-histories that is shown in Dickens's intuitive apprehension of the relation between the inner and the outer life that is manifested by gesture, mannerisms, speech-habits, facial expressions, gait, physical characteristics and such that he documents so accurately in his novels (the idea now sedulously propaganded that Dickens's characters make merely theatrical gestures and facial signs is demonstrably false). He proceeds always from such intelligent observations and sensitive insights as Russell Brain admiringly records, to an ordered and systematic inquiry into what light may be thrown by such insights on the subjects that are the province of the great novelist. Dickens is always to be seen asking questions as to the *why* of human conduct – What is their motivation? Why are people what they are (heredity or nurture)? Why do people in similar circumstances and under the same pressures behave differently? Is there such a thing as free-will, admitting the force of heredity, conditioning by the social and psychological forces of infancy and adolescence, and the constrictions of emotional and moral habits? What explanation is there for apparently pointless, or perverse, or even self-stultifying action? How do murderers feel and behave after breaking the most powerful human taboos in doing to death friend, kinsman, mistress? What are madness and associated states of temporary aberration or derangement due to drugs, fever and delirium, suicidal states? Dickens explores all these and many related questions by the means proper to the novelist, of course, and not by writing essays in his fictions as novelists have frequently done. But his approach to such questions and topics is neither emotional nor theatrical: it is so systematic as to be almost academic. Hence his interest in human life after the callow *Pickwick Papers* is not just in people as such (whatever the Chestertonians may allege) but includes them in the examination of questions that we now tend to consider the province of the psychologist and sociologist – though in happier days it was otherwise and Dickens, like Shakespeare and Tolstoy, shows the advantage of the artist's insight which is not reductive nor generalizing and abstract, but always sympathetically human. Dickens sees people as at once the products and symptoms of their society and the producers of it. Similarly he shows his interest in ethical matters by exploring the behaviour of characters, chosen for the purpose, in such a way as to undercut theory and extend our views by presenting situations in a new light, disturbing our preconceptions and prejudices. Where judgment on behaviour is in question Dickens puts before the reader facts that must be taken into consideration before forming such judgment, facts that would otherwise have lain outside our perceptions even.

Of course the method is not evident as such except in such a tale as I am about to point to. The procedure, though it must have been pondered at some level, appears generally to be spontaneous, the ideas completely dissolved into novelistic material of action, dialogue and characterization. But one way in which we can see that Dickens evidently did do some deliberate thinking is by recognizing that he habitually examined alternatives–people he posits who in the same situation have responded to it in opposite ways and so become different persons with, alternatively, tragic or relatively happy outcomes. Thus the girl-child who learns she is illegitimate in Dickens's society, which held that the child inherited a stigma from the guilty mother, could respond either by acceptance and docility or by aggression and resentment: in the one case is produced Esther Summerson in *Bleak House* and in the other Miss Wade in *Little Dorrit*, who is so much alienated from everyone that she has no need of a Christian name and has to write out her case-history for her own relief, as her justification. Being able to communicate in no other way, she hands it to some-one to read whom she senses is sympathetic because a fellow-sufferer from life, Arthur Clennam. Dora, who adopts and exploits the rôle of pet provided by her habitat, has an alternative in Pet Meagles who outgrows that character but finds it has fatally circumscribed her possibilities of happiness. These cannot be chance occurrences since a great deal of Dickens's characterization is seen to have been formed or used in such a way. Another instance of his rationale is the characterization of Pancks in *Little Dorrit* and Wemmick in *Great Expectations*. Pancks is presented as a human machine (a steam-tug), humourously, but the humour is entirely controlled by Dickens as a means of developing for us this character's functional uses. When he argues with Arthur, in their Socratic dialogue, which ends with Pancks's definition of 'The Whole Duty of Man in a commercial society', cornering Arthur with his final query: 'What else?', Pancks is being subtly ironic, acting Devil's Advocate in order to ridicule the Victorian theory, which as a human steam-boat he has to exemplify in his working life. But in fact, no one can be a mere machine: while in his working life, as the grasping hand of Casby the Patriarch, his business is to rack-rent the inhabitants of Bleeding Heart Yard, he compensates in his own time by looking for people to *give* money *to*, for those who are missing heirs. Thus he is able to release the Dorrits from prison and set them up with wealth (paying the expenses of the inquiry out of his own pocket); eventually Nature, whom Dickens evidently thinks can't be trifled with, drives him to rebel outright against his 'proprietor'. Dickens's grounds for optimism, legitimate because psychologically sound, are dramatized thus by embodying them in the history of Mr. Pancks and enacting it before our eyes, with humour, irony, drama, pathos, wit and a final scene of fantasy revenge. Wemmick is a similar but distinct case of the completely split man, so much so that Pip feels Wemmick is actually twins who replace each other according to circumstances, one who earns his living in the Office and the other who had to invent the Castle to make a healthy life possible– healthy physically, morally and spiritually.

Such characters are means of pursuing an argument and yet thanks to Dickens's art don't in general strike us as schematic. Even less so do the more complex characters who embody, like David Copperfield and Pip, the basic problems of living in their society. However amusing or merely entertaining at times, or partially irrelevant, it may at first sight appear, such an enquiry is conducted by Dickens responsibly, with his eye always on an object of ultimate importance. Thus it is not surprising that Dickens re-read *David Copperfield* when undertaking a comparable novel, *Great Expectations*. But David was not a true alternative to Pip except that while David achieves happiness and fulfilment by coming to terms with and accepting his society, Pip ceases to be wretched and saves himself from shipwreck by freeing himself from participation in that society. The very close alternative to Pip's is the subject of a late short story which though subsequent to *Great Expectations* I propose to examine first because it shows indisputably how Dickens's mind operated in creating, and for what purpose.

George Silverman's Explanation, though written rapidly for an American magazine (published in 1868 and therefore one of Dickens's last undertakings in fiction) is one of his best written and most accomplished, as well as one of his most significant works, but it is because it is so thoroughly representative, and so undisguisedly so, that I cite it here. It is laid out in three sections, corresponding to the phases of the protagonist's development, each having its own locale, a method that is easily apparent in *Great Expectations*[1] and only less obviously the essential structure of *David Copperfield*. Dickens has tried perhaps too realistically at the start to show the difficulty the narrator has in bringing himself to rehearse his sufferings, but there is absolutely nothing, not a sentence, in this tale, once it is launched, which is not required for the demonstration of a child whose conditioning is similar to Pip's but whose reactions to it were almost the opposite. George writes his history not as Pip does, with detachment, and not as an apologia, for he is bewildered and is trying to explain how he came to be where and what he is, to find out what went wrong.

'My infant home', he eventually begins, 'was a cellar in Preston.' In wretched poverty and deprived of all affection, light and warmth, he was constantly accused by his bad-tempered mother (a Mrs. Joe Gargery in character, always frowning), whenever he was hungry, cold or frightened of the dark, of being 'a worldly little devil'–the sense in which 'worldly' affected him suggests that it is expected to be understood in a sectarian or Evangelical context. His parents die frighteningly in the cellar of fever and he is brought to the surface by the authorities, knowing nothing except what it feels to be cold and hungry and ashamed of being 'worldly'–that is, with a sense of guilt, which of course he can't help since worldliness seems to him to mean 'yearning for enough of anything (except misery)', yet for which sin his mother used to beat him. He cannot therefore regret his parents but is told by his rescuers that this too is horrible worldliness. The police teach him the virtues of cleanliness and order, and feed him well, and he is then taken in charge by an unctuous sectarian tradesman, Brother Hawkyard, who undertakes to educate George as a good deed. As George is probably still infectious he sends

---

[1]Dickens has emphasized this for the reader by marking the sections as 'This is the end of the first' (or 'second') 'stage of Pip's expectations'. The true artist, exhausted and yet triumphant, is shown in what he writes about the novel as he ended: 'It is a pity that the third portion cannot be read all at once, because its purpose would be much more apparent; and the pity is all the greater, because the general turn and tone of the working out and winding up, will be away from all such things as they conventionally go. But what must be must be. As to the planning out from week to week, nobody can imagine what the difficulty is, without trying. But, as in all such cases, when it is overcome the pleasure is proportionate.' The extra difficulties he gave himself by undertaking weekly publication and thus shorter portions than his usual numbers, make it even more remarkable that *Great Expectations* is such a tight, economical and yet infinitely suggestive and complex work of art.

the boy to lodge at a farmhouse in the country to recuperate, first
charging him not to tell about the fever or he'll get turned out. George
knows that he was at this time a mere animal, 'sordid, afraid, unadmiring'
–the choice of words is striking; he thought that the shadows on the hills
from clouds were frowns, like his mother's, at him, the guilty one, as he
comes to the farmhouse built up against an imposing ruined Jacobean
mansion.

Here begins the second phase of his moral life. The powerful impression
made now by the countryside and the deserted great house on the boy's
sensibilities, that is, by art and nature together, their morally poetic action
upon him, is finely conveyed; Wordsworth himself never described more
convincingly the moral influence of natural surroundings and of the
works of man's imagination. George ends, recalling them:

> I have written that the sky stared sorrowfully at me. Therein I have
> anticipated the answer. I knew that all these things looked sorrow-
> fully at me; that they seemed to sigh or whisper, not without pity for
> me, 'Alas! poor worldly little devil!'. . . . How not to be this worldly
> little devil? How not to have a repugnance towards myself as I had
> towards the rats? I hid in a corner of one of the smaller chambers,
> frightened at myself, and crying (it was the first time I had ever
> cried for any cause not purely physical) and I tried to think about it.
> One of the farm-ploughs came into my range of view just then;
> and it seemed to help me as it went on with its two horses up and
> down the field so peacefully.

This bears fruit. A girl of his own age in the farmer's family attracts him
as Estella does Pip, but because Sylvia is kind as well as pretty. It occurs
to George that if he is infectious and she caught the fever from him she
would die like his parents, therefore he must keep away from her. He
can do this only by avoiding meals and hiding from her; he is even
pleased that this means he has to live on 'broken fare' because 'so much
the less worldly and less devilish the deed', and pleased also to see from
afar that Sylvia looks healthy still thanks to his sacrifices. This unselfish
action was, he knows, 'the humanizing of myself' and softened his
thoughts of father and mother. Thus begins a sense of achievement and
self-respect founded in self-sacrifice which is even heightened because he
must not explain to the kindly farmer and Sylvia why he is unsocial and
ungracious. This makes him 'timidly silent under misconstruction'. All
this becomes the unalterable pattern of George's existence.

After a start he earns his own education, forcing himself to stomach the odious patronage of Brother Hawkyard and his sect and resolutely suppressing a suspicion, which in fact becomes a certainty, that Hawkyard has embezzled George's inheritance from his grandfather and is quieting his conscience by paying a very little of it out for George's support. Determined not to be worldly, George, quite unnecessarily, and of his own volition gives the man a document vindicating him, renouncing his inheritance for ever rather than appear to be ungrateful, for 'without him, how should I ever have seen the sky look sorrowfully down upon that wretched boy at Hoghton Towers?' he says, confessing to 'an inexpressible, perhaps a morbid, dread of ever being sordid or worldly. It was in these ways that my nature came to shape itself to such a mould.' He wins his way to Cambridge, and thus becomes a scholar and a Fellow, takes Holy Orders and is soon a university coach of some repute. Again he shows how this 'mould' has made him automatically yielding of his rights: his scrupulous unworldliness obliges him to return 'immediately' on request from the grasping mother of an idle pupil, half the fees, because the young aristocrat doesn't take a degree in spite of George's work. The mother, Lady Fareway, thus finds that George's fear of being thought mercenary can be exploited, and by forcing on him a poor living on her estate gains, as well as a clergyman, a secretary for herself and a tutor for her talented daughter, for nothing. George however refuses to attribute mean motives to her and is content in fulfilling his own standards of conduct and with the joy of instructing an eager pupil, Adelina Fareway.

But now the final and fatal repetition of this pattern of self-blame, self-sacrifice and over-compensation for his guilty cellar-self takes place inevitably. Adelina Fareway the pupil is everything that could make George happy. He falls in love with her and he even sees that she unconsciously loves her very congenial young tutor. Adelina is almost of age and will then possess her own fortune, and is of a 'daring, generous character': George could be rich and happy, and he is already a gentleman (there is no question of social distinctions between them to complicate the purely moral-psychological conditions). But 'No. Worldliness should not enter here at any cost' – and George again over-compensates. He is not satisfied with forbidding himself to win Adelina, he must complete the sacrifice by putting her into another man's hands. He now has a likely pupil studying with him in his vicarage whom he deliberately throws into Adelina's company, resolutely encouraging an attachment between them, for it is enough, George felt, that 'though poor, Mr.

Granville had never lived in a cellar in Preston'—this does not raise a class issue, the different poverty that disqualifies George in his own eyes is a matter of his past guilt of moral savagery and has nothing to do with snob values either. George heroically marries the lovers himself in secret, 'and I was at peace'.[1] He has undertaken to break the news to Adelina's ambitious mother; he is prepared that she should be angry but not that she would accuse him, to his horror, of being a 'worldly wretch', of having been in a conspiracy with Mr. Granville to gain Adelina's fortune and take a percentage for himself. George is of course incapable of justifying himself or defending his interests, as always, and resigns everything, losing his living and his reputation owing to Lady Fareway's malignity. Though little over thirty, he is now white-haired and broken-hearted. 'If I have unwittingly done any wrong with a righteous motive, that is some penalty to pay', he says, and 'I almost suspect I was a repulsive object'—since having sacrificed everything he has *still* incurred the charge of being 'a worldly little devil'. He lies broken-hearted in the churchyard to write his 'explanation', though to him it explains nothing. Though George is a clergyman, religion doesn't enter into the tale any more than Class. Dickens has kept the question of irrational guilt incurred in childhood and its part in the development of the life of feeling and its influence on character and conduct entirely clear of such extraneous matters, though it is relevant and appropriate that George should become a clergyman as part of his programme. The uselessness of a high ideal of conduct that is simply automatic because it is founded on fear and guilt and does not allow a reasoned response to each situation as it arises, is the point of this case-history, where George's intentionally noble behaviour, originally right in the case of the fever-infection and Sylvia because spontaneously evolved, is wrong in the later contexts, not noble but inappropriate, merely compulsive and therefore self-defeating. The relevance of George's case to Pip's helps to make clear the purpose of that earlier spiritual adventure, *Great Expectations*. Pip was by definition 'morally timid and very sensitive' too, owing to his early conditioning

[1]At dawn on the wedding-day George goes out to see the sunrise on the seashore and feels that Nature approves his actions; he sees that in such signs as 'the orderly withdrawal of the stars, the calm promise of coming day, the ineffable splendour that then burst forth', etc. Thus the help he once got from nature when felt to be sympathetic to his anguish, is now invoked again as a sanction. Dickens's intelligence is shown here in his remarkable comprehension of the psychological truths on which Wordsworthian beliefs were based, while showing clearly his own dissociation from them as beliefs.

by his unjust and ill-tempered sister, who demanded gratitude for bringing the child up 'by hand' when that hand was so hard upon him that he could feel only resentment. But Pip does not end as George does broken and bewildered and still saddled with the original guilt from which he had tried so sedulously to escape—for Lady Fareway was, as George suspects, right in accusing him: in making Adelina's marriage he *had* done it for his own profit, his 'percentage' being the self-approval he gained from it. George ends, in spite of his life-long and resolute efforts to become of good repute, back where he started, repulsive to himself. [The logic that shaped George's history and the compassionate insight with which it is interpreted, show that, whatever may be deduced from the obsession Dickens revealed in the sixties about his 'readings', his powers as a creative artist were unaffected as late as 1868 anyway.] The elements which *Great Expectations* and *George Silverman's Explanation* have in common (such as Sylvia and Estella, Hoghton Towers and Satis House, the guilt-inducing mother and mother-surrogate, the striving of both boys towards peace of mind *via* intellectual cultivation and usefulness, among others) are not reworked from *Great Expectations* because the writer was worn out and running out of resources, but because he was pursuing what I have shown to be his regular creative method. Having succeeded with Pip, Dickens posits an alternative case: suppose Pip hadn't had the qualities which made him able to free himself from his early conditioning and its burden of guilt and shame? (The shame is absent from George's case.) Reversing Dickens's progress, we can discover from George's history what was crucial to Pip's case, what made the book not a case-history but the history of a successful progress towards spiritual freedom. Pip, we are shown, though this seems not at all noticed, is fully human in having impulses flowing freely in different directions, and it is by ordering these according to a code he acquires by trial and error and self-examination of an open kind—the process is laid before us—that at the crisis of his life, which occurs half-way through the novel, he is able to master his immediate reactions and control them, substituting a 'better' mode of feeling and action, not of course by forcing them on himself as a duty, but by understanding himself and his needs more fully so that his new self is produced of free choice, a choice that is seen to be steadily prepared for, unconscious of it though Pip has been, by undercurrents of feeling since his first association with 'his' convict.

Pip's business in telling his history is to explain and chart for us what he calls in chapter VI 'my inner self'—it will be noted that with his outside we have no concern and the only person we get any kind of description of Pip from is Herbert on one occasion, from whom we then hear that Pip was 'a boy whom nature and circumstances made so romantic',[1] confirming for us a deduction we ought to have made. The sense in which *Great Expectations* is a novel at all is certainly not to be arrived at by applying to it the ordinary conventions and assumptions derived from Victorian novels in general. The succession of events are as carefully chosen, and almost as exclusively, as those in *George Silverman's Explanation* for a similar purpose, and just as in that there is in *Great Expectations* no love interest in the usual sense, no love scenes, and a refusal to be limited to the everyday 'reality' of commonsense experience. But whereas George's is *only* a case-history, and explicitly a morbid one, Pip's is so fully human as to be representative in its age. Dickens's preoccupations in *Great Expectations* are with the fundamental realities of his society and focus on two questions: how was it that a sense of *guilt* was implanted in every child, and with what consequences? And what part does *Class* play in the development of such a member of that society? The novelist is concerned with the effects of these two sanctions, guilt and shame, and it is an inseparable feature of this concern that he constantly insinuates the question: what is 'real' in such a context? for Pip is continually in doubt and perplexity as to whether the real life is that social one with its rules of right and wrong, into which he was born, or the life of the imagination that grows out of natural feeling, into which he was inducted from the opening chapter, his first distinct memory. Of course it is in the working out and presentation of these inquiries that the value of the novel lies, in the minute particularities of the individual life which are yet so skilfully invented as to carry overtones of allegory and to be exemplary. The pertinacity and concentration of Dickens's mind on his theme has made the two questions, in which the third is implied, so interwoven as to be inseparable eventually, and his Shakespearean genius as a creator has produced the wonderful plot which is not only exciting to read and faultless in execution but strikingly classical in its peripeteia. Every detail of the plot, moreover, expresses some aspect, some further aspect, of the theme, and one that is necessary for its full apprehension by the reader. A remarkable feature of the novel is the complexity of the irony which informs the plot from beginning to end

---

[1]'Romantic' here is used basically in the sense it bears in Jane Austen's novels, meaning to feel excessively about things and not be directed by reasonable considerations.

(the rewritten end which is demonstrably superior to the one first intended and which perfectly completes the intention and meaning of the novel)—an irony which inheres in the title; yet the novel is affirmative and constructive, not, like other novels shot through with irony (e.g. *Huckleberry Finn*, *The Confidence Man*, *Le Rouge et le Noir*), pessimistic or nihilistic.

And whereas Dickens's difficulties, ever since they first appeared in *Oliver Twist*, in reconciling the reader's demands for realism with his own need, for his creative intentions, of a non-rational symbolism of situation and action, a freer form of dealing with experience than his inheritance from the eighteenth-century novelists provided, he has at last, in *Great Expectations*, managed to reconcile realism and symbolism so that in this novel we move without protest, or uneasiness even, from the 'real' world of everyday experience into the non-rational life of the guilty conscience or spiritual experience, outside time and place and with its own logic: somehow we are inhibited from applying the rules of common sense to it even where we hardly recognize that it is symbolic action and can not possibly be plausible real life. The novel is also remarkable for having no wide divergences of prose style either, as even *Bleak House* has; almost the only rhetoric is the passage where Pip tries to explain to Estella his feelings for her, where the effect of weak egotism is required and deliberately obtained through rhetorical language. There is a consistent sobriety of language without losing idiomatic identity for the characters, who range widely nevertheless, as from Jaggers to Joe, from Wemmick to Herbert, from Miss Havisham to Mrs. Joe, and this personal idiom is even what distinguishes Magwitch from Orlick. While Dickens works here, as in *George Silverman's Explanation*, with the minimum in word, setting and characterization, he does not sacrifice in *Great Expectations* scope, range, richness or imaginative complexity. This is the Dickens novel the mature and exigent are now likely to re-read most often and to find more and more in each time, perhaps because it seems to have more relevance outside its own age than any other of Dickens's creative work.

Dickens, as I've argued, from *Dombey* onwards worked schematically by translating ideas into characters and their relations to each other, and by choosing or arranging illustrative settings for this, and he proceeded commonly by picking up an idea he had thrown out marginally before and developing it thoughtfully in a more suitable context. Thus the exemplary situation of the illegitimate child Esther who is made to feel 'guilty yet innocent' (by the mere fact of her birth)[1] is thoroughly explored in Pip's comparable situation which, unlike Esther's, is not static, an initial fact only, but cumulative; while in the same novel Richard Carstairs had been shown as the tragic victim of illusory expectations, 'great' indeed, sacrificing a real happiness and hopeful work for a delusion which falsifies all reality, the realization of which kills him. From these previous disjointed ideas Dickens now deduces a coherent and compelling analysis of what was *fundamentally* amiss with his society. In the world of Esther and Richard it was seen as a litigating society where base competitiveness and greed and desire for power over others ruined the innocent; now it is seen as a society that first makes and then executes criminals, with a quite arbitrary conception of justice, a society in which all are therefore guilty inescapably–there are no innocent, only those more or less aware of guilt, ranging from the blindly self-righteous to the repentantly self-accusing.

One of the principal reasons for the homogeneous tone of the novel is that it is told us by a narrator who is firmly kept before us as remote from the self who is the subject, a self that is seen in growth from childhood to adult status. Unlike David Copperfield the narrator Pip is not identified in sympathy with that child, boy or youth; far from it, the wry glance he directs at his follies and shortcomings and mistakes warns us off any easy sympathy with the youthful Pip. The frequent humour or amusement in the narrator's tone–which is not inconsistent with the narration's being painful, pathetic and at times even terrible–guarantees the narrator's detachment for us and underplays (very notably if we think of David's) the exposed self's sufferings, so that there is no bitterness about others' treatment of him, only a clear insight into the causes of his mistakes. We thus grasp, without being told, that the narrator is now truly a free man, freed from the compulsions of childhood guilt and from shame imposed by the class distinctions that closed round him in his boyhood, and from the unreal aspirations imposed on him by his society–a society from which when he grasps its true nature he is finally seen to recoil. Yet we have also seen that the guilt and the shame were necessary to produce the complex sensibility of an adult who can free himself by renunciation, contrition and publicly manifested repentance. This is Pip's history and in this light it is seen to be a novel comparable with apparently

[1]Dickens here, as so often, seems to have arrived independently at an insight close to Blake's in 'Songs of Experience' rather than to be merely translating theological dogma into psychological fact.

more sophisticated novels of the major novelists of our European tradition such as *Crime and Punishment* and *Under Western Eyes*. Pip is not apologizing for himself nor, like George Silverman, explaining his conduct in order to assert the truth when he has been maligned, but telling us dispassionately how he became the man who can now write thus about his former self. After all, only half this novel is concerned with the formation of the Pip that Magwitch finds (his 'brought-up London gentleman') awaiting him; the other half is devoted to showing Pip's self-regeneration and how he reverses his life-stream–the second half of the novel is a reversal for Pip of the first half both in direction and in detail of action and impulse.

The critics who despise Pip as weak don't apparently notice his strengths, and those who, like H. House, dismiss his history as 'a snob's progress' are unable to appreciate the delicacy, subtlety and intention of Dickens's searching investigation into Pip's feelings, successfully presented in all their complexity and psychological truth: unlike such critics, Dickens refuses to simplify, and the marvellous persuasive power with which Dickens establishes the inevitability of Pip's feelings, given the circumstances in which he finds himself, leads us also to believe in Pip's better choices when he makes them. Pip is framed as a victim, an unconscious victim deceived by accident and intention, impelled into a position of maximum exposure to destruction and saved only because, as Dickens believed and has intimated in earlier novels in marginal cases, there is reason to have faith in human nature inasmuch as it contains in itself compensatory powers, inherent impulses towards spiritual regeneration, because we cannot but crave health. The novel structurally hinges round the return of the convict patron, the peripeteia, and never was there a more wholly thematic plot-structure; but the novel also, as for a traditional use of the three-decker form, is divided into three stages which are also thematic divisions (comparable to those of George Silverman's history) and marked as such, with Pip ending the first stage of his expectations by leaving the village for London when the morning mists are rising; the second stage ending with Magwitch's return towards midnight as Provis; and the third of course ends with Pip's leaving 'the ruined place' hand in hand with Estella, as the evening mists disperse.

Pip says his 'first and most vivid and broad impression of the identity of things, seems to me to have been gained on a memorable raw afternoon' when he found himself crying in the churchyard from fright, misery and cold (George's cellar experience); he had been looking at his parents' grave. [David Copperfield's first consciousness included the churchyard outside his window where his father lay buried.] On the marshes Pip knows also of the existence of the gibbet for hanging malefactors, and it turns out that he is to learn now that a prison hulk is part of his habitat. Dickens like most great novelists was quick to pick up ideas and make them his own (not, in his case, at the conscious level probably) and we may note here substantial evidence for his expressed admiration for the opening scenes of Hawthorne's allegorical masterpiece *The Scarlet Letter*[1] (1850) where Hawthorne had started by setting out the conditions of human society in the same terms but more forthrightly. However Utopian a new colony may be in intention, he states, 'the founders have invariably recognized it among their earliest practical necessities to allot a portion of the virgin soil as a cemetery, and another portion as the site of a prison'—that is, death, and sin or crime (offences against the laws of God and man) are the basic facts in any society and, Hawthorne adds, therefore not only is a burial ground needed but the settlement's soil inevitably bears 'the black flower of civilized society, a prison'. Whether Dickens adopted Hawthorne's ironic diagnosis of society or transferred

[1] *The Scarlet Letter* was so influential on English novelists and the Victorian reading public that it is really part of the English 19th century tradition, as witness its influence on, e.g., Dickens and George Eliot (who also greatly admired it—*v. Anna Karenina and Other Essays*, 'Adam Bede', where F. R. Leavis discusses the influence on that novel of *The Scarlet Letter*). Its steady sales here from the beginning in innumerable cheap editions showed that it was recognized as a classic of our own. The highly stylized settings and the schematic technique of *The Scarlet Letter* seem to have an affinity in the very deliberately selected simple settings of *Great Expectations*, as well as in its salvationist outcome and its exploration of the effects of guilt. Hawthorne opens his novel outside the prison, uses the Scaffold for public expiation, has his little settlement surrounded by woods where lurk the Devil and his instruments, all as the background for the sinful consciousness of Hester Prynne and Arthur Dimmesdale, with the incidental revelation by Hawthorne, with devastating irony, that the society that condemns these sinners is far more really evil. The two characters have to work out their own salvation by suffering, contrition, confession, self-abnegation and atonement, and, in the case of Hester the survivor, by a life of useful work and humble acceptance of her lot. Miss Havisham's being seen by Pip in a vision as first and last hanging from a beam reminds one of Hester forced to stand on the Scaffold at the beginning and end of her sufferings. Though the likeness of *Great Expectations* to Hawthorne's novel is pronounced in these respects, yet Dickens's masterpiece is unique—thus one creative genius can make use of another's work without being parasitic or even imitative. I provided a critique of *The Scarlet Letter* in its context of Hawthorne's whole creative *oeuvre* in my essay 'Hawthorne as Poet' (1951) which is available in the volume *Hawthorne* in the Twentieth-Century Views series (Prentice-Hall).

the irony into the 'great expectations' which such a society produces, he sets his scene in the same way, to investigate the human condition.

Pip's initial sense of guilt was inevitable, the result of the Victorian (or Evangelical) theory of the relation between parent and child: Mrs. Joe is supported in her demand for gratitude from Pip by public opinion. Pip is made to feel that he has committed a sin in being born, not because his is a specifically sinful birth like Esther's, but simply by being a child who has to be reared. Thus he feels, like her, 'guilty and yet innocent', and so is morally bewildered from the start. Even if he had never met the convict the guilt would have been there which made him harbour the suppressed wish to be rid of his sister, and therefore feel himself a candidate for the wicked Noah's Ark on the horizon to which society banished those who broke the law. Hence the convict limping out of the churchyard who had escaped from his lawful punishment looked to Pip's 'young eyes as if he were eluding the hands of the dead people, stretching out of their graves to get a twist upon his ankle and pull him in'.

Thus the churchyard, where his dead relatives are very present to him, and the gibbet, guns firing for escaped convicts, and prison Hulks, are the prominent features of little Pip's moral consciousness. And through no fault of his own he is now involved with crime, since the terrifying convict faces him with a dilemma in which, having no parents to protect him and not daring to confide even in Joe (whom he loves but knows can't protect him against Mrs. Joe), the lesser evil is to become a criminal himself. The escaped convict, starving and leg-ironed, requires him to steal food from his mother-surrogate and a file from Joe his almost father. The requirements are perfectly chosen for the purpose of setting up the dilemma and riveting the sense of guilt Pip already carries within him. Pip's feelings of guilt are explored convincingly–everyone recognizes an element in his own childhood–he knows now that the gibbet and the Hulks would be his deserts if all were known, and this makes another link with the convict, projecting Pip on to that side of the social division, the only one he yet knows of. His projected guilt in the next chapter– seeing the natural features running at him, the accusing looks of the clerical-coloured cattle and so on–is all established abundantly with wonderful imaginative sympathy with a child's state of mind. Pip's fear of the convict is tempered by a natural human sympathy for a wretched creature, which creates further moral confusion–he knows it is right to feed the starving (a point slyly reinforced by its being Christmas Day) and the minimal expression of this feeling creates a bond between the two. We note that this involvement on Pip's side arouses gratitude for the feeling, as well as for the food and file, in the convict who has already become for Pip 'his' convict. This becomes the unbreakable chain binding Pip to him, through no fault or will of Pip's. Dickens establishes this paradigm with an unbelievable economy of art and with the minimum of direct explanation:

> Pitying his desolation, and watching him as he gradually settled down upon the pie, I made bold to say, 'I am glad you enjoy it.'
> 'Did you speak?'
> 'I said, I was glad you enjoyed i t
> 'Thankee, my boy. I do.'

The repetition underlines the point, and the convict is not only 'my' convict to Pip, Pip has now become 'his' boy. And Pip can never again feel the separation from the criminal that is felt by the consciously self-righteous, a fellow-feeling which is kept alive constantly by Dickens throughout the first half of the novel. Part of it is decent human sympathy for the hunted outcast, reinforced by good Joe's expression of similar feelings when the convict, in order to save Pip from the charge of theft, makes a false confession of having himself robbed the blacksmith's; and part is Pip's guilty knowledge that he is himself one who might be sent to the Hulks if all were known, which is kept alive in Pip's consciousness by a succession of events that he recognizes as a recurrence of 'this taint of prison and crime . . . starting out like a stain'[1] and which makes him, for instance, see the finger-post as pointing to his destination in the Hulks; when he gets home he runs into the sergeant holding out the handcuffs to him, and much more to the same effect, testimonials to the inexhaustible fertility of the novelist's imagination.

Thus there is a great difference between Herbert's good-citizen's disgust for the convicts going down on the coach with Pip in chapter XXVIII (the chapter is one of the highlights of the first half of the novel) – 'What a degraded and vile sight it is!' Herbert says, and Pip's own very mixed feelings, so confused that he can't deal with them and daren't try to sort them out. Dickens with perfect art brings out the combination of

[1]Pip makes this reflection after visiting 'Wemmick's greenhouse' in Newgate while waiting for Estella and 'thought with absolute abhorrence of the contrast between the jail and her'. She then refers to the inmates of Newgate, which he points out to her, as 'Wretches!' with disdain, not knowing she is the child of such. The point that emerges from the deadly irony that thus pervades the novel is Father Zossima's 'All are responsible for all'.

Pip's conscious distaste with his unwilling and only partly conscious sympathy, in Pip's own description of how the convicts are treated by the respectable passengers who must share the same coach[1] however they may resent being alongside criminals. Having described the convicts with an undercurrent of indignation he winds up that it 'made them (as Herbert had said) a most disagreeable and degraded spectacle', where the bracket shows Pip's dissociation from Herbert here. Following this, the excessively violent expressions of the 'choleric gentleman' and Pip's sympathy with the convicts' coarse reactions (which, he says, he felt he would have had himself ' "if I had been in their place and so despised" ') mark him as having too much imagination to be in Herbert's camp, even though these very convicts' association with Pip's secret guilt–one of them had brought the two one-pound notes from Pip's convict long ago –brings to the surface his helpless state of guilty involvement that Dickens establishes as non-rational:

> I could not have said what I was afraid of, for my fear was altogether undefined and vague, but there was a great fear upon me. . . . I felt that a dread, much exceeding the mere apprehension of a painful or disagreeable recognition, made me tremble. I am confident that it took no distinctness of shape, and that it was the revival for a few minutes of the terror of childhood.

Pip's unwilling sympathy with convicts and his inexplicable terrors have been fed by a tug-of-war between conscience and human sympathy from the start, and Dickens takes pains to show that it is precisely because he was 'morally timid and very sensitive' that he is alive to the case for both sides. For instance, he senses on Christmas Day, after returning from his rendezvous with his convict, the odiousness of the villagers' self-righteousness and their gloating over the chase the soldiers are about to undertake–'I thought what terrible good sauce for a dinner my fugitive friend on the marshes was. They had not enjoyed themselves a quarter so much, before the entertainment was brightened with the excitement

---

[1] I suspect Dickens had in mind Fielding's allegory of the coachload of travellers and servants that represent Fielding's society in *Joseph Andrews*, and their character-istic reactions to the man robbed and left naked by the wayside. Dickens's has the great advantage of not being an obstrusive parable like Fielding's but a delicate creation of a complex attitude that raises issues at once moral, psychological and sociological. Fielding's is comparatively simple-minded–he is satisfied with the satiric contrast between the selfishness of social man (even when allegedly Christian) and the spontaneous human sympathy that the classless poor can afford to manifest.

he furnished'; we may note the partiality revealed by the word 'friend' here. This unwilling sympathy is kept alive by Pip's being taken on Joe's back in the voluntary participation in the chase by which the villagers show their solidarity with the forces of the law. (This is neatly reversed in the second half of the novel when Pip steers the boat rowed by his friends down the river to assist his 'fugitive friend' to escape the pursuing officers of the law, the half-way stage being the involuntary journey with convicts on the same coach that I've already discussed.)

Pip's sympathy remains an inextricable mixture of decent feelings and guilty ones, a remarkably adequate paradigm for the creation of a sense of guilt that, Dickens implies, is at once a source of psychological disorder and yet a condition of moral growth. It is this sense or conviction of shared guilt, guilt by participation even if involuntary or forced, that is the reason why Pip is able, when his patron is revealed to be the convict, to overcome ultimately his natural spontaneous horror of the man and his despair at his own impossible position, and to find his painful way out of his terrible plight. His sensitiveness is shown in the delicacy of feeling that comes natural to him, as in the circumlocution evolved by the child in his desire to spare the convict's feelings when he has to mention the leg-iron (there are many such incidents, including his sense that Joe gives him extra gravy to comfort him whenever he is scolded); and this basic sensitiveness, a product of his uncomfortable position in Mrs. Joe's household and the cause of his suffering more than a hardened or happy child would, is what makes him peculiarly vulnerable to the influences that he is exposed to in his visits to Satis House. Though the sufferings are minimized by the amusement with which the adult Pip recounts his memories, there is sufficient poignancy in the recollections to make them moving as well as vivid. The chain of cause and effect that binds Pip involuntarily to his convict is riveted link by link before our eyes, but what matters is that we should register the shades of Pip's changing feelings towards these facts, so finely imagined that, while showing Pip to be a victim, they yet prepare us for his *volte-face* which would otherwise not be, as it is, plausible and psychologically convincing. The moral confusion inevitably set up by such a society is illustrated when the fugitive is recaptured: Pip, fearful that 'his' convict will think he has betrayed the man and is 'a fierce young hound' (from which Pip shrinks as naturally as George Silverman does from the charge of being 'a worldly little devil') tries to convey in dumb-show that he is 'innocent', though knowing that his spontaneous feeling is 'wrong' since it reveals a wish to defeat the

Law: he is again 'guilty yet innocent'. Joe's introduction of the Christian ethic in his refusal to judge others and his ready forgiveness of the wrong done him by a 'poor miserable fellow-creature', which ends with a confident appeal to Pip to endorse him, makes the whole thing impossible for the child to cope with, so he tries to bury the memory of it thereafter. Nature had seemed to him to condemn the hunt with 'the shudder of the dying day in every blade of grass' and the cattle had seemed to reproach the hunters, but this is in contradiction to the social indoctrination he has picked up as to what is right and wrong, and had not the sergeant declared: 'I am on a chase in the name of the king'?

ii

At this point Dickens lets this theme rest while in fact the introduction of the new subject, shame as a product of social distinctions, is really a further complication, deepening the guilt and moral confusion by which Pip is already ravaged. Again Dickens refuses to simplify the subject of his inquiry. Pip's knowledge of false social values – the snobbery produced by deference to social status and property-owning – does not derive from Miss Havisham and Estella, for Mrs. Joe and Uncle Pumblechook and the tradesmen of the market town had surrounded the boy with it, but that made no real impact on him because he detested these people. What Satis House does when he is (again involuntarily) precipitated into it by mercenary relatives is to give social status and property an impressive content and an imaginatively overwhelming context for him, apparently only seven or eight at this time.[1] We note that Pip is already able to recognize Estella as 'a young lady' though she is only his own age. It is because she is so confidently his superior, and is 'very pretty', and her beauty is enhanced by the symbolic jewels which Miss Havisham declares are Estella's property, that he is impressed by her in spite of her being 'insulting' to himself. Together with the tragic figure of Miss

[1] If Pip seems excessively young to have been so momentously struck by Estella's beauty and grace, we may recollect that when Dickens was removed from Chatham to London at the age of nine, he was stricken by the loss of what were the equivalents of Estella and her romantic ambience: 'Cobham park and hall, Rochester cathedral and castle, and all the wonderful romance together, including a red-cheeked baby he had been wildly in love with, were to vanish like a dream'. – Forster, *Life*, on Dickens's own information.

Havisham and their extraordinary surroundings, Estella is part of a hither-to undreamt-of alternative to the flat and dull life of the village and the marshes. At Satis House (the name 'meant more than it said', Estella tells him) he learns for the first time that his hands are coarse and his boots thick–that there are standards by which he is not ordinary as he'd sup-posed, but degraded. Estella's manifestations of class superiority are all unpleasant, from her deployment of the weapon of U-vocabulary (' "He calls the knaves, Jacks, this boy!" said Estella with disdain', suggesting the arbitrariness of such distinctions) to dumping his dinner on the ground 'as if I were a dog in disgrace', which completes his humiliation because he had noted that his convict, when he had fed him on the marshes, ate like their dog–the equation, that as the convict was to him, so he was to Estella, is evidently what brought the tears to his eyes–'the girl looked at me with a quick delight in having been the cause of them'–and he ends with the admission: 'Her contempt for me was so strong, that it became infectious, and I caught it'. Next time she slaps his face hard to express her enduring contempt, which he has doubted.

But this is not the whole truth about Class by any means, nor does Dickens intend that the reader should suppose he himself thinks so. We learn in due course that Estella is an upstart and is being trained to be proud and disdainful to revenge Miss Havisham on the opposite sex. Miss Havisham herself, apart from her obsession, is to be respected: though a lady she is not offensively so, and her cousin Matthew Pocket and his son are unequivocally admirable, while Mrs. Pocket, who is a snob because she is a fool, and Drummle who is a country squire and a mean boor, are both despised or deplored by the more intelligent members of their class. Herbert inducts Pip at their first meeting in London into a true code of manners with grace and right feeling; he is invaluable as a civilizing in-fluence on the young ex-blacksmith. Dickens undoubtedly believed that there was a respectable content in the idea of a gentleman, and that Pip did well to leave behind him the limitations of the village and the vulgar little world of the market town, as Dickens saw them. Dickens didn't share the lip-service now given to the idea of equality, which he detested when he saw it operating in America and satirized in *Martin Chuzzlewit*; and the reluctance in our day of critics to believe this, or to believe sin-cerely in the existence of any distinctions except those based on money, must not prevent us from recognizing that for Dickens class distinctions were valid since ideally they represented an aspiration towards distinction and fineness. Herbert has grace and style: 'he had a frank and easy way with him which was very taking' and expressed 'in every look and tone, a natural incapacity to do anything secret and mean'; 'he carried off his rather old clothes much better than I carried off my new suit' Pip noted; and Herbert is contemptuous of snobbery. The convict's money did not make Pip a gentleman, it only gave him the opportunity of making himself one by study and the society of such as Herbert, and this point is wittily made by Provis's innocently assuring Herbert that Pip shall make a gentleman of him (Herbert) by money. Dickens distinguishes between a Pumblechook's or Trabb's sense of money as the measure of position and achievement, and Pip's ability to feel the real superiority of Matthew and Herbert Pocket who are not at all well off, which again is a quite different thing from Pip's appreciation of Wemmick as essentially a good fellow. Pip takes Matthew Pocket's point that a gentleman is from the feelings outwards; he can appreciate these things because he is not a snob but has real delicacy of feeling himself – a quality not now thought well of, I gather, but Dickens valued it so highly that he considered it indispensable and constantly indicates its presence or absence in his characters in all novels. When Joe has laboriously explained to little Pip why he never protects the child (or himself) from Mrs. Joe, Pip notes: 'I had a new sensation of feeling conscious that I was looking up to Joe in my heart'. Dickens is tracing the growth of a moral sensibility in *Great Expectations*, in which a capacity for such appreciation plays a major part.

The real influence of the experience of Satis House, which includes Miss Havisham's being a living witness to the reality of passion, Estella's aloofness, the poetic impact of the candle-lit house (outside time and the commonplace life of the forge kitchen) with its 'extinct' brewery and 'ruined garden' – is that Pip is awakened to the knowledge that there is a life of the imagination, feelings different from the mean self-interest of the Pumblechook ambience or Joe's amiable ignorance. Of course he is more bewildered than ever, and cannot reconcile the two worlds he now inhabits separately; he can only feel that 'there would be something coarse and treacherous in dragging' Miss Havisham and Estella and their life 'before the contemplation of Mrs. Joe'. The immediate effect of his acceptance of Estella's view of himself is to start being worthier of her by self-education and self-improvement, at which he works long and hard *before* he has any 'expectations' and without which goal he would have had no desire to accept the offer brought him subsequently by Mr. Jaggers, or would have been unable to profit by it. There is also another proof of the enrichment of living that the entry into Satis House had brought to Pip:

> Whenever I watched the vessels standing out to sea with their white sails spread, I somehow thought of Miss Havisham and Estella; and whenever the light struck aslant, afar off, upon a cloud or a sail or green hill-side or water-line, it was just the same. – Miss Havisham and Estella and the strange house and the strange life appeared to have something to do with everything that was picturesque.

– That is, he saw for the first time that these things were 'picturesque'. He had previously said, describing his visits to Miss Havisham:

> What could I become with these surroundings? How could my character fail to be influenced by them?

Dickens is showing, as he did in *Bleak House* through the incarnation of the values of 'Passion and pride' in Lady Dedlock and Chesney Wold, his conviction that we need something besides 'real' life. Pip expresses his difficulty by his dissatisfaction with himself and his daily round: 'What I wanted, who can say? How can *I* say, when I never knew?' But Satis House and its inmates provided him with forms that fed his imagination, without which there is no true growth; he feels now that there is an alternative to the life of 'dull endurance' and 'flat colour', and sees his surroundings through other eyes. But that the boy who had admired Joe and believed in the sanctity of his parlour and honoured the forge should be unable to relegate the Estella who showed such odious characteristics is proof that his world had collapsed in the face of the evidence of Satis House that 'whoever had this house, could want nothing else' and that what this represented was irresistible to him. Estella represents it, and though he later admits her to be what she is (" " I know it, Herbert", said I, with my head turned away, "but I can't help it" ') he must 'adore' her. When Herbert sensibly advises Pip to try to 'detach himself from her' therefore, Pip can only express his knowledge that this is impossible by a metaphor: 'I turned my head aside, for, with a rush and a sweep, like the old marsh winds coming up from the sea, a feeling like that which had subdued me on the morning when I left the forge, when the mists were solemnly rising, and when I laid my head upon the village finger-post, smote upon my heart again.'

Pip's relation with Estella is a constant throughout the book, till the finale, and is symbolically represented for us in repetitive forms at their first meeting, to make the point clear, with Dickens's endless resources of creative representation. They are first set to play cards, the suitably named 'Beggar my neighbour' (which is a game of pure chance), the only game Pip knows:

> I played the game to an end with Estella, and she beggared me. She threw the cards down on the table when she had won them all, as if she despised them for having been won of me.

–the situation between them could not have been exemplified more concisely and yet naturally. The relation is re-enacted to enforce the conclusion, which we have no excuse therefore for not arriving at, that there can be no profit for Pip from his adoration of Estella and that we are not to expect a love affair or a love-interest in this novel (a remarkable sacrifice for a novelist and a risk for one writing for a Victorian public). It is a guarantee that Dickens has a serious object more consistently in view than anywhere else but in *Hard Times*. Then follows the scene already mentioned, of Pip's being treated by Estella as a dog and her enjoyment of his humiliation. Next, when he walks in the ruined garden, he finds 'Estella was walking away from me even then'. When he begins to walk, boylike, on the row of casks that smelt sour, 'I saw *her* walking on them. She had her back towards me, and never looked round, and passed out of my view directly.' The final version winds up the subject forever:

> So, in the brewery itself. When I first went into it, and, rather oppressed by its gloom, stood near the door looking about me, I saw her pass among the extinguished fires, and ascend some light iron stairs, and go out by a gallery high overhead, as if she were going out into the sky.

Her name of course means a Star, and she was first seen by Pip as a star, carrying a candle in the darkness *and going off with it*, leaving him in the dark alone.

There is here an illustration of the technique Dickens invented for presenting the extraordinary class of experiences that are needed to embody his theme. I don't mean only the truly poetic and frequently haunting use of language ('I saw her pass among the extinguished fires') but the gradual and often imperceptible movement from everyday experience to an implicitly symbolic but plausibly real experience which then shades into one overtly unrealistic, as this one becomes immediately after Pip has seen Estella go out 'high overhead, *as if she were* going out into the sky' when he thinks he sees Miss Havisham hanging by the neck on the beam, though his eyes are admittedly 'a little dimmed by looking up at the frosty light' from following Estella's disappearance into the sky. Thus Estella is always, as predicted here, ahead of, above, and indifferent to Pip, out of his reach, even when he has become a gentleman for her sake. We should also have gathered that Pip's attachment is unrealistic as well as hopeless, for he doesn't love *her*, she is unlovable and unloving, he only loves what she represents for him.[1] He repeatedly recognizes indeed that he is never happy when with her, as well as in his final speech to her when he learns she is to marry Drummle (in chapter XLIV). This rhetorical outpouring is generally held against Dickens as though he endorsed it, whereas in fact it is in keeping with his keen exposure of Pip's case: Estella embodies Pip's aspirations ('You are part of my existence, part of myself', etc.) and it is made clear that he is not so much wretched at losing her (he never expected to win her) as humiliated that she should degrade his dream by marrying a stupid brute like Drummle. [The speech seems to me to be reminiscent of Catherine's similar rhetorical speech about her feelings for Heathcliff in *Wuthering Heights* ("I am Heathcliff. If all else perished and he remained", etc.) and if so shows Dickens's intelligent use of a passage that had lodged in his memory once.] Pip in fact makes the suitable comment on his speech himself: 'The rhapsody welled up within me like blood from an inward wound, and gushed out', he says. The idealization has been exposed as an illusion even to Pip's reluctant mind.

It is nevertheless his idealization of Estella and his involvement imaginatively and emotionally with the poetic influences of Satis House that made him strive to educate himself for years and that makes him jump at Jaggers's offer, for if he had not known Miss Havisham and Estella the manly life of the forge and affection for Joe and Biddy would have held him back. Dickens holds no brief for village life. He takes pains here to show only its deprivations culturally, socially and morally. The best of it is to be found in Joe who has a good heart but is illiterate,[2] and who is lost outside the forge and the village inn–Dickens admits none of the compensations of the village community such as George Eliot brings to

---

[1]Sometimes the reality is forced on his notice, as when he sees her 'quick delight at having been the cause of' the tears in his eyes, or the 'bright flush on her face' at the pleasure of seeing the boys fighting on her account, or that when she lets him kiss her, first as a boy and later as a man, he can get no gratification from it.

[2]Dickens's conception of Joe was of a 'foolish, good-natured man' originally: subsequent accretions of virtues tend to disguise this but though gentle and affectionate he remains a very limited person and one who did not protect little Pip from Mrs. Joe, as he ought, he knew, to have done, which deprives him of Pip's confidence.

life for us in *Adam Bede* and *Silas Marner*. Once Pip has grown up he can visit Joe and Biddy at the cottage but Joe can never be comfortable out of it, and this is not Pip's fault, though Pip, very much to his credit, feels that it must be when the fiasco of Joe's visit to the young men in London has occurred; after all, that is only a repetition of Joe's impossible behaviour at Miss Havisham's in the early days which is nothing to do with any conceivable snobbery on Pip's part, and the anguish Pip suffered then is what anyone in the circumstances at his age must have felt. Dickens indeed makes us feel it with him. That Estella is a living symbol for Pip is shown by his inability to fall in love with Biddy, whom he recognizes as kinder, and more suitable for his future life as a village blacksmith, at the time when no alternative 'real' life seems possible: he confides in Biddy but he can't take advice from her, Mr. Wopsle's great-aunt's grand-daughter who was down-at-heel and is not much more literate than Joe. In fact, her advising him not to want to be a gentleman because she 'don't think it would answer' is irrelevant to his problems, and as regards Estella, she can tell him only what he has always told himself 'in the singular kind of quarrel with myself which I was always carrying on'. Just as he had felt that though Joe's intellectual superior he had to look up to him for other reasons, so he knows that Biddy is better than Estella but alas! 'How could it be, then, that I did not like her much the better of the two?' Pip's real difficulty is in deciding which is 'real' life. Critics of the novel who pick on the story to despise Pip and condemn his creator fail to grasp the complexity provided for us, and the reasons for inhibiting easy conclusions or for passing judgment at all.

Again, when Jaggers comes to make Pip (not yet out of his apprenticeship) the offer of a patron—who must be Miss Havisham on circumstantial evidence—Pip can't help seeing that Jaggers despises Joe, despises him for his not knowing his own interests as well as for his manners. Jaggers being a brilliant and successful professional man from London, Pip is inevitably affected by this and so is insensibly inclined to patronize Joe, at first only by 'encouraging' him. Pip now openly produces Estella's 'coarse and common' formula with confidence as appropriate for village ways, and confesses to resenting the clergyman's reading the parable about the rich man and the Kingdom of Heaven in church as inappropriate to Pip—all this is surely very natural in a village boy (neither the village circle nor the town tradesmen nor the relatives of Miss Havisham he met in Satis House were any help here, on the contrary). He does not mean, at any time, to drop Joe, and at first he plans to help

Joe to fit himself for 'a higher sphere' though he has already tried for a long time without success to teach Joe to read, and feels aggrieved because Biddy points out that Joe wouldn't acquiesce: everything is made hard for him. We must realize both how formidable his difficulties are and that his feelings are by no means those of a snob. Pip himself, the mature recorder of his own exemplary history, does not deal tenderly with himself, recording mercilessly every least attractive impulse, but we should notice that these are mitigated always by generous misgivings, permeated by uneasy self-criticism, and contrary movements of feeling of a self-corrective kind. How, in his circumstances, should he know which of his voices to listen to? Dickens is really showing the evolution of a self from the contradictory influences of the various social, moral, religious and psychological forces present in his age, and the daunting problems of an adolescence like Pip's. We must recollect–Dickens can assume its knowledge in his readers–that Victorian theory held it right and indeed obligatory to rise socially and culturally if possible, and Pip is only trying to act in accordance with this ethic, even if we ignore his desire to rise into Estella's orbit. In fact, Pip's divided feelings make him 'more and more appreciative of the society of Joe and Biddy' as time runs out, and the night before he leaves he notes that he 'had an impulse to go down again and entreat Joe to walk with me in the morning. I did not.' The desire not to be seen off is surely known to us all in adolescence, but Pip shows grace in being 'aware of my own ingratitude' (not such a common virtue), constantly thinking of getting off the coach and walking home for another evening with them, until it is too late. None of this is 'a snob's progress' and few in the circumstances could be confident of showing up better.

Once in London, settled with Herbert Pocket and exposed to Mrs. Pocket and the emanations of class consciousness from his fellow-students, as well as to the cynical materialism of Wemmick and Jaggers, the regrets and softer feelings haven't much chance, though it is important to note that he never loses them. And Herbert's conversation and company are undoubtedly preferable to that of the forge kitchen and The Jolly Bargeman. But in assimilating himself to Herbert and Mr. Pocket, Pip necessarily increases his difficulties in relation to Joe whose coming on a visit distresses Pip because of 'a keen sense of incongruity'–Biddy has foreseen this, so it undoubtedly existed as a fact, but says in her letter that she trusts to Pip's 'good heart' to solve the problem. Pip's analysis of his feelings when the visit is about to take place show them to be not those of a snob or a brute but wholly natural:

> I had little objection to his being seen by Herbert or his father, for both of whom I had a respect; but I had the sharpest sensitiveness as to his being seen by Drummle, whom I held in contempt.

This seems the sensitiveness to social contempt common to adolescents. Joe's insistence on having his message "What larks!" sent to Pip is a sign of Pip's real difficulty, the normal one in growing up, the need to assert a new personality in the face of the determination of kin and neighbourhood to keep the child or boy they knew unchanged, to force a now uncongenial rôle on the person they can't admit to have the right to have changed. Trabb's boy's jeering at Pip's better clothes and manners is a humorous presentation of this subject. Pip can't still be 'the little child what come to the forge' and Joe's playmate, though Joe demands he should. Joe himself explains that he is 'wrong out of the forge, the kitchen, or off th'meshes'. This is evident, and that Pip, who could use more of the world than this, should have forgone that extension of experience is unthinkable. The alternative to being the grown-up child Joe would for Pip have been to be like Trabb's boy, who must grow up into a Trabb if he is to get a living there. Pip could only meet Joe on home ground, but here Estella had blocked the road: the first time Pip sees her after going to London she remarks that his old company ' "would be quite unfit for you now" ': how can he then go from Satis House on to Joe's, as he'd intended?

Thus Dickens shows the effects on the poor lad of these influences, hopes, fears, desires, and false and true idealisms, making it impossible to pass judgment on him at this stage. Dickens is interested, as I've shown in examining previous novels, in the question of freewill. He sees that it is complicated by heredity and nurture, noting of Estella that her innate likeness to her mother, by which Pip recognizes Estella's parentage eventually, is a different thing from her acquired likenesses to Miss Havisham which came from being in Miss Havisham's company and sharing her thoughts, which, Dickens says, is the kind of likeness to each other visible in married couples.[1] Allowing for all these things, Dickens sees that there is still some margin for freedom of choice and therefore for a moral

[1] One is prepared for Dickens to make use of Estella's heredity—her gypsy mother murdered her rival—by making Estella murder the brutal husband who ill-used her, in the original ending when she wasn't to marry Pip; but Dickens did not, either because it would have been too melodramatic or because he held that nurture is stronger than nature.

judgment,[1] though the margin is narrowed by the pressures of environment and by all previous experience, especially that of childhood, as Pip's case is designed to illustrate. But it is at the point of the greatest pressures on Pip that Dickens shows him able to make true decisions, to decide action of the greatest moment by free spiritual choice: Pip could have abandoned his convict at several different points after Magwitch's return, even as late as the trial, but Pip makes each decision not to do so freely in the light of his whole previous experience of what he has felt to be his mistakes and what he now feels to be rightful demands on the self he has become. By now he is twenty-three and by Dickens's reckoning should be a man.

iii

To show the relation between shame and guilt, while keeping them distinct, is part of Dickens's undertaking. He shows that the effects of Pip's introduction to the idea of shame (at being 'coarse and common') is to reinforce his sense of guilt, which becomes then social as well as moral. This is demonstrated by the episode of the two one-pound notes, an episode which shows the economy with which Dickens works throughout *Great Expectations*, as in George Silverman's tale, though this being a novel needs fully imaginative realization. It keeps alive Pip's sense of guilt because he knows the gift must come from 'his' convict since the messenger stirs his drink with Joe's old file that Pip had stolen; his sense of guilt makes him think the messenger's cocking his eye at him (to imply a secret understanding) is 'as if he were expressly taking aim at me with his invisible gun', a loaded simile which we remember when Magwitch, having thus fired his money at Pip, lays Pip low on his return. This image naturally causes the boy to have nightmares, but behind them is the real nightmare, the thought 'of the *guiltily* coarse and common thing it was, to be on secret terms of conspiracy with convicts–a feature of my low career that I had previously forgotten'. Thus the old guilt about his forced theft gets fused with social shame because he can imagine

[1] This is made twice in our novel in an interesting way. When Pip reproaches Miss Havisham for leading him on in the false supposition that she was his patron, she replies: '"You made your own snares. *I* never made them."' Pip seems to be recollecting this when he subsequently defends himself against Orlick's charge of having ruined him (expressing Pip's sense of guilt at having had Orlick discharged from his post as porter at Satis House) with '"I could have done you no harm, if you had done yourself none".'

what Estella would say about his being, though already 'low' connected with convicts in addition (there is now yet another convict in his life, the messenger). Pip continues as to the revival of his sense of guilt by this message from the past he had hoped buried:

> I was haunted by the file too. A dread possessed me that when I least expected it, the file would reappear . . . and in my sleep I saw the file coming at me out of a door, without seeing who held it.

The irrational dread, and the consequent fantasy forcing itself on him in dreams, are psychologically true. And he is right. The file reappears duly as the source of the instrument with which Pip's sister is struck down. Though Pip is morally convinced that instrument was wielded by Orlick, he can't be sure, and, in another sense, he feels he himself was responsible: hence it does indeed come at him without his being able to see who held it. Finally, the two one-pound notes reoccur as central in the scene of Magwitch's return. They are revelatory to Pip that he won't be able to get rid of his troublesome visitor from the past by repaying them, and they are central also to the moral issue of his indebtedness to Magwitch, having first appeared as Magwitch's down-payment on his ownership of 'a brought-up London gentleman', which Pip had had to accept though he tried to return them to the messenger, who had disappeared.

The next link in the chain of shame and guilt follows in the fight with 'the pale young gentleman', a class episode[1] from which Pip again emerges as 'guilty yet innocent'–the fight is forced on Pip and he only defends himself of necessity, he is even at a disadvantage from being overawed by Herbert's social superiority in his alarming knowledge of the ritual of boxing and its techniques: winning therefore leaves Pip morally even guiltier, expecting vengeance from the Law because he knows that low boys can't be allowed to injure (possibly murder) young gentlemen. So getting bound apprentice next at the Town Hall seems to

[1]The characteristic humour of this novel appears in the satiric note struck about the class assurance of superiority in Herbert's management of the fight, which is picked up when Pip and Herbert meet again as young men when it turns out that though beaten then Herbert remembered the fight as a victory for himself over 'the prowling boy'. This time Herbert, before he recognizes in 'Mr. Pip' his 'prowling boy' of old, says innocently: '"We shall be alone together, but we shan't fight, I dare say"'–immediately after which he makes the identification of Pip, the innocent cliché having been the memory-rouser presumably. This is a good instance of Dickens's keen and consistent interest in how the mind works.

him another guilt-proving ordeal and he is reproached with not enjoying himself in addition!

Thus when it is proved that the attack which ultimately kills Mrs. Joe was made with the leg-iron the availability of which is Pip's responsibility, though involuntary, Pip immediately feels that he must be the criminal: again he is 'guilty yet innocent'. Legally he is of course innocent, but he holds himself morally guilty because in his heart he detested his sister and his accumulated sense of guilt had just then been activated by Mr. Wopsle's having thrust on him a part in the popular melodrama of George Barnwell who ungratefully murdered his uncle. Pip is thus in even more confusion as to his identity than usual when the news of the murderous attack on his sister is told him. Garis says that the reading of *George Barnwell* and the leg-iron striking down Pip's sister are 'both theatrical "pretexts" for Pip's false sense of guilt' (as part of his case against Dickens's art generally). But Pip's sense of guilt is not false, as we have seen, and they are not '*theatrical* pretexts' but psychologically sound devices used perfectly legitimately within the world Dickens has created as Pip's. The sense of guilt provides its own logic and guilty fantasies, and those related by Dickens are right in the context created already. By this logic Pip's irrational sense of guilt is greatly heightened, so that when his sister dies that doesn't help him, on the contrary, for he now expects to meet her accusing ghost everywhere, and feels guiltier than ever because he can't feel any regret or tenderness for her now she is dead, as he knows he 'ought'. Dickens, with his keen interest in the self-deceptions of civilized man, makes Pip note that to compensate he 'was seized with a violent indignation against the assailant from whom she had suffered so much' – believing him to be Orlick but of course still *feeling* as though it was himself. Hence when he confronts Orlick in the unearthly scene in chapter LIII we are not surprised, having been led by stages to comprehend the nature of this scene, that Orlick (in the rôle of Satan the Accuser of Blake's theology) says: 'It was you as did for your shrew sister. I tell you it was your doing – I tell you it was done through you.'

Pip must surely be entitled to sympathy for his explanation in chapter XIV of his misery at losing his simple belief in the merits of his home and the satisfactions of a blacksmith's life, and in suppressing this not to hurt Joe. It was a stroke of Dicken's genius to choose the calling of blacksmith, since the smith was indispensable in an agricultural community dependent on horse-drawn ploughs and a society dependent on horse transport, doing work requiring exceptional strength as well as skill, a kind of work

that was both a craft and an art, which even had a mystique; and therefore he was highly respected on many grounds. Yet his work dirtied the
hands and covered the smith with 'sut', in an age when a gentleman was
known by his clean hands and refined appearance. No wonder that Pip
was haunted by the dread of seeing Estella looking in at the forge window
and seeing him grimy. Still, he had spells of feeling that the forge life
'offered me sufficient means of self-respect and happiness' though these
were sooner or later dispelled by memories of 'the Havisham days'. Inevitable therefore that he should accept a patron's offer to make a gentleman of him by educating him–it is the chance to be better educated that
Pip tells Jaggers he 'had always longed for'–even if he hadn't been sure
that the patron must be his old friend Miss Havisham 'up town' to whom
he had often mentioned this desire.

How could he know what London was, where he hopes to fulfil his
dream and make a fresh start? He encounters on arrival a London that is
characterized as 'ugly, crooked, narrow and dirty' (all terms morally as
well as literally unpleasant) and we note that Mr. Jaggers's office is in
'Little Britain, just out of Smithfield'–Smithfield was then as well as a
cattle-market the place where cattle were publicly slaughtered. Pip looks
in there while waiting for his guardian:

> So I came into Smithfield; and the shameful place, being all asmear
> with filth and fat and blood and foam, seemed to stick to me. So I
> rubbed it off with all possible speed by turning into a street where I
> saw the great black dome of Saint Paul's bulging at me from behind a
> grim stone building which a bystander said was Newgate Prison.

–we are left in no doubt of the relative standing of church and prison,
the former blackened by the prison in front of it which blots out most of
the great church. The parallel between Newgate and Smithfield is underlined when Pip is then conducted round the prison and told, with awful
immediacy, that ' "four on 'em" would come out at that door the day
after tomorrow at eight in the morning to be killed in a row'. The word
'killed' instead of 'executed' makes the identification with 'the shameful
place' inescapable, and the whole tells us with the force and simplicity of
Blake's poem 'London' what aspects of the metropolitan culture the
village boy is to find representative of the nation. Evidently a society
that butchers people as callously as animals, it is later, at Magwitch's trial,
to pass sentence of death with sickening inhumanity on the 'two-and-
thirty men and women' at once, and one at least of them we know to

have been made a criminal by the refusal of his society to do anything for a child but drive him to thieve from hunger and thence to prison and a life of crime.

Jaggers is the representative figure-head of London, and Pip's introduction to his office and himself in a throng of clients reveals shatteringly that his great abilities and unsparing labours are habitually devoted to defeating the purpose of justice: yet he is paradoxically rewarded for this by high reputation, wealth and a unique status (still the characteristic feature of the legal career). The fascination and high spirits with which Dickens explores his case must not divert us from taking the impact of the horror Jaggers evokes.[1] Jaggers's self-respect inheres in his professional reputation and he can't be bought off (his substitute for integrity) but his work being what it is his only satisfaction is gained from the visible exercise of personal power–over his housekeeper (whom he exhibits cruelly as a wild animal he alone can handle), his clients, his guests, and the Law itself–Pip is shown him at work in a police-court where 'he seemed to be grinding the whole place in a mill', terrifying prisoners, officials and witnesses alike. He is as decent as circumstances permit but his potential goodness is powerless in such a morally perverted society, in which he acquiesces because he profits by it, though that state of things has made him uncomfortable enough to have made an effort to rescue one child, Estella, from becoming, like other children 'so much spawn, to develop into the fish that were to come into his net'. It is true that God or Nature has been revenged on him, since he has no private life, no real home, thinks it proper to conduct experiments on his guests as to their potential criminality, has no idea of conversation except as a cross-examination, has no manner except bullying ('he even seemed to bully his sandwich as he ate it', says Pip, and his characteristic gestures, of biting his forefinger and deploying his handkerchief to terrify, are not engaging either). [The only person ever to intimidate him is Joe, who turns on the bully in a pleasing scene.] His objection to anything not evidence is revealing, especially in the scene where he and Wemmick, having been

[1] It is extraordinary how people can read the novel without taking the impact, some critics complaining of the 'unpleasant' tone of the discussion between Wemmick and Jaggers about whether Drummle will beat his wife or cringe (which is actually more damaging if we remember that Jaggers has a personal responsibility for Estella) as though this were out of character. We must not forget 'the two brutal casts' which Pip says were 'always inseparable in my mind from the official proceedings' between Wemmick and Jaggers, and that Jaggers has no life that is not 'official'–of the office.

drawn by Pip into an unprofessional confession of harbouring 'poor dreams' once, that is, a confession that their sordid 'real' life is not enough, turn together on the wretched client who sheds a genuine tear, and by this display of strength of mind 're-establish their good understanding'. Here, as in *Great Expectations* generally, comedy is in the service of a very serious master. Jaggers is probably Dickens's greatest success in any novel. This is because he is truly in and of the novel, brilliantly created in action, gesture and dialogue, and exemplifying in his situation the theme of the book, as does even his manner, admired by Wemmick: '"Suddenly-click–you're caught!"'

But even Jaggers cannot escape a sense of guilt for the way he earns his living, for his whole mode of life, and he betrays this by his habit of washing his hands of his unsavoury clients at the end of the day, like Pontius Pilate in disclaiming human responsibility thus, though Jaggers needs heavily scented soap to drown rather than wash off the contamination of which he thus shows himself conscious. Pip had said of Estella: 'It was impossible for me to separate her from the innermost life of my life'–everyone has an 'innermost life', except Jaggers, for whom life is therefore only self-assertion. Hence his daring the thieves with his massive gold watch and chain and by leaving his doors unlocked at night –his need for the assurance of power is strong enough even to make him risk his life nightly to prove it. The tremendous creative effort Dickens put into Jaggers shows how serious a criticism of his society–a Newgate London–he felt him to represent. Jaggers is the richest of all Dickens's characters who live for the exercise of power–that so many are to be found in leading positions in his later novels shows how important Dickens saw this characteristic, a psychological perversion, to be in revealing what he found wrong with the life of his time. Wemmick, with his dual life of office and Castle that must be kept separate even to the extent of requiring twin selves with different ethics, is a variation on the Jaggers conception and extends the implications of the idea, for Wemmick keeps guilt at bay by rejecting his office self altogether in his home existence, a grimly realistic fact of Victorian life rather than a whimsicality as it may seem in the way it is presented in the private life of Wemmick.

Wemmick is necessary also to establish other aspects of the theme. What seems at first a jocular description of Pip's London home, Barnard's Inn, acquires sinister implications which reinforce the impressions of Newgate London–the window he throws up in order to get some fresh air nearly guillotines him, he has a sense that someone is dead and buried on the premises, and that the whole place is verminous and rotting away – and that this is the 'realization of the first of my great expectations'. But this is only a preliminary:

> So imperfect was this realization of the first of my great expectations, that I looked in dismay at Mr. Wemmick. 'Ah!' said he, mistaking me; 'the retirement reminds you of the country. So it does me.'

This is more than a joke. That Dickens intends us to realize that this break in the continuity of memory of nature – of what is really 'the country' – is a proof of the breakdown of full humanity in social living is proved by what immediately follows this when Pip tells us, Wemmick having said 'Good day' to indicate the conversation is ended:

> I put out my hand, and Mr. Wemmick at first looked at it as if he thought I wanted something. Then he looked at me, and said, correcting himself,
> 'To be sure! Yes. You're in the habit of shaking hands?'
> I was rather confused, thinking it must be out of the London fashion, but said yes.
> 'I have got so out of it!' said Mr. Wemmick – 'except at last.'

Later Pip learns that he shakes a client's hand when sentence of death is to be carried out, in order to be assured that the client doesn't bear him a grudge for failing to get him off, his own office morality consisting solely in doing the utmost to get a client off, however guilty he knows the client to be.

Thus, Jaggers being his guardian, Pip's fresh start in London amounts only to a closer involvement with crime and guilt. He goes down to see Miss Havisham on the coach with the convicts. He finds that Orlick the suspect is now porter of Satis House. On consideration Pip feels obliged to tell Jaggers that Orlick ought not to be in a position of trust, so Orlick is dismissed, necessarily, but Pip though, or through, having acted for the best has Orlick on his conscience as though the situation of being 'guilty yet innocent' were the human condition, inevitable; and Orlick has yet another grudge to notch up against Pip. Turning Orlick out of a job drives him, it appears, into a life of crime, into working for the master-criminal Compeyson, and it is through Orlick's spying and knowledge of old of Pip's circumstances that Magwitch is tracked down for Compeyson and caught by the law again, as a returned transport – a turn of events Pip could not have then foreseen and hardly deserved, but Dickens is consistent in showing in *Great Expectations* that the logic of events is not just nor are consequences foreseeable. Thus Orlick's accumulated grievances against Pip drive him to attempt Pip's murder (at one level – at another, we see that Pip is drawn back to his past to face the causes of his guilt in confrontation with Orlick): Pip is then only saved by the power of friendship (by Herbert and Startop) directed by Trabb's boy who alone knew the paths across the marshes to show them the way in time. Trabb's boy is an unconscious instrument of Providence, for Pip notices that Trabb's boy was rather disappointed at finding he hadn't been killed. The sense that life consists of traps and mines that cannot be foreseen or evaded becomes dreadfully ominous in the detailed account of the Eastern tale (in chapter XXXVIII) with its laborious preparations for setting such a machine in motion, a tale that enacts that overthrow of all his hopes that Pip is about to endure from the revelation of who his patron is. Another instance, with an equally powerful simile, is when Pip finds Compeyson has been sitting behind him at the theatre:

> For if he had ever been out of my thoughts for a few moments together since the hiding had begun, it was in those very moments when he was closest to me; and to think that I should be so unconscious and off my guard after all my care, was as if I had shut an avenue of a hundred doors to keep him out, and then had found him at my elbow.

This has nothing to do with Nemesis or poetic justice but provides a similar forceful conception of the nature of life: life is shown as a dangerous enterprise where we must make decisions without being able to foresee their outcome or consequences and where intention or will go for nothing. Nevertheless, Dickens shows, in spite of our having to live blindfolded, and in spite of being handicapped by nature and fettered by the social condition, we *can* achieve contentment and self-respect if not happiness. This is what Pip is shown winning his way to in the face of apparent total disaster; the second half of the novel is devoted to it.

iv

I can never understand the righteous indignation of the Dickens critics at Pip for not being delighted to find Magwitch is his patron, or (admitting he might be shocked, having always supposed it would be Miss Havisham) that gratitude should not overcome all other considerations.

Why, one of them demands, should he 'recoil in horror' from Magwitch? As though Dickens had not taken the greatest pains to make this inevitable and to give it justification! 'Pip's horror is not openly explained, although there is the suggestion that it is founded on the connection established between criminality and his own fortune' (Dabney). Professor Christopher Ricks thinks Pip behaves badly. Behind these and similar attitudes to Pip's reactions is an assumption that the critic in his position would have behaved differently. Perhaps all Dickens's art is wasted in the light of democratic sentiment of such theoretical strength that no realities can affect it. Not to understand Pip's sickened sensations and his refusal to take the ex-convict's money, though he wouldn't have minded being supported by Miss Havisham's, seem to be mostly American (Miss Havisham's having an even greater disadvantage in being 'a crazy old maid's', we gather). It seems necessary to make clear exactly what Dickens establishes in the peripeteia scene in chapter XXXIX. Pip's reaction is shown to be much more complex and fundamental than a genteel squeamishness due to Magwitch's manners and eating habits, though Dickens's brilliant evocation of the man's personality ('there was Convict in the very grain of the man') and speech-idiom reinforces the more serious horrors of the actualities behind his professed love of 'his boy' on which his claims to much more than gratitude are based–'You're my son–more to me nor any son'. Even ignoring the art with which the scene has been led up to, from the very first chapter of the novel, so that it carries the added power of a hidden man-trap that has been suddenly sprung under the studious young man just about to go peacefully to bed, it must still be evident that the scene is the highest proof of the fineness of Dickens's imagination. The incidents that lead up to the revelation are truly dramatic, and Pip then, without warning, sees that all the facts that he had interpreted one way, relating them to Miss Havisham, have now to be interpreted as referring to the convict, whom he has known only as a violent criminal: it is this realization, and that, further, it means he has no claim on Estella whatever, that makes him first tremble at the prospect of such an overthrow of all he had believed his life based on, and then turn dizzy. Nothing else could be expected. But, it is argued, on second thoughts he should have welcomed his benefactor in the spirit in which he had been approached, and been grateful for the money which had been honestly earned and cannot rightly be considered tainted. Pip is therefore dismissed as a snob and held as evidence for condemnation of the idea of a gentleman. Dickens didn't intend this, since Herbert Pocket, who is certainly not a snob, has no false pride and is earning his living in an office as a clerk, reacts to the horror of Provis's presence and his claims on Pip equally. Perhaps a Victorian gentleman's view of having such a patron attached to him as father and house-mate cannot really be understood nowadays, particularly in a country that has accepted violence[1] as a way of life, but Pip's sense of the impossibility of offering the proud, fastidious Estella such a father-in-law and one who will always be there, or even of explaining him, must surely arouse sympathy. [That Provis is Estella's father is an irony to be revealed later.]

But the major shock for Pip is that Provis's claims simply wipe out all that Pip has worked and suffered for, though Provis has actually already blighted Pip's life and prospects by stipulating from the start that Pip should not be prepared for earning his living—the convict's idea of a gentleman but not Dickens's—thus condemning Pip, as we've seen, and as he knew, to an uneasy life without purpose and to incurring a burden of debt through boredom—Dickens knew the necessity for a vocation and hard work, and makes Jaggers disapprove of the patron's stipulation also. Has Pip studied with such zeal[2] so long in order to read books in foreign languages for Provis's self-gratulation? For it is at once made plain to Pip that he has been plucked out of the forge and educated in London at Magwitch's behest less from gratitude than as a means to an end, in which the boy was merely an instrument. This makes it plausible that the convict should have laboured to transmit his savings to England for someone whose only claim on him is once having got him food and a file—though we see that a deeper claim was Pip's service in telling him Compeyson had also escaped, which made his own freedom useless but

[1]Thus Garis, *The Dickens Theatre: A Reassessment of the Novels,* 're-interprets' *Great Expectations* as 'an embodiment of Freud's theme in one of his most important works, *Civilization and its Discontents*', because he can't see any creditable evolution in Pip, and wants to explain what he feels to be the unsatisfactoriness of Pip, Herbert and Joe—unsatisfactory because non-violent characters who would have liked to be, or ought in a better state of society to be, uninhibited characters like Orlick, he thinks, A modern tendency to explain Orlick as acting out the suppressed desires of Pip at least, is in line with this rejection of the merits of civilization.

[2]Dabney complains that because there is no detailing of Pip's studies there is no reason for believing in them, that he is merely *stated* to be educated. Of course it is in his reactions and conversation that our conviction lies, and a realistic novel was ruled out by the nature of Dickens's undertaking. George Silverman's much more specialist education is even more briefly but still sufficiently indicated for a similar purpose.

enabled him to punish Compeyson by dragging him back to prison, earning himself transportation to Australia and his first chance to go straight and make good. Pip's place in Magwitch's memory was therefore assured; but his reasons for determining to educate Pip are based on more plausible grounds than gratitude, a quality in which it is always unwise to place confidence and which Dickens himself, we know, discounted.[1] Stronger than gratitude was the desire to revenge himself on the society that had unjustly discriminated in Compeyson's favour at his last trial because Compeyson was privileged by education and manners, and the need to show to his own satisfaction that he is not the inferior of the 'colonists' as they insultingly maintained – for even in the colonies his manners and lack of education deprived him of a social position in spite of his honestly-earned wealth. Dickens's understanding of these essentially human motives, which are not base, and with which we must sympathize, enriches the character of Magwitch and makes him much more than a convenience like Orlick or an unplausible character, a mere mouthpiece for Dickens, like Biddy. Thus his affection for Pip is for the idea of his 'brought-up[2] London gentleman' and Pip is to be his puppet. Magwitch makes this very plain and it is this which revolts Pip, with reason, for he had not supposed this to be his function for his patron. Assuming the patron was Miss Havisham whom he was fond of and who had certainly affectionate feelings for him, and who, he thought, meant well by him as to Estella ultimately, and whose money was derived honourably from her father's brewery (a highly respectable traditional English way of making a family's fortunes), there was no reason why he shouldn't accept her help in achieving an education and status, though Dickens implies he ought to have had a profession and have justified himself by working at it. So it is natural that Pip should now feel, as he says, a Frankenstein in reverse, for he is bound to a compact he never voluntarily or knowingly assented to, forever to be linked to a monster. 'Provis' reveals himself by saying:

> 'Yes, Pip, dear boy, I've made a gentleman on you! It's me wot has done it! . . . I tell it, fur you to know as that there hunted dunghill

[1] *V.* Forster, Book XI, Section III

[2] Obviously Magwitch desired to 'own' a real gentleman – one brought up in London, the capital, and it is the bringing-up as to which he has made specifications. Dabney renders the adjective 'bought-up', I don't know on what authority but it is clearly wrong, though it suits Dabney's 'theme': *Love and Property in the Novels of Dickens.*

dog wot you kep life in, got his head so high that he could make a gentleman–and, Pip, you're him! . . . You shall show money with lords for wagers, and beat 'em! . . . And then, dear boy, it was a recompense to me to know in secret that I was making a gentleman . . . I says to myself, "If I ain't a gentleman, nor yet ain't got no learning, I'm the owner of such. All on you owns stock and land; which on you owns a brought-up London gentleman?" This way I kep myself a going.'

Dickens even explains how Magwitch brought primitive superstition to aid his undertaking: ' "Lord strike me dead!" I says each time–and I goes out in the open air to say it under the open heavens–"but wot, if I gets liberty and money, I'll make that boy a gentleman!" "Lord strike a blight upon it", I says, wotever it was I went for, "if it ain't for him!" ' The psychological truth is as convincing as the lively expression of it.

The reader will, and is meant to, find this pathetic, but we cannot but sympathize also with Pip, to whom it represents a nightmare he has done nothing to deserve and can never wake up from. Provis not only says he is Pip's owner, he at once behaves accordingly with complete confidence: he turns the ring on Pip's finger (hadn't he paid for it?), takes the watch out of Pip's pocket, demands to be read foreign languages to and 'While I complied he, not comprehending a single word, would stand before the fire surveying me with the air of an Exhibitor'. Surely anyone would find this rôle insufferable, even if one's handler were not known to one as a violent criminal. Pip now realizes that he has been bought and paid for and that he is merely a valuable property to Provis; Miss Havisham was a lady, which would have made all the difference, and Pip could have respected himself as a *protégé* in such a relation. Pip knows his 'owner' only as the wild beast struggling murderously with another convict in the ditch who terrified his childhood, and in fact the man is still desperately lawless, drawing his jack-knife when he hears Herbert's footsteps and sleeping with a pistol on his pillow.

It is intolerable and yet Pip sees that he cannot go on being supported by this man's money if he is unwilling to play his part as Provis's gentle-man-exhibit. He now reflects that it is owing to Magwitch that he has no means of earning a living and wishes that he had been left in honest in-dependence, if not content, at the forge. Even assuming Estella would have him, he cannot support Estella without Magwitch's money, which he can't take now, or Miss Havisham's, which he now knows is not destined for himself. And Magwitch even anticipates that Pip may be in love and that money (his money) will 'buy' the girl, thus laying his hands on Pip's dream too. Magwitch's blind egotism undercuts the pathos of his position as a man also deluded, who also had great expectations (of being loved by 'his boy') which are now seen ironically by us. The horror and despair of Pip's position is completed when Herbert points out that Pip cannot reject his patron since he may then have the returned transport's blood on his conscience for ever. Pip says 'I am afraid the dreadful truth is, Herbert, that he is strongly attached to me. Was there ever such a fate!' Here 'attached' neatly combines both the bond of affection of Provis for his creation and that chain, forged link by link by Pip's fate without his knowledge, that we have had demonstrated in the making and that now fetters him apparently without hope. This is marked as 'The end of the second stage of Pip's expectations'.

We now see the part to be played by Pip's 'guilty' past. The dormant sympathies Pip had, as we've seen, for the guilty and the law-breakers (being consciously one himself) are activated next by Magwitch's telling the story of his life. The arbitrariness of 'justice' in this society is again emphasized by the greater consideration shown for the really vicious Compeyson than for his tool; and the heartlessness of the respectable, compared with the sympathy and good offices shown the boy Magwitch by social outcasts and unfortunates, makes the class issue now a matter of the difference between righteousness and charity. It is a characteristic Dickens touch that whereas the prison visitors only give the boy tracts that he can't read,

> 'A deserting soldier in a Traveller's Rest, what lay hid up to the chin under a lot of taturs, learnt me to read; and a travelling Giant what signed his name at a penny a time learnt me to write.'

This, though picturesque, is not sentimental, and is recognizable as corresponding with the actual state of things, as we repeatedly find – e.g. one of Mayhew's vagrants told him how he woke up frozen in a haystack covered a foot deep in snow and said, 'An old farmer came up with his cart and pitchfork to load hay. He said: "Poor fellow! have you been here all night?" I answered, "Yes". He gave me some coffee and bread, and one shilling. That was the only good friend I met with on the road. I got fourteen days of it for asking a gentleman for a penny.'

Pip cannot help reflecting that it is society which is guilty towards Magwitch, whereas Compeyson, starting with the advantages of being educated, made himself into a criminal. Magwitch is evidently not named

'Abel' for nothing: one sees who is Cain, and remembers the title in *Our Mutual Friend*: 'Better to be Abel than Cain', a maxim Dickens is already promoting in *Great Expectations*. So that at the end of Abel's history Pip says:

> He regarded me with a look of affection that made him almost abhorrent to me again, though I had felt great pity for him.

'Almost' is a sign that Pip has begun to slip over from abhorrence to sympathy with him, in spite of being unable to accept the affection yet, and to realize the true nature of the Cain-like society which he had elected to join to become one of the privileged. He had already reflected consciously that it was for the expectations represented by Magwitch's patronage that he had deserted Joe, thus deepening his sense of guilt.

Returning to Satis House and finding the truth about Estella, he has no further illusions to cherish and only realities face him when he comes back. He has Magwitch's safety on his mind to create a real demand on him, a demand whose validity he now recognizes and it is this, together with the sympathy, and self-reproach, that makes him find his convict more tolerable. An admission of the bond between them is elicited by Pip's suffering him to take his hands affectionately, though he had resented the man's desire to do so on their first meeting in London. Pip is surprised to find that their positions have been reversed by these undercurrents of feeling from the time 'when I little supposed my heart could ever be as heavy and anxious at parting from him as it was now'. Finding that Compeyson is dogging him increases his concern for Provis. His misery at losing Estella makes him feel for Miss Havisham who had been deceived like himself once, just as her sight of Pip's misery had woken her to the realities of her use of Estella for revenge: thus freed from being the woman of Pip's vision deliberately hanging in martyrdom by the neck, she burns up in what seem to be Dantean flames of penitence; Pip kisses the dying woman's lips in forgiveness of the harm she had done him, his own hands and arm being scorched by his involvement with her. These things take place neither exactly in a real world nor in a wholly symbolic context, though the dispersal of 'the heap of rottenness and all the ugly things that sheltered there' is one of the many suggestive notes of a double meaning, and the intensities of this last experience of Satis House prepare us for the astonishing chapter LIII when Pip involuntarily goes back through the phases of his early life to the sluice-house on the marshes. The portentousness of Wemmick's warning note 'DON'T GO HOME' that reverberates through chapter XLV is not exhausted there but remains in the reader's mind to sound its warning note again now though ignored by Pip when, in answer to the summons, he reluctantly retraces his steps immediately before he intends leaving England with his convict: 'Towards the marshes I now went straight, having no time to spare.' 'I left the enclosed lands and passed out upon the marshes':

> There was a melancholy wind and the marshes were very dismal. A stranger would have found them insupportable, and even to me they were so oppressive that I hesitated, half inclined to go back. But I knew them, and could have found my way on a far darker night, and had no excuse for returning, being there. So, having come there against my inclination, I went on against it. The direction that I took was not that in which my old home lay, nor that in which we had pursued the convicts. My back was turned towards the distant Hulks as I walked on.

The gravity and loaded meaning of all these words, the suggestion of an ordeal unwillingly undertaken and yet inescapable, prepares us for the realization that we are in the presence of a mystery, that Pip's back being turned towards the Hulks, for which in childhood he believed himself destined, is one of the reverse symbolic actions of the second half of the book. Pip is keeping a tryst, he knows not with whom, but we can see that the journey takes place in his 'inner self', as we proceed with intimations of a spiritual pilgrimage: Pip passes the lime-kiln with its hellish vapours and takes the road that goes down through a stone-quarry and up again, in the dark. Anyone who has read *The Pilgrim's Progress*—and in Dickens's time everyone had—would recognize that Christian's pilgrimage through the Valley of the Shadow of Death was being echoed. Sure enough, in the sluice-house Pip encounters his Apollyon; in Bunyan's allegory Christian had had to meet and overcome the Devil's advocate in the Valley of Humiliation. Old Orlick tells his enemy to prepare to die and worse, and faces him with charges of his guilt, as Apollyon had Christian. Like Christian, Pip admits those sins of which his enemy accuses him, expresses contrition and hope of forgiveness, is fought with flame and wounded; similarly, his devilish assailant is unexpectedly routed only after the man had given up hope of saving his life. That *The Scarlet Letter* and *The Pilgrim's Progress* were drawn on by Dickens as sources for inspiration and method for this novel shows us the kind of undertaking *Great Expectations* was, and how we should respond to the presence in it of these forces and parallels. The reliance on re-collections of *The Pilgrim's Progress* and the recognition of Orlick as performing the part of Apollyon in this scene, are so obvious when one sees it is so that one wonders that this is not a commonplace. This realization would have spared us the antics of critics searching for Freudian explanations of this scene and of the rôle of Orlick. The ordeal that culminates in the admission of guilt, and in repentance, suffering, humiliation and a fight for life was in a popular English literary tradition treating spiritual experience. Dickens has made sketchy indications of Orlick's being in the Devil's service from when he was first introduced – refusing to spend Sunday properly, frightening little Pip with his intimacy with the fiend, and so forth – but he has been unable to resist the temptation to make Orlick a character-of-all-work, in league where necessary for the plot with Compeyson and Drummle, and even brought in to make a comic scene at the end (robbing Pumblechook for us to re-member the old humbug with his mouth stuffed with flowering annuals and Orlick pulling his nose, for which Orlick deserved, we feel, to escape his spell in the county jail, where we leave him).

The difficulty of integrating symbolic scenes with a novel overtly realistic in parts is cleverly managed by Dickens the novelist, but not so perfectly that we don't feel an occasional jolt. Thus the problem of re-turning Pip from the realm of the ordeal and spiritual regeneration is rather startlingly solved by his returning to consciousness in the incon-gruous but thoroughly mundane presence of Trabb's boy, and yet having Pip express a conviction that the ordeal had lasted more than two days and nights, and 'thinking a thanksgiving' as he passes the vapour of the kiln again, safe with his friends. The ordeal entailed physical and moral suffering and endurances but this was subsidiary to admissions of guilt in forms that Pip had never allowed to come to the surface before now when, under stress and duress from Orlick, he has to answer accusations that reach depths of guilty conscience he cannot avoid with death staring him in the face – 'I felt that I had come to the brink of my grave', Pip says. Pip has worse than death to endure, the certainty of defamation in the minds of those most dear to him since with his body disposed of in the lime-kiln Provis and Herbert will think he has run away: thinking of Provis now as Estella's father, his imagination feverishly connects her with this too – 'I saw myself despised by unborn generations – Estella's children and their children'. He accepts even this in the face of his 'miser-able errors' for which he prays for forgiveness. Having virtually died in enduring the agonies of death and anticipating extinction, he can now be reborn; this is delicately indicated – we note that next morning he wakes up in London to a new world, Wordsworth's vision of a London all bright and glittering in the smokeless air, and he adds, 'From me, too, a veil seemed to be drawn, and I felt strong and well'. The gradual process we noted, by which Pip had been unconsciously shedding his acquired egoism, and false views of life, has been accelerated by the encounter with Orlick and the ghosts of his early terrors and guilt. Pip is now content to forgo all his worldly possessions and wordly hopes:

> Where I might go, what I might do, or when I might return, were questions utterly unknown to me; nor did I vex my mind with them, for it was wholly set on Provis's safety.

Thus, in the next step of reversing and rejecting his past self, the journey down the river in the boat that he steers 'freshened me with new hope' –the hope of a new life in which he has renounced all his great expectations and accepts that he has his own way to make. When it darkens light seems to come from the river more than the sky, and 'the oars in their dipping struck at a few reflected stars' – the tact with which Dickens offers the evidence so sparingly but adequately should be respected. Even when the law cuts in at the last moment to claim its own and Magwitch is wounded in the struggle, Pip's new self is equal to the demands he now makes on it, which are far greater than Magwitch himself is willing to make.

> I took my place at Magwitch's side. I felt that that was my place henceforth while he lived. For now my repugnance to him had all melted away, and in the hunted wounded shackled creature who held my hand in his, I only saw a man who had meant to be my benefactor, and who had felt affectionately, gratefully, and generously, towards me with great constancy through a series of years. I only saw in him a much better man than I had been to Joe.

The significant operative idea is in the last sentence, and carries the novel on after Magwitch's death to Pip's necessary accommodation with Joe.

The strength of Pip's resolution is shown in the trial scene and at Magwitch's death-bed. Again *The Pilgrim's Progress* is invoked. The trial and the scene in court are deliberately written of in terms that recall the trial of Faithful with Christian in attendance, and the capital letters with which Dickens sprinkles the pages of chapter LVI show the allegorical intention, that we must identify Pip's society with Bunyan's Vanity Fair, giving the Sessions, the hanging Judge, and the heartless spectators the condemnation that Bunyan gives his. It shows us why Pip prefers to stand trial, as it were, with his convict, by identifying with him in the eyes of his world. Pip says:

> He held my hand while all the others were removed, and while the audience got up (putting their dresses right, as they might at church or elsewhere) and pointed down at this criminal or that, and most of all at him and me.

'Audience', and one which considers trials and church services equally social occasions; and an audience which has come to watch as an entertainment 'two-and-thirty men and women put before the Judge to receive that sentence [of Death] together', a society both heartless and self-righteous which can, now it is fully known, no longer inspire Pip with social shame. To make this clear he has stood by the dock 'holding the hand that he stretched forth to me'—we must realize that this is again a purely symbolic gesture and additional proof that the trial scene is essential and not literal truth for in real life no one would have been allowed to hold the hand of the criminal in the dock: Dickens of course knew this and so also did his readers, since the public were then connoisseurs of criminal trials (no doubt Dickens's reason for pillorying that interest here). Pip's change of attitude to his society and to his convict are therefore seen to be independent of Magwitch's personality—the assertion of some critics that Dickens has worked a trick (by turning the old lag into another Joe) to secure Pip's acceptance of him now is unjustified.

Thus we get to Pip's revelation to the dying man of his daughter's existence and Pip's love for her, which has again been criticized adversely, as if Pip were concocting a deliberate lie. But Pip speaks only the truth about Magwitch's lost child: 'She is living now. She is a lady and very beautiful. And I love her.' This is a selection of true facts designed to give the dying man the greatest gratification he could receive, and even if it possibly had a false suggestion (that she might marry Pip), who could censure Pip in these circumstances? Pip produces these facts in all unselfishness, and with an obvious effort, one of the last it is necessary he should make to free himself from the Pip who, among other things, had assured himself, in his original revulsion against his convict patron: 'Never had I breathed, and never would I breathe—or so I resolved—a word of Estella to Provis' (the parenthesis shows that Dickens had already prepared for the last step in Pip's retraction). The fact that Estella is already Mrs. Bentley Drummle does not detract from Pip's obligation to confess his knowledge of her and love for her to her father.

Dickens had clearly given a great deal of thought to the problem of convincingly freeing Pip from the bonds of selfishness, shame and guilt. Thus in the magnificent scene of Magwitch's return, when Pip thinks of him only as the convict who once sent him money out of gratitude, he returns the two one-pound notes with two 'clean and new' ones and with a patronizing conventional remark. Silently Magwitch burns the notes, showing Pip both that he is now rich himself and that the return of money is not what he has come for. Pip takes in both these points, but he doesn't see the meanness of spirit revealed in his believing that kindness and gratitude can be repaid with money, or that what was then a large sum for a poor man to give is a negligible sum for rich Pip to repay. But his enlightenment as to such matters is shown us when he tells Joe and Biddy before leaving England to work under Herbert as a clerk:

> 'And when I say that I shall never rest until I have worked for the money with which you have kept me out of prison, and have sent it to you, don't think dear Joe and Biddy, that if I could repay it a thousand times over, I suppose I could cancel a farthing of the debt I owe you, or that I would do so if I could.'

A convincing proof of a change of heart, and a proof of the understanding of what spiritual health is by the novelist himself, a man who had by perpetual hard work made himself rich but who freely gave his money and services in the spirit of true generosity to those less fortunate than himself. The suggestion of one critic that *Great Expectations* was written because Dickens now felt guilty at being a rich man is absurd; as is another's suggestion that Dickens used the story of Miss Havisham who had been jilted and deceived by her professed lover because, having separated from his own wife, he needed to express his sense of guilt thus. Miss Havisham is so evidently marginal as a picturesque convenience; the significance, which swallows her up, is the whole context of Satis House, and as the producer of Estella she is the parallel to Magwitch the patron of Pip. Pip and Estella are equally victims of an *idée fixe*.

Pip is now left with his relations with Joe to put right. Here the ironic mode of the novel comes into operation again. The revelatory dreams Pip has in his fever after the trial (his trial as well as Magwitch's) prove the genuineness of his renunciation of a privileged position in such a society as he has learned his London to be the centre of. He remembers:

> that I suffered greatly, that I often lost my reason, that the time
> seemed interminable, that I confounded impossible existences with
> my own identity; that I was a brick in the house wall, and yet en-
> treating to be released from the giddy place where the builders had
> set me; that I was a steel beam of a vast engine, clashing and whirling
> over a gulf, and yet that I implored in my own person to have the
> engine stopped, and my part in it hammered off; that I passed through
> these phases of disease, I know of my own remembrance. That I
> sometimes struggled with real people, in the belief that they were
> murderers, and that I would all at once comprehend that they meant
> to do me good . . . .'

When he finds it is Joe who is nursing him it is easy in his weakness to
return to childhood and his old easy relation with Joe: 'I fancied I was
little Pip again'. But Dickens neither simplifies nor sentimentalizes the
situation: that no one can be a child again is one of the stern realities of
experience. Pip can now withstand the maddening effect of the repetitiveness and illiterate formulations of Joe's conversation and exercise
the tact of goodwill, and remembering his debt and Joe's goodness, kiss
Joe's hand in true affection. But the relations of Pip's childhood are impossible as Pip, growing stronger, also grows older. The bond of affection
is even enhanced by Pip's new humility but contact becomes difficult to
sustain though Pip is ashamed to find that this is so. It is not Pip's fault,
for Joe feels the strain too and starts calling Pip 'Sir' compulsively and
Pip, though distressed and remorseful, doesn't see how to check Joe's re-
treat from a Pip who can no longer be treated like a child. It is ended by
Joe's returning home without warning. Now Pip has a final decision to
make: instead of being Herbert's clerk should he not offer to return to
the point where he left the forge?–go back to work for Joe and, if Biddy
will have him, marry her and settle in the village; that is, lead the life he
would have done if Miss Havisham and Estella had not intervened for
good or ill to propel him into becoming a gentleman.

This is the part of the novel that has been most misinterpreted and for
which Dickens has got least credit. It is necessary that Pip should make
the decision to go back and try, and indeed he has 'a sense of increasing
relief as I drew nearer to them, and a sense of leaving arrogance and un-
truthfulness further and further behind'. He is to receive a shock comparable to the revelation of his patron–he doesn't count in Biddy's life.
His real sacrifice is in finding he can't make this premeditated recompense,

for Biddy has married Joe and his pilgrimage ('I felt like one who is toiling home barefoot from distant travel') is frustrated, his return an anticlimax. He can't solve his problems by going back to an earlier point in life and cutting out what he has become in between, he must go on, living with his contrition and difficulties. He leaves the village for good, but this time begs Joe and Biddy to accompany him to the finger-post, instead of, as originally, shrinking from their company to it. Biddy, by marrying Joe and without thinking it necessary to tell Pip of their intention, has made it clear that Pip does not belong to her world and that she belongs to Joe's. She is neither married off arbitrarily by Dickens to show that Joe is the true gentleman who must marry the true princess to fulfil the fairy-story that the novel is (according to Professor Harry Stone) nor because 'Pip has found that he has forfeited his right to her' (Dabney). He had thought it right to offer himself to Biddy to make amends and show his new humility, not because he really believed it would make him happy, and he has to be shown that such an escape from guilt would no more have answered than his becoming a blacksmith again to please Joe. Dickens has made his point repeatedly, that he believes that education and the society of educated people with high standards of integrity like Matthew and Herbert Pocket, represent, other things being equal, a more desirable social habitat than a village-market-town society of Gargerys, Wopsles, Trabbs, Pumblechooks, Hubbles and Orlicks.[1] Dickens has intimated that there are real distinctions to be made, based not on money or birth but on cultivation and intelligence and talent. Joe is described by Pip as 'this gentle Christian man', which is neither a gentleman nor even a wholly satisfactory practical character; it seems to represent an uneasy gesture of the novelist's towards making a special status for Joe, to get over the difficulty Joe now presents in having outgrown the original role of 'a good-natured foolish man'. Joe, in spite of Dickens's effort to elevate him here, really represents the novelist's final disenchantment with the Romantic image of the child that Dickens has reached by the path I have traced. In the next and last novels we get only sociologically realistic children: in *Our Mutual Friend* the deformed and psychologically warped Dolls' Dressmaker and in *Edwin Drood* 'the hideous child' Deputy who stones Durdles home nightly–inevitable products of their environments. Dickens even as early as *Oliver Twist* had recognized the

[1]These names were evidently chosen as ugly and grotesque, to suggest yokels; they are quite different from the alarming sharpness and hardness suggested by the London names like Wemmick, Jaggers, Skiffins, Clarriker.

need for sociological realism by providing the more plausible charity-school product Noah Claypole to offset or supplement the purely Romantic image of untouched innocence and goodness embodied in Oliver.

And we should not be misled by the apparent virtue of the simple, wholesome rule-of-thumb morality, 'Lies is lies', which Joe produces for Pip's guidance; we must note that Joe's wits, after his own introduction into Satis House, 'brightened by the encounter they had passed through', (Pip notes), realized that some deception was the best, the necessary, means of managing Mrs. Joe in this matter. Finding it as impossible as Pip had done to explain Miss Havisham to his wife, he systematically lies to her, to flatter her into a good humour, involving Pip without consulting him in advance: if this is humour at all it is also something much more. Dickens really needs to make no comment on the inadequacy of simple-minded people thereafter. He has deliberately made his point thus, and it is unmistakable; yet it seems not to have been taken by readers, another instance of the unintelligent reading he habitually receives.

It is rather odd that American critics should write with such confidence regarding the facts of the English social system in the past as they do with regard to the actualities of the class system operating in *Great Expectations*, pooh-poohing the idea that Pip had any right to feel that Biddy was not suitable for him as a wife. 'Pip is now educated, but Biddy is a school-mistress' says Mr. Ross H. Dabney flatly. 'In Dickens's terms there is more of a class barrier between Joe and Biddy than between Pip and Biddy.' This is simply not the case.[1] Biddy was emphatically not the

[1]There is plenty of available information as to the social position and educational level of the village schoolmistress in Victorian England. A good source for the later, and therefore most favourable, phase is *Lark Rise*, Flora Thompson's auto-biography of a cottage childhood in Oxfordshire. In her childhood, as long before, the village schoolmistress had only to teach the elements of the three Rs and needlework. Her first teacher was satisfied to marry the squire's gardener, a later one had the ambition of being received at the front door of the manor house but was deflected to the kitchen. 'At that time the position of a village schoolmistress was a trying one socially . . . . In the 'eighties the schoolmistress (now the new type 'fresh from her training-college') was so nearly a new institution that a vicar's wife, in a real dilemma, said: "I should like to ask Miss — to tea; but do I ask her to kitchen or dining-room tea?" '. (Equals would of course take tea in the drawing-room.) The old type, like Biddy, would naturally take tea in the kitchen at the rectory or the manor house, Flora Thompson shows. Biddy and Pip were of an earlier generation altogether, the age of the dame-schools kept by such as Mr. Wopsle's great-aunt or rather better, like Biddy, but certainly not our idea of a

comparatively educated kind of later schoolmistress who had had a course at a teachers' training college, like Miss Peacher in *Our Mutual Friend* (but who was still very limited and knew only what she had to teach). Biddy was self-educated just enough to teach the merest elements in the old-style village school, and had never known, or felt the need of, any more enlightened company than that of the forge kitchen, as far as we know. As soon as Pip began to educate himself by systematic study she lost contact with him, and once he returns from London makes this clear by calling him 'Mr.'; her letter, sent to inform Pip of Joe's impending visit, nicely defines the degree of her literacy and her difficulty of communicating with Pip on all grounds. George Eliot, whose authority cannot be questioned here, shows a village schoolmaster of great natural ntelligence and superior abilities, Bartle Massey, who is yet highly respectful to the excellent Rector and never expects to be treated as an equal socially. Bartle, like Dinah the Methodist preacher in the same novel, speaks in the dialect , and so would Biddy have been tied to the Gargery kind of idiom if Dickens had not falsified her in this respect, thus obscuring another difference from Pip–the outward sign of a

teacher. 'Biddy had imparted to me everything she knew, from the little catalogue of prices, to a comic song she had once bought for a halfpenny', is Dickens's way of conveying this fact. Jane Eyre when destitute was considered a phoenix of a village schoolmistress, we remember, but this was because she had been educated at a boarding-school to be a private governess and was a lady; and she had herself replaced by someone more appropriate as soon as she inherited money– Charlotte Brontë knew all about these matters. Clothes were also an immediate class-index in the 19th century, as we can see from the discomfort suffered at Wuthering Heights when Catherine Earnshaw comes home to the farmhouse after her stay at the Grange unsuitably–impossibly–dressed like a young lady; and Biddy did not even belong to the farmer class. Cottagers had a recognizable women's costume. Biddy would neither have dressed nor spoken like a lady, her hands would have been coarsened by rough work as Mrs. Joe's substitute (in the days when everything from floors upwards had to be constantly scrubbed), and unlike Pip Biddy is shown to have taken to the Hubble and Gargery households as congenial enough. For all these reasons (and more) there *was* a real barrier between Biddy and Herbert's Handel which had nothing to do with 'snobbery' unless any manifestation of real differences that are more than merely social in fact though classified for convenience under that head, are to be dismissed thus. To say that there was 'more of a class barrier between Joe and Biddy' is nonsense, if only because there is no suggestion that Biddy had anything to overcome in marrying Joe–she was doing well for herself, like Flora Thompson's teacher who married the squire's gardener. Dickens assumes the reader understands all this without being told, and of course his readers did, Biddy inevitably suggesting to them the Irish peasant.

real cultural difference and a limitation of interests, experience and knowledge. Dickens cheats over her ability in these circumstances to deflate Pip by having Joe explain that she is exceptionally quick, but she is still not plausible in her rôle. A coarser style of repartee would have carried more conviction in her case (as it does in Susan Nipper's), but then Pip's idea of going back to marry her would have been more obviously impracticable. Dickens avoids idealizing Biddy and so should the modern critic.

The preference of critics generally for the originally-planned ending to the novel instead of the one printed seems to me incomprehensible. Estella was to marry after Drummle's death a new character, specially introduced for the purpose, a doctor who had defended her against Drummle's brutality (Jaggers's prediction had been correct as to Drummle's marital conduct). She was subsequently to see Pip accidentally in London walking with Joe and Biddy's boy whom she thought Pip's, and to kiss the child for auld lang syne. This has the complete inconsequentialness of life, but is quite unsuitable for the conclusion of such a schematic novel. Dickens's second thoughts produced the right, because the logical, solution to the problem of how to end without a sentimental 'happy ending' but with a satisfactory winding-up of the themes. This he has done with dignity and economy. And we don't, I think, ask how it is that Estella is now poor, since Miss Havisham's fortune was described as having been 'tied up on' her (the tying, being by Jaggers, would have been too skilfully done for her to have been stripped even by a husband) and since Drummle himself was by definition rich, avaricious and mean, why should he lose his fortune? Dickens could easily have made them the victims of a defaulting trustee or bank, so this doesn't matter, what is essential is that Estella should be stripped of the attributes that made her both desired by Pip and at the same time out of his reach. Dickens recreates the memory of the spell of Satis House in the appropriate reunion there, the right place at evening, which follows on Pip's shock at finding the house gone:

> There was no house now, no brewery, no building whatever left, but the wall of the old garden. The cleared space had been enclosed with a rough fence, and looking over it, I saw that some of the old ivy had struck root anew, and was growing green on low quiet mounds of ruin . . . . I could trace out where every part of the old house had been, and where the brewery had been, and where the gates, and where the casks.

We are not surprised to find Estella there too; it seems inevitable, as she belongs to the place in his memory. That Pip should marry Estella without the jewels that had enhanced her beauty for him (that is, stripped of her pride, social superiority, aristocratic grace, youth and fortune, and also of the illusions Pip had had, lost when he learnt of her parentage) shows him to have recovered from the spell Satis House had cast over him. Estella is now saddened, a poor widow, has passed through Drummle's distasteful hands, and has nothing left but the site of Satis House. The old Pip would have shuddered away from her, and he says she is almost unrecognizable. But for the first time she is not walking away from him—he notes 'She let me come up with her'. She has gone through a process comparable with Pip's self-knowledge and humiliation so that they can truly come together at last.[1] Her appeal for Pip now is that they have this experience in common, as they have a common past history, both having been made use of and having much to regret. This fits them for each other and no one else. So they leave 'the ruined place' hand in hand, in a 'broad expanse of tranquil light', a picture that is not theatrical, nor is it Academy art, nor a happy ending, but a true symbol of the successful end of Pip's pilgrimage. And this does offer an answer to the implicit question in the novel. How can one live without the crushing burden of guilt that this society imposes, yet without cutting oneself off from all society? It would have been easy for Dickens to have made his protagonist more than a gifted man—Jaggers is merely that—one who, like Dickens himself, was a man with a vocation who could respect himself therefore; but he would have evaded the problem. Pip, who has been much criticized as weak, uninteresting, tame, and otherwise lacking in spirit and force, was designed for the purpose as representative of the ordinary man, but with greater sensitiveness so that he cannot rest under the load of guilt and shame that other ordinary men managed not to notice. But it is the very fact of this awareness that makes Pip able to exercise moral choice, and even in such a constricting society as Dickens saw his to be. Pip's moral sensibility is shown to be the product in fact of

[1]She had been improving in self-knowledge as she grew up, Dickens shows in flashes. It is a pity he didn't go into these more fully as some, like the influence on her childhood of her awareness that Miss Havisham's relatives were intriguing against the adopted infant and that she couldn't protect herself, are interesting and expressed with great force. We are entitled to complain that Estella isn't given more scope, for unlike Biddy she is potentially someone to take seriously, though remaining for most of the novel a classical example of the child who, being unloved, can't feel affection therefore, only hostility.

the very conditions that made his sufferings: Dickens wrote of himself that he couldn't resent his unhappy experiences in childhood 'for I know how all these things have worked together to make me what I am'. We see Pip at the end freed from the oppressive fantasies and fears that were the result of his guilt, and equally from the shame that produced his false aspirations after a gentility of unearned income. He is content to work as a clerk under Herbert having resigned himself to the knowledge that in such a society there can be no great expectations–the charge that he ought to have worked in some capacity to bring about a better state of society ignores Dickens's (and Hawthorne's) point that this is the human condition: we cannot escape the necessity for the prison and the grave-yard.

A Shakespearean (in two senses) comic under-plot is seen in Mr. Wopsle's career which counterpoints Pip's: dissatisfied with the social position of parish clerk and indignant at social discrimination (because, he believes, if the Church were 'thrown open' he would rightfully be the parson) he goes up to London with the ambition of becoming a great tragedian and reviving the drama–*his* 'great expectations'. Conceit blinds him to the humiliating reality and unlike Pip he never learns the truth of things. The account of his deception is apparently humorous but really rather painful because of the indignities Wopsle incurs, also because Dickens, who was steeped in Shakespeare and saw as many of the performances of the tragedies as he could, implies disgust at the production (a travesty of *Hamlet*) and at the audience who are worthy of nothing better. The whole plays a part in characterizing Newgate London, along with Barnard's Inn, Smithfield, the hotel where Pip is humiliated because they can't provide a decent tea for Estella, Herbert's counting-house, Jaggers's performances in the police-court and with his clients in the street, and his dinner-parties in Gerrard-Street. The state of the theatre and its public is part of this degradation of a society, which no one felt more intensely than Dickens.

CHAPTER SEVEN

THE DICKENS ILLUSTRATIONS:
THEIR FUNCTION

W AS it necessary or desirable to have Dickens's novels illustrated? Why did Dickens's original publishers, all of them, think it essential to pay artists to illustrate novels, to illustrate even short pieces of light reading like *Sketches by Boz*? And even if illustrations were desirable or necessary then, do we, sophisticated intellectually, and capable readers of far more difficult novels than Dickens's, need them now? Mr. Lynton Lamb, in his *Drawing for Illustration* (Oxford, 1962) not only admits that 'No work of imagination should need illustration' but that some 'fail to get satisfactory illustrations from any artist' because, he feels, there are 'some great novels that seem to me to be closed to *any* kind of illustrations' – he makes this clear by specifying Jane Austen's ('I am embarrassed by the idea of seeing them illustrated') and adding 'It is the same with Shakespeare for me'; we would probably all agree with him, and add that *Wuthering Heights*, *Jane Eyre* and even the novels of George Eliot (though – significantly – not of Thackeray, Trollope or George Meredith) come into the same category. This is what every sensitive reader must surely feel, and it is encouraging to have the validity of such a prejudice confirmed by a very distinguished and widely successful professional in the field of book-illustration in our own time. Yet Mr. Lamb also says – he is writing for young artists wanting to go in for illustration and gives them a brief history of this profession to start with – that in the second decade of the 19th century novels not only were expected to be illustrated but that the illustrations, being drawn by established artists, 'were sometimes more eagerly awaited than the text', and that the sixties, a time when the Victorian novel was in its prime, 'was a decade particularly distinguished for its illustrators and for the poetic and literary insight that they showed'.

Thus we have to ask why Dickens's novels differ from both Jane Austen's and the (quite other) post-Romantic novels of Charlotte and Emily Brontë, in having been able to secure what are generally agreed as being satisfactory illustrations from several contemporary artists, and why–a different thing–Dickens's publishers originally insisted on having illustrators for them. The second question is more conveniently answered first, since the answer is a matter of social history, and incidentally supplies an explanation for the other issue. The satiric art of the 18th century had a social focus in the coffee-house and an aesthetic meeting-point, between literature and visual art, in Hogarth, whose moral series of prints were accessible to the illiterate and implied a moral and fictional narrative which the viewer inevitably supplied for himself (there was of course a long tradition of popular art in woodcuts behind the popularity of Hogarth's art). Hogarth's moral and satiric work was known to the ale-house, the farm, the inn and the cottage, as well as to the frequenter of the London print-shops and coffee-houses. His pupil Gillray succeeded him, with an almost equally popular commentary on the social, political and literary scene throughout the Napoleonic period, establishing the mode of satire at a finer level of wit than Hogarth and in a convention more suitable for illustration of fiction, as we can see from the use made of Gillray's stylization of life by Dickens's two greatest illustrators, Cruikshank and 'Phiz' (Hablôt K. Browne). Cruikshank was born in 1792 and, says Mr. Ruari McLean in his monograph on the artist,[1] 'was actually Gillray's direct successor employed to finish plates that Gillray had started and was too ill to complete. The prints, brightly coloured and exhibited close against the panes of the printsellers' windows, were an exciting feature of daily life in London to which there is no genuine parallel today. Their importance can be better understood when it is remembered that there were then virtually no illustrated papers or magazines, and that "the man in the street" usually could not read.' Thus we have a public which, even when highly literate, was accustomed to a visual art going hand in hand with the presentation of political ideas and their discussion and with a moralistic literature, and that part of it which was semi-literate or illiterate had at least had this visual education. All were accustomed to taking in ideas in a stylized art form and had an imagination formed by the tradition of moral satire independent of literacy. Thus when the novel ceased to be entirely an expensive three-volume product for the upper classes and library-subscribers, because it was discovered that cheap part-publication was feasible to reach a larger public altogether, the parts *had* to be illustrated, and artists like Cruikshank who were caricaturists became also famous illustrators of books.

[1] *George Cruikshank* by Ruari McLean (Art and Technics, 1948) has a representative selection from Cruikshank's enormous output of etchings.

Younger men like H. K. Browne imitated and adapted Cruikshank and Gilray in their turn. 'When most of us think of "Dickens-characters" ', writes Mr. Lynton Lamb,' we think of drawings by Cruikshank and "Phiz" rather than of later ones. . . . And although Cruikshank is the best of them all we are apt to forget that the only Dickens books with his illustrations are *Sketches by Boz* and *Oliver Twist*. He has conveyed the idea of "Dickens's London" better than any other artist', etc.[1] The suitability of Cruikshank and 'Phiz' for Dickens was not accidental; the principle of convergence that novelist and artists seem to exhibit so successfully is due to their all belonging to the tradition of a visual-literary moralistic-satiric art with its roots in Pope[2] and Hogarth. Dickens's brilliantly imaginative translation of Hogarth's visual art into his own[3] and for his own related purposes enriched with an extra dimension of Dickensian fantasy, has been mentioned in the essay on *Dombey* earlier in this book, and other instances of the kind can be found by the reader interested in this aspect of Dickens's creativeness.[4] A visual training of the kind Hogarth

[1] Lynton Lamb should be consulted for an appreciation in aesthetic terms by a fellow-craftsman of the 'Morning Streets' and 'Public Dinners' illustrations in the *Sketches by Boz* and of 'Oliver asking for More' and 'Fagin in the Condemned Cell' in *Oliver Twist*.

[2] I have always been struck by how Hogarthian is Pope's history of Sir Balaam in the third *Moral Epistle* (the first one on the use of riches), which in its four parts reads like a poetic narrative of a series of Hogarth's moral satires on contemporary life, of the form of *Marriage-à-la-mode*, but whose illustrations have been lost; in fact, Pope's story of Sir Balaam precedes Hogarth's inventions of the kind. Pope seems there to be describing a moral series of paintings or drawings, while Hogarth seems to work from a written narrative of dramatic fiction which he is illustrating— the two arts are not parallel but overlapping.

[3] Dickens had a set of Hogarth's series hanging in his hall at Gadshill, his last home, and later removed them to the walls of his own bedroom.

[4] Even as late as *Little Dorrit*, e.g. the account of the clever *arriviste* Fanny's wedding in Rome to the moronic socialite Edmund Sparkler in chapter XIV which begins: 'The day came, and the She-Wolf in the Capitol might have snarled with envy . . . the murderous-headed statues of the wicked Emperors of the Soldiery . . . might have come off their pedestals . . .' ending 'So the Bride had mounted into her handsome chariot, incidentally accompanied by the Bridegroom; and after rolling for a few minutes smoothly over a fair pavement, had begun to jolt through a Slough of Despond, and through a long, long avenue of wrack and ruin. Other nuptial carriages are said to have gone the same road, before and since.' Dickens's idea of Society marriages seems to have been formed once for all on Hogarth's *Marriage-à-la-Mode*. The numerous Hogarthian scenes in *Dombey* (the christening, the wedding, in Dombey's study, as well as the scene quoted above in Warwick Castle, which is very close to the first plate of Hogarth's series) suggest to me a

and Gillray had provided implied a sharpening of the wits, a habit of vis-ualizing character and situation as types, and an instinctive practice of moralizing a spectacle, with an expectation of wildly exaggerated characteristics and of a satiric intention. This is what Dickens is to be found almost unconsciously satisfying in his early novels, and learning to refine on and bring into relation to a fuller apprehension of life in his maturer work, but he remained a great admirer of Hogarth, and an intelligent one, all his life. [A related influence, *The Beggar's Opera*, also a part of this popu-lar inheritance from the Augustan age, which added music (the songs sung to popular airs) and stage drama to the stylized satiric presentation of contemporary society, was also a strong and lasting influence in Dickens's art: openly acknowledged in the introduction to *Oliver Twist* along with Hogarth, it can be seen more subtly present as late as *Little Dorrit*—as in Rigaud-Blandois's various apologias which depend on the cynical under-mining of values centring, as in Gay's satire, on the word (and idea of the) 'gentleman', and in the cynical attitude to Society derived from Gay in terms of which the Merdle-Barnacle party in chapter XII is conducted. There 'Bar' has a long speech explicitly quoting Captain Macheath on law and lawyers and admitting Gay's point that the company in the drawing-room is really no better ethically than that hanging on Tyburn Tree.]

Thus thanks to this rich tradition and the visual education it provided, even those who took their instalments of fiction orally could fix those in their memories by the two or more full-page pictures that came with each, with the added help of the descriptive pictorial cover that Dickens always had drawn to summarize the plot and themes and show the lead-ing characters in appropriate combinations and context, with the addition of the meaningful frontispiece and often a vignette on the title-page (which, as in the case of the very memorable one on the title-page of *Little Dorrit*, for instance, can be seen to stand half-way between a popular emblematic cut and a Blake-like symbolic vision). Lynton Lamb merely says, and this is the conventional view, that 'The illustrations were of real

generally Hogarthian inspiration, that the subject of Hogarth's *Marriage-à-la-Mode* was behind the drama of Mr. Dombey's second marriage, with Carker playing the part of the Lawyer-paramour—it was originally intended to end with Edith's moral disgrace and general disaster, and with Walter Gay coming to a bad end like Hogarth's Idle Apprentice. On reading *Sketches by Boz* the Regency wit Sydney Smith (b. 1771) deduced that 'the soul of Hogarth has migrated into the body of Mr. Dickens'.

importance in establishing the success of the series by fixing, as each part appeared, the identity of a character and the continuity of the action'.

This was generally realized by both novelists, readers and illustrators. Even as late as 1853 I note that Surtees, introducing a new hero with *Mr Sponge's Sporting Tour*, starts chapter IV with: 'We trust our opening chapters, aided by our friend Leech's pencil, will have enabled our readers to embody such a Sponge in their mind's eye as will assist them in following us through the course of his peregrinations.' But du Maurier wrote in an essay 'The Illustrating of Books. From the serious artist's point of view' in The Magazine of Art in 1890: 'What does not the great Dickens himself owe to Cruikshank and Hablôt Browne, those two delightful etchers who understood and interpreted him so well! . . . Our recollections [of his characters] have become fixed, crystallised and solidified into imperishable concrete by these little etchings in that endless gallery, printed on those ever-welcome pages of thick yellow paper, which one used to study with such passionate interest before reading the story, and after, and between. One may have forgotten what Mr Pecksniff has thought, or said, or done in this world, but what he looked like, never!' Similarly, William Black, himself a Victorian novelist, wrote of Millais's illustrations to *Framley Parsonage*, that they were 'illustrations that remained vivid to the mind when the characters in the novel have all faded away into shadow or downright oblivion'. This however was, naturally, as far as possible from being Dickens's idea of the function of his illustrators.

In showing in a previous essay how the illustrations to *Copperfield* draw attention to the novelist's theme and make apparent his deeper intentions, I have shown that Dickens made the illustrations that he had to have, to satisfy traditional expectation and need, serve the purposes of an altogether new art of the novel. The illustrations of Dickens's novels up to *Bleak House* are a unique addition to the text, not only visualizing a scene for us in its historical social detail, and giving a visual embodiment to the characters which expresses their inner selves for us inescapably, besides being a visual embodiment of dramatic flash-points: the illustrations are frequently indispensable even to us, the highly-trained modern reader, in interpreting the novels correctly because they encapsule the themes and give us the means of knowing with certainty where Dickens meant the stress to fall (since his touch is often lightest where most meaningful, and tactfully indirect). Even we lose much if we don't read the Dickens novels with their original illustrations, and this is true of no other English novelist. For fortunately Dickens was not only a genius as a novelist, he was also a gifted editor and had an intuitive as well as an informed understanding of the problems of providing a diverse and even largely semi-literate and illiterate public with, not something it would have no effort to absorb as entertainment, but with what he himself wanted to write yet which must be presented in a form that such a mixed readership could cope with and get *something* out of—if not all that there was in it to get. It was part of his genius that he was able to seize the opportunity presented by the well-established custom of employing artists as illustrators. It was not his merit of course but his good fortune that the age in which he wrote was that of the great age of English illustration[1] both in technical achievement, in craftsmen like the famous brothers Dalziel who could carry out the artist's designs, and in the many gifted exponents of the art of illustration such as Cruikshank, 'Phiz', Leech, Keene, Doyle, among others.

Thus Dickens was able to carry with him on his progress from entertainer to artist both a public that even when literate was not educated in reading fiction that had broken with the eighteenth century novel,[2] and also a public that without the illustrations would hardly have been able

---

[1]'Keene . . . for a threepenny weekly made drawings that are on a level with the finest in the world'—Sickert (quoted in *Charles Keene* by Derek Hudson). Keene, though an artist of such stature and originality that he was recognized by great French painters as their master, worked hard for forty years as a contributor to *Punch* and as a book illustrator. He would have been the best successor to 'Phiz', having the right requirements—experience in illustrating Victorian novels, humour, dramatic feeling, and the capacity for satire and burlesque, as well as the speed of execution and the poetic feeling—for Dickens. Keene, though his powers were primarily those of a great artist in his own right, was still able to earn his bread and butter happily in illustration, thanks to its status in the nineteenth century. It should be noted that Keene also was in the direct tradition, having a special admiration for and debt to Hogarth and Bewick. There is no profit in making a fundamental distinction between Keene as illustrator and his contemporaries, as did Sir Lionel Lindsay in his book on Keene, *The Artists' Artist*, where he states: 'Cruikshank, "Phiz" and Leech are publishers' hacks; du Maurier at his best a fashionable satirist; of the English artists of the 19th century Charles Keene alone invented a world we can believe in.' Dickens's tribute to Leech and Henry James's to both du Maurier and Leech bear witness to the veracity of the worlds created for them by the Victorian illustrators and their imaginative stimulus for creative writers.

[2]Scott's was essentially a continuation of this 18th century tradition and not, like *Wuthering Heights, Jane Eyre and Oliver Twist*, the new novel into which the insights and experiences of the Romantic poets had been channelled.

to cope with a novel doled out in portions at intervals of as much as a month, or even a fortnight, much less the novels of Dickens with (after *Oliver Twist*) their enormous numbers of characters and range of scenes. Cruikshank, twenty years older than Dickens and already famous, was naturally engaged by Dickens's publisher to make the collection of Dickens's early journalism, *Sketches by Boz*, attractive for publication in book form, and his etchings for the book, many of which are independent of the text and exist as works of art which are recognized classics of their kind, were rightly admired as such. But whether he was, as artists and art-lovers always allege, Dickens's *best* illustrator is another matter, which is of interest in deciding the whole question of the function of the Dickens illustrations. When Dickens started as a *novelist*, after some puerile attempts at fiction in story form which can be seen in *Sketches by Boz*, it was, as we all know, through being engaged at the age of 25 to furnish a story for illustrations by Seymour in the projected form of cockney sporting plates for a Nimrod Club, an engagement which Dickens accepted while, characteristically, refusing to provide sporting scenes and rejecting the subordinate rôle generally. According to him:

> I said that it would be infinitely better for the plates to arise naturally out of the text; and that I would like to take my own way, with a freer range of English scenes and people, and was afraid I should ultimately do so in any case, whatever course I might prescribe to myself at starting. My views being deferred to, I thought of Mr. Pickwick, and wrote the first number; from the proof-sheets of which Mr. Seymour made his drawing of the club. I connected Mr. Pickwick with a club because of the original suggestion; and I put in Mr. Winkle expressly for the use of Mr. Seymour.

Mr. Winkle was unnecessary, it turned out, since Seymour committed suicide before the second number and later artists were never in the position of being able to dictate to or make any such demands on the novelist: Dickens saw to that. After temporary aid had been called in (a weak illustrator called Buss) Dickens himself made the excellent choice of H. K. Browne, who signed himself thenceforward 'Phiz' in harmony with Dickens's pen-name of 'Boz' (which however Dickens soon dropped, though it had earned for him the title of 'The Inimitable Boz'). The fact that Browne was younger even than himself and obviously not a formidable artist like Cruikshank was no doubt an attraction for the novelist; but Browne's real merit must have been that he was decidedly in the Hogarth tradition–Dickens had wisely rejected Thackeray who had applied for the vacent post, and who would have had nothing to offer for Dickens's purposes. [He also rejected the young Leech, with less reason, for Leech's illustrations later to some of Dickens's Christmas tales are both finely executed and appropriately enchanting, and Leech was a widely successful illustrator all his life.] Thus, having had illustrators thrust upon him in his literary beginnings, Dickens had, in learning to work with them, soon realized that they could be made to serve his own purposes as collaborators, as well as the publishers' in promoting the sales.

In fact, Seymour did well to remove himself from the Pickwickian scene. As we can see from the arrangement of the characters up the stair-case in his drawing of 'Dr. Slammer's defiance of Jingle' which was used in the second number of *Pickwick*, Seymour could make an elegant and memorable design, but his Pickwick is unconvincing (he had even had originally, it seems, the misguided idea of making Mr. Pickwick a tall, thin man) and his scenes are weak too–compare his plate 'The Pugnacious Cabman' with similar street-scenes and character-pieces of both Cruikshank and 'Phiz', to see his inferiority for Dickens's purposes. Dickens now had two admirable artists at his disposal, but he did not choose the distinguished illustrator of *Sketches by Boz* for his next novel, *Oliver Twist*; Bentley, the publisher for whom Dickens was editing *Bentley's Miscellany*, a magazine in which *Oliver Twist* was published in instalments, himself engaged Cruikshank to illustrate the novel. Cruikshank seems to have sent his plates to be printed independently of the author. Dickens objected to some but only just succeeded in stopping the very trite last illustration and having that replaced by one less unsatisfactory. While some of the illustrations to *Oliver Twist* have been immensely admired, with justice, the illustrations as a whole are very uneven, and it seems to me that there is no doubt that Dickens did the best for himself and his readers in electing to stick to 'Phiz' after that (sometimes supplemented by Cattermole and others) until in his late novels he no longer needed any illustrations. It seems to me evident that the kind of free connexion with a text, and preferably with a non-novelistic text such as most of *Sketches by Boz*, was what suited Cruikshank best, and that where the text of *Oliver Twist* offered similar opportunities to *Sketches*, the illustrations to the latter are the better. The 'Public Dinners' where characters of the beadle kind lead in the infant objects of charity, would have done well for the novel, since it superbly incarnates the theme of the early satiric part of *Oliver Twist*, while the 'Seven Dials' and 'Monmouth Street' he did for the *Sketches* show how much the novel lost by not having any such illustrations – how odd that Cruikshank did not take the opportunity, which his 'Seven Dials' suggests he could have taken successfully, of supplying more vigorous illustration for the crucial scene of the recapture of poor Oliver by Nancy and Sikes! Cruikshank neglects most of the opportunities he had for helping the reader by illustrating the key points of the novel, since he took no directions from the author – other than the very fine 'Oliver asking for More' and the supremely imaginative success of 'Fagin in the Condemned Cell'. It is odd that Mr. Lynton Lamb asserts the superior *dramatic* power of Cruikshank as well as the undeniably superior bite, depth, solidity and luminous texture of his drawings compared with 'Phiz's', for Cruikshank did not adequately illustrate the recapture of Oliver, or illustrate at all the intensely dramatic court scene where Fagin feels the moral condemnation of the court in the accusing eyes focused on him; and when he takes such an opportunity as the important scene of Oliver's trance (in which Oliver *feels*, without seeing, the terrifying presence of Fagin and Monk at the window) there is nothing supernatural, no thrilling sense of the mystery of Oliver's vision, and no horror, all of which the text demands. The pictures of Bill Sikes after the murder of Nancy are crude and none of these drawings containing the Artful Dodger and his set convey the combination of a degraded humour with brutality that Dickens has created there. Yet *Oliver*, with its sequence of satiric, melodramatic, tragic, and potentially symbolic scenes, was surely stimulating for any artist with flexibility and who would be willing to be directed by an intelligent sympathy with his author's aims.

It seems to me that this is where Cruikshank was lacking. He was too independent and much too egotistical – it is significant that in his old age he claimed to have originated the plot and incidents of *Oliver Twist* and alleged that he gave Dickens all his ideas for that novel, an absurd delusion; overflowing with invention and fantasies, Cruikshank had an impish sense of humour which was quite undisciplined. It does not matter that Fagin's hook nose, whiskers, oval face, short figure and glaring eyes were Cruikshank's own characteristics which his sardonic sense of humour must have enjoyed copying from his mirror for the villain. But his habit of putting recognizable people into his illustrations necessarily interfered with the proper purpose of the novelist's art: in his 'Public Dinners' in *Sketches by Boz* the second man in the procession is recognizably the young Dickens and the fourth unmistakably himself, so

that it is not surprising that the two complacent figures leading the procession should have been traditionally said to be Chapman and Hall the
publishers (though Mr. Arthur Waugh has since declared this to be a
myth). This is Cruikshank's sense of humour, but he does not show the
right kind for Dickens's work, and there is no humour, as distinct from
an interest in the grotesque, in his illustrations for *Oliver Twist*. While
this might have been largely not inappropriate for the Dickens phase that
ended with *Chuzzlewit*, after that Gillray's style of caricaturist's wit was
no longer suitable, so Cruikshank could never have been the ideal illustrator for the tender and idealistic side to Dickens's novels such as is
present as early as *The Old Curiosity Shop*–Cruikshank's children are
drawn in that curious earlier 19th-century convention which makes
them appear dwarfed adults, with large heavy heads, unchildlike faces
and minute feet. Though one would have liked to have seen Gillray's and
Cruikshank's idea of the Pecksniff clan gathered in Mr. Pecksniff's 'best
parlour' in chapter IV,[1] this style would not have done for the humorous
side of *Dombey* and *Copperfield*, which though humorous is yet tender,
domestic and poignant. 'Phiz' was not only more pliable, more educable
and more suitable in his wider range of feeling and his freedom from an
assertive ego; in spite of what the art critics have said, it seems to me he
is even, for Dickens's purposes, the better artist. Mr. Ruari McLean, who
also prefers Cruikshank, writes:

> A comparison of Cruikshank with 'Phiz'–thumbing through
> *Sketches by Boz* together with, say, *Martin Chuzzlewit*–shows how
> much greater an artist Cruikshank was, with ten times more per-
> sonality in his characters and life in his scenes–and with an infinitely
> greater sense of making a picture.

Yet it still seems to me that if we take up this challenge and compare
Cruikshank's illustration for *Sketches by Boz* of 'The Pawnbroker's Shop'
with 'Phiz's' very similar scene which illustrates young Martin's encounter
with Tigg in the pawnbroker's, we feel and see that though admirable as
a composition and an etching Cruikshank's pawnbroker's interior is too
tidy, unimaginative and static to be interesting, and there is no sense of
the essentially painful element, the sordid and degrading, inherent in the
situation and in the relation between customers and pawnbroker, which
'Phiz' captures and makes us aware of. Nor is there the humour that is

[1]Though 'Phiz's' 'Pleasant little family party at Mr. Pecksniff's' serves the
purpose admirably.

necessary for a Dickensian treatment of the text. It is 'Phiz's' that has the vivid dramatic quality, the feeling and the humour, and we see in the stance of both men behind the pawnbroker's counter, in the expression of the one on the tilted chair, in the woman with the baby at the breast, the Hogarthian use of the pictures on the wall, the expressive attitudes and faces of *all* the other characters, the whole *mis en scène* and its dramatic lighting, that 'Phiz' has immersed himself imaginatively in the life of the novel and found a corresponding visual art for expressing it–not as an independent picture but as an illuminating contribution to the novel. This is what the readership needed, and Lynton Lamb implicitly admits 'Phiz's' value to the reader, even to the modern reader, when he says that in spite of what he feels to be 'Phiz's' general inferiority to Cruikshank aesthetically, 'But, touch by touch, our knowledge of the visible world in which Dickens's characters moved and had their being, is extended and consolidated' [by 'Phiz'].

There is a well-known woodcut by Cruikshank called 'Our Library Table' which shows Harrison Ainsworth the novelist conferring with Cruikshank 'his pictorial coadjutor' on *Ainsworth's Magazine*, 'Cruik-shank', it has been observed, 'characteristically laying down the law'. Now Dickens was not an author who would submit to this, though, also characteristically, he delighted in Cruikshank's society and maintained a convivial friendship with him after dropping him as an illustrator. For 'Phiz' there was no question of independence: Dickens seems to have given out the subjects as well as criticized the drawings for alteration before they went to press. Thus in the course of *Pickwick*, when they were newly working together, Dickens writes to him, of the drawing submitted for his approval:

> I think the Sergeant should look younger, and a great deal more sly, and knowing–he should be looking at Pickwick too, smiling compassionately at his innocence. The other fellows are noble.

Unfortunately we have few of the memoranda that Dickens supplied to 'Phiz' for his use or that 'Phiz' made for himself at Dickens's coaching sessions, which indicate the nature of the instructions Dickens gave, and not very many of his criticisms remain either as given by letter direct to 'Phiz' or indirectly through Forster–with Forster Dickens evidently felt freer to express the exasperation or disappointment that he frequently felt, it seems, at his artists' efforts. We shall never know how much of 'Phiz's' success was due to empathy and how much to Dickens's patient explanations of what he wanted. A great part of these explanations must have been verbal, as we can see from such accidental evidence as this in a letter from Dickens to Forster: 'Of course she hates Carker in the most deadly degree. I have not elaborated that now, because (as I was explaining to Browne the other day. . . .)'. It is to 'Phiz's' credit that whereas Cruikshank was weak in those respects where Dickens's growth was taking place, 'Phiz', a whole generation younger than Cruikshank, was amenable to the new influences enough to be carried out of the limittations of the tradition of the grotesque, the satiric and the moralistic, that he, like Cruikshank, had inherited as an illustrator, though, very intelligently, he kept to the Hogarthian tradition wherever it was most suited to the text–and, as we have seen, Dickens long continued to see and feel in this tradition at times himself.

How Dickens and 'Phiz' together tackled the problem of carrying along a mixed and incompetent readership in the train of the Inimitable's progress from the concocter of hand-to-mouth entertainment to the serious and responsible artist who could and did risk alienating important sections of his public, is worth examining. As I have already said, it seems to me there is no question that Dickens rightly chose 'Phiz' as the most suitable artist he was likely to get for his purposes in the period between *Pickwick* and *Bleak House* when Dickens was developing as an artist and had to reach and conquer the higher levels of his society, which at first were strongly resistant to what was felt to be, compared with Thackeray's, a vulgar form of fiction and later, compared with George Eliot's, an unintellectual one.[1] Dickens was still experimenting for *The Old*

[1] Mrs. Archer Clive, rich and well-born and herself a novelist, read *Chuzzlewit* on its appearance and notes: 'Finished *Martin Chuzzlewit*, and I don't care that one character should be hanged and one married. If they had changed situations it would have been nothing to me, nor to Archer.' Such expressions of contempt were part of a hostile attitude to Dickens, felt to be for long a writer of novels for the vulgar only (and which G. H. Lewes continued to allege them to be to the end). The feelings of Miss Jenkins, the aristocratic Rector's daughter in *Cranford*, on the subject of people of her circle's lowering themselves by reading the parts of *Pickwick* (a vulgar form of publication, she held) are well known. Less so now is Miss Charlotte Yonge's distaste (she also was County and highly educated) which is put into the mouth of the pattern young lady in *The Heir of Redclyffe* (1853). The invalid brother is rebuked for being 'nearly walled up' in 'cheap rubbish', which turns out to be the new fiction published in monthly parts, and he makes his sister read him ' "the part of *Dombey* that hurts women's feelings most, just to see if she would go on–the part about little Paul–and I declare, I shall think the worse of her ever after–she was so stony hearted, that to this day she does not know whether

Curiosity Shop, for which both Cattermole and 'Phiz' were employed, Cattermole doing the 'Gothic' interiors of the curiosity shop, the churches and tombs and of the vaulted chambers in the ruins, and also the sentimental scenes, 'Phiz', much more satisfactorily, the satiric and humorous illustrations.

Actually, 'Phiz' shows himself here better able than Cattermole even to bring out the potentialities of Gothic architecture (which to Cattermole are only antiquarian) in playing off its sinister antiquity and symbolic suggestions against the youthful innocence of Little Nell. 'Phiz' successfully shows it as embodying the threat to Nell represented by Quilp and his malignity. This can be seen in 'Phiz's' illustration 'Nell Hides from Quilp', where the dwarf is shown as an inhuman bestial figure in exactly the same tradition of heraldic monster as the two stone ones above which flank the archway and which stand, threatening in posture, beside the niches which are empty of their guardian saints—as are likewise the niches below the monsters, against one of which niches Nell crouches from Quilp with his uplifted stick (he repeats the attitude of the monsters above who raise banners)—crouches against the empty niche for the protection that is not forthcoming. In the shadow of the archway is a sinister figure with a sack or burden on its back. All this is either mentioned or implied in the text—for instance, Quilp is described when raising his stick (actually, to direct forward the boy with Quilp's trunk on his back) as 'looking up at the old gateway, and showing in the moonlight like some monstrous image that had come down from its niche and was casting a backward glance at its old house.' Whether by Dickens's direction or by his own sympathetic comprehension of the text supplied

he is dead or alive" '. The superior young man in the novel says: ' "those books [Dickens's novels] open fields of thought; and as their principles are negative, they are not likely to hurt a person well armed with the truth" ' [meaning Miss Yonge's, the correct, religious views–Keble's] but adds: ' "it would be a pity to begin with Dickens, when there is so much of a higher grade equally new to you" '. Trollope's skit on Dickens in his early novel *The Warden* is another placing of Dickens as eminently vulgar, crude and sentimental, and a demagogue. Hans Andersen mentions that Dickens, being a Radical writer, was not considered respectable socially in his earlier phase. The turning-point here was *David Copperfield*, for obvious reasons. Sydney Smith, who moved in the best social and intellectual circles, 'was deterred by the vulgarity of the name' ['Boz'] but after reading *Nickleby* admitted: 'I stood out against Mr Dickens as long as I could, but he has conquered me'; he made advances to Dickens (to Dickens's great joy) and their friendship, valuable to both, lasted till Sydney's death. Others such as Bagehot stood out to the end against the vulgar art.

him here, 'Phiz' has supplied the visual equivalent not merely of an episode in the story but of its meaning in the novel as a whole, and much more successfully than Cattermole's sentimental picture of Nell on her death-bed, 'At Rest', with its very obvious and trite appurtenances of the Madonna and Child above her bed-head, the open window for the de-parting soul, the hour-glass and the song-bird on the window-sill, the prayer-book in the dead girl's hand, the contrast between her youthful simplicity and the decayed Gothic magnificence of her surroundings – all easily taken in (because conventional and hackneyed) even by the illiterate who could only listen to instalments read aloud.[1]

'Phiz's' low-life and below-stairs scenes here are also full of interesting detail giving new force to the tradition of caricaturing such (e.g. those in Miss Brass's kitchen and wherever Dick Swiveller – a younger Micawber – is present, as well as traditional satiric representations of the Brass family. But his 'Quilp defies the Dog', with a telling view of Thames-side through the opening of the shed, is much more than this and emphasizes Dickens's idea – the animal nature of Quilp's face and body-attitude in goading the chained dog opposite him brings out the inferiority of the animal to the human in ferocity and malice, as the fearsome hatred of Quilp's belabouring the gigantic wooden figurehead (a substitute for Kit) in 'Revenge is sweet' is made more frightening by Sampson Brass's shrinking away from it in spasmodic terror. 'Phiz' shows he is trying to respond to the real and new elements of painful feeling in this novel which, while escaping Dickens in direct handling of Little Nell, the character deliberately chosen to embody it, Dickens successfully captured

[1] V. Forster's reported anecdote of the charwoman who was unaccountably impressed by its being a son of Dickens who lay ill in a house she worked for, and explained her knowledge of the author of *Dombey*, though she could not read, by the fact that 'she lodged at a snuff-shop where there were several other lodgers; and that on the first Monday of every month there was a Tea, and the landlord read the month's number of *Dombey*, those only of the lodgers who subscribed to the tea partaking of that luxury, but all having the benefit of the reading; and the impression produced on the old charwoman revealed itself in the remark with which she closed her account of it. "Lawk ma'am! I thought that three or four men must have put together *Dombey*!" She may well have meant that she assumed multiple authorship was needed to account for the pictures as well as the text, and would of course have been right in essence. Such readings as this were tra-ditional in England, as we know from many sources, such as the member for Parliament who said that *Pamela* was read aloud in his constituency by a village blacksmith and that when the reader reached the surrender by Mr. B. to Pamela's matrimonial intentions, the villagers rang the church bells for joy.

in such indirect and apparently unconnected episodes as the description of the sufferings of giants at the hands of dwarfs when the giants have been discarded as too decrepit for circus display, the rigorous disciplining of the performing dogs, the domineering of the artful Codlin over his partner the kind unselfish Short, and other symbolic aspects of the world of the fairground travellers (symbolizing the essential truth about the real world), where Dickens presents the suffering and the pathos of helpless innocence and simple goodness with complete and astonishing success, free from the sentimentality that is evoked in him by 'the child' here (Little Nell, whose ambiguity of age the artists uneasily reflect in various places, with unconscious appropriateness). 'Phiz' has not undertaken a full-page representation of the most touching and pregnant scene in the book (the end of chapter XVIII), but suggests its painful pathos in a vignette of 'Jerry's Dancing Dogs', unambitious but on the right lines, in chapter XXVII. In the drawing of the giants waiting on the dwarfs, though his dwarfs are excellently spiteful and domineering, the giants are comical instead of pathetic so he loses the point – this and other signs, such as mawkishness in representing Nell[1] shows the difficulty of a Gillray-type art's being requested to do something outside its range and suggests the effort 'Phiz' must have made to cope successfully with *Dombey*'s demands on him. In the plate 'Miss Monflathers Chides Nell' while he has as a foundation a Hogarth-type satire (there is even an ambiguous placard on the wall of the boarding-school: 'Take Notice! Mantraps') yet Little Nell's feeling of being hemmed in by scornful, hostile female presences is quite successfully established in spite of the superficial presence of the comic spirit. It was not to be expected that 'Phiz' could tackle satisfactorily the scenes where Nell travels through the industrial Midlands in chapters XLIV and XLV, to which only a Martin combined with a Doré could have been adequate; Dickens's nightmare vision of the breakdown of civilization and the death of humanity in a dehumanized landscape where industrial processes dominate and poison life at its sources, and where the rhythm of machinery has replaced the movements of

[1]Though this is almost wholly confined to Cattermole's contributions – which include the final stages of Nell's martyrdom and her transference to a better world in the arms of angels, something 'Phiz' could never have produced, one feels, and which actually make the novel seem more sentimental and religiose than the text, and are therefore doubly unfortunate though it was in fact Dickens who requested Cattermole to supply the angels. This does however make my point that the illustrations inevitably contributed an interpretation of the text and if they didn't intelligently help the reader they could be harmful.

Nature, is more powerful than the subsequent use of it in *Hard Times*. Now seen to be a prophetically wise insight, this remarkable passage never deserved the cheap sneer it received in House's *The Dickens World* (a sanctioned academic text for Dickens students), where it is dismissed as 'a piece of metrical excitement. . . his horrible imaginings stream on in an almost hysterical rhythm', and is described as 'recording the ordinary Southerner's surprise at what they see' in 'the industrial midlands'.

In *Chuzzlewit* we see 'Phiz' has taken pains to help the enlarged readership by establishing the characters of Pecksniff and his daughters so that their rôles shall be comprehensible to the artless class of reader in spite of the deceptive irony of the early chapters, and again by responding to the changed rôle of Mercy Pecksniff when, upon marrying Jonas, she becomes a figure for compassion, by altering his rendering of her, taking out the satire, while Charity's likeness to her father is stressed in contrast. The high spirits of the scene where poetic justice is achieved by Charity's being left in the lurch by her bridegroom is as congenial to 'Phiz' as to the Dickens of this first phase, where a stock situation of popular humour has been appropriately invoked by the novelist and treated by the artist.

But the real test of 'Phiz''s suitability for Dickens was whether he could rise to the necessary partnership in *Dombey*, Dickens's first major, complex novel, and the first conceived as a serious whole, though the working out is neither so ambitious nor so realistic as the original conception to be found in Forster's *Life*.[1] Dickens, we have evidence, took more than ordinary pains to get his artist to supply a not inadequate visual equivalent of his text which until it reached the elopement and the pursuit of Carker had the demerit, for a popular art, of being rarely dramatic, never spectacular, and where humorous, oddly indirect and devious. Dickens

---

[1]Forster, Book VI, §ii, where Dickens's outline of his 'immediate intentions in reference to *Dombey*', which Forster says Dickens sent him with the manuscript of the first four chapters, is given. Paul was to survive until the age of ten and the situation was to be altogether more interesting, curiously suggestive of a memorandum in Henry James's notebooks for the kind of subtle fiction we think of as his alone. Dickens wrote that Mr. Dombey 'for all his greatness, and for all his devotion to his child–will find himself at arms' length from him even then; and will see that his love and confidence are all bestowed upon his sister, whom Mr. Dombey has used *–and so has the boy himself too, for that matter–*as a mere convenience and handle to him' etc. The italics are mine. Going along with the intended moral disintegration of Walter Gay and Edith, this unpleasant likeness of Paul to his father (only lightly hinted at times in the novel itself) would have made *Dombey* more akin to Dickens's late novels and more substantially realistic than it is.

explained to 'Phiz' in detail the plates that he wanted to summarize the theme and embody ideas rather than illustrate actual episodes in the text. Forster knew that Dickens was exceptional in the demands he made on artists because he had a function for them other than just making the novels attractive visually: Forster says

> even beyond what is ordinary between author and illustrator his requirements were exacting.

–Forster well knew this since when Dickens was abroad, as he was during the writing of *Dombey* and *Little Dorrit*, for instance, he conveyed through Forster his requirements and even angry criticisms at not getting what he wanted from 'Phiz' and any other of his illustrators. Dickens also knew it. He wrote to Forster:

> You know how I build up temples in my mind that are not made with hands (or expressed with pen and ink, I am afraid), and how liable I am to be disappointed in these things.

To avoid unnecessary disappointment, Dickens himself produced by selection and admonition and the suggestion of a real man as an indication of what world Dombey belonged to, the face and appearance of Mr. Dombey–he made 'Phiz' supply him with sheets of drawings (which Forster rightly thought worth reproducing in his *Life*) of types of faces for Mr. Dombey for himself to choose from, before the artist even started on the book's illustrations, knowing that once fixed the appearance could not be changed, and feeling the importance of providing the readership from the start with an adequate embodiment of the most important figure in the book, the one on whom it all hinged. What was this conception that made Mr. Dombey different from Mr. Pecksniff or Ralph Nickleby or any comparable figure in the previous novels? Forster, who was very inward with Dickens's state of mind about this, tells us that he had 'a nervous dread of caricature' in 'Phiz's' interpretation of Mr. Dombey; naturally, since something in the nature of caricature had hitherto been a characteristic feature of the art of both the artist and the novelist, for the same reason–it was basic in the tradition to which they both belonged as artists with roots in the Hogarth complex of visual and literary art (an art extraordinarily homogenous, where Pope's poetry, Gay's *Beggar's Opera*, Fielding's *Jonathan Wild*, Swift's fantasies, Hogarth's didactic art and Gillray's political satire, shared the same conventions and aims). In the preface to *Martin Chuzzlewit*, the predecessor of *Dombey*, Dickens wrote, defending his own method: 'What is exaggeration to one class of minds and perceptions, is plain truth to another'. But in *Dombey*, in its very opening which sets the tone of a subtler art where irony springs from the pathos of the domestic scene, we see that Dickens has given up the old easy type of satire with its fierceness and exaggeration, for a delicate and tender sympathy with ordinary people, people no longer held at arm's length (though of course peripheral figures such as Major Bagstock and the villain Carker get the old treatment inevitably). If we think what Miss Tox, Mr. Chick, the Toodles parents and the Blimber family, even Mrs. Skewton, would have been in any earlier novel of Dickens, we can see how differently they are conceived in this. Yet there was enough of the old Dickens effects in *Dombey* for 'Phiz' to find plenty of congenial subjects there in his old style, and to be able to wind up with the marriage of Captain Bunsby and Mrs. MacStinger to which he gives the full Hogarthian treatment, very appropriately, providing a richly humorous picture packed with detail, corresponding to, and even better than, the disappointed nuptial party of Charity Pecksniff.

Dickens's conception of Mr. Dombey was not of a caricature and not even of a man to be satirized merely or mainly; evidently this man was conceived by Dickens as a complex creature, unhappy, misguided, even tragic, stupidly proud, callous to women's claims (here Dickens put his finger on a Victorian representative fact, and through the cases of the first and second Mrs. Dombeys and Florence, explores its various aspects with real feeling). Even and while really loving his boy, Mr. Dombey is yet jealous of his loving others and views him almost wholly as an extension of his own ego. Dickens went over the sheets of heads the artist had drawn for him, marked those which were on the right lines, and indicated for his benefit a certain 'Mr. A' who better embodied what Dickens had in mind as Mr. Dombey's type–not because he wanted Mr. A's likeness used, as Forster explains:

> A nervous dread of caricature in the face of his merchant-hero had led him to indicate by a living person the type of city-gentleman he would have had the artist select.

With regard to *Dombey and Son* in particular Forster says, reproducing these attempts of 'Phiz's' to satisfy his master:

> In itself amusing, it has now the important use of showing, once for all, in regard to Dickens's intercourse with his artists, that they

certainly had not an easy time with him; that even beyond what is ordinary between author and illustrator, his requirements were exacting; that he was apt, as he has said himself, to build up temples in his mind not always makeable with hands; that in the results he had rarely anything but disappointment; and that of all notions to connect with him the most preposterous would be that which directly reversed these relations, and depicted him as receiving from any artist the inspiration he was always vainly striving to give.

'*In the results he had rarely anything but disappointment*'; '*the inspiration he was always vainly striving to give*'—what a revelation! And undoubtedly reliable, coming from the confidant and intermediary.

After the initial trouble about getting the appearance of Mr. Dombey fixed, Dickens settled down it seems into hopeful resignation about the illustrations, writing: 'Browne ['Phiz'] is certainly interesting himself, and taking pains. I think the cover very good: perhaps with a little too much in it, but that is an ungrateful objection.' What is important is that 'Phiz' was able to rise to Dickens's demands for a quite new kind of illustration, which the new art of *Dombey* needed if Dickens's readership was to be kept (in fact, the sales soared). The first example comes early on, and would alert the readers accustomed to pondering the pictures that a complicated effect of pathos with probably a tragic outcome was to be the keynote of the new novel, and it has besides the function of lending point to the climax of chapter III, 'In which Mr. Dombey, as a man and a father, is seen at the head of the home-department'. This illustration has the cross-page title of 'A Slighted Child'. Mr. Dombey is seated centrally, but turned to the left, where the nurse holds up for his delectation the infant Dombey of the right sex, while the wrong one hovers on the right, *outside the frame of the picture*, marking her exclusion from the family piece; with her mourning frock and her hands wrung with anguish little Florence is a pathetic sight. She casts a longing look towards her father's chair, whose back, together with a leaf of the folding-door, bars her off. Yet though Mr. Dombey has his back almost to her the tormented expression on his face shows his consciousness of the presence, or existence, of his unwanted daughter; his stiff posture and frozen yet divided gaze show he is an unhappy man, and his eyes, instead of being fixed on the baby Paul, as his position directs, are slewed round against his will because of the hovering, timid, resented presence of Florence. The nurse Polly has on her comfortable round face an obviously unnatural expression of distress and alarm—she knows there is something wrong about the situation, which is new to her. Above her head and looking as though about to fall on the baby and crush him, is the chandelier which is described in the text as being, like all those in the mourning house, 'muffled in holland' and which 'looked like a monstrous tear depending from the ceiling's eye'—the artist has chosen to make it not a symbolic tear but an ominous bundle in its felt weight and threatening position in the picture: the whole illustration is emblematic therefore. Even the tiny baby is sat up in a precocious way with an unchildish look, adding to the sense of discomfort and something tragically wrong conveyed in every detail of the picture. This is an immense advance on Cattermole's deathbed of Little Nell, which was an unconvincing concoction of commonplaces. Yet, though 'Phiz's' picture here is original, it is simple and direct enough in execution to convey some at least of its import to even the unsophisticated reader or illiterate listener and viewer. And it is recalled in a similar, really a companion, piece towards the end of *Dombey*, 'Let him remember it in that room, years to come!' where the adult Florence stands in the same relation to her back-turned father, but herself facing away from him and evidently about to leave him forever, he thinks. Thus Dickens and 'Phiz' together had already arrived at the solution to the problem of illustration as exemplified ideally here in a French critic's comment on Chagall's illustrations to an edition of La Fontaine's Fables:

> Look carefully at one of these engravings, and the engraving all by itself will start telling you the fable. Chagall has managed to capture the very seed of the fable. As you look, the whole thing will germinate, grow, flower. The fable will step out of the picture.

Yet the Dickens-'Phiz' solution was still a form of *popular* art, accessible to all readers.

That Dickens was intimately concerned in all the *Dombey* illustrations we know from his involvement with the other principal ones of the kind. For 'Paul and Mrs. Pipchin' Dickens had great expectations (not unconnected with his own childhood experience of the original of Mrs. Pipchin—he was evidently recapturing in Paul's bewitched attraction to the alarming figure his own at about that age),[1] and he expressed a

---

[1]The same situation recurs in *Great Expectations* in Estella's memory of her childhood relation to Miss Havisham: "I who have sat on this same hearth on the little stool that is even now beside you there, learning your lessons and looking up into your face, when your face was strange and frightened me!"

violence of disgust and anger proportionately when they were disappointed. Artists have consistently argued that Dickens ought to have
been pleased with this plate, and grateful to 'Phiz' instead of abusing
him, since it is remarkably successful in itself and what more could
Dickens have wanted? We know what he wanted for this subject that
he had given out himself, since he wrote to Forster of 'Phiz's' version of it:

> It is so frightfully and wildly wide of the mark. Good Heaven!
> in the commonest and most literal construction of the text, it is all
> wrong . . . I can't say what pain and vexation it is to be so utterly
> misrepresented. I would cheerfully have given a hundred pounds to
> have kept this illustration out of the book. He never could have got
> that idea of Mrs. Pipchin if he had attended to the text. Indeed, I
> think he does it better without the text; for then the notion is made
> easy to him in short description, and he can't help taking it in.

Lynton Lamb quoting this and reproducing the etching alongside in his
text-book on illustration for artists, comments: 'we cannot help feeling
that he [Dickens] was wrong. It is a lesson to us all', a conclusion that all
artists and art-critics seem to agree on (at least, I have not found a dis-
senter). But, as a novelist employing an artist for his own specific purpose,
Dickens was not wrong, and on examining the novel, the etching, and
Dickens's statement of his grievances, one feels for the author. The lesson
is to all who undertake illustration, not to make a picture which, however successful on its own, does not represent the spirit of the text from
which it arose. Dickens specified some of the reasons for his pain and
vexation, such as that Paul ought to have been down low in the shadow
of the old lady's draperies, as he tells the reader in the novel—'in a nook
between Mrs. Pipchin and the fender, with all the light of his little face
absorbed into the black bombazeen drapery', whereas 'Phiz' has seated
Paul up on a high chair with the light full on his face (no doubt the
novelist's distribution of the light was impracticable, but the seating
wasn't). We can see also that the cat in the picture is not a witch's cat,
that the interior of Mrs. Pipchin's parlour as depicted is not sinister but
cheerful and cosy with the kettle comfortably singing on the fire, nor is
Mrs. Pipchin the well-fed old dragon with the stooping figure and the
hard eye as created for us in the text—she is here gaunt, towering,
youngish and not uncanny. 'Phiz's' attempt to indicate the threatening,
clutching nature of her plants which figure powerfully in the text, is
perfunctory and hardly noticeable, and there is nothing 'necromantic'

in 'the three volumes–Mrs. Pipchin, the cat and the fire', which is their stipulated effect on little Paul. Dickens's anger at the artist's ignoring what he had taken so much trouble to build up for the reader visually with words and which 'Phiz' has replaced or rather supplanted by a quite other visual picture, one which for the purposes of the novel is wrong (and the worse the more memorable it is as a picture), is understandable then. And the more the novelist believed the illustrations were important to the success of the novel with its public, the worse the artist's treachery seemed. Dickens ultimately realized that he could dispense with illustrators, but that was because Dickens had by then become an institution, and moreover the character of his creative art had again changed; *Dombey* however was early days.

Dickens's bitter conclusion about his artist, that it is better to withhold the text from him and coach him as to what is wanted, for then 'he can't help taking it in', is the familiar exasperation of the creative literary genius at having to work with an uncomprehending visual talent that is deaf to the written word or else heedless of it, wanting to work out its own idea.[1] But 'Phiz' *did* do better when on subsequent occasions Dickens carefully described what was wanted–gone for ever were the days when a Cruikshank was allowed to send drawings for *Oliver Twist* direct to the press without Dickens's being able to stop them on the way. And equally a matter of a dead past was the enthusiasm Dickens had expressed and apparently genuinely felt for Cattermole's olde-tyme architectural, and distressingly sentimental, illustrations of Little Nell, as to which he had written to Cattermole in 1841:

> Believe me that this is the very first time any designs for what I have written have touched and moved me, and caused me to feel that they expressed the idea I had in mind. I am most sincerely and affectionately grateful to you, and am full of pleasure and delight.

Yet he had not apparently felt so, as he might have with more reason, about Cruikshank's contributions to *Oliver Twist* and *Sketches by Boz*, or 'Phiz's' to *The Old Curiosity Shop* itself. But no doubt Cattermole's idea of illustration would not have satisfied him by the time of *Dombey* or

---

[1] A more intelligent and cultivated Victorian illustrator showed both in his practice and in words that he comprehended the necessity for the artist to collaborate with, not supersede, the author, declaring: 'as with Hablôt Browne, the achievement is most successful when an author's text has been followed to the letter, and the drawing is one with the page it illustrates, so that each is the complement of the other' (G. du Maurier, op. cit.).

even *Chuzzlewit*. Mr. Arthur Waugh, in his little paper on 'Charles Dickens and his Illustrators' for the Nonesuch Press, says of Dickens's profuse directions to Cattermole for *Master Humphrey's Clock* (which included *Barnaby Rudge* and *The Old Curiosity Shop*) – rather exaggerating – that they show 'the author throned in the chair of authority, with his hand guiding the pencil of the artist at his own free will. "The Inimitable" has now become "the Indominatable" as well.' He considers that Dickens was 'absolute dictator' as regards *A Christmas Carol*, but this can't mean more than that Dickens gave out the subjects and criticized the drawings before passing them; Dickens can't have been responsible for Leech's excellent artistry and sympathetic response to the spirit of the story. Mr. Waugh, remarking on the change Dickens shows in his concentration on getting the illustrations to *Dombey* right, describes him on the accepted lines as 'edgy' and 'querulous' about them, but this is unjust, for it seems to me that Dickens, conscious that he was breaking new ground for which the old style of illustration wouldn't do, and that he needed the right illustrations to enable his public to follow him, was trying to educate his artist on these lines. We can see that Dickens was not simply fussy or arbitrary by comparing what he complained about with what he let pass because though incorrect it didn't matter, such as 'Phiz's' turning Mr. Peggotty's boat-home upside down, which made a better picture, though Dickens had described it as standing right way up and roofed in, like a Noah's Ark.

Dickens provided 'Phiz' with instructions, which survive, for an important picture that, not answering to any particular part of the text, incorporates the whole spirit and ethos of Dr. Blimber's educational practice along with a detailed criticism of it, not too refined to be understood of the many and essential for the briefing of that part of the audience incapable of understanding Dickens's points about the traditional Classical education – a very different thing from understanding the humanitarian case against Yorkshire schools and a barbarous Squeers family. Dickens writes that the subject is to be 'Doctor Blimber's young gentlemen as they appear when enjoying themselves'; gives details of the ages of the boys to be shown in addition to Paul, their expressions, and dress, where the Doctor and Paul were to be in the procession, with the additional hint that 'Mrs. Blimber is proud of the boys not being like boys, and of their wearing collars and neck-kerchiefs'. Dickens explains that the young gentlemen were to be 'out walking dismally and formally', evidently having envisaged the excursion for himself. 'Phiz' certainly worked this out with intelligence, humour and suitable supporting detail, unless Dickens also suggested the details verbally, for there is a whole symbolic background ('Phiz's' backgrounds to his street scenes and outdoors with crowds of characters in the foreground standing out, are generally very good). This background to the dismal procession is nowhere described in the novel, nor is the humorous detail with its critical point in the foreground figures of low boys jeering at the young gentlemen who, as Dickens desiderated, are uncomfortably dressed like adults and with every expression on their faces from the stuck-up, through misery, blankness and boredom down to the outright imbecility of Toots, while Paul's innocent surprise is set off against them all and contrasts comically with his companion, the self-satisfied Dr. Blimber. Two Huckleberry Finn figures in the foreground turn rude somersaults in mockery of the genteel enslaved boys, while far back in the picture common children disport themselves on sand, cliffs and by the sea, flying kites, riding donkeys, and enjoying themselves in ways proper to youth, the whole forecasting the Blake-like lyrical coda that Dickens contrived as a separate ending to the novel, to round off his theme, where we are shown a new Paul and Florence roaming free along the sea shore followed humbly by a now repentant and loving Mr. Dombey: this could have provided, and really needed to drive home the theme of *Dombey*, a final and wholly different kind of illustration from anything known to Dickens's artists–one from the artist-poet of *Songs of Innocence*. If Dickens never read Blake, then it is an extraordinary coincidence how wonderfully his novels incarnate the *Songs of Innocence and Experience*; he is indeed the Blake as well as the Shakespeare of the novel.

This and the other major illustrations to *Dombey* represent a great enlargement of the powers of an artist who had hitherto been most at home in Hogarthian satire and in figuring the mean, the ridiculous, the pretentious, the contemptible and the depraved. 'Phiz' has now shown himself equal to the demand for something other than that he should establish the characters memorably in order to hold together the instalments for unintelligent readers and to make clear to them who is being satirized and who is to be taken seriously; more delicate distinctions are being required in *Dombey* and a greater range of feelings than merely to chronicle fierce and violent actions or comic overthrows as he had mostly done hitherto. He must now, in *Dombey*, and in spite of Dickens's assertion that he can't read effectively, have done so almost too intelligently in order to make the striking picture called (ironically) 'Mr. Carker in the hour of triumph',

where Dickens must have got more than he bargained for from his illustrator. 'Phiz' has either been wicked, his sense of fun having got the
better of him, or has over-responded with unconscious sympathy to the
text of Carker's meeting with Edith Dombey at Dijon, where she un-
deceives him–refusing to become his mistress–in the hotel room where
there is, symbolically, a choice meal spread untouched. The writing of
this chapter is excited and theatrical, and the dialogue is conducted in the
language of melodrama; 'Phiz' has accordingly drawn what is unmistakably a stage performance with an actor and actress taking the parts of
villain (baulked) and tragic heroine (vindicating herself and denouncing
him), in conventional melodramatic postures with the appropriately exaggerated expressions and the larger-than-life gestures of those treading
the boards; there is even a tragedy-queen fold to Edith's draperies. [This
is quite a different thing from 'Phiz's' general fondness for setting his
drawings in stage dispositions, a way of achieving a composition suited
to the stylized comedy of Dickens's early novels.] Even the Hogarthian
adjuncts–the picture on the wall of Judith beheading Holofernes and the
statue of the Amazon on horseback charging with raised lance–are dramatic as well as related to the situation of Edith cutting down Mr. Carker,
and so appropriate to the dynamic theatrical performance taking place in
the foreground. This illustration inevitably stresses the artificiality of the
written scene–did Dickens notice, one wonders? But of course the readership was accustomed to the idiom of melodrama, *the* popular art–in
fiction, on the stage and in pictorial forms; so this illustration would not
seem risible at that date and to those readers, nor perhaps to 'Phiz' himself (though to Cruikshank, who belonged to a tougher age, we can be
sure it would have been a piece of deliberate caricature). But, with the
very different illustrations to *Dombey* that I've already described, it shows
'Phiz' in perfect sympathy with the spirit of the novel at every point.

'Phiz's' amiable desire to oblige in *Dombey* and his attempts to extend
himself to answer adequately the new demands the text made on him,
are the cause of such a very surprising effort as 'On the Dark Road', the
first of what are known as 'the dark plates' where 'Phiz' tried out a new
technique for an element in Dickens's work that he seemed to feel needed
another medium than that which he had hitherto found adequate. This
etching certainly conveys a terrible vitality in its dark brightness and impression of speed. 'Phiz' found only one situation in the next novel, *David
Copperfield*, that this new technique suited, while as might be expected
Bleak House and *Little Dorrit* abounded with such opportunities. He there-

fore provided ten dark plates for the former and eight for the latter.
Those in *Bleak House* are mostly successful and some really very beautiful.

The wider range and purpose of the illustrations to *Dombey* must have
helped the readers to keep up with the new direction that Dickens's genius
had set itself on, and tactfully helped it to bridge the gap between the old
and known, and the new and puzzling. Yet it is undeniable, even on such
evidence as we have[1] at present, that it was the novelist's own devoted
care that took 'Phiz' along with him in *Dombey*. The relation of novelist
to artist is shown in the letter to 'Phiz' of March 10, 1847, when he writes:

> The first subject which I am now going to give you is very im-
> portant to the book. *I should like to see your sketch of it, if possible.*
> [Dickens's italics.]

He then goes on to describe in detail how this subject is to be executed,
ending:

> Lettering: Major Bagstock is delighted to have that opportunity.

The subject is Mr. Dombey's introduction to Edith and Mrs. Skewton
by the Major, and Dickens's title is of course double-edged. Dickens also
gave instructions as to the faces, expressions, postures, and described for
'Phiz's' benefit the characters, of the people he wanted in this picture. He
did not hesitate to have such sketches redrawn to his taste, making such
criticisms as 'Florence too old, particularly about the mouth', 'Edith

---

[1]That is, have in the Nonesuch edition of what were then available of Dickens's
letters, until the collection of many times as many which only two volumes, at
intervals of four years, have so far been released by the editors, and which have
not yet therefore got to the interesting period which starts with the conception
of *Dombey*. No doubt the subsequent volumes may provide more evidence of
the relation of Dickens with his artists, but few of us mature Dickens critics can
hope to survive to see the whole corpus of the letters at this rate of progress. But
that we shall have more evidence as to Dickens's instructions to 'Phiz' is unlikely,
in the light of this footnote (in the original two-vol edition only) to Fitzpatrick's
Life of Charles Lever (1879): 'Mr Hablôt Browne in a kind letter writes:- "Some
years ago when I was about to remove from Croydon, I had a bonfire to lessen
the lumber, and burnt a stock of papers containing all Lever's, Dickens's, Ainsworth's and other authors' notes as they were almost solely about illustrations. I
did not at the time attach any importance to them, nor did I think anyone else
would; but I was blamed by several autograph collectors for wilful destruction
of what they considered valuable."' This artless admission gives further grounding
for Dickens's grievances against 'Phiz' as insufficiently impressed with the importance of the work of illustration entrusted to him. It must be mentioned, however,
that 'Phiz' resented being dropped by Dickens after *A Tale of Two Cities*.

something too long and flat in the face'. He proposes to take 'Phiz' down to Leamington solely to get the atmosphere and show him the Pump-room where he wanted a scene set. By 1853 he is writing to 'Phiz' as a matter of course:

> I send the subjects for the next No.: will you let me see the sketches here, by post. Thirdly, I am now ready with all four subjects for the concluding double No. and will post them to you tomorrow or next day.

He is seen thoroughly in command of the medium as well as the artist:

> My dear Browne, Don't have Lord Decimus's hand put out, because that looks condescending; and I want him to be upright, stiff, unmixable with mere mortality. Mrs. Plornish is too old, and Cavaletto a leetle bit too furious and wanting in stealthiness. (Dec. 6, 1856)
> I hope the Frontispiece and Vignette[1] will come out thoroughly well from the plate, and make a handsome opening to the book' (*Little Dorrit*).
> The doll's dressmaker is immensely better than she was! I think she should come out extremely well. A weird sharpness not without beauty is the thing I want (to Marcus Stone, who succeeded 'Phiz').

Yet 'Phiz' was really happiest in the crowded Hogarthian satiric scenes that *Dombey* still offered him for illustration, such as the christening of Paul, the second marriage, and the dinner-party given to the friends of each side of that marriage.

But with the next novel, *David Copperfield*, there were no such opportunities, for the scene here is completely domestic with scarcely any perceptible degree of caricature or satire, other than Uriah Heep's incongruous presence and Mr. Creakle's brief appearances; a new style of drawing altogether would therefore seem to be indicated. This 'Phiz' found, and the delicacy with which he adapted the Hogarthian formula, where pictures, statues, domestic animals, furnishings, and so on are all used to make a satiric or moral comment—adapted this so that it became a quite different pointing to a subtler kind of meaning altogether, is proof of his intelligence as well as of his docility, for Dickens couldn't have suggested this to him. I have already given some indication of what he

---

[1]This vignette is the Blake-like vision of Little Dorrit stepping through the prison door with shafts of light striking in with her and through her. It looks from the letter quoted here that Dickens may have ordered this vignette and frontispiece and given 'Phiz' his instructions for them.

has achieved by these means in illustrating *David Copperfield* in my essay on that novel, but it must be further noted that 'Phiz' has managed to make every plate a complete picture on its own as well, and put in abundant detail to furnish it imaginatively without spoiling the composition,[1] and with real feeling as well as, sometimes, wit. For instance, in the plate 'Changes at Home' where, as I've described in my essay on *Copperfield*, David has opened the door on the unexpected scene of his mother nursing a new baby, the baby's robes, the mother's skirts and the draperies of the cot beside her, correspond to the curves of her bowed head, and of the baby's head and body reaching up to the breast, in a touching rhythm, and both mother and child look so delicate and solemn that the expression on David's face might be suspicion of an impending loss.[2] It is remarkable how 'Phiz' has modified his usual satiric tendencies to suit the subtler tone of this novel, as in the Sunday church service, the scene in Creakle's school where Steerforth, obviously seen through David's eyes as heroic, is exaggerated preposterously as such as he defies Mr. Mell, or where David and his friend sit in the Misses Spenlow's drawing-room pleading for Dora, with the sympathetic pictures of romantic courtship on the wall. His success in keeping the reader in mind of the ideas on which the book is constructed I have shown already.

Though 'Phiz' had done so well by Dickens up to now, his work for *Bleak House* is—not wrong, for there is nothing inappropriate or sentimental or vulgar, but disappointing. He does nothing to actualize the

---

[1]In the convenient collection of 'Phiz's' plates reproduced by A. Johannsen: *Phiz. Illustrations for the novels of Charles Dickens* (U. of Chicago Press, 1956) the author makes a very few brief comments on the aesthetic aspects of the plates, but in one of more general bearing on the *Copperfield* illustration 'Our Housekeeping' he says: 'Although the illustration shows confusion such as probably never was and more than Dickens himself described, it actually makes the appearance of the room more real'. This suggests the intelligent sympathy with which 'Phiz' worked in translating novel into illustration.

[2]The distinction between an aesthetic judgment on the illustrations as pictures and an appreciation of their success as illustrations is to be seen in this dismissal of 'Changes at Home' by the authority mentioned in the previous footnote: 'As a drawing, 'Phiz' failed to make it interesting. Aesthetically it lacks balance and has no centre of interest.' The conflict of the two different points of view is shown when Mr. Johannsen writes of another memorable *Copperfield* illustration that 'I Make Myself Known to My Aunt' 'is not a successful composition artistically, although one writer considered it the best in the book'. It is certainly one of the most memorable, which readers of *David Copperfield* in the illustrated edition memorize automatically, so perfect for the purpose is it.

Chancery fog, and the frontispiece, which attempts an impression of Chesney Wold when the waters are out in Lincolnshire, is ineffectual. Though the principal characters are well established and drawn larger than previously, there is little in the way of background and almost no interesting detail,[1] none of the atmosphere that is special to each Dickens novel and which makes *Bleak House* so different from the other novels and akin only to *Little Dorrit* and *Great Expectations.* 'Phiz's' imagination seems to be failing – he gets little of the horror that is in the text into his drawing of Lady Dedlock and Jo looking into the 'Consecrated Ground' at her lover's grave. Excellent as are the groupings of characters in the *Bleak House* pictures, as always, the bareness around and between them suggests a drying up or exhaustion of the artist's faculties and interests. He had collaborated with Dickens for twenty-three years altogether, up to 1859 when Dickens dropped him, feeling either that 'Phiz' had failed him, or that he had outgrown 'Phiz', or, more likely, that he no longer needed an illustrator at all. Indeed, *Great Expectations* was printed in instalments without any illustrations, and Marcus Stone was only engaged to do some wood-engravings (a small number) for it when published in book form in order to provide the orphaned son of Dickens's old friend with a job; he was kept on for *Our Mutual Friend* mainly for the same reason one feels, but did little good for that, as he had done none for *Great Expectations*. The last novel, *Edwin Drood*, was another matter altogether, and an illustrator was at least necessary to give definition to the course of such a multiple mystery tale and a tantalizing cover suggesting but not revealing the whole plot was essential.

Everyone feels the impoverishment of 'Phiz's' work in the two last novels he did for Dickens, but there are different explanations. Noting the decline Lynton Lamb remarks:

> The story of Dickens and his illustrators is that as his prestige grew the quality of the illustrating declined. We lose the sense of setting: the character of interior, street, or landscape . . . the larger the figures become in the picture, the less important they seem.

This may have been because 'Phiz' was overworked; his degeneration seems most likely to have been due to physical strain, which resulted in

---

[1] Except for the tempting subject 'Attorney and Client' which he has handled in the old Hogarthian witty mode which, as I explain in my essay on *Bleak House*, is here inappropriate: 'Phiz' conveys nothing of the sinister ethos that emanates from Mr. Vholes in the text of the novel.

paralysis at last, and the speed required to get the drawings to press now that very much larger editions had to be published with Dickens's enormously increased popularity and the much greater reading public anyway. In keeping with this explanation is what has generally been noticed, that the etching of many plates is poor; Johannsen says they lack atmosphere and 'the printing of the backgrounds are as heavy as the fore-grounds. . . . Perhaps Browne left the etching more and more to his assistants, as he certainly did the printing. This let-down in the plates is more noticeable in the succeeding novels.' Lynton Lamb has a related comment:

Editions were small enough to allow the early Dickens illustrators such as George Cruikshank or Hablôt K. Browne ('Phiz') to draw with an etching needle on the actual copper plate from which such a masterpiece as 'Fagin in the Condemned Cell' was printed. It was a method that perfectly suited Cruikshank's talent, But, for the larger editions of the mid-nineteenth century, etching was too slow: text and illustration had to be printed together. Other craftsmen had to engrave from the illustrator's drawings blocks of the same nature as the letterpress type. Sometimes he drew his illustration on the surface of the block; sometimes the engraver copied it; or, later, it was photographed on to the surface before it was engraved. But in all three cases the engraver had to *interpret* the illustrator's work . . . . Cruikshank had drawn naturally with the etching needle: his illustrations are true originals, not interpretations of something drawn in another way.

In fact, illustrations to the novels from *Bleak House* onwards would have been unnecessary but for the habit of having illustrations, that had become less and less necessary as the Victorian reading-public had become educated up to a more subtle kind of reading, and had become accustomed to Dickens's mature art. Perhaps it was a perception of this that made Dickens not only drop 'Phiz' but risk publishing *Great Expectations* without any pictures. He must have sensed that he had dragged his reading world into his mature art which, in *Little Dorrit*, *Bleak House* and *Great Expectations*, needed no illustrator if only the reader could now carry in his memory the characters and the themes without visual aids. Yet the few wood-engravings Marcus Stone did for *Great Expectations* could not have been much help in this respect even if they had accompanied the original instalments, and they did nothing else for the text—in fact, less than nothing. Can we imagine satisfactory illustrations to this novel? The answer makes us aware that it is a quite different art from even *Little Dorrit*, or any other of its predecessors. 'Phiz' could have done well enough by the few residues of satire such as the Pocket household, Barnard's Inn and the Wemmick-Jaggers office with its squalid clients, at any rate better than Marcus Stone, predestined to Academy art; the Doré who was inspired to do his best work by London's slums, docks and poorer residential quarters and by Dante's Inferno could have furnished splendid visual accompaniments to the most striking parts of *Great Expectations*—to its Newgate London, the world of Miss Havisham in the ruined brewery, the purgatorial fires suffered by Miss Havisham in Satis House and Pip's ordeal in the sluice-house on the marshes; but who then except Arthur Hughes (and not even he adequately) could have furnished the innocent eye and the imagination combined with the technique to convey visually Pip's childhood experiences? To see that such a variety of artists as 'Phiz', Doré and Hughes at least would have had to be invoked to illustrate adequately Dickens's last great novel (admitting *Our Mutual Friend*'s inferiority) is to realize its complexity, range and unique greatness.

Something different is required in the case of *Little Dorrit*. For much of this novel 'Phiz' would have been adequate in his prime, but the only illustration in which he succeeds in capturing the essence of the text is 'The Pensioner-Entertainment', where Mr. Dorrit's ecstatic expression of satisfied patronizing is turned on the humble old man eating off a newspaper on the window-seat, offset by the embarrassment of Clennam and Amy, while Miss Fanny flounces as far as possible from the distasteful spectacle of the pauper guest, contempt in every curve of her person and expression. Otherwise one would have thought the humour too had worn out of 'Phiz', he makes such a poor thing of the splendid dramatic scene Dickens has outlined in Book the Second, chapter III. Yet perhaps this very scene shows why Dickens no longer needed an illustrator and why illustrators no longer took pains with his work. It is worth quoting also to show how Dickens now thought in terms of truly dramatic humour, not stagey, and can create the spectacle so admirably in words that we conjure up the vision for ourselves inevitably. It depends for its full effect on what has gone before in the first half of the novel, where Miss Fanny was a humble dancer whom Mrs. Merdle saw as a threat to her son Mr. Sparkler and patronized with cheap presents before paying her off with a bank-note:

For a moment the lady, with a glass at her eye, stood transfixed and speechless before the two Miss Dorrits. At the same moment, Miss Fanny, in the foreground of a grand pictorial composition, formed by the family, the family equipages, and the family servants, held her sister tight under one arm to detain her on the spot, and with the other fanned herself with a distinguished air, and negligently surveyed the lady from head to foot. The lady, recovering herself quickly—for she was Mrs. Merdle and she was not easily dashed—went on to add that she trusted, in saying this, she apologized for her boldness, and restored this well-behaved landlord to the favour that was so very valuable to him. Mr. Dorrit, on the altar of whose dignity all this was incense, made a gracious reply; and said that his people should—ha—countermand his horses, and he would—hum—overlook what he had at first supposed to be an affront, but now regarded as an honour. Upon this the bosom bent to him; and its owner, with a wonderful command of feature, addressed a winning smile of adieu to the two sisters, as young ladies of fortune in whose favour she was much prepossessed, and whom she had never had the gratification of seeing before. Not so, however, Mr. Sparkler. This gentleman, becoming transfixed at the same moment as his lady-mother, could not by any means unfix himself again, but stood stiffy staring at the whole composition with Miss Fanny in the foreground,' etc.

Dickens is here his own illustrator and any artist who tried to emulate this in his own medium, as 'Phiz' actually did, could only make a shot at one of its changing moments and necessarily, in fixing that, lose the rest of this inimitable film sequence.

As for *Our Mutual Friend*, du Maurier and Charles Keene could no doubt have done a good deal with the respectable social life—Dickens's forecast of the *fin de siècle* young men, the Podsnap family, the Veneerings' dinner-table and the Lammle circle, Bella and the Wilfer household and the Milveys—but all these come alive of themselves; it is the submerged part of that society that needed an artist's interpretation and comment—the waterside and the world of the doll's dressmaker, Limehouse Hole and the weir of Rogue Riderhood's last phase, the tormented life of Bradley Headstone—all of which are right outside the ambience and beyond the talents of the Early and Mid-Victorian illustrators. When one sees how inept Marcus Stone was with 'The Garden on the Roof', missing all the weirdness Dickens wanted in the doll's dressmaker, all the character and distinction of Lizzie, completely disregarding the unearthliness of the 'Come up and be dead' speech and not even hinting at its thematic importance; or how he throws away in his 'Not to be shaken off' the opportunity the text gives in the dramatic confrontation of the now criminal Bradley Headstone with his twin Rogue Riderhood; the poverty of his comprehensive cover-design, which Dickens's other artists made a valuable accessory to the novels–then one feels Dickens had better have left the bereaved Stone family to starve. Of Marcus Stone and of Luke Fildes, one notes that their abandonment of the Hogarth-Gillray-Cruikshank tradition, which was indeed unsuitable for Dickens's late work, left them with nothing to fall back on but Academy Art and photographic naturalism; they cannot make use of caricature even when a touch of it is necessary (as for Mr. Sapsea and Silas Wegg). In Luke Fildes' groups of characters, in his young ladies of Miss Twinkleton's academy, his scenes between young men and Jasper, the faces are not distinguished from each other, much less memorable, there is no definition and no purpose in the whole, the settings are dull and the interiors without charm or that suggestiveness that always characterizes Dickens's descriptions of insides and outsides. The whole convention is savourless and to illustrate Dickens thus is pointless. George Eliot rightly resented having similar illustrations attached to her novels in the collected edition, though she distinguished in favour of the delightful and appropriate little vignettes on the title-pages which are views in the Bewick tradition of George Eliot country and help by feeding the reader's imagination with the right images of the background and atmosphere of the novels. One sees how Marcus Stone threw away his opportunities in illustrating Trollope's wide-ranging and interesting novel *He Knew He Was Right* (1869), Stone apparently having no conception of what illustrating a novel meant. And even Millais's much-admired illustrations to other Trollope novels do not do more than provide distinguished visualizations of some of the characters–they don't bring out the meanings in the novels, as du Maurier's illustrations to fiction of the sixties and earlier seventies do, at his best. Yet Dickens could have found better illustrators for his later novels if he had been more alert to what was happening in art, which in some quarters corresponded to his own development as a novelist. It is relevant to inquire into this relation between Dickens's change from *Bleak House* onwards and the development of the art of illustration, which Dickens anticipated in a sense in his own art.

Not only did he, with *Bleak House*, surpass the ability of the traditional illustrators to accompany him. It is evident to us, looking at the scene from this side, that a general change of taste was in progress which required more and different things from illustrated books than previously, and which eventually was seen as a complete revolution, and recognized approvingly as such by the art critics of late in the century, whose own taste was formed in the sixties and after. Thus Joseph Pennell in his *Modern Illustration* in 1895 says, with the assurance of being generally endorsed in such a judgment: 'I suppose that among artists and people of any artistic appreciation, it is generally admitted by this time that the greatest bulk of the works of "Phiz", Cruikshank, Doyle, and even many of Leech's designs, are simply rubbish. . . . Leech was the successor in this work of Gillray and Rowlandson, and though his designs appealed very strongly to the last generation, they do not equal those of Randolph Caldecott, done in much the same sort of way. . . . The change from the style of Cruikshank, Leech [etc] . . . to Rossetti, Sandys, Houghton, Pinwell, Walker, Millais was almost as great as from the characterless steel engraving of the beginning of the century to the vital work of Bewick.' He sees *Once a Week*, started in 1859, as the connecting link. Writing in 1897, Gleeson White similarly, in his compendious work *English Illustration, The Sixties*, testifies to the predominance of a taste in illustration that had completely lost touch with that of Dickens's reading-public of the thirties, forties and fifties. Gleeson White exhibits a radical reaction against the line of caricature and satiric-moral illustration, which he fulminates against. It is evident that his, the then 'modern', idea of illustration was that of an art existing in its own right as 'pictures', which were to express the Pre-Raphaelite concept of Beauty and also refined comedy, domestic sentiment, naturalism in depicting scenery and correctly academic composition. Thus he deplores illustrations prior to the sixties except for Millais's to Trollope and Fred Walker's to Thackeray, which correspond more to his requirements, and far from finding any contribution to the success of Dickens's novels in Cruikshank's and 'Phiz's' illustrations, he considers them blemishes: 'Even the much-belauded *Fagin in the Condemned Cell* appears a trite and ineffective bit of low melodrama today. . . . We recognize the power of the [Early Victorian] writers, but wish in our hearts that they had never been "illustrated", or if so, that they had enjoyed the good fortune which belongs to the novelists of the sixties', though reluctantly admitting that 'the idea of *Once a Week* owes more to these serial novels than to any previous enterprise'.

This is of course an incontrovertible fact. This periodical's lavish illustrations to fiction and verse by a galaxy of existing successful artists and illustrators, supplemented by new blood, continued by extending and enriching the earlier tradition of novel-illustration and yet ultimately impoverishing it by excising the wit and humour, the satire and moral comment, so that it ceased to be a popular and educational factor in the age succeeding Dickens's. In fact, it rose in the world socially and became Art. That it met a need is shown by the success of similar illustrated periodicals that closely followed–e.g. *The Cornhill* (less thickly illustrated) and the abundantly illustrated *Good Words* were both founded in 1860, and the need for such periodicals was due to the need for fiction in instalments *accompanied by* attractive (i.e. striking and interesting) illustrations, the taste for which had been formed by those writers, artists and publics now written off by the Gleeson Whites and Pennells and who show what this soon led to–a separation out of illustrator and writer so that the illustration was conceived as a picture in its own right, and illustrations not so conceived were so down-graded as to be eventually despised. Gleeson White says of Thackeray's own designs for 'Lovel theWidower' in *The Cornhill* (which actually were ghosted by better artists): 'Like the "Phiz" plates for Dickens's works, and many of John Leech's sketches, they have undoubtedly merit of a sort, but not if you consider them as pictures pure and simple'. He asserts the low intrinsic value of the work of 'Phiz', Cruikshank and Leech, among other pre-sixties illustrators, for, he says, only 'certain qualities which are not remotely connected with art belong to them'. Here one sees 'art' should be understood to have a capital A. He specified Millais's illustrations to Trollope as the right kind of thing, but these in fact do Trollope a disservice by ignoring the comedy, the humour and the recurrent satiric vein in his work. This new taste approves above all of the idyllic type of pictorial illustration. In accordance with this changed taste we may note that collections of the new illustrations, as worthy to be Art and independent of a text, were provided from the sixties onwards, and evidently were at once successful. *The Cornhill Gallery*, of illustrations from *The Cornhill*, was published in 1864 and so popular as to be republished next year; the wood-engravings, of Millais' drawings, mostly to Trollope, were published handsomely as *Millais' Illustrations* in 1866, while illustrations from periodicals owned by one publisher (from *Good Words*, *Argosy*, *Sunday Magazine* etc.) were published in an anthology suggestively called *Touches from Nature* in 1876. Others followed, showing that the conception of illustration as picture was now established generally and that it was indeed high time to drop 'Phiz' after *The Tale of Two Cities* appeared at the end of 1859. We may note further that Ruskin found Keene's art 'coarse' and that the poetess Alice Meynell considered it 'obscene'. Gleeson White doesn't select for reproduction any of Keene's illustrations to *Evan Harrington* in *Once a Week* (which were admired by Meredith himself) and praises Millais and Walker in contrast; yet writing in 1928, when late Victorian taste had lost its authority, Forrest Reid in *his* book on *Illustrators of the Sixties* says: 'somehow Keene's *kind* of beauty appeals to me more than theirs', and acutely remarks of Fred Walker's illustrations; 'In the drawings for *Denis Duval* he may clothe his figures in the costumes of a bygone age, but the drawings themselves breathe precisely the same idyllic Victorian spirit as his modern illustrations'. The idyllic spirit had indeed completely replaced the comic spirit in illustrations of fiction, and from the sixties onwards Victorian illustrators when they aimed at the poetic tended to interpret this sentimentally or solemnly.

Arthur Hughes is an exception here, and as regards his possibilities as the illustrator of the Blakean side of Dickens's art we may cite Forrest Reid's testimony to Hughes's achievement. Hughes made 231 drawings for the first five volumes of *Good Words* (1860–5) and of these Reid wrote: 'Here, in these figures of children, he at last enters his own world–a world very close to that of Blake's *Songs of Innocence* . . . faithful to the imaginative side of childhood'; and he makes an important point in Hughes' favour when he says of his unforgettable illustrations to George MacDonald's *At the Back of the North Wind* (1870) that 'The artist was unhampered by George MacDonald's strong moral purpose'. In effect, Hughes could express tenderness without sentimentality and ideally he would (if he had been available at that date!) have been a far better collaborator for Dickens in *The Old Curiosity Shop* than Cattermole ('Phiz' would still have been needed too); but Dickens's public would not at that period have been able to assimilate, or be helped by, such an artist as Hughes, nor could Hughes have developed such an art as his without the influences that emanated from the Pre-Raphaelite movement. Beside his imaginative innocence that enabled him to recapture the child's view of the world Hughes had an indescribable poetic quality, such as Dickens combines in his later novels with a wholly adult recognition of the squalor, corruption and degradation inherent in Victorian society, but this Hughes could not have interpreted. There was therefore no one adequate illustrator possible for *Bleak House*, *Little Dorrit*, *Great*

Expectations or *Our Mutual Friend*. There is now, judging by the recent biography and its reception by reviewers, a wholesale revolt against du Maurier's work as an artist, based mainly on his undeniably deplorable novels, and on his alleged defects of character and personality (which were not, however, noted by his contemporaries, including his admiring friend Henry James). But as an artist du Maurier did not deteriorate until the late seventies, and Dickens had much better have got him for *Edwin Drood* (and such associated stories as *Hunted Down* and *No Thoroughfare*) than anyone else working in illustration then. Of the illustrations du Maurier made for *The Notting Hill Mystery* which ran as a serial 1862–3 Forrest Reid says: 'never, I should think, has a story of this class found such illustrations–illustrations that cover its poor horrors with a veil of dark romance at once sinister and poetic, and that linger in the memory long after the tedious and involved plot is forgotten.' And du Maurier's earlier work is successful in the grotesque and satiric modes also, and, in addition, as we may see from his sensitive and intelligent illustrations to Mrs. Gaskell's *Wives and Daughters*, he was throughly capable of interpreting civilized social life and its painful situations in memorable and moving compositions. He was thus qualified to be the Dickens illustrator of the most difficult period of the novelist's art in that respect.

The Christmas books which Dickens produced annually as money makers (also from a feeling that it brought his readers closer to him and helped keep their loyalty) were all well done by pictorially, and undoubtedly created some special bond between the novelist and the public. They are linked very strongly with the novels–*A Christmas Carol*, so delightfully adorned and interpreted by Leech, being a bridge between *Pickwick* and the subsequent more serious Dickens, while *The Chimes* clearly associates with *Hard Times*, for example. For *The Battle of Life* Dickens tried the experiment of a number of aritists, either to do it justice (he over-valued it, but we tend to do the opposite no doubt because it was this trivial tale for which he broke the continuity of his creation of *Dombey*, very visibly to the novel's detriment) or to make sure of an extra large sale. It wasn't worth the pains Dickens and his team lavished on it, and the combination of artists must have been confusing for the readership in spite of a graceful pseudo-Blakean frontispiece by Maclise, and a lovely interior of the reunited sisters which pleased Dickens as well as it does us. For *The Chimes* Leech, Maclise and Stanfield all did their best, and Leech's pictures are again perfect for the purpose; *The Cricket on the Hearth* which associates with the idealization of domestic life in Dickens's middle phase from *David Copperfield*, and which was nearly as popular as that novel, has some of Leech's enchanting interiors and vignettes, preceded by an elaborate frontispiece by Maclise covering the whole story which gave that preview of the tale that Dickens always had provided for his novels. No doubt the proliferation of artists was to make the buyer feel he had value for money and to promote the sale of Dickens's annual Christmas offering as a gift-book, and it is true that the illustrations alone must have accounted for the sales of the gloomy and obscure story of *The Haunted Man*, of which they are much the best part, though the chopping and changing from one artist's style to another's throughout its pages is disconcerting, to say the least. Altogether the collected Christmas stories re-published in one volume under the title *Christmas Books* (not to be confused with the inferior *Christmas Stories* volume) show the work of seven artists and gave Dickens as well as his public great satisfaction – he was less critical of these illustrations since he knew the texts were not important like those of the novels – that is, not likely in any case to be taken seriously by his readers. But in one case, that of *The Cricket on the Hearth*, where Dickens had initiated the airing of serious themes – later to be consolidated in *David Copperfield* – the illustrations actually do the tale a disservice: their charm and quaintness underplay the text instead of confirming and reinforcing its implications as they might have done if more seriously conceived, or if Dickens had taken the trouble he did next year for *Dombey* to see that they should be. The fact is that Dickens himself had wrapped up his serious interests here in fantasy and fairies (sub-titling it 'A Fairy Tale of Home') and Leech and Maclise followed suit. That Dickens was not at bottom satisfied with the consequences is evident in the strange afterthought, with its Hans Andersen-like melancholy, attached to the 'fairy tale':

> But what is this! Even as I listen to them, blithely, and turn towards Dot, for one last glimpse of a little figure very pleasant to me, she and the rest have vanished into air, and I am left alone. A Cricket sings upon the Hearth; a broken child's toy lies upon the ground; and nothing else remains.

A confession of regret unique in Dickens's creative work and which acknowledges a mistake he never repeated.

Finally, I think it worth suggesting that just as in the previous century of Pope, Gay, Hogarth and the novelists who admittedly fertilized themselves on the dramatic satire of *The Beggar's Opera* and Hogarth's pictorial satires, so in the Victorian age the influences of literature and art were not merely mutual but inseparable. In general Dickens can be seen and felt to have passed through a similar development to the illustrators and humorous artists of his age–an age which covered an 18th-century tradition lasting into the Regency Period up to the latish Victorian revulsion against the Early Victorian heritage. For instance, Dickens hailed Leech (giving excellent reasons) as an improvement on Rowlandson or Gillray in subtlety and as effectively more persuasive therefore as a satirist: 'his opinion of Leech in a word was that he turned caricature into character' Forster summarized. Dickens, however, never accepted anyone as an improvement on Hogarth, whose merits as a satirist and moralist he showed he thoroughly appreciated in specifying why Cruikshank's teetotal series, The Bottle, is essentially inferior to Hogarth's Gin-Lane. Yet nevertheless Dickens was not so much a chameleon to these changes of taste as an anticipator of genius and an influence directing them himself in some respects, it seems to me. The inmates and visitors at Chesney Wold might have been written in for Keene to illustrate; we recognize the debilitated cousin in all his detail of dress, action, attitudes and speech-habits as a genuine Keene. Keene had a nice ear for the articulation and idiom of such types as well as a fine eye and hand for their embodiment (like Dickens he used to mime his characters first to be sure he had got them right), and with the immortal dictum: 'Better hang wrong fler than no fler' Dickens would seem to have added just the necessary element of satiric caricature to be doing a Keene himself. Yet Keene had only recently started drawing for *Punch* when *Bleak House* was appearing and had not got into his characteristic stride. In *Our Mutual Friend* the society gathered round the Veneerings' dinnertable is recognizably that of Keene's and du Maurier's art worlds which, incidentally, Dickens had already occupied with masterly authority in the drawing-room drama of Book the Second, chapter XII of *Little Dorrit*. Lady Tippins's interior monologue at the Lammle wedding might have been a drawing with words from *Punch*, though at an exceptionally brilliant level of social comedy, for Dickens always transcends his models. Eugene and Mortimer with their languid and self-conscious insolence and their contempt for moral earnestness anticipate du Maurier's renderings of the socialites influenced by the currents from Wilde and the aesthetes of the *next* generation–Eugene and Mortimer were created in 1864 when du Maurier had only recently begun to contribute to *Punch* and *Once a Week* and was not yet a social satirist.

Rightly therefore, implicitly recognizing the dependence of the Victorian artist on the creative genius of the masters of language, du Maurier wrote, for the instruction of the young illustrator:

'And if the dissapointed author says to him: "Why can't you draw like Phiz?" he can fairly retort: "Why don't you write like Dickens?" '